797,885 Books
are available to read at

www.ForgottenBooks.com

Forgotten Books' App
Available for mobile, tablet & eReader

ISBN 978-1-331-76253-9
PIBN 10231378

This book is a reproduction of an important historical work. Forgotten Books uses
state-of-the-art technology to digitally reconstruct the work, preserving the original format
whilst repairing imperfections present in the aged copy. In rare cases, an imperfection in
the original, such as a blemish or missing page, may be replicated in our edition. We do,
however, repair the vast majority of imperfections successfully; any imperfections that
remain are intentionally left to preserve the state of such historical works.

Forgotten Books is a registered trademark of FB &c Ltd.
Copyright © 2015 FB &c Ltd.
FB &c Ltd, Dalton House, 60 Windsor Avenue, London, SW19 2RR.
Company number 08720141. Registered in England and Wales.

For support please visit www.forgottenbooks.com

1 MONTH OF FREE READING

at

www.ForgottenBooks.com

By purchasing this book you are eligible for one month membership to ForgottenBooks.com, giving you unlimited access to our entire collection of over 700,000 titles via our web site and mobile apps.

To claim your free month visit:
www.forgottenbooks.com/free231378

* Offer is valid for 45 days from date of purchase. Terms and conditions apply.

English
Français
Deutsche
Italiano
Español
Português

www.forgottenbooks.com

Mythology Photography **Fiction**
Fishing Christianity **Art** Cooking
Essays Buddhism Freemasonry
Medicine **Biology** Music **Ancient**
Egypt Evolution Carpentry Physics
Dance Geology **Mathematics** Fitness
Shakespeare **Folklore** Yoga Marketing
Confidence Immortality Biographies
Poetry **Psychology** Witchcraft
Electronics Chemistry History **Law**
Accounting **Philosophy** Anthropology
Alchemy Drama Quantum Mechanics
Atheism Sexual Health **Ancient History**
Entrepreneurship Languages Sport
Paleontology Needlework Islam
Metaphysics Investment Archaeology
Parenting Statistics Criminology
Motivational

THE LOGIA

OR

SAYINGS

OF THE

MASTER;

AS SPOKEN BY HIM;
RECOVERED IN THESE DAYS,
AS WAS FORETOLD BY HIM.

J. TODD FERRIER.

PUBLISHED FOR THE ORDER OF THE CROSS, PAIGNTON,
BY PERCY LUND, HUMPHRIES AND CO., LTD.,
THE COUNTRY PRESS, BRADFORD; AND
3, AMEN CORNER, LONDON, E.C.

BT 308

gift of Robert H. Perks

Swald of   1950.

DEDICATION.

To the Members of the ANCIENT CHRISTHOOD ORDER who have for untold ages been dwellers within this planetary system, ministering unto the children of the Earth in things that are of God and the Soul, the true Seers and Prophets in all ages and amongst all peoples, the Interpreters of the Divine Wisdom and Manifestors of the Divine Love ;

And very specially to those of them who formed the inner group of the Master's most intimate friends, and heard from Him these Logia, and beheld His sorrow in the days of His Gethsemane ;

And of these we would name two who have been with us once more as the Messengers of the Highest, and who now minister from the Heavens, namely, ANNA BONUS KINGSFORD and EDWARD MAITLAND, who were known under other names in the days of the blessed Manifestation and were very near to the Master :—

To these we dedicate this volume.

iii.

347808

PREFACE.

SOME who turn to these pages in the hope of finding an ordinary biography of the Master, known to the West as Jesus Christ, will meet with disappointment ; for it is not the biography of the Master with which we are concerned, but the restoration of the Teachings which He gave. A true biography of Him would be indeed profoundly fascinating and full of interest ; but it need not for one moment be supposed that such a biography would accomplish that which the marred fourfold biography of the Evangelists failed to do. It could not effect that for which the Manifestation of the Blessed Life was made and the Sin-offering Oblation offered ; for only through the Teachings which He gave, the right understanding of them, and the making of them concrete in experience, could the supreme purpose of the Manifestation be achieved. It is possible to admire a biography and worship the subject of it, and yet utterly fail to apprehend the purpose and aim of the life— just what the West has done all through this era. After eighteen centuries of supposed interpretation and progress, the World that professes to worship the Master and follow Him, marks its most singular failure in the revelation of the conditions of that world. The nations that have most loudly acclaimed Him Prince of Peace and Redeemer from sin and wrong, and claimed Him as their Saviour and King, have followed only too surely the false prophet whose materialistic teachings have misled the whole world. They have set up the image of the Beast of every kind of gross materiality upon the planes of the earth, and even within the Temple of Life, and bowed down to it, and oppressed those who would not bow down and worship. They have made friends of the Dragon of Oppression to wound and crush each other, all of them praying to the Prince of Peace to give them the victory to the utter overthrow and abasement of each other. The peoples who have most loudly proclaimed the Gospel of Love have cherished and revealed the deepest hates. Those who should have been initiated into the knowledge of the true glory of life, have set upon it false values, accounting man as nothing unless as an earning and fighting unit. The most ostentatious spreading of religious wares has been done by the very nations whose vision of life has been so false that true religion can scarcely find room to make itself manifest. These have mostly killed the true expression of the Soul's life, whilst with clanging cymbals they have announced themselves the devout followers of Him whom they believe to have been meek and lowly in heart, and in life the Saviour of all.

In the following pages there is no biography as such, though the Sayings reveal the several degrees of the Manifestation. In these Sayings the true Way of Life is set forth in such manner that it must be obvious unto all who truly seek an entrance into the Kingdom. The Path of Jesushood is most clearly and emphatically revealed; the deeper experience of Christhood is unveiled; and the perfect Atonement is made manifest in which the Soul is one with the Lord. There is thus the threefold manifestation of Jesushood, Christhood, and the Lord-consciousness, in which the Lord speaks directly through the Soul—the Way of Life, the Light of Life, and the Divine Pleroma. Of these beautiful states of Soul-realization the Sayings are the exposition and interpretation. And to these remarkable revelations of the value and destiny of the human Soul, the high life unto which it is called, the path to be followed, the nature of the realizations that would become its heritage, there is added the true nature of the Oblation known as the Sin-offering, the reason for it, the path along which it would take the Master, the duration of it, and the tragedy of its awful sorrow and anguish.

These Teachings were designed to aid Souls in different degrees of spiritual attainment. All had to pass through the first initiation, or the baptism of John in the Waters of the Jordan, ere they could find Jesus—come to the state of Jesushood. Whilst all could find Jesus in this sense, there were many who could not proceed further, so that the several degrees of Christhood could only be found by the few, especially the higher degrees of that state in which it was said that the Soul had found Christ. To the elect Souls only—those who had found Jesus, then Christ—was the Lord made manifest.

For the same purpose as the Sayings were originally spoken, are they restored and given to all who may be able to follow. For their appearing they require no apology ; they are their own apologia. They are not likely to appeal to those who prefer the ways of human and priestly traditions to those of God and the Soul. But in the hearts of many they will find response, and especially in those who were once within the Household of the Faithful, or the Order of the Christhood in the ancient days. To these it will be no barrier to the discernment of their source and meaning, that they come to them in terms and arrangement differing much, and often fundamentally, from the teachings given in the New Testament records ; for these know that the light of truth is in itself, and that it is not dependent upon any formula, or school, or institution, or authority begotten of men. It will be no occasion of offence to such Souls that the beautiful Teachings of the Master, and His strange and remarkable Sayings, should be separated from the false environments in which they were placed, and the historical and Jewish garments in which they were clothed. Such Souls will now be able to perceive and understand many things, to trace something of their own past history and the ancient heritage which was theirs, and is now once more to be entered into—the true promised land. To the question, Whence know we these things ? they will find an answer in the Sayings, and themselves come into the blessed consciousness that the dawn of the Resurrection morning has broken upon the world, and that the Lord has risen indeed, and that He calleth them. Nay, they may now discern the arising of the Christhood, of which Order they themselves were once members. And those who belonged to the groups of disciples in the days of the blessed Manifestation through the Master, many of whom are now upon these outer planes, will also discern the signs of the times, and know that the Oblation of the Sin-offering is accomplished.

CONTENTS.

			Page.
DEDICATION	.. ..	..	iii.
PREFACE ..	.. ..	..	v.
CONTENTS	.. ..	..	ix.

INTRODUCTORY .. ..

PART I. THE BAPTISM OF JOHN 11

  The Voice in the Wilderness.
  The Waters of the Jordan.
  The Coming of Christ.

PART II. DISCIPLESHIP 21

  The Finding of Christ.
  The Call of Disciples.
  Not to be called Masters.
  Purity, and the Value of Life.
  Concerning Offences.
  The Little Ones of the Kingdom.
  Heavenly Treasures the Great Requisite.
  The Lost Sheep of the Fold.
  The Good Shepherd.
  The Younger Brother.
  The Marriage Feast.
  The Woman who found the lost Coin.
  Stewardship and the use of Talents.
  The Virgins and the Marriage Festival.
  A Vision of Hades with its Gehenna and Gehinnom.
  The Different Soils of Life.
  The Work wrought by the Enemy.
  The Soul as a Fisherman.
  A Cohort of Angels at Bethphage.
  The Fig-Tree that withered away.
  Healing the Obsessed.
  The Way of the Birth from Above.
  The Holy Breath.
  Bringing back the Supposed Dead.
  The Giving of Sight to the Blind.
  Concerning the Law of Divorce.
  The Humble of Heart.

CONTENTS.

Page.

PART III. DISCIPLESHIP 83

Within the Secret Place.
The Prayer for Initiates.
The Doctrine of the Logos.
When the Kingdom Cometh.
The Shepherds of Bethlehem.
The Way of the Birth of Jesus Christ.
The Benedictus—A Song of Israel.
The Magnificat—A Song of the Soul.
The Story of the Magi.
The Presentation in the Temple.
Gloria in Excelsis.
The Children of the Bethlehem.
The Flight into Egypt.
Witnessing for the Father-Mother.
The Nourishing of the People.
The Law of Ceremonial.
Concerning the Works of God.
The Healing of a Leper.
An Event of Great Moment.
The Vision of one who was Blind.
The Demons and the Swine.
The Stilling of the Waters.
Coming Events—The Vision of Peter.
The Foundation of God's Church.
The Prophecy of Peter's Denial.
A Story of the Passion.
Going through Samaria.
In the Days of the Regeneration.

PART IV. THE CHRISTHOOD (Epistolary) 147

The Elect Ones.
Epistles of Christ.
The Abrahamic Allegory.
Remembering the Divine Graciousness.
The Mystery of God.
The Gifts of the Spirit.
Spiritual Discernment.
Love Transcendent.
The Veil of Moses Lifted.
The Grace of the Lord.
The Earthly and the Heavenly.
The Rising from the Dead.
The Imprisoned World.
The Divine Conqueror.
Experiences of the Oblation.
The Burden of the Oblation.
The Restoration of Israel Foretold.

CONTENTS.

Page.

Part V. The Christhood (of the Soul)...   189

The Marriage in Cana.
The Perfect Union.
The Mount of Transfiguration.
The Manna of Life.
The Bread of Life.
The Lord as the Vine.
The Beatitudes of the Immortals.
The Return of the Presence.
The Night and the Dawn.
The Greater Works.

Part VI. The Christhood (The Great Oblation)   209

The House of Mary.
The Anointing.
The Gethsemane.
The Sayings of the Cross.
Fragments from the Garden of Sorrow.
The Burden of Ransom.
The Way of the Cross.
The Forty Days in the Wilderness.
An Echo of the Sin-offering.
The Great Lament.
The Exceeding Sorrow.
The Recovery of the Logia anticipated.
Preparing the Guest Chamber
The Eucharistic Supper.
The Eve of the Passover.
The Humiliation and Condemnation.
The Crucifixion.
After Ten Days.
Sin Remitted or Retained.
Sharers of the Oblation.
The Closing Scene.
The Last Allegory.
The Great Request.

Part VII. Vistas of Events to Come   259

Going through Samaria.
The Well of Jacob.
The Woman discovering Christ.
In the House of Simon.
The Way of the Debtors.
The Woman in Simon's House.
The Seven Fishermen of Galilee.
The Mystery of the Fish.
The Mysterious Soliloquy.

xi.

CONTENTS.

Page.

Washing the Disciples Feet.
The Case of Simon Peter.
A Story of the Oblation.
The Sleep and Awakening of Lazarus.
The Sorrow of Maria Magdalene.
A Vision of the Lord.
The Prayer of the Aftermath.

PART VIII. THE APOCALYPTIC VISIONS 301

SECTION I.—

The Overthrow of the Great City.
The Ancient Church Unveiled.
The Glory of Adonai.
The Church in Ephesus.
The Church in Smyrna.
The Church in Pergamos.
The Church in Thyatira.
The Church in Sardis.
The Church in Philadelphia.
The Church in Laodicea.

SECTION II.—

The Throne of the Eternal One.
The Book that was sealed.
The Opening of the Seven Seals.
The Travail of the Christhood.
The Loosening of the Four Breaths.
The Hosts of the Tribulation.
The Song of the Redeemed.
The Seraphim and the Golden Censers.

SECTION III.—

The Voices of the Seven Trumpets.
Lucifer, Star of the Morning.
The Measuring of the Temple.
God's Two Witnesses.
The Voice within the Temple.
Woman Clothed with the Sun.
Her Persecution and Preservation.
The Beast that rose out of the Sea.
The Lamb that spake as a Dragon.
The Twelve Tribes of Israel.
The Coming of the Messenger.
The Mystery of Babylon.
The Overthrow of all False Systems.
The Lord Alone Reigneth.

CONTENTS.

Page.

The Word of God the Redeemer.
The Seven Arcs of Light.
The Angel of the Sun.
The Binding of Satan.
The First Resurrection.

SECTION IV.—
The New Creation.
The Holy City.
The Restored Eden.

INDICES.

1.	GLOSSARY AND INDEX	390
2.	SUBJECT INDEX OF THE LOGIA	395
3.	GENERAL INDEX	397

INTRODUCTORY.

INTRODUCTORY.

THIS volume of the Sayings of the Master contains His chief utterances, those given in parable, allegory, and those spoken to the inner groups of interested friends. The accepted records are believed to contain these Sayings in practically perfect form ; yet in the four Evangelists the reports of what He did say are so maimed as to misrepresent His meanings, and not infrequently give to them quite a foreign meaning. In many things the four Evangelists contradict one another. As they stand in these records, some of the Sayings could not have been the utterances of the Master, for they are a contradiction of the state of Christhood, and even of Jesushood. Nor would they ever have been accepted as His, had the meaning of these two blessed states of Soul attainment been understood.

In the present volume, which is naturally the complement of *The Master : His Life and Teachings*, the Sayings are brought into truer relationship and freed from their oft-times Jewish setting. They are presented in the form in which they were spoken. The allegories, which were changed into narratives by the writers of the Gospel Records, will be found to contain other and deeper meanings than the narrative form implies. Many of the profound Sayings of the Master are to be found mixed up in the Pauline Letters, much corrupted as to their meaning, and placed amid environments that were foreign to them. For the real mystic Sayings in the Pauline Letters, formed part of the Logia spoken by the Master to the inner group of initiates. These Sayings we have presented in a separate section that they may be the more easily recognised, and we have brought together portions which were separated when made use of by the Pauline writers, when they sent out their letters to the first communities of the New Religion.

INTRODUCTORY.

It might be well here to say a word about those Sayings, and how they came to be put into the Letters to the Churches. They had been embodied in a larger treatise for use amongst the members of the Brotherhood composed of the intimate friends of the Master. That treatise was known amongst the brethren as the Logia of St. John. It had been preceded by the evangel of St. Matthew, the very record concerning which there has been so much guesswork on the part of scholars. That evangel contained the initial teachings on the way of the redeemed life. It made quite obvious what was meant by purity in life, compassion and pity, illustrated by parable wherein the life of the Divine Way was set forth, the nature and value of the individual life, the law of the Soul's growth, culminating in the realization and consciousness of Jesushood. These were the Teachings given in a more general way, and expounded to all who cared to inquire and follow the path indicated in them. But the Logia of St. John contained the deeper Teachings, such as could only be spoken to the inner groups composed of those who had attained to Jesushood, and who had become initiates for the Christhood. In that greatly treasured document the Christ estate was dealt with, its nature and various degrees expounded, the path to be traversed ere the Soul could enter into its realizations. It contained the allegories whose profound teachings none could receive who had not passed through some degree of the Christ consciousness. Some of these allegories contained the mystery of the Sin-offering and Oblation. There were also Teachings on the history of the human Soul and the World, the Ancient Order to which the members of the inner group had belonged, portrayals of the betrayal and crucifixion of the Christhood as distinguished from that of the personal Master, the spiritual event named the Resurrection and the arising in the age of the coming again of the Son of Man, of the Ancient Order of the Christhood, with the conditions that would prevail, and the events that would transpire in these days.

It was from that document containing the true Gnosis that Paul derived his mystic Sayings. He secured these during his visit to Jerusalem, when he is said to have gone up with Barnabas to consult the Brethren. He found

INTRODUCTORY.

himself confronted by their united opposition to the interpretations which he chose to put upon the Sayings of the Master, as these had orally been conveyed to him. The main subject of discussion between him and them was not that recorded in the Acts of the Apostles, but the doctrine of the Redemption and the Sin-offering. He was given the privilege of reading the Logia of St. John, and from that he took portions and built them up into his several theses, but without understanding them. And he often applied them to himself in a personal way, and thus destroyed their deep significance in relation to the Master as He bore the burden of the Oblation. That many of the Sayings were beyond his power of spiritual understanding, is most evident from the interpretation he put upon them and the setting he gave to them. Some of the Sayings which contained hidden in them profound depths of Soul history in relation to the Oblation, a pathos and mysterious sorrow none could understand who had not been with the Master in most intimate fellowship, Paul mixed up in various letters in detached fragments ; and in not a few instances he made use of some of these to express personal experiences, through which he said he had passed during his arduous labours amongst the churches.

This action on the part of Paul destroyed the real meaning of the Sayings, and hid from the mystic Souls the true spiritual relationship of them. As a consequence, the wrong interpretation of the Redemption was given to the new communities created by Paul and his followers. It was not the doctrine of the Redemption taught by the Master, and believed in and taught by the Brotherhood. Had the interpretation of Life, the Fall, and the Redemption given by the Master been understood by Paul and those who followed him, and had the Churches been also taught the same, there would have been a very different order of religious expression in the West to-day. The Churches would have been truly Christian, for they would have understood Jesushood and Christhood ; their message would have brought the redeemed life into beautiful individual and social manifestation, for it would have taught a real Redemption, and not a mythical one which,

A—I

INTRODUCTORY.

after eighteen centuries, has left the West as pagan as it was in the last days of the Roman Empire.

By those who are able to discern it will be observed how valuable these Pauline Logia are. Indeed they will find in them priceless treasures. In all the epistolary literature they have been the most magnetic, because they are the most spiritual. But their magnetic light was veiled.

In addition to the Pauline Logia, others are included in this volume, and it will be a surprise to the reader to discover that these are important parts of the Apocalypse of St. John. But St. John the Seer was the Master.

The Apocalypse is one of the most profound writings in sacred story, and contains more Planetary and Soul history than other writings. It was given by the Master to a few of His most intimate friends, and one of them embodied it in the original Logia of St. John. Afterwards it was enshrined in a separate document, and, in that form, it came into the hands of those who did not understand it, after the Brotherhood was broken up and its members were scattered. Throughout all the ages of this era it has remained a sealed book, though the attempts at interpretation have been many. For ages it was the cause of much controversy regarding its authorship, and whether it was an inspired writing worthy of a place amongst the canonical books; but at last the authorities who were set up to decide upon the different books, admitted it into the New Testament Records. Why it was worthy to be regarded as a divinely inspired writing none of the ecclesiastical councils appear to have known; for even until this day the ecclesiastical schools have no key by which to interpret it. In earlier ages it did not escape serious alterations at the hands of editors, though in this respect it suffered less than other portions of the Logia of St. John.

The Apocalypse has remained a Mystery Book to the several Churches, though in its message it has much to say to them. It has been supposed by many to contain the history of the overthrow of the Roman Empire, the deliverance of the Jews from their captivity, and the restoration of the Temple service with a glorified Jewish nation to which the nations of the world would pay tribute; whilst others have believed it to relate chiefly to the later

INTRODUCTORY.

effects of the Roman Empire upon the West, whose chief fulfilment was to be made manifest in " the last times." Upon these aspects, many have been the books written. But others have looked upon its series of visions as appertaining to the Divine Judgment upon the World, as that Judgment has been understood and interpreted by the Churches.

But the teaching found in the Apocalypse is much more. Little have the Churches imagined what wealth of sacred story it contained. Had they known what the series of visions comprising the book meant, they would have found in them remarkable histories of the Soul and the Planet, histories dating back to long ages prior to the times spoken of as the beginning of human history in the Sacred books, and indeed of anything that science knows. They would have discovered who the Elect-Souls were who are spoken of, even the Ancient Christhood Order, and the nature of the ministry which they rendered to the children of this world. They would have found remarkable events foretold, whose history upon these outer planes was to be written during the three terrible days, in which the Oblation or Sin-offering was to be made—three planetary cycles which have only been completed within these days. In addition to these they would have found the present times embodied, and many events in the fashioning, events in which the blessed effects of the Sin-offering Oblation will be made manifest.

The Apocalypse contains the history of the Redemption, the Resurrection, and the Regeneration. And through the outworking of these it reveals the overthrow of all the materialistic systems, religious, scientific and national, which are expressed under the hieroglyphs, the Beast, the second Beast, the Dragon, the false Prophet, the Beast which assumed the appearance of the Lamb, the Devil, Satan and Abaddon, with the scarlet Woman and the great City of Babylon over which she reigned. For all the merely materialistic systems which have oppressed the Children of the Most High, are to be overthrown, not only the gross systems of government, the sensualism in the midst of societies and nations, the great military tribunes, the scientific inquisitions which impose upon the dumb creatures

INTRODUCTORY.

the most awful cruelty imaginable, but also the ecclesiastical systems which have failed themselves to enter the Kingdom, and, by their wrong conception of the Redemption, have prevented from entering that Kingdom those who would have done so. All the systems founded by the materialistic spirit, including those which have assumed the religious nomenclature, like the Beast which took on the appearance or likeness of the Lamb, will be cast out from the New Heaven and the New Earth which are now in process of becoming. The day of the Judgment of God is now upon them, to purify them, and to remove all that cumbers the ground. They are to be judged, not because it is wrong to have earthly Houses of Prayer, for we have some most noble Sanctuaries with the history of saintship written upon their walls ; nor because such Sanctuaries have had attached to them Priesthoods of various orders and degrees of ministry, for in themselves these may be most beautiful and helpful if kept pure, free from all bondage, and full of light ; they are to be judged, because they have lamentably failed to be the channels of Divine Revelation to the World, in which the true laws of being and the path to the realization of the prefect life should have been rightly interpreted, and beautifully manifested. They have failed to be what they have always professed to be, namely, the true interpreters of the Divine Nature, Love and Wisdom ; for, as systems, they have not known these : had they understood and realized these blessed truths, they never would have crucified afresh, and continually in one way or another, the Lord of Glory, through persecuting and oppressing those who were sent by Him unto them. For it has been the ecclesiastical systems, from the pontifical to the most rationalistic and democratic, which have slain the Seers and Prophets in all ages, and contributed in no small way to the death of the two witnesses for God within the Soul—the Intuition and the higher or spiritual Understanding. Ecclesiastical Christianity has failed as fully as rabbinical Jewry. It has mistaken the letter for the Spirit ; the husk for the kernel. It has always grasped at the phenomenal and missed the truly substantial. Upon tradition it has set great store, but utterly failed to rightly appraise the inward life. Its nomenclature teems with shibboleths, but the

INTRODUCTORY.

meaning of the terms it uses it has never understood. The meaning of Jesushood it knows no more of to-day than when, as a system, it was first inaugurated. In the cave of its Adullam it has hidden the light of the Christhood, for it has never known the Path to the realization of that blessed state. Ahab and Jezebel have ensnared it; in its ramifications are to be found even unto this day the Abattoirs and Shambles, Distilleries and Breweries, houses of the Wine of Sodom and Gomorrah—the testimonies to the barbaric conditions amid which the Church sits as Queen.

But the purification of the Temple for the Soul and the Planet has begun, and in its process there shall be cast out every evil thing, and all who love to treat as human merchandise the most sacred verities of life, and all who buy and sell the Dove or the Spirit of purity, love and peace.

May these precious Logia be found of all for whom they have been restored, and may these be aided in their spiritual realizations, even until they reach the high estate of their Christhood as in ancient days. To this are they called, that they may make manifest Jesus in the ways of their living and show the children of this world how to live, and be the vehicles once more through whom the Light of the Eternal Love shall be radiated and His Glory revealed. To each one of these Souls is the Word of Life spoken—

" Arise ! Shine ! for thy Light is come ! "

PART I.

THE BAPTISM OF JOHN

Wherein the Logia of the Master reveal that John the Baptizer was none other than Himself Baptizing with the Waters of the Jordan or the Truths of the Spirit, at Bethabara or the House of the Crossing, unto the Purification of Life for all who sought to be Initiates of the Jesushood, and come to know the Christ of God, and the High Life and Service unto which He called the Soul.

THE LIGHT AMID THE DARKNESS

*There was a man sent from God whose
name was John. He came into the
world to bear witness unto
the Light of God which
lighteth every man
as he cometh up
out of the
world.*

THE BAPTISM OF JOHN

Amid the wilderness of Judah[1] was a Voice heard proclaiming the Word of the Lord.

The Voice in the Wilderness

It was the Voice of the Messenger of the Lord of whose coming the holy prophets spake, to prepare the way of the Lord, and to proclaim unto Israel His appearing.[2]

From afar was the Voice heard calling from the East side of the Waters of Jordan[3], to make the ways of life pure in the waters of purification, and receive of the Spirit of Truth that baptism, which maketh clean the heart and prepareth the life for the coming of the Lord.

Unto the Waters of the Jordan did many gather that they might be baptized therein, even unto the making clean of all their ways ; for they responded unto the Voice of the Messenger to prepare for the coming of the Lord, to make crooked ways straight and rough places smooth, that their lives might be lived in righteousness before Him, to exalt desire and purpose of mind through purifying them, and make clear the inner life of the Soul with its spiritual uplands and divine heights, that the true life might be manifested.

And the Voice that was heard calling unto the Waters of the Jordan, spake saying :

" Bring forth fruits meet for repentance, O ye dwellers in Jerusalem[4], and ye inhabitants of the wilderness of Judah !

Say ye not any more that ye have Abraham and the Fathers, and that ye are in the line of the Prophets of the Lord.[5]

For out of stony places hath the Lord had to raise up children unto Abraham, because of the going down of the children of Jacob into the wilderness which was made of the land of Judah, and into Egypt where they were oppressed by the things of the flesh, and into Goshen where gross darkness overtook them, and they were led into the awful Desert of Sin where they were afflicted by the fiery serpents and viperous creatures.[6]

NOTES.

[1] The Wilderness of Judah was not a strip of land in Palestine, though there was a wilderness of Judea. What is referred to is the spiritual condition of the land of Judah, for it had become as a wilderness, all confused and confusing. But Judah was not a country, but the Soul of this Planet. It was the term used by the Ancient Hebrews to designate the Planet-Soul. Her land had become a veritable wilderness. The religious history of the world testifies to this fact.

[2] As Judah was no mere section of the Jewish nation, neither was Israel. The Israelites were the Ancient Christhood Order, those who had attained and were the Cross-bearers in ministry unto the children of this world. As the appearing of the Lord upon this world could only be of a Soulic kind (for the Lord is not any man), His appearing could only be apprehended by Souls who knew Him. And the Ancient Israel had once known Him as a conscious Presence.

[3] "The Waters of the Jordan" was meant as a symbol of truth. Water is the cleansing element in the outer; so is truth in the inner realms of our being. But the river Jordan referred to was not the river of Palestine so named by the Jews, but that of the Spirit which flowed through the land of man's nature, and which divided the East from the West, the inner from the outer. The Waters of Jordan were the truths held as knowledges become vitalised by the Spirit, and filled with power to cleanse even the leprosy of a Naaman.

[4] Jerusalem in the terms of the Hebrew Mysteries meant this Earth as a spiritual system. That was the City that once was so glorious, and which was to be restored to her former glory.

[5] A direct negation of all the religious claims of the Jews.

[6] A whole world of history is contained in these allusions. They indicate what took place in the ages after the "Fall." Abraham, Isaac and Jacob were planetary names and were meant to express three states of planetary consciousness. Abraham was the father of all, because all have proceeded from the Divine. It represented the Divine Estate of this Earth. To raise up children unto Abraham— to aid Souls to evolve into a high state of consciousness—was now a difficult process because of the stony or non-spiritual conditions. The history implied in the paragraph as relating to Israel will be found interpreted elsewhere.

THE BAPTISM OF JOHN

The Voice in the Wilderness

Behold! Out from these things hath the Lord called you unto redemption, to change the hard and stony nature through the washing of purification, to raise you up as seed unto Abraham that ye should inherit the Blessing which the Lord gave unto him."

And John[1] continued to baptize all who came unto Him ; with the Waters of the Jordan did He baptize them in the Name of the Holy One.

He called upon all who came unto Him to bring forth fruits meet for repentance, that their lives might be a true returning unto the ways of purity.[2]

As He proclaimed His message, there came to Him certain of the Pharisees and Levites, demanding to be informed upon whose authority He taught these things, and who He Himself was.[3]

And He said unto them: " I am a voice crying in this wilderness of Judah unto all who may hear of her children, calling upon them to purify themselves of evil, and to prepare for the coming of the Lord unto them,[4] to repent truly of their iniquities, transgressions, and sins, and bring forth within their hearts those fruits which are alone worthy of a turning unto Him."

But they inquired yet farther concerning His authority, and questioned whether He were Elijah returned, or another of the prophets.

And when He answered that He was neither, they pressed Him to tell them who He was, and whether He laid claim to be the Christ.[5] But for answer He said,

" I baptize you with these truths of the Spirit in the Name of the Holy One, that ye may return in your lives unto the Lord ; but in the midst of you there is One whom ye know not[6]: He baptizeth with the Fire of the Holy One.

He it is who will purge the house of Judah and cleanse the courts of the Temple of the Lord[7]; for He will winnow the chaff from the wheat upon the threshing-floor, with His Fan which is in His right hand, and He will consume away the chaff, and gather in to His granary all the wheat."

NOTES.

[1] John the Baptist was none other than the Master Himself in the first part of His mission, that of the baptism of those truths necessary for the purification of the life. He was the Man sent from God to bear witness of the Light of Life, even that Light which illumineth all who rise above the domination of the elemental world. The Baptism of John came first, then the Baptism of the Holy One—the Eternal Christ. John must be the fore-runner of the Christ. Purification is absolutely essential to the redeemed life. For a man to know Jesus he must be pure; to know Christ he must pass through Jesushood.

[2] The true returning is not in matters of belief, but purity, pity, compassion and love. The way of Jewry was the denial of these. Its religion was along the path of blood ; its Sanctuary was a religious abattoir. They traded in the lives of the creatures in their daily meals and daily sacrifices. There can be no real following of Jesus without purity and compassion.

[3] This is just what the leaders and priests did : it was the old story in their history. Upon whose authority say ye these things ? What are your credentials as a new teacher ? And in the modern world it is even as it was in the ancient times. Tradition circumscribes everything. The Scribes and Priests claim still to sit in the seat of authority.

[4] The coming of the Lord relates to the coming into the life of those gracious influences breathed forth from Him. Unfortunately it was made to relate to the coming of the personal Master, owing to the way in which the writers of the records presented what they found in the original document by St. Matthew, wherein the Master's ministry was described. The expression has depths of meaning which will be unfolded later.

[5] The Master only laid claim to have been sent from the Father-Mother. He sought no titles ; He required none. The application of the three terms expressive of His state and ministry to Him personally was a great calamity.

[6] This refers to the descent of the Logos or Adonai to overshadow the Master. He was the One who baptised with the power of the Highest. The Baptism of His Fire was the energising of the entire being from the Divine World. It was the Divine Flame within the Soul carrying up the life as in a chariot of fire to the Heavens.

[7] The real Temple of the Lord is the Holy Place within every one's own Soul ; and its courts reach to the outer life. To purge the House of Judah is to purify the entire planetary conditions, to purge away all the evil elements which cause so much disorder, disharmony, disease, pain and sorrow. To cleanse the courts of the Temple of the Lord, is to make clean every one of the Souls' vehicles—body, lower mind, heart and higher mind ; and to bring back to the Soul the use of all its inherent attributes.

THE BAPTISM OF JOHN

The Voice in the Wilderness

And some of the priests who were of the house of Levi inquired of Him concerning the One of whom He spake these words, and whether they were related to Himself.[1]

But He said : " He of whom I have spoken unto you was before me. He came unto His own, yet His own received Him not ; for they knew Him not, having lost the memory of His countenance.[2] But unto all who were able to receive Him, unto them did He give Power, even the strength to become Sons of God ;—those who were born, not of bloods, nor of the flesh, nor of the will of man, but of the Holy One.[3]

And He has been in the world, but the world has known it not ; for He of whom I spake is the Word, the Christ who is to come.[4] And the Word will be made manifest through those within whom He takes form, and His Glory shall be revealed through them, full of grace and truth.[5]

I saw the Heavens open and the Word revealed ; for the Spirit of the Lord descended even as a dove descends in her flight. And when it had rested upon Him, I heard a Voice saying unto me, ' Behold ! it is the Lamb of God, even He who taketh away the sin of the world.'[6]

Of Him do I bear record that He is the Son of God."

NOTES.

[1] How ready those in authority were to find occasion in which to entrap Him to say something upon which they might build up a case against Him ! When opportunity presented itself, they bemeaned themselves, anxious to overwhelm Him if possible ; for His interpretations of life were opposed to theirs, His doctrine of purity, pity, compassion and love was far above such as their traditions taught.

[2] This saying has had a Jewish interpretation in Biblical exegesis ; for it has been taken to refer to the Master coming through the Jewish nation, and that they failed to recognise Him. But the words were spoken by the Master concerning the coming of the Adonai to those who had once known Him in blessed realization, but whose condition prevented them from entering again into that consciousness. These were of the Order of the Christhood in ancient days.

[3] There were some of these Souls equal to the vision, of whom were the true Seers and Prophets, some who were able to receive the Power that enabled them to reveal the Son of God. These Souls were of that Divine Order which attached no importance to racial, traditional and social claims, for their love and purpose in life were not begotten of these, but from the Holy One whose dwelling was with them.

[4] The Logos or Adonai is here referred to. He is never a man, but His Presence is with all who attain the Christhood, and through them He is made manifest. The world has not known Him, because none of the Planet's children had reached the high state of the Soul's evolution in which He becomes present to the inner consciousness, and in vision He can be beheld. And He is the Eternal Christ, of whom the microcosm is within the Soul to be unfolded until the perfect day of the realization of Christ. He is the One who makes manifest through His Christs.

[5] The Glory of the Presence within those in a state of Christhood, which is also the Light of Life—the radiations of that Presence. The grace is the Divine Love manifest, and the truth is the Divine Wisdom revealed.

[6] The opening of the Heavens must be understood esoterically. It was the opening up of the innermost realm to the vision of the Master. He beheld Adonai in that moment once more. Often had the vision been His, for He came forth from the inner realm in order to be the Vehicle of the Manifestation and the Oblation or Sin-offering. He knew that the Lamb of God was the Divine Love of Adonai in a sacrificial capacity, and that He alone could bear up and take away the awful sin of this world which had been written by its children.

19

PART II.

DISCIPLESHIP.

*The Logia of the Master showing how the Initiation
of several of the Disciples took place, and the Way
of Jesushood, into the higher degrees of which
they were led ; also the interpretation of the
mystery of the Soul in its nature and
attributes, its history, state and require
ments ; the Divine Love and Compassion for Souls and the way in
which He vouchsafes true Healing
and Blessing ; together with
glints and gleamings of
the inner meaning
of the Kingdom of
the Heavens, and
the great possi
bilities of all
Souls.*

DISCIPLESHIP

The Finding of Christ

There came unto the Master two who would be disciples of Christ, and these inquired of Him, saying: "Teacher, where does Christ dwell that we may seek unto the finding of Him?"[1]

And He said unto them: " Come and see " ; for it was about the tenth hour with them. So they entered in and abode there.[2]

Now, these two were Andrew, the brother of Simon Peter, and John, the son of Zebedee. And they brought Simon also to the place whither they had gone.[3]

When the Master beheld Simon He said unto him : " Thou art a fisher upon the Sea of Galilee : if thou wilt follow Christ, thou shalt be great as a fisher amongst men ; for with the Understanding shalt thou perceive heavenly things, and interpret the secrets of God."[4]

And Simon said unto the Master · " Yea, we have left all, that we may follow."

The Master saith : " Unless a man take up his cross and deny himself, he cannot be His disciple. He who loveth the ways of life in the flesh, loseth the life of the Spirit ; but he who loveth not the ways of life in the flesh, cometh into the Life Eternal."[5]

And Simon said : " Lo, we have left all ; what shall our gain be ? "

The Master saith, " He who would be His disciple, must leave all things—Father, mother, wife, husband, son, daughter, brother, sister, friend, goods and land.

For if one be not prepared to give up unto the leaving of these, he cannot follow Christ.[6]

But if a man give up all things for the Kingdom of the Heavens, he shall receive in this world the coming of Life, and hereafter, that Life in fulness."[7]

Of those who accompanied the Master there was one named Philip : he was of Bethsaida in Galilee, the city of Andrew and Simon

Philip found Nathanael when he was sitting under the Fig-tree, and saith unto him : " We have found one in the city of Nazareth, who has revealed unto us Christ."

NOTES.

[1] In the accepted record of this event it is made quite personal, and that the two wanted to follow Him and so accompanied Him home. But they were disciples of the Master and were in Jesushood, and they wanted to proceed farther in the blessed realizations.

[2] Here the meaning is made clearer by the expression " The tenth hour " ; " for it was about the tenth hour with them " ; and the ninth hour esoterically is the Jesus state found and entered into. They could " Come and see " where Christ dwelt, for the tenth hour was the first degree of Christhood.

[3] The Names said to have been given to the disciples of the inner group were Initiate Names. The terms signified the special qualities which each one spiritually represented. Thus in the case of Simon who also became Peter—the higher Mind, first in its outward look seeking the meaning of life by that means, then the inward look and the coming of the Light to the Understanding.

[4] Here we have stated succinctly the high office of Simon Peter or the illumined Understanding. Simon Peter is a fisher or seeker for knowledges contained within the heavenly arcane, and which are to be found within the Sea of Galilee. And what is the Sea of Galilee but the precious waters gathered up by the Soul in its experience ? For all interior knowledge is begotten of the Soul's own history.

[5] Herein is the step made obvious. The Cross of Self-denial must first be borne. No Soul can come into higher things without the bearing of it.

[6] Herein is the second step in varying degrees revealed. The Cross of self sacrifice must become a reality in the life. It is the second step of the threefold Path. But its meaning was not materially literal. That would have been in many instances a violation of the love by which the Cross of self sacrifice is borne. What was meant was the emancipation of the Soul from the dominion of any or all of these.

[7] The Kingdom of God is within. It comes as a consciousness, gradual but surely, to those who give up all to find it.

DISCIPLESHIP

Nathanael saith unto Philip : " Can any such good thing come out of Nazareth ?"[1] But Philip counselled him to come and see.

The Finding of Christ

When the Master beheld Nathanael also coming, He saith of him : " Behold, an Israelite indeed, in whom is no guile."[2]

Nathanael saith unto the Master : " Whence knowest thou me ? " And He saith to him, " Before Philip called thee, I beheld thee sitting under the Fig-tree."[3]

And Nathanael was filled with wonder and awe ; and he saith : " Thou art, indeed, the revealer of the Christ of God ! Thou art of the Ancient Kings of Israel."[4]

And the Master saith unto him, " Thou shalt behold greater things than these. Hereafter thou shalt behold the Heavens opened unto thee, and the angels of God in their ministry as they descend and ascend in their service for the Son of Man."[5]

" Do not seek to be called Rabbi : for one alone is the Teacher, even the Spirit of the Lord who is in you.

ot to be .alled Masters

Call no man on the earth by the sacred name ; for only One is your Father-Mother in the Heavens, and all ye are brethren.

Be careful that no one gives you the title of Master, like those who love to be thought of as masters of cere-monies and knowledges ; for one is your Master, even the Lord.

Remember that the greatest one is servant of all, and that he who would be great in the Kingdom of the Heavens must be servant of all.

So serve ye, that the life of the Kingdom may be made manifest through you.

Be ye of an humble mind and spirit that through you your Lord may be exalted."[6]

NOTES.

[1] Nazareth in the Logia uniformly represents a spiritual state. The real Nazarenes were in that state, hence the designation. It implied the purity of life associated with the early Nazarites, but was a further stage and higher degree of the same life. There is therefore deep meaning in the sayings that the home of the Master was at Nazareth, and that it was at Nazareth where they sought to overwhelm Him and bring His ministry to a tragic close.

[2] " An Israelite indeed " was one who was not merely such nominally, but one in spirit. He was a true child of the King Eternal, a companion of the Order of the Christhood.

[3] The Master was not merely clairvoyant ; He had the power to discern the inner life of a Soul. He knew what was in a man. It is in this way the meaning of the Fig-tree is to be understood. In the Mystery Teachings, the Fig-tree was the symbol of the Divine Wisdom, and to sit under it was to be a learner of the true Sophia.

[4] In this saying of Nathanael's there is a revelation of his own knowledge of what a Christhood was. He shows that he knew that only one who was in Christhood could perceive such interior things. And farther, his statement implies that he was conversant with the history of the Ancient Kings of Israel, those Kings which in the Apocalypse are said to have come from the Sun. These Kings were in the great Order of the Christhood, and were not rulers of men, but the Illuminati.

[5] This prophecy finds fulfilment in every one who sits under the Divine Fig-tree. It is not to be confounded with ordinary clairvoyance, which unhappily for many is not dependent upon purity of life ; for it is something truly psychic, that is, truly Soulic. It is of the Soul's vision.

[6] The state of Christhood precludes the very thought of ambition of any kind. One is the Great Teacher, even the Spirit ; and though the teacher on the human Kingdom is the direct vehicle of the Spirit, he will always remember that it is not of man, but of God. Whilst the vehicle may be revered for his work's sake, he may not seek titles such as the Schools give to their great ones. The Christs are never Masters of Assemblies. Not a few have endeavoured to associate the Master with the Head of an Occult School. The Master was distinct from all such things.

DISCIPLESHIP

" Not that which entereth through the eye or the ear, defileth a man,[1] but that which proceedeth from the heart when its desires are impure ;

For out of the heart are the issues of good and evil. —

To eat the bread of this world with unwashen hands, defileth no man ;[2] but to eat of the Bread of Heaven with unwashen hands is not only to defile himself, but also the sacred Bread which he eateth.[3]

For when the hands are unwashen, the ways of the man's life are impure ; his heart seeketh only those things found in the paths of evil, and his hands do them.

But when the hands of a man have been made clean, then are his ways those of compassion and pity ; he is full of goodness and righteousness."

" Are not two sparrows bought for one farthing ? Yet the heavenly Father-Mother taketh notice of them.

Of how much more value is a man than a sheep ? Yet the heavenly Father-Mother careth for the lambs of the fold.[4]

The ox knoweth the crib wherein its owner hath placed it, though the owner knoweth not unto what end the ox was fashioned : but in the day wherein the owner of the ox understandeth why it was fashioned, he who killeth the ox shall be as one who slayeth a man.[5]

The horse is a useful creature. He hath under-standing, though he is held and guided by bit and bridle ; but do those who use him know that when he looketh at them, he doeth so with the eyes of a man-child ?[6]

The dog is a faithful companion. How great is his affection and beautiful his devotion ? When he respondeth to his master's call he doeth so with the impulse of a child ; for he is a little man-child.[7]

Hurt not therefore one of these little ones for whom the Heavenly Father-Mother careth.

NOTES.

[1] These Sayings were in answer to questions which had been asked. Those who neither understood His Teachings nor His way of life raised difficulties where there were none. In the Records of the New Testament it is stated that the Master said " Not that which entereth into a man defileth him, but that which proceedeth from him," which is so obviously a misstatement that it is surprising any one of spiritual discernment could ever believe it. How many indeed do defile their bodies by what they eat and drink ! If the Churches had not been ensnared by the delusion foisted upon them that flesh-eating was a divinely appointed means of sustenance, they would have perceived in such a statement the hand of the betrayer.

We have to both see much and hear many things which of themselves cannot defile, but which do defile if assimilated and made part of the life's thought, feeling and action.

[2] This does not mean that uncleanness in person is acknowledged as of no account. It has reference to Jewish traditional washing of the hands. Those who followed the Master knew how pure He was, and how much purity meant in those who were with Him.

[3] The Heavenly Bread cannot be defiled ; but it can be brought down in its meanings and uses, as the religious history of the world can testify. For the unwashen hands referred to are the ways of a man's going. " Who shall ascend into the Hill of the Lord ? He who hath clean hands and a pure heart."

[4] The care of the Oversoul whom we speak of as the ever Blessed One, the Father-Mother, for all true life, is something the western world has yet to learn. It professes much belief in this direction, but by its conduct it negatives all.

[5] Who knoweth now whether the Oxen are mere temporary sojourners on this Planet, being only as the goods which become chattels for man, having no conscious perpetuated life beyond this existence ; or whether they have spiritual being hidden in their seemingly dull forms ? Man's dominion of this world is one full of astounding darkness, and ignorance of those things he should have known. The day is hastening when these words of the Master will become true in human experience.

[6] So also with the Horse man uses and abuses : it is more than it appears to be.

[7] The Dog and the Horse were once upon the Human Kingdom as Souls ; but in the last terrible human descent into the Animal Kingdom, they became so impoverished that they could not rise with the race. Many of their attributes are most human.

DISCIPLESHIP

Sayings Concerning Offence

If any one hurts or destroys one of these little ones, it would have been better for that one had he never been born.[1]

Whosoever offendeth against them, offendeth against the heavenly Father-Mother whose little ones they are.

But whosoever receiveth them to minister unto them, the same ministereth unto Him.

And whosoever giveth even a cup of water to refresh these little ones, shall in no wise lose the reward of compassion and pity.

It must needs be that not one of these little ones should perish, but that they also should enter the Kingdom.''[2]

There were brought unto the Master some who were as little children in their experience, being weak in those attributes whereby the Soul rises to its full estate.[3]

Those who brought them desired that the Master should lay His hands upon them and bless them.

And when some of the disciples saw it, they requested that the Master should not be troubled.

But He, when He heard of it, said unto them : " Suffer those who be as little children to come unto me ; of such is the Kingdom of the Heavens built up."

And He laid it upon them to pray much, lest they entered into temptation.[4]

The Rich Young Man

And behold there came unto Him one whom He had loved,[5] *and he said unto Him : " Master, what may I do that I may enter into the Eternal Life ? "*

And the Master said unto him : " Thou knowest what is good. If thou wouldst have Eternal Life, keep the commandment through which it cometh."

And he replied, " I have kept the commandments from my youth : wherein do I yet lack ? "

And the Master said unto him : " What thou hast, give in service unto those who need, and follow the way of Christhood. If thou doest this, then shalt thou have the heavenly treasure of Life Eternal."

But he turned away sorrowfully.

NOTES.

[1] The cruelty of men and women towards even the creatures has rebound. The law of cause and effect most surely follows. The memory of such deeds will haunt them in the day of their judgment and remembrance. If this were rightly understood there would soon be an end to the monstrous customs of using the creatures for food, clothing and medicine ; and abattoirs, shambles, and vivi-sectional laboratories would have no place.

[2] The little ones of the Planet's Household—the creatures—are also to come up into higher planes and enter upon the Human King-dom, and evolve and deepen in experience until they also, after their order, attain to the Life of the Kingdom of the Heavens. Not only must every human Soul be preserved, but also those not yet upon the human Kingdom.

[3] Many people are yet as little children in their spiritual experience, and not a few men and women who have been born through the older races. These must likewise be cared for and treasured as Souls. And there are very many who once were strong, but who became greatly impoverished through tragic Soul history, and in their new beginnings are weak and faltering like little ones learning to walk. These have to be led to Jesus, by which is meant the pure life and way of love of the Jesus state.

[4] This was spoken to the anxious disciples. Their very anxiety on behalf of the Master led them to do what He could not approve of. Their intention was beautiful, but their judgment was at fault. None could judge for the Master what work He should do, nor when it should be done. These things had to be left to Him to decide.

[5] The incident was fraught with much grief for the Master. He had loved the inquirer long ages ago in other service, and He loved him still. When he came making inquiry, the Master recognised him. He knew what temptation had most assailed him and taken him captive ; but He appealed to what was once the highest in him, for He knew the way of life. " Keep the commandment through which that life cometh. Give thyself with all thine attributes to the burden of the Cross."

DISCIPLESHIP

Heavenly Treasures the great Requisite

"*Lay up no treasures of the earth for yourselves, treasures whose nature is as those things which corrupt or which moths destroy; for they are like thieves who break into a house to steal.*[1]

Lay up your treasures in the Heavens, treasures which will not corrupt nor tarnish,[2] *and such as no one can steal from you; for the treasures which are of the Heavens are imperishable.*

Let your heart be filled with them. Wherever the treasure be found, there let your heart be also.

No one can have two masters and be faithful unto both. For in obeying one he would be unfaithful unto the other.

So men cannot both serve God and Mammon.[3]

Therefore, be not anxious about the morrow as to what ye shall have to eat and drink, and with what raiment ye shall be adorned; for your life is more than these.[4]

Behold the birds of the air and learn ye from them: they sow not, neither do they gather into barns, yet are they provided for by the Father-Mother in the Heavens.

And ye are greater than they.

Consider also the lilies of the field: they toil not, neither do they spin, yet are they nourished, and clothed in garments whose glory is even greater than that associated with Solomon's reign.

And the Father-Mother clotheth these.

Perceive ye not how much more your life is than these, and how the Father-Mother knoweth all your needs?[5]

Therefore, seek as the first thing, the Kingdom of God and the manifestation of His righteousness, and the heavenly treasures shall be added unto you.

By taking thought for the coming of the Kingdom of the Heavens and the fulfilment of righteousness, ye shall add unto your stature in Jesus Christ.[6]

Judge not after the manner of men, even though ye yourselves be condemned by them. For the con-

NOTES.

[1] It is not necessary to be absolutely impoverished, but it is very essential that no undue value be given to the things of sense. Where false value is assigned to earthly things, the tendency always is to corrupt the life and eat away the spiritual qualities of the Soul. Unto many have material things become like thieves robbing them of what heavenly treasures they possessed.

[2] True treasures are of the Soul. They have within themselves the preservative power of things Immortal. Pure Religion never corrupts a Soul, nor a nation. It would never lead those who possessed it to conduct which could only tarnish the life. By this sure standard the religious life of a nation may be judged. The treasures of Heaven are the precious gems of purity, pity, compassion, love, righteousness, justice.

[3] It is possible to render service unto more than one at the same time, though it would be difficult in a state of servitude where the demand of the one were for the entire service of the other. But in the Divine Service there is no such bondage, for the freedom unto which the Divine Love sets free the Soul, is perfect. Yet it is impossible to serve equally two opposing principles such as are represented by the terms, God and Mammon.

[4] How infinite the contrast between the state of mind in the professedly Christian world to-day, and the state of life recommended here ! That world is infinitely more anxious about business and gain, than Soul-culture and blessed realizations. Its ways are a comedy in that they bring into false settings the things believed to be true and sacred ; and they are also a tragedy, for in them they have crucified in themselves the Lord of Glory.

[5] It is not to be imagined that what is meant is inaction and indifference ; for service is essential upon every plane and zone of life, and it is beautiful. By service the Soul grows stronger and richer ; but the end of all the service must be the culture of life.

[6] The Kingdom of the Heavens is within ; it is the coming of the Kingdom of the God within into manifestation. And in the degree of that coming so is the becoming of Jesus Christ within.

DISCIPLESHIP

Heavenly Treasures the great Requisite

demnation which they mete out, shall be again meted out to them. For, with the measure with which men judge others, will they themselves be judged.[1]

Give not the Holy Things, the things of the Lord, unto those who be like all who turn to rend the giver of good; for they would trample them under their feet.[2]

But as men must ask for those Holy Things to be given to them, let them seek to understand the meaning of them, and they shall find it; let them knock at the door of the innermost realm, and it shall be opened unto them. For, whosoever truly asketh, receiveth from that realm; whosoever seeketh with the heart, findeth that realm; and whosoever knocketh with humble spirit at the door of that realm, shall find it opening unto him.[3]

For, though men have known evil, yet do they give good gifts unto their children; how much more then would the Father-Mother give good things unto those who ask?

If a son of His asked for bread, would He give him a stone? If he asked for fish, would He give him a serpent?[4]

Nay, the Father-Mother would give him the heavenly bread; He would make known unto him the mystery of the Kingdom of the Heavens."

NOTES.

[1] The Law of Righteousness is eternally just. Its operation is unfailing. If any one imagines it can be defeated, the hour of awakening will come. But the operation of the law of cause and effect is not unmerciful. The Eternal Justice is a very different quality to that made manifest in civil and criminal courts. The burden it imposes is not only one of restitution but of redemption. The law of Divine Love demands that the Soul who does wrong to another should do service by which that wrong would be undone ; and in the service both are blessed.

[2] The innermost experiences of the Soul may not be told to everyone. Few could understand them ; many would misunderstand and misinterpret them. Nay, there are not wanting those who, whilst professing to be willing to hear that they may learn, only turn to rend the one whose heart and Soul have been laid bare. Well did the Master understand what even religious men and women could do when tradition bound them.

[3] The way to the understanding of the Innermost Things is always the same, in every religious expression, in every age, and amid every race. No man however gifted can impart that knowledge which is of God and the Soul. Divine ministries aid the life in its forward endeavours, but the way into the Kingdom is by means of desiring, praying, yearning—asking, seeking, knocking. Never Soul entered the Kingdom by other means. The three-fold Path must be trod. The cross must be borne in self-denial, self-sacrifice, and self-abandonment.

[4] The Bread is the shew bread of the spiritual priesthood, which is found of those who enter the middle court of the Temple of Life in the spirit of reverent sacrifice ; the Fish is the sacred mystery of Life which is hidden from the view of all but those who enter into the holiest of all—the innermost shrine where God overshadows the Soul. Both terms had deep mystic meanings.

DISCIPLESHIP

Parables concerning the Divine Love

Unto many who came to Him, the Master spake of the way of the Father-Mother in His Love towards all His children, even unto all who had gone far astray in their ways. For there were those who were accounted sinful amongst the many who drew near unto Him, and thus in parable did He show the way of the Love of the Father-Mother unto them.

" There was a shepherd into whose care one hundred sheep had been committed. He led them amidst pastures which belonged to his lord, and cared for them one by one ; for he knew them by name and called them, and they knew his voice and followed him.[1]

Now adjacent to the pastures there was a wilderness not owned by his lord, and into this many other sheep had strayed and been lost.[2]

Whilst he tended his flock, one of the sheep lingered behind the others, and strayed into the wilderness where it became lost.

When the shepherd discovered that one had wandered away, he committed the ninety and nine into the care of another shepherd who served his lord, and betook him into the wilderness to search for the lost one until it was found.

And as he sought it out he called it by name, and the sheep knew his voice ; so he at last found it, but in a bruised and wounded state. And he tenderly lifted it upon his shoulder and brought it back to the fold.[3]

In like manner does the Father-Mother through His shepherds seek His lost children.

For if a man would do so much for his lost sheep, think you the Lord of our Life would do less to find His children who are lost?[4]

Nay, for they are of more value than many sheep.

Because He so loves, He has sent the Good Shepherd into the wilderness to seek until He find all who are lost.

For many are now there, having gone far astray in their wanderings.

NOTES.

[1] Though this parable is obvious in its meaning when interpreted in relation to the children of this world, and is full of beautiful encouragement to all Souls to approach the Father-Mother, yet it contains greater depths of meaning than are apparent. In this parable the deeper significance is hidden, but in the allegory of the sheep it is revealed.

The pastures were the true spiritual planes of this system which at one time were in perfect equilibrium, and, being so, Souls were truly nourished upon them. The reference to the sheep knowing the shepherd and each having been named by him, belongs to the teaching in the allegory, though here it is also true. For each Soul has a name and a number in the Divine Household. The universe is built up upon numbers with their signs.

[2] It was the Wilderness of Judah, the changed planes of the Planet with all the terrible conditions which had arisen. Many were the sheep lost amid its labyrinths. It was easy to enter the wilderness and get mixed up in its labyrinthine ways, but it became most difficult to get out again. Herein is a description of what the Souls of this world have experienced at the hands of the evil conditions which arose. It is more easy to get into bondage to desires that are wrong and ways that are sad and evil, than it is to arise out of them.

[3] In these sayings there is reference to great spiritual events, though they are here necessarily veiled.

[4] The tragedy of this fallen world became the tragedy of the Divine Love, for in order to effect the Salvation of the Planet and all her children, infinite sacrifices had to be made. And it reveals what the intrinsic value of one little world is amid all the hosts of celestial systems, and how great is the value of a human Soul in the Divine Scheme of life, when the ministry of the Heavens becomes so extended that not one of all the human children is left without it.

DISCIPLESHIP

The Good Shepherd loveth the sheep : He knoweth them all by name and calleth them.[1]

Parables concerning the Divine Love

He leadeth and guideth amid the pastures all who hear His voice and who follow Him.

Through the portals He leadeth them into the fold where they are safe,[2] *and where the wolf cometh not.*

For the wolf cometh up out of the wilderness to kill and destroy.[3]

The Good Shepherd even giveth His life for the sheep ; He goeth down into the wilderness to find that which has been lost.

He hath power to lay down His life in the finding of them, and He has power to take up life again ; this power hath He had bestowed upon Him from the Father-Mother.

And when He findeth any of those sheep which have been lost, He beareth them back to the fold ; and great is the joy in the presence of the Angels of God when the lost ones return unto Him."[4]

" There was a father who had two sons.

Upon both he bestowed his blessing and committed unto them much of his possessions, that in freedom and love they might serve him within his estate.

And for a time the service of both was good, and their devotion beautiful ; so the father had occasion of great joy in them.

But there came unto the younger of the two sons one who did not love the father, and who desired to do an evil thing unto him ; and he laid temptation in the way of the younger son, and drew him from his father's household and estate.[5]

When the younger son had left behind him the father's house and estate, the tempter led him into a far country, robbed him of all his possessions, and left him in a desert land desolate and impoverished.

And he languished so greatly from want of nourish-

NOTES.

[1] The use of the expression the Good Shepherd was meant in relation to Adonai. One is the Good Shepherd, even the Eternal Love made manifest in Him. The Master has always had this term applied to Himself by readers of the New Testament ; but He would not have so accepted it, though He had been in the position indicated in the allegory. It is quite true that He gave up His life—gave up His Christhood consciousness with all the most blessed realizations which accompany it, and is thus said to have laid down His life— but that giving up must always be associated with Adonai. It was the Divine Love who stooped through the Master even unto the uttermost.

[2] The portals are the several initiatory states through which the Soul passes as it enters ever more and more fully into the consciousness of spiritual being. The Fold has many Houses or departments, each with its distinctive portal.

[3] The wolf represents a state of mind brought about through the influences of the Astral World upon it. For the Astral World became the wilderness through the changing of all its elements. The wolf cometh to kill and destroy, because the mind in the state represented by it, killeth the best aspirations of the Soul and destroyeth its beautiful hope.

[4] The mere statement that there is joy in the Presence of the Angels of God when a Soul returns into a found state, implies what is meant by being found. When the Soul finds a man, the whole being becomes changed. The wilderness life that once delighted him only brings him pain and sorrow, and he seeks unto that land of pure delight found in the life of purity, compassion and love. The joy is begotten of the returning of a Soul into these blessed possessions.

[5] This parable is also an allegory of the going down of the Soul in what is called the Fall. The enemy who came was the materialising influence, a power that does not love the Father-Mother, because it destroys what He loves. It was that spirit which robbed the Soul of all its beautiful spiritual possessions, and thus took it into a desert land where it languished.

C—I

DISCIPLESHIP

Parables concerning the Divine Love

ment, that he would fain have partaken even of those things which only the swine do eat.

And he sorrowed in his loneliness and shame ; and no one came to comfort and aid him, for he was in an enemy's land.[1]

But there came a time when, amid his sorrow and shame, he recalled all the way he had been led by the one who deceived and betrayed him ; so he purposed to find his way out of the desert land.[2]

And he arose and left the place in which he had so long dwelt in sorrow and shame ; and he retraced the way back to his father's house, in the hope that he might be forgiven for all the sorrow he had caused through his mistake, and be nourished in his weakness and impoverishment.

As he journeyed thither, so great was the shame of his condition within him, that he felt he was no more worthy to be accounted his father's son, and that he was less in his estate than a hired servant.[3]

But he resolved to be even as one of these, if his father would receive him.

And lo, whilst he was yet a long way off, the father beheld him coming, and in his joy went forward to meet and welcome him.[4]

And he who had gone so far away said unto the father : ' Father, I have sinned against thee in the sight of heaven, and am no more worthy to be called thy son ; wilt thou receive me and make me one of thy servants ? '

But the father said unto him : ' Nay, for thou art my son, even though thou hast been perishing for lack.

Come, there is still thy room awaiting thee, and all the goods thou didst leave behind. Thou hast been lost unto me, but now art thou found ; it is meet that we should rejoice together '[5]

And the son bowed his head upon his father's neck and wept sorrowfully, grieving that he had ever gone away from so great a love.

So is it when the Kingdom of the Heavens cometh within those who have been lost but are found again.

NOTES.

[1] The enemy land is that far country into which the Soul goes when it leaves the paths of purity and good, and descends in its desires until it would fain gratify them amid the swinish elements. No one can aid or comfort the Soul in that state.

[2] The first awakening of the Soul to the consciousness of its low estate. The new purpose is full of deep pathos, and it is sad though beautiful. The going away is easier than the coming back. The journey to the enemy's land is less difficult than the finding of the way back to the Kingdom of the Father-Mother.

[3] In the return of many of those who originally belonged to the Ancient Order of the Christhood, this very experience has been passed through. Some of them were betrayed unto the uttermost, and their coming back into the Kingdom of the Father-Mother has proved a painful process for them. But they were always of humble spirit ; and in their return, humiliation has been great within them.

[4] The Ministry of the Divine Love meets a Soul long ere it reaches the Kingdom itself. When once the setting out on the homeward journey is begun, the ministry of Angels draws near. Were it not so, no Soul could reach the Kingdom. But for the Grace of God revealed in manifold ministry, no Soul could be saved unto Life Eternal.

[5] There is a pathos in these words, subtle and wonderful : subtle in that they covertly reveal that each Soul has a place in the Great Temple of Life ; wonderful because they show the graciousness of the Divine Love towards the individual. Amid all the hardships met on the way, as a Soul is returning from the far country, there is this to remember which is full of hope, that the place which it ought to fill still awaits it ; that the treasures so long left are ready for its use.

DISCIPLESHIP

Parables concerning the Divine Love

For every one who has gone away from the land of the great Father-Mother, and has known the bitterness of betrayal by all those who be enemies unto Him, has indeed been a sojourner in a strange land that has been desert.[1]

And their return unto the Father-Mother is in like manner ; for though amid the impoverishment of the desert land they have often partaken of those things in which there is shame and bitterness, yet when they come to themselves and arise out of their shame and purpose to come unto the Father-Mother, they are met on their way.

And every one who cometh back feeleth conscious of the great loss sustained by them,[2] and how unworthy they have become in their own sight to be spoken of as His sons.

For within them the sorrow is great, because of the impoverishment of their life, and it is with meekness and lowliness of heart that they return.

But in the Heavens the joy is great ; for in the return of every Soul there is found one who had been lost.

And the welcome is such as no one could conceive ; for the blessed ones meet upon the threshold all who find their way thither.[3]

Upon the wanderer are new garments placed, that he may be clad as becometh a Son of the Father-Mother, even the white raiment so pure and beautiful, which those wear who dwell within the Heavens.[4]

And unto him are given new shoon to replace those he has worn whilst wandering ; for his ways will be no more those of the desert land, but such as befitteth the house of the Father-Mother, and one who is restored to sonship.[5]

Even the seal of union will be given unto him, that seal which will reveal him to be the Son of the Father-Mother.[6]

And within the Heavens shall the Pascal Lamb be partaken of ;[7] for all will be full of great joy through partaking once more of the Divine Love."

NOTES.

[1] There are many who in this life have not seemed to go far afield in their ways, and these doubtless imagine that they have never been prodigal in their ways. But not one of the children of this world escaped scatheless. Indeed, all went down into the depths, though some by reason of their attributes went farther than others.

[2] Not the eternal loss in ultimates, which, though possible, is rare indeed ; but the loss within their own consciousness of those powers once possessed and exercised by them. For, though through the return they will come into the possession again of these attributes, during the return the consciousness of the limitations is sometimes very great.

[3] The Angelic Ministry is little understood. So real is it and so blessed, that not a Soul is left without it.

[4] The new garments are the raiment of the redeemed life.

[5] The new shoon represent the new ways of the understanding. The feet were spoken of symbolically as representing the thought and ways of life.

[6] Those who rise up out of the fallen conditions and return into the unfallen state, or life of purity, goodness and love, are sealed with the name of Son of God, for they are in the path to that most glorious realization.

[7] The Pascal Lamb was the Divine Love in its sacrificial capacity, by which it accomplishes within a Soul its redemption, and ultimately its regeneration.

DISCIPLESHIP

"A King once made a great festival on behalf of his son, to celebrate the marriage of the latter; and he sent out his servants with invitations unto all who should be guests on that occasion.[1]

When the appointed time had come, there were excuses sent by some of those who had been bidden; and these greatly grieved the King, for they were not such reasons as should have prevented them from being present to participate in so important an event.

One said: ' I have bought some new land, and I must needs attend to it.'[2]

Another said: ' Five yoke of oxen have I procured, and I must put them to the trial; so I cannot come.'[3]

And there was one who for excuse said: ' I am married to a wife, so I need not come.'[4]

Then the King sent out his servants unto them, saying: ' Come now, for all things have been got ready; leave your land, your goods, and your friends for a little while, that ye may be of the marriage feast.'

Yet they would not come.

And the King being full of grief that they should treat his son so unkindly, sent back his servants, saying unto them: ' Go ye out to the highways and fields where they be, and constrain them to come in.'

And the servants returned unto the King and said, ' It is done, thy command hath been obeyed.'

So they went into the marriage feast.

Now of those who had been invited there were some who had been impotent and blind and halt; for the King had desired to have them present.[5]

These were clad in wedding garments provided by the King.

But some murmured that these were present as guests, and that they had apportioned unto them places at the table of the King, and such royal raiment.[6]

Unto those who so murmured the King said: 'Friends, I do ye no wrong. These did I invite because they were ready to accept; and they are worthy.[7]

42

NOTES.

[1] It is a parable of the Christhood coming into manifestation. All who should have been able to respond were invited. They should have shared the glory of so happy an event.

[2] A new earthward interest. Men and women soon find a reáson for not responding to the appeal of the Divine Love and Wisdom. It is easy for them to secure new land to till.

[3] The ' It ' is the symbol of the body, and to have a five-fold yoke was to have awakened unto the consciousness of a new power of the senses, which are five.

[4] Here the Soul is married to the life of the Earth, for it did not require to come. The earth ties are supreme, so the Soul suffers, and the Christhood loses its guest.

[5] Of those who enter the Kingdom many have been in these states. They have come to know Divine Healing, and have followed. The Divine Judgment as to fitness is remarkable for the way in which it differs from that of men. Priesthoods, Schools and Churches have had their day of power in judging as to fitness. Those whom they accounted impotent, blind and halt have found the way into the Christhood whilst they have remained outside.

[6] Honour is done unto all who are worthy, of whatsoever race, nation and religion. In the Kingdom of the Heavens there is no such racial and social caste as men believe in and practice. The Lord of all the Earth doth righteously.

[7] Whosoever willeth to enter into the marriage festival of the Christhood estate is acceptable ; and whosoever responds in fulness to the King's behests may attain unto the perfect day of realization.

DISCIPLESHIP

And I would say this unto you ; when ye make a feast, call not your kinsmen and friends only, for they can recompense you again.[1]

But rather call ye those who are unable to recompense you—the poor, the maimed, the halt and the blind.[2]

For in ministering unto these, ye shall have the recompense of joy, that ye served those who could not recompense you.[3]

In like manner is it in the Kingdom of the Heavens.[4]

In the coming of that Kingdom the Lord of Life sendeth forth His messengers to invite all who will to come ; and those who be infirm and poor, those who be maimed and blind, are also called to share in the joy of its coming.

For in its coming, sight is given to the blind, hearing to the deaf, healing to the maimed, strength to the impotent, raiment for all who be unclothed, and the bread of life for everyone.

In the Kingdom of the Father-Mother, those who be of humble heart are exalted ; those who be poor in spirit are enriched ; those who have been cast down and left wounded by the wayside are lifted up and comforted ; and all the impoverished ones who have cried in their hunger for bread, are nourished from the Lord's table.

NOTES.

[1] The ecclesiastical and social orders have always followed the way of caste in their fellowship. Their feasts have been for their kinsfolk and friends, for those who moved in their own circles, or circles to which they aspired. The Church has repeated the ways of Society; within its fellowship caste is as strong and manifest as within the social fabric. Even the various religious communities are like so many different castes. There is no real inter-communion amongst them. They are like families who are jealous of each other's estate and each desires to be first in point of prestige. Their feasts, such as they are, are for themselves.

[2] When feasts are made for those who be poor, maimed, halt and blind, they are in their origin and ministry acts of mere charity— not charity understood divinely, but as understood by the social and religious orders. To minister unto those who are not able to recompense us must never be regarded in that light, but as a most blessed privilege of serving our Lord and making consecrate our gifts in His service.

[3] The whole trend of the West has been to seek reward for any service rendered. It has penetrated all circles. It has grown to be an important element in life for the people. There is so little that is selfless in any department of service. Yet it is only in selfless ministry that the recompense can be realized of supreme spiritual joy. The servant is always worthy of his or her hire; and gifts of love should be given : but the service must be selfless, and the gifts not accounted as recompense.

[4] When the Kingdom of the Heavens has been firmly established on this world, the present inverted social orders will be changed ; they will be brought into a state of true equilibrium. The poor, the maimed, the halt and the blind—not only those who are so literally, but the vast multitudes, rich and poor, who are in such states of impoverishment spiritually—will then be invited to the Feast of the Divine Love, and have rendered unto them a selfless ministry.

DISCIPLESHIP

The Woman who found the lost Coin

" *A woman lost a coin which she accounted of great value, and sought most carefully everywhere to find it, even calling upon her friends to aid her in the search. But they failed to find it.*[1]

Then, when she was alone, she bethought her that she might search within her own house for it, if haply she might find it.[2]

So she secured a light and went from room to room, diligently seeking as she went; and at last she was rewarded, to her great joy, for she found it in the upper room.[3]

And she ran to her friends to tell them of her good fortune, and said unto them: ' Rejoice with me, for I have found my treasure within my own house, and in my upper room; for there it had been overlaid and hidden.'

So is it when the Kingdom of the Father-Mother is found.

The treasure which is of greatest value is discovered to be lost, and men and women seek everywhere without, that they may find it.

But they discover it not, because it is not there.

Then doth the woman within their house, get the light that revealeth all things; and with it she maketh search, sweeping the rooms as she proceeds, until she cometh to the upper room, and there she maketh the discovery that the Kingdom of the Heavens had hidden the treasure of its realm there.[4]

And when the sacred thing is found and its beautiful superscription discerned, great is the joy within that house, even the joy of the Angels of the Heavens who are in the Presence of the Father-Mother "

The Unjust Steward

" *A certain rich man had a steward who was unjust in his actions, and who wasted his lord's goods.*

His lord called upon him to render a full account of his stewardship; and when he had done so, his lord dismissed him because he had been so wasteful and unjust.

46

NOTES.

[1] The inner meaning of this parable will be most difficult to apprehend, except where a Soul who was once in Christhood is again returning to that state. There is implied in the parable the loss of something esteemed of great value to the loser, so much so, that everywhere is it searched for, if haply it might be found. It could not therefore relate to the evolution of a Soul towards the consciousness of the Divine Life, for in that instance there would be no sense of loss. It is not a parable illustrating growth, but rather one in which there has been attainment of high estate, and then through some cause not named in the parable that possession has been lost.

Here the Woman is the Soul, and the coin is the sacred possession which has been lost by her. Those Souls who once were in the consciousness known as Christhood are always the true seekers for the Kingdom of the Heavens ; for they do not seek mere knowledge, even though it may be termed the Sophia, but they seek for the realization of the blessed life.

[2] The Soul, in its seeking for the recovery of its lost treasure, does search everywhere at first. But nowhere does it find satisfaction until it seeks within itself. It is within the woman's house that the treasure has been lost.

[3] The light by which it is discovered, overlaid in the upper room, is the Intuition illumined from the Divine Sun. Through the Intuition are all things made known unto the Soul. And it is in the upper room or sanctuary where the Divine Presence alone is realized.

[4] Within the sanctuary of every Soul lies hidden the treasure of the Divine Life. In many it is only yet latent, for they have not yet come up into the realizations which it gives. But when a Soul has once had these, and they become lost to its consciousness, they are preserved for it within the sanctuary against the day of its return.

In these days there are those who are finding their lost treasure.

DISCIPLESHIP

The Unjust Steward

Then the unjust steward went unto those with whom he had traded, and said unto them, severally: ' How much owest thou to my lord ?' And one replied: ' One hundred measures of oil.' And the unjust steward said : ' Take this bond which maketh it fifty.'

And unto another he said : ' How much owest thou my lord ?' And this debtor replied, ' One hundred measures of wheat.' And to him also the unjust steward said : ' Take this bond, for it maketh it fifty.'

And in like manner did he act towards all who had been his lord's debtors.

When his lord discovered what he had done he was grieved, and sent unto him that he would speak with him.

So when the unjust steward came back, his lord inquired of him why he had done this thing against him.

And the steward said : ' When thou didst dismiss me thy service, I knew not what to do.

I have not strength to dig, and my shame preventeth me from going forth to beg. So did I this evil thing in the hope that these thy debtors might receive me into their houses.'

And his lord had compassion upon him, and forgave him, and restored him to his office.

Thus are Souls tempted by the unrighteousness of mammon to do evil, hoping thereby to get gain.

They think themselves to be the wise ones in their day, and forget that they are the habitations of the Eternal One whom they should remember as their Lord, and serve as His faithful stewards.

Be ye His stewards.

Make not for yourselves gain of the mammon of unrighteousness, nor be tempted to go in that way ; for it will fail you, and lead you into sorrow and loss.

But be ye tabernacles of the Eternal Love, that, through you, it may be manifest what righteous steward-ship is and how it is faithful in those things which are accounted least, as well as in the great things."

NOTES.

The first or general meaning of the parable must be obvious to all. That it is meant to present the conduct of Souls in their use of the Divine Treasures within themselves which had been committed into their trust, is evident to any serious reader. And the half measure of response of Souls to their indebtedness to the Divine Love and Wisdom, is strikingly illustrated, for it is just what has been wrought through the unjust stewardship of those who should have been the helpers and teachers of Souls.

The parable also reveals the Divine graciousness towards those who have erred and confessed their wrong, and in this it should encourage faltering and sorrowing ones, for all have in a measure been unfaithful stewards in our use of the fine spiritual elements in us, and the attributes we have acquired.

Yet beyond all this lies a deeper significance, its innermost meaning. That must imply a high state of consciousness. For Souls do not become cognisant of any great responsibility passed on to them, such as is indicated by the position of the steward in the parable, until they have attained a degree of Christhood. It is in this direction that the meaning of the parable for the disciples is to be found.

The picture is that of one who is fully conscious of his stewardship, one who knows the powers that lie at his hand for his service, one who is cognisant of the treasures within the House of his Lord, and who is there to administer those treasures and use those powers as in the sight of his Lord.

But even in those who know much, and who desire high and holy things, great is the temptation to yield to influences of a personal order, and serve the personal first.

How often those who are entrusted with the most sacred service, allow the clamour of lower desires and feelings to weigh with them and take them away from the true Path of faithful service unto their Lord ? They act as if they were anxious to make sure of both worlds in the sense of the worldling.

DISCIPLESHIP

The ara e of the Talents

" *The coming of the Kingdom of the Heavens shall be even as the coming of a great one who has been journeying in distant lands, and the calling together of his servants and the delivering unto them of powers for service.*

For, in the Kingdom, unto one is given ten talents, unto another five, and unto another one ; unto each servant according to the power to use.[1]

And when the Kingdom in its coming shall be accomplished, those who have been endowed with the talents for the Lord's service shall be brought together.

And it will be found that the possessors of the talents have enriched the Kingdom of their Lord through the uses unto which their powers were put in His service.

He of many talents will find himself enriched and increased in power for service ; for the ten will have become twenty, the five ten, the two four, and the one two.

For they who be faithful, thus fit themselves for higher and fuller service in the Kingdom of their Lord.[2]

For in the coming of the Kingdom, the Souls of all who serve are enlarged, and their lives made blessed.

And if there be found those who, having had talents for service bestowed upon them, do not put their powers to use for the Kingdom, and think that the service of the Lord is not the service which they thought it to be, or desired that it should be, these will suffer loss.

For the treasures of the Kingdom can be given only unto those in whom it is coming, even those treasures which the Lord bringeth with Him.

Herein is the mystery of the Kingdom of the Heavens in its coming, and the justice of its judgment.

Unto all who have of its treasures, and use these for their Lord, shall more abundantly be added ; but from all who have and yet serve as if they had not, shall be taken away the power of that which they have."

NOTES.

[1] The various talents represent the various powers of which the Soul has become conscious in its awakening to Divine realities. In the first awakening the talent may be only one ; that is, though the Soul has all the attributes of a Christhood latent within itself, yet only one of these may at first be called forth into activity. Then come two, then five, even in some, ten.

The coming of the Kingdom of the Heavens is the conscious becoming of the Divine Life.

[2] The Kingdom of the Lord is enriched to the extent of the Soul's awakening and realization. Every one whose face is turned homeward, that is, towards the blessed realization of the Divine Life, adds to the multiple consciousness of that kingdom upon the earth, and thus enriches it.

And in this thing will they themselves be greatly enriched, for the one attribute will have become two-fold in its power, the two four, the three six, the four eight, the five ten, and up to the ten, which also will have become doubled, for·every attribute of the Soul becomes twofold in its ministry. It has its positive and negative, its active and passive modes. Nor does it rest content in its ten attributes—the House of Christhood, but goes on to the realization of the full power in the twelve, which number with the Soul makes thirteen, the number of Divine Christhood.

The training of the twelve Apostles is the realization of the twelve attributes, which in due course become twenty-four—the number of one of the Ancient Ones.

Herein is the blessed mystery of Christhood.

Thus every awakened Soul grows through the use of its attributes in spiritual service until the day of perfect realization.

But those who fail to respond to the awakening and put their powers to wrong service, or refuse to make use of their attributes, suffer loss ; and it may be that their loss will prevent them from entering the Kingdom or consciousness of the Christhood for many days. This is no harsh Divine Judgment, but the natural corollary of their own indifference.

DISCIPLESHIP

The Parable of the Virgins

" *And in the days of the coming of the Son of Man shall the Kingdom of the Heavens become as in the days when the Virgins went forth to meet the Bridegroom.*[1]

Of these Virgins five were wise and five were foolish ; for whilst they awaited the coming of the Bridegroom, these latter all slumbered and slept.[2]

When they awakened, hearing the cry that the Bridegroom was coming, they found that it was all dark around them, for they had permitted their lamps to burn out ; and they had no oil wherewith to replenish them.[3]

Then they besought those Virgins who had been wise, to give unto them of their light to enable them to go forth to meet the Bridegroom.

But the Virgins who had been wise said that that could not be ; that they must go unto Him who alone could supply the oil for their lamps.[4]

And whilst they tarried in the darkness, behold the Bridegroom appeared unto the Virgins who had been wise, and they went in with Him unto the Marriage Feast.[5]

Then when those Virgins who had been foolish found oil for their lamps, and came forth unto the house of the Bridegroom, they found that the door had been shut.

And they knocked at the door, seeking to be admitted to the marriage festival.

But those who were appointed to keep the door said unto these foolish ones : ' *The Bridegroom has come and only those who were ready have been permitted by Him to enter in.*'

And when they pleaded with those who kept the door, to let them in as they were known unto the Bridegroom, they were answered by those within that it was too late, as they could not enter now.

And they went away most sorrowfully.

But when the Bridegroom heard of it, He was filled with grief, and sent His servants after them to bid them yet come.[6]

NOTES.

[1] Two expressions in this parable require explaining, as they were mystery terms, having an entirely esoteric meaning. The first is " the Son of Man," and the second is " Virgin."[1] The term Son of Man is an ancient one in which Adonai in manifestation through a Soul is denoted. It was not used to designate the vehicle of the manifestation, for it was impersonal in its meaning. Thus, the coming of the Son of Man was the becoming of the Divine within a Soul unto manifestation.

The term Virgin expressed a Soul-state. It signified a Soul unfallen in its nature.

[2] The Virgins, said to be wise, are those who have again awakened to the consciousness of the becoming of Christ within them which is the coming again of the Son of Man, for the Bridegroom is the Lord Presence within the Soul, and in the higher degrees of Christhood the Soul is married to its Lord—that is, it becomes one with Him. Within that Soul the light of His glory shines. The flame of its lamp is kindled from the Lord. ·

The foolish virgins are those who have failed to awaken to the higher realizations, Souls in whom the consciousness of the light that once was in them has slumbered and slept, still virgin because they have not fallen in their innermost desires and feelings, whose substances are still pure.

[3] The light of their lamps had gone out of their consciousness, they had lost and had not found again the knowledge of their Lord. Therefore they had no oil.

[4] Many of those who were of the Christhood of most ancient times are still in this condition. And they seek everywhere for oil but of Him from whom it alone can come. Divine knowledge is not to be had from any man. It is something born within from the Presence, and the Soul must seek there.

[5] The Festival of the Christhood.

[6] The door is never shut to any Soul. Many find it difficult to reach. But the true seeker will always find. Yet the true path must always be followed. The royal road is the only way. There can be no entering into the marriage feast by any who do not find the door and pass through it. Even the Virgin Souls who have lost their inherent Christhood light must find that light once more ere the feast of Christhood can be partaken of.

The parable anticipated the days in which we live.

D—I

53

DISCIPLESHIP

And they returned and entered in, though the hour was late ; and they also partook of the marriage feast with their Lord.

The Parable of the Virgins

And the house was filled with the joy of it.

Even so shall it be in the days of the coming of the Son of Man.

And in those days, may ye also be ready to enter in with the Bridegroom.

May your loins be girdled, and your lamps burning brightly."

Dives and Lazarus

Now, amongst those who came to listen to the Master were some few who loved riches and hated poverty.[1]

In order to help them to overcome the desire, and to seek supremely the riches of the Spirit, He spake this parable unto them.

" There was a very rich man who fared sumptuously every day.

His garments were made of fine linen, and he arrayed himself in a purple robe.

At his gate from day to day there sat one who had been greatly impoverished, and who suffered so sorely that he would fain have shared with the dogs the portions left over from the rich man's table.

But he of the sumptuous desires, cared not whether the impoverished one was tended, nourished and comforted.[2]

And it came to pass that both passed from these states into the world that is unseen, and there their estates were reversed.[3]

He who had been so greatly impoverished here was much enriched there.

His wounds were healed and his raiment was the white linen of those who have overcome.[4]

But he who had lived in sumptuousness found himself much impoverished and unable even to quench his great thirst ; for the fires of the Hadean World consumed him.[5]

NOTES.

[1] There have been those who believed that absolute poverty was essential to attainment of Life Eternal, and have given up all they possessed in the hope of finding it. Many of the Monastic systems had this end in view. Yet it cannot be shown that these found the high state of Christhood. One who would find Christ must be poor in spirit—that is, humble. He must be poor in respect of this life—that is, he must set no store upon anything of a material order. Whatsoever may have come to him must not be held in any other light than as means for service. His life must be selfless.

It is quite possible to be poor and yet long to have riches. But no Soul who loves divinely could become rich.

[2] None who understand will deny the hardening effect of the love of wealth. Many otherwise noble men and women have been brought down by the love of having in possession. There never would have been any impoverished ones had the rich used their wealth rightly. The beggar at the rich man's gate would have been unknown.

[3] This is a great truth. The states of Souls in the Beyond are so frequently the reverse of what men would have anticipated. It is the inner spirit that matters, the heart's desire, the Soul's yearning. The outward life, with its phenomena, is often a mask.

[4] Those who have passed through and have overcome are indeed of the poor of this world. Rarely have they much of the earthly treasures, and they desire them not. They set no store upon earthly riches, but seek alone the spiritual and divine. And they give up all earthliness that they may find the Kingdom in fulness.

[5] The purgatorial fires are within a Soul ; they are kindled and fed from the astral elements.

DISCIPLESHIP

And in that condition there came unto him a vision of his own estate, and also that into which the impoverished one had passed; for he beheld Lazarus as if he were in the bosom of Abraham, whilst he himself had been cast out of the Kingdom of Abraham.

And he anguished sorely, and sorrowed over his estate.[1]

Then he prayed that Lazarus, whom he had despised in his earth life, would bring unto him the water that would cool his tongue and quench his thirst, for there was none such where he was.

But no one could go down to him, so great was the gulf between them.

And he cried out the more that Lazarus might be sent unto him, lest he should be consumed amid the fires.

And there was sent unto him this message: ' Child, in thy sorrow and pain remember thou how thou didst for thyself and others when thou wast upon the earth spheres, and repent. Thou beholdest how Lazarus is comforted and enriched. Be thou also poor in thy spirit, humble and just in all thy ways; then wilt thou rise, out of thine anguish and thy pain, and be comforted.' "[2]

In speaking unto many who came to Him to inquire of the Way which He taught, the Master made use of this parable to illustrate what He meant.

" A sower went forth to sow his seed. As he scattered it, some fell by the wayside, and there the fowls of the air gathered it; some fell upon stony ground, and seemed to grow more quickly, but not having depth for nourishment, it soon withered; some fell amongst thorns and thistles, and was choked ere it could reach maturity; but that which fell upon the good ground bore abundant grain, even thirty, sixty and one hundred-fold."

And some who had become disciples of the Way which He taught, said unto Him: " Wilt thou interpret this parable for us ? "

56

NOTES.

[1] Gehenna is within a man or woman. It is the state of the Soul when it is beginning to awaken to the consciousness of its own evil. It may be here or beyond. There are many in the hell-states who are absolutely unconscious of it. It is when the consciousness of the state dawns that sorrow and anguish come. In such an awakening there is hope. It begins a new epoch for the Soul.

[2] Here there is no harsh condemnation ; but there is justice. The Divine Justice is full of the goodness of the Lord. It is healing. There is healing for all, even in the worst hells here and beyond ; but those in these states must be purified, for true healing is by the process of purification, and purification is the redemption of the Soul.

The parable had yet deeper meanings, but these could only be given to the groups of disciples who had found Christ. It was retrospective and prospective : it revealed what the Jewish Church had done with its riches, and it foreshadowed what was coming through the new Church to be raised in the name of Christhood. Jewry clothed itself in the fine linen and purple robes of priesthood that was no true priesthood, but it starved the Souls of the children. They were spiritually as Lazarus—children of a lazar house.

But its deepest and most poignant and sorrowful application had relation to the Christhood. Ecclesiasticism did indeed fare sumptuously. It drew material treasures to itself, and it held the spiritual treasures in the sacred Mysteries. Of course, it did not understand these latter, though it set them forth in symbols. But it made of the Christhood an impoverished state. The Christ, as a conscious blessed realization, sat Lazarus-like at the gates awaiting recognition.

Here we may not say farther : those who understand will behold what the West did with the Christ-Vision.

DISCIPLESHIP

And unto them He said : " Unto you who seek for the Kingdom of the Heavens are its Mysteries to be made manifest.[1] Hear, therefore, the interpretation of the parable of the sower.

The sower of the seed of the Kingdom of the Heavens is the Lord of Life and the seed is His Word of Love and Wisdom.

Through those whom He sends He scattereth the seed. As it is scattered, some falls upon those who are represented by the byway or hardened ground, where it cannot find any soil amid which to fructify ; and in them the seed is soon lost sight of, for the birds of the air or the shallow and fleeting things of this world soon eat it up.[2]

The seed sown upon the stony ground represents those in whom are possibilities of fructification, but who have not yet acquired depth of desire and feeling ; for though the seed appear to germinate and grow somewhat as if it would come to fruition, yet the lack of depth prevents it from arriving at that state in them.[3]

The ground which brought forth thorns and thistles which choked the growth so that no maturity could be reached, represents those in whom the seed has taken root and grown into manifestation, but over whom the cares and customs of the world exercise so great power that these choke the life and prevent its unfoldment.[4]

But the good ground is the willing heart and mind that receives the word of the Divine Love and Wisdom, and cherishes it unto fulness of growth in understanding and manifestation. In them the Word bringeth forth thirty, sixty, and one hundred-fold."[5]

NOTES.

[1] The Mysteries were the knowledges containing the history of the Soul and the laws of its growth ; the Planet and the System to which it belonged, with the history of life upon the former, and the history of the whole system ; the Fall and the Redemption ; the Christhood and the Regeneration ; the nature and ministry of the Divine Love and Wisdom. These Mysteries had to be withdrawn from the ken of men and women owing to the manner of their life, for they could only be truly understood through realization. There were found in different schools remnants of these knowledges and these were taught to their several initiates. But the true knowledge of the mysteries was not occult, but spiritual ; they were not mere skeleton knowledges of the mind, but realizations within the Soul.

Herein is the difference between occult and mystic knowledge. In the one it is something believed in because it has been taught ; in the other it is something understood through Soul vision.

[2] A sad commentary upon the religious history of this world for thousands of ages.

[3] This is true where Souls are even growing. It is most difficult to get deeper than the superficial soil of their nature. Many do receive with joy a message which touches their emotional nature, and they become moved for a time ; but by and by the influence passes.

[4] These represent many of the elder Souls of the Planet and not a few of those who once belonged to the Christhood Order, whose service in the world was upon the more outward planes.

[5] Only the few come into the full realization of the Divine Life latent within, for the conditions have prevented many from entering in. But the day is hastening when it will become the blessed realization of all who once knew that high Life and many who were then on the way to it. The numbers indicate states of consciousness in the Soul.

DISCIPLESHIP

He spake also this parable concerning the trials which befell a sower of good seed.

The Parable of Wheat and Tares

" The Kingdom of the Heavens, when it cometh, is like one who sowed good seed in the fields belonging to his household.[1]

But when the blade appeared above the ground, there were found beside it tares which some enemy had sown.

And the servants said unto the householder : ' Shall we weed out the tares from the wheat ? ' But he counselled them not to do so, lest hurt should come to the wheat. For he said : ' The harvest will reveal which is wheat and which is tare ;[2] and then the harvesters will separate them and gather the grain into the granary, but the tares they will burn up with fire.' "

And some of the disciples asked Him to interpret for them the meaning of the parable. And He thus explained it .

" The sower of the good seed is the Son of Man.[3]

The fields are the hearts of men and women, the human soil of this world of life.

The servants of the householder are the children of the Kingdom of the Heavens.[4] The good seed is the corn of the Divine Love and Wisdom, the truth which springeth forth into life and becometh bread for all Souls.

The enemy is the evil one, the devil who ever denieth and destroyeth good.[5] And he worketh through his servants.

These are they who are not children of the Kingdom in their desires and ways, and who lend themselves to his service.[6]

The night in which the tares are sown is the darkness within men and women, during which they spiritually sleep.[7] They see not, neither do they hear with the understanding, the things of the spirit.

In this darkness the enemy worketh, sowing the tares of wrong desire, impure feeling, unrighteous thought and ignoble purpose, causing these to grow up with the

NOTES.

[1] The coming of the Kingdom of the Heavens is the becoming within a Soul of the new life, a consciousness of the heavenly influences upon it and within it.

[2] Wheat is for bread, knowledge to be ground for nourishment. Tare is very like the wheat at first, because it is materialized and perverted truth.

[3] The Son of God, Adonai, the Overshadowing Presence of the Soul. All truth comes from the Word who breaks the bread of God for all. And the supreme truth or wheat for the Soul is that state of Christhood unto which all heavenly ministry leads us.

[4] There is distinct reference here to those who had become Christs, and therefore the Order of Ancient Christhood. They were always spoken of as the Children of the Kingdom, because they realized in wonderful fulness the Life of God within them. Of them were the Prophets and Seers, the children of Zion.

[5] The negativing spirit that works against the upwardness of the Soul.

[6] Alas that this should be so. It is true of many on these planes ; it is also true of many who have passed over. All the exoteric and non-spiritual presentations of things essentially spiritual and divine, have sown tares ; and all the evil things begotten from the lower astral plane, have been fuel to feed and perpetuate evil desire in every form.

[7] Even where the good seed has taken root it is well to watch and pray.

DISCIPLESHIP

good seed that is in them ; for these tares are most like the wheat in their early growth.

The harvest is the ingathering of fruits within each life at the consummation of one of the Soul's ages, and the ingatherers are the Angels of God.[1]

These separate the good from the evil, the wheat from the tares. The wheat or good is gathered into the granary of the Soul for nourishment and service,[2] but the tares or evil elements and those which cause stumbling are burnt up in the consuming fire which purifieth all things.[3]

Then the righteous ones shall be as lights in the Kingdom of the Heavens ; for the Glory of the Father-Mother shall be within them."[4]

The coming of the Kingdom of the Heavens within the Soul is like a man finding goodly pearls ; for whilst he is seeking out these unto the finding of them, he discovers one of inestimable value and gives himself up to the gaining of it.

And when he hath come into the possession of it, he accounts all else that he possesses of little value compared to it.[5]

The coming of the Kingdom within the Soul is likewise as the discovery of hidden treasure. When the Kingdom is becoming in a man he makes the discovery that within the soil of his own nature there is buried sacred treasure. So he gives up all else that he may be able to devote himself to the finding of it.

And when it is found he comes to possess all things with it.[6]

NOTES.

[1] The Divine Judgment of a Soul is in cycles. These are great epochs in its life's history. In every life there is, in a sense, this judgment. For the Soul gathers up all the good which it has appropriated into itself for future use, like grain stored ; but the evil influences which have deeply impressed it remain also, and these by and by have to be eradicated. This is expressed by the Western term Destiny and the Eastern term Karma. But in the great cycles when judgment comes upon a Soul it is that of the weighing of it, so to speak, in the balance, when, if it be equal to it, a new and higher experience is entered upon. If it be unable to respond to the new vibrations and higher initiations, then it must needs remain for another cycle.

[2] This is the good resulting from experience, the gradual discern ment of truth and its appropriation in so far as it could be understood and assimilated.

[3] Evil generates astral fires, and these have to be extinguished through overcoming the evil. Evil is burnt up in all-consuming fire of the eternal energy within the Soul. In this sense God is a consuming fire.

[4] That is, those who have overcome the evil influences spoken of as the tares, and have become good ground or elements for the Word of God, the Life, the Love, the Light of the Eternal One, shall radiate the glory of His Countenance.

[5] The Priceless Pearl is the Christhood Estate. It is found only of those who seek goodly pearls—purity, goodness, compassion, love.

[6] The great treasure is the consciousness of the Divine Presence within, and all the riches of the wisdom of God which proceed from it.

DISCIPLESHIP

The Master spake this parable unto the disciples concerning the process by which the Divine Wisdom was acquired.

The Parable of the Net

" The Kingdom of the Heavens is like a net let down into a great sea.[1]

Those who be fishermen[2] upon the waters, let down their nets to catch what may come to them ;[3] and when they land their nets, they separate the fish, the good from the bad, taking the good fish into their vessel, but throwing away the bad.

In like manner is it with those in whom the Kingdom of the Heavens cometh.

The power of the Kingdom within them causeth them to let down their nets into the sea whence knowledge and experience come ; and they bring up fish good and bad.

And being true fishers, knowing the good from the bad, they separate them, taking the good into their vessel with them, but throwing away the bad."

And those who were present when He spake the parable asked Him if He would further unfold to them its meaning. And He said unto them :

" The Kingdom of the Heavens is the Life of the Lord of Glory within a Soul.

As that Life grows, so does it become realization.

In its growth and becoming, it lets down its net into the deeper waters, for it seeks the deeper reaches of experience, and the more profound knowledges.

But in its experience the life gathers bad as well as good ; for the fish of hidden knowledges are not all of the same quality ; and some are bad.[4]

But those who are fishers indeed, those in whom the Kingdom has gained power, are full of discernment and come to know the good, and they gather these into their vessel. For these are high knowledges to be made use of by the Soul.

The bad they put away, those knowledges which are not good for the inner life ; for they cannot make use of them."

NOTES.

[1] The great sea is the sea of Life, and it is full of mystery. Every Soul must needs go forth upon that sea, and upon it no one escapes being confronted with the Mystery of Being. The Kingdom of the Heavens cometh through Revelation in a Soul ; but in the process of its becoming a realization, the Soul passes through profound experiences. This was so in the unfallen days when there was nothing bad within the sea ; but since the going down of the Soul, the experiences have had a mixture of evil.

[2] Fish and Fisher were mystery terms : the one signified hidden knowledges ; the other, one who sought out these.

[3] The nets let down by the fishers into which were gathered the fish, symbolized the letting down of the mind by the fishers to secure the knowledges. For in the evolution of the Soul, apart from the abnormal conditions which have arisen out of the evil which overtook the race, the Soul acquires experiences through the mind, and grows in heavenly wisdom. In this way is the knowledge and understanding of things stored up within the Soul, which in later ages become unto it what is known as Intuition—the power to perceive heavenly secrets.

[4] But the mind, amid the present conditions, gathers into itself much that is not of permanent value, and which is often distinctly hurtful. Many knowledges now acquired in the way of the Soul cannot be taken up into the vessel for sacred use. The knowledges concerning the Soul itself, its nature, past and future, are often so bad that they hurt the Soul. The meanings now given to the mysteries by ecclesiasticism are hurtful ; they are fish which are not good. And many things of an occult order have an influence over the Soul which is more than hurtful. Many have been made to suffer through the knowledges which have come in this way. Not a few have suffered shipwreck. These things the Master knew. He beheld the effects upon many around Him. The true fishers understand. They know what is good and what is not. They are the mystical Souls whose kingdom is from the Heavens.

E

DISCIPLESHIP

When the disciples accompanying the Master drew nigh unto Bethphage[1] which lay on the way to the Mount of Olives,[2] there met them a great concourse of angelic ministrants who carried in their hands palm trees with which to proclaim their citizenship of the Heavens, and the victory that overcometh the world.[3]

The Angelic Cohort at Bethphage

And these were heard by the disciples proclaiming the coming of the Lord and His Christ, saying .

" Hosanna to the Highest ! For from the House of David hath He brought His Son : Blessed be He who cometh in the name of the Lord."[4]

And He led the disciples into Bethany.[5]

And on the way thither He spake to them of the Temple of God, and how it had been desecrated.[6]

" The way followed by the teachers and leaders of the people has turned the Father's House of Prayer into a house which is no longer a house of prayer, but one inhabited by thieves.

The Sanctuary of the Soul has long ceased to be the altar of God ; for the offerings within it have been the things sacrificed unto idols.

The Temple of the Lord has become the house of those who bought and sold the Dove,[7] and the money-changers.

But in the coming of the Lord to His Temple, those who have wrought these things and turned the House of Prayer into one for the exchange of merchandise, shall be scourged and driven out, that the House of Prayer may be restored.

And though those powers who sit in the chief seats and work such things upon the Temple, shall also destroy the Temple which My Heavenly Father-Mother raised up for you, yet after three days it shall be raised up again.[8]

And out of the midst of it shall Praise be perfected unto the Most High, even through those who will be accounted as babes and sucklings."

NOTES.

[1] Bethphage was a term used in the Mysteries to denote a stage of spiritual initiation. It meant the House of Young Figs, and therefore the beginnings of knowledge in the Divine Wisdom. The Fig was the symbol of interior knowledge.

[2] The Mount of Olives in the ancient Mysteries signified the state of spiritual experience in which the Soul recovered much of her past, for the mount meant an elevated condition. It was in such a state that a Soul was able to bring forth from its treasure house the ancient wisdom it had learnt. The disciples, as will be observed, had not yet reached that stage, but were on the way to it.

[3] The story in the records is full of glamour. What is said to have taken place at Bethphage is just such as He would have shrunk from. Was He meek and lowly of heart ? There is an element of the ecclesiastical tableau about the story as told in the New Testament absolutely at variance with the character and spirit of the Master, and utterly out of keeping with His sublime mission.

The Hosts were those of the Lord, and the disciples, having attained to Bethphage, could feel the beautiful atmosphere which they intensified and hear the blessed song of gladness being sung, not only over the Master, but over their return into some degree of the ancient Christhood estate.

[4] The Christ-coming as a consciousness. This was true of those who followed the Master in His ways. And in a yet deeper sense it was true of the Master ; for the culmination of the Christ-Manifestation through Him was at hand.

[5] The House of Christhood, where was the house in which the Lord loved to dwell.

[6] The Temple of the Soul which should be sacred to the Presence.

[7] The things of the Spirit have been as those things of which men and women make merchandise.

[8] The Christhood Vision given through the manifestation. It was destroyed by the misrepresentation of the nature of a Christ hood ; and it is only now after the three days of the Oblation that it is being restored.

DISCIPLESHIP

The Fig-Tree that Withered

Now as He approached the city where He was to suffer so many things at the hands of the chief priests and scribes, He beheld a fig-tree, whose leaves were out of time and whose branches bore no figs.

Though He was an hungered and would fain have found wherewith to satisfy Him from the tree, yet He could not find anything.[1]

So He spake concerning that tree, saying : " Henceforth no man shall eat fruit of thee."[2]

And that tree withered away.

Then the disciples inquired of Him how it was that the tree withered away.

And He expounded unto them how it came to pass that life had died within it.

" A certain one had a vineyard in the midst of which was a Fig-tree.

This tree should have borne much fruit, but did not. Then the owner of the vineyard, being desirous that it should not be cut down, but if possible preserved, counselled his steward to care specially for it, in the hope that it might yet bear fruit.

For three years it was helped by him, but without avail ; so it was decided to cut it down, as it only cumbered the ground."

" Have faith, and all things shall be possible unto you.

Without faith ye can do nothing.[3]

When the Lord of the Vineyard cometh, ye cannot have fruits to garner for Him unless ye have faith.

Learn ye from the story of the Fig-tree in the vineyard.

The Fig-tree was the Wisdom of God in the midst of His vineyard, the ancient Church.

That Holy Wisdom was given unto the Church of Israel, and it once blossomed and bore much fruit.[4]

But there came a time when the vineyard was let out to others ; and these, not understanding the Fig-tree, hurt it so much that it could no longer bear its fruit."[5]

NOTES.

[1] To those who understand the esoteric meaning of this incident a profound pathos will be observed in it. A more terrible indictment of the condition of Jewry in His day it is difficult to imagine. The Jewish Church stood as the repository of the Divine Wisdom. It claimed to stand alone amongst the nations as the channel of Divine Revelation and Manifestation. It had elaborate sacrificial ritual and tradition, but its pretensions bore no fruit. It had many leaves, but no Figs upon its branches. The Divine Wisdom was not to be found in it. There was no interior vision to be found ; all was exoteric and barbaric. The Master would fain have found a venue for the Teachings He had to give, but Jewry could not provide it. He hungered and would fain have found something worthy upon that tree, but could not.

[2] He knew it was withering away and indeed almost dead. It had often been helped by the true seers and prophets who came unto it—the remnants of the Ancient Israel ; but though these came to it and gave their message from the Lord during a long period, covering long ages, yet it could not be enlivened and made to bear fruit.

[3] True spiritual perception, the discerning of the true meaning of things.

[4] The Ancient Hebrew Community formed the Ancient Church of God. The members were of the Order of the Christ, and as such knew the Divine Wisdom. They were the true Israel, the world's Cross bearers, prophets, teachers, seers. The religion they gave to the world was rich indeed. The terms applied by the Jews to the mountains, hills, valleys, rivers, lakes, cities, villages and districts contain a wealth of esoteric teaching. So also did the various orders of sacrifice which they materialized and degraded.

[5] The effect of their materializing and degrading genius upon the sublime things into whose possession they came through joining the schools founded by the later Hebrews for the teaching of the Ancient Wisdom. The Jews were not true Hebrews ; they were not of the same race or order.

E — I

69

DISCIPLESHIP

And on one of His journeys the Master met some people who had heard of Him and the work He did, and these had with them a young man who was said to be obsessed of evil.[1]

And they desired that He should heal the young man, for though they had been to some of the disciples to have the evil spirit cast out, it still prevailed, and it threw him down, greatly afflicting him.

And the Master stretched forth His hand and touched him, commanding the unclean spirit to leave him:[2] and from that hour the young man was restored.

And there were those who marvelled at what was done.

But He spake unto them of the Love of the Father-Mother, how it ever blessed those who besought blessing; and of the majesty of His Power, for He was over-ruling all things that such blessing as they had witnessed might come. And He said:

" O the faithlessness and perverseness of the children of this world from generation unto generation ! How long has He who hath ever loved you, borne with you, and made manifest His tenderness ! How long shall it be ere you come to know that He is even with you now, to the end that your healing may be accomplished !"

And when they had withdrawn, He spake unto the few friends who were with Him :

" Let these words find a place in your hearts; for the day is approaching in which you will understand many things.[3]

The Son of Man who is being made manifest will be delivered into the hands of sinful men and women who will crucify Him.[4]

But in the accomplishment of the work which the Father-Mother hath given us to do, shall the Son of Man rise again from the dead and be made manifest through many."[5]

But they understood not what He meant, for the hour of their enlightenment had not yet come; and they hesitated to inquire of Him as to its meaning.

*Casting
out Evil
from the
Obsessed*

NOTES.

[1] Obsession was not uncommon in those days. Evil entities often found embodiment in some afflicted Soul. The realm of the shades —the " valley of the shadows of death "—contained many entities of magnetic character strong enough to persist for ages, and which sought not only to communicate to those upon these planes, but to gain power over them so as to live their old life through them. They produced epilepsy and kindred forms of evil, and men wrought wickedness through their victims.

[2] Obsession was not easily overcome and healed. The worst forms of it were only subject to the Christs, as in this case. They are overcome only by the power of the Divine Spirit.

In our own time obsession is not uncommon, and many are the evils arising from it. Before it medical science is powerless; and so are all those who seek to be healers who are not in the state of Jesushood. There are some cases where none have power to drive out the obsessing entity, but one in Christhood.

[3] These things the disciples were soon to understand. They were to come into the knowledge of the power of Christhood, and become true therapeuts. They were to arrive at the knowledge of the condition of the world upon all its planes, and the causes of so many of the sad tribulations by which men and women were overwhelmed.

[4] The Son of Man was a mystery term denoting the Christ state in a Soul as well as the Adonai in manifestation through such an one. Here it referred to the Christ-Vision. The Son of Man was to be delivered up into the hands of those who would crucify the vision through misrepresenting the Christhood.

[5] An allusion to the work of the Oblation during the three days of the Passover or Sin-offering, and the effect of that work upon the arising of the Christhood.

DISCIPLESHIP

Nicodemus shown the Way of the Higher Birth

There was one of the rulers within the Synagogue who was attracted to the teachings of the Master; but he had fear of the other rulers, and so would not show that the Teachings had influenced him.

The same came at night to the Master to further inquire concerning the things of which he had already heard. He was afterwards known by the name of Nicodemus.[1]

Unto the Master he thus spake: "Rabbi, I perceive that thou art a teacher from God; for no man who was not from God could teach as thou dost."[2]

But the Master said unto him: "Of many earthly things have we spoken, and you have found it hard to receive these as true, but how will ye receive the many deeper things of which we have yet to speak?[3]

Verily, as I said unto you, ye must be born again to understand these things."

Nicodemus then said · "But how can these things be attained? Must a man pass through the womb again to be born into the life of which thou speakest?"[4]

The Master said unto him: "The life born from ties of the flesh has the life of the flesh; bu' the life born from the Spirit has the Life of the Spirit. Unless a Soul be born of the Spirit it cannot perceive the heavenly nature of these things.[5]

Marvel not, therefore, at my saying unto you that ye must be born again.

No one ever ascended into the Heavens of the Son of Man until he was born of the Spirit.[6]

No one knoweth the Father-Mother except God's Son be born in him.[7]

The Son of God within you must, therefore, be lifted up upon the Cross, even as in your Scriptures it has been said that Moses was lifted up in the wilderness when the fiery serpents were destroying the people.[8]

For the Son of God who is within must be brought forth into manifestation, not to condemn the world in His appearing, but that through His revealing the world may be saved.

NOTES.

[1] No one should be condemned because he or she comes in secret to inquire about divine things. Men and women are often placed in the like position to Nicodemus, where persecution awaits them from those who are in authority, should it be known that they are inquiring after other religious expression than that authorized. For a chief within a synagogue to seek out the Master, that he might learn from him, meant much ; for his seeking was not begotten of mere curiosity, but genuine desire to hear and learn.

[2] A true perception of an inspired teacher, showing that Jewry did not meet his needs.

[3] The Master had spoken to him concerning the mysteries of nature and the Planet, and interpreted these as seen from the inner realms. These had seemed strange and wonderful to him, difficult to reconcile with his traditional knowledges.

[4] The doctrine of the re-incarnation of the Soul is here tacitly acknowledged by him, and he wondered whether he would have to await other times ere he could enter into the experiences of the new life.

[5] Souls have been reborn time after time, coming through generation after generation, without having arrived at the blessed state referred to. It was not to be found merely by means of re-incarnation, though in the spiritual evolution of the race that was also essential. But mere incarnation did not change the inner life; the new state came through the quickening of the Soul by the Holy Breath.

[6] To be born from above is to enter into a high degree of spiritual consciousness, and to have the power to ascend in state into the Heavens of the Son of Man. This last degree is only reached in the state of Christhood, for it is the outcome of the Christ consciousness.

[7] The Divine Father-Motherhood can only be apprehended by those in whom there is the beginning of the Christ-consciousness, and the Divine Nature in the duality thus expressed can be known by realization only unto those who have reached the spiritual state designated the Son of God. It was the state of the Immortals.

[8] The reference is to the original Hebrew Mystery which embodied a history of a spiritual order. The Cross upon which the Son of God within must needs be lifted up, is verily the sign of the Divine Presence within. The mystery of the Cross is the greatest in the universe of Being. To understand it by means of realization is to know indeed the Father-Mother.

DISCIPLESHIP

**The Holy
Breath**

For God the Father-Mother so loves this world that He has sent His Beloved One into it, that through Him it may be saved.[1]

And he who entereth into the understanding of these things and receiveth them, passes from the life of the flesh to the Life of the Spirit.[2]

And the way of the Spirit is even as the breath of nature. The breath bloweth, and thou canst tell where it listeth ; but thou canst not tell whence it beginneth, nor whither it shall end.

Thus is it with everyone who is born of the Spirit. For the Breath within quickeneth them into the Life Eternal,[3] *even the Life of the Son of God."*

There dwelt upon the shores of the Sea of Genesaret one who was a Ruler in a Synagogue, a man just and kind whom the people honoured and loved.

The same had a little daughter who was subject at times to illness which made her appear as if she were suffering from an Eastern fever.

On one of these occasions she became so ill, apparently, that the parents grew most anxious concerning her, and sent for the Master to come to them.

**' Talitha
Cumi '**

The Master knew the Ruler, and He at once went to his home to minister unto his child.

But, whilst the Master was on His way, a message was sent to Him that He was not to trouble to come, as the child had passed away.

But the Master nevertheless went to the home. And when He entered the room where the child lay, He found both the parents and the friends mourning for the loss that had come to them.

Then said He unto them : " The child is not dead ; she only sleepeth."

And those who had come to mourn, scornfully laughed at Him.

But the Master beheld the Soul of the child and knew that she had not been withdrawn ; so He requested the mourners to retire from the room, and, when they had done so, He spake unto her, saying, " Talitha Cumi " ; and she returned and arose from her couch.[4]

74

NOTES.

[1] The world can only be saved through a Christhood. Salvation is healing, but true healing can only come through purification of life. To be saved is to be made whole, and to be made whole is to be in a state of equilibrium. To save the world men and women must be brought back to rectitude, purity of thought and feeling, pity, compassion and love ; and only through those who are in a state of Jesushood and Christhood can the world of men and women be shown this way of salvation. The coming of the Beloved of the Father into the lives of those who once knew Christhood is the hope of the world.

[2] Another reference to the new consciousness. It lifts a Soul into the realm of the Breath.

[3] The Holy Breath is a blessed reality. It becomes a conscious experience in those who attain Christhood. It is the Life-stream of the Eternal One, ever Blessed, and it flows through those who have risen into the consciousness of the Eternal Life.

[4] We give this incident because of the association of it with the previous conversation, and the significance of the teaching underlying what occurred. It contains but little actual Logia, but great depths of understanding of the Soul. How few there are who understand the Soul in its nature and the manner in which illumination comes to it. How few understand even in these days the possibilities of the Soul in its power to transcend the lower planes ! How few know what Soul trance is ! The maid was not dead except to the influences of the outer world ; the personal consciousness was in a state of quiescence, and the vehicle seemed lifeless, so those near her thought she had passed away.

Those who have had the experience of profound Trance-sleep will understand this incident. In such a state, the body is sometimes so absolutely cold and lifeless that the uninitiated might easily mistake its condition for that of a body from which the being had departed.

DISCIPLESHIP

he Story
f the
lind Man

On one occasion when the Master was walking with the disciples, they drew near to one who had been blind from his birth.[1]

And one of them said unto the Master: "How came it to pass that this man was born blind? Had he so sinned that it befell him to be so born; or was he bearing the burden of the sin of his parents?"[2]

And the Master explained that the blindness was not the outcome of the man's sin, nor of his parents' wrongdoing, but for some spiritual purpose in the man himself:

"Neither did any sin, this man or his parents to bring upon him this blindness; it has for its meaning the holy purpose that within him the work of God may be made manifest. Things are not always what they appear to be."[3]

Turning to the man who was blind the Master said unto him:

"If thou wilt go down to the pool of Siloam[4] *and anoint thine eyes with the waters which thou shalt there find, thy blindness will pass away, and thou shalt see."*

And when he returned, having gained his sight, the Master saith unto him, "The works of God must be wrought in the light of day; in the coming night no one will be able to do the works. I am the Light of the world, saith the Lord, he who followeth Me shall not walk in darkness, but shall have the Light of Life."

And the man who had been blind said unto Him: "Master, where is He that I may find Him and follow on to the Light of Life?"

And the Master saith unto him: "He is now nigh thee, for He it was who opened thine eyes and enabled thee to see. He is within thee, even as I said unto thee."

Then did he who had had his eyes opened, bow himself worshipfully.

NOTES.

[1] This incident was not what the narrative of the fourth Gospel would make it appear to have been. It was no ordinary blindness with which the man was afflicted. The story itself reveals as such. Had it been the result of defective nerve, or iris, or pupils, it would have been an ordinary case of blindness. But it was not that, but the lack of power to perceive. It was a spiritual blindness, a great Soul limitation that had befallen the one afflicted.

[2] This question was in harmony with Jewish belief. They attributed such afflictions to the Divine Judgment. Yet the question meant more, for it implied the doctrine of re-incarnation and Karma ; it recognised a history in the Soul, and it likewise acknowledged the power of parenthood over the attributes of a child.

[3] But the blindness was not due either to the man's own past, or the way his parents had taken, showing that there are afflictions which arise independently of these. The incident is most striking in that it relates the limitation of the afflicted one to the Divine purpose. Within the man some work had to be accomplished to the end that God might be made manifest in and through him. Who was he ? What was he ? His name is hidden in the story, for there are some things that may not be told. There were reasons for this silence then, and there is reason now. The fact remains the same that he had been unable to perceive from birth the inner things of the Spirit.

[4] Herein is revealed the nature of the blindness, and the means by which it alone could be taken away. " Go wash in the Pool of Siloam " and the anointing of the eyes with its waters will restore the power to perceive. For the Pool of Siloam contained the waters of knowledges of one who was sent.

DISCIPLESHIP

In His ministry unto men there came to Him those who sought to find occasion of stumbling in Him, to inquire concerning the law of divorce; and these asked Him whither it was lawful for a man to put away his wife for any reason whatever.

The Law of Divorce

But the Master said unto them: "Is it not written in your scriptures that God made both male and female, and that when two come into the marriage bond they become as one? If that is your law, then it is unlawful for any one to put away his wife."

But they said unto Him: "Under the law of Moses a man can put his wife away, and take unto himself another."

To which the Master replied: "If any man harden his heart against his wife, and put her away that he may marry another, he committeth adultery; and if another be married to her in that state, he hath made them also to commit adultery.

This is what your law teacheth. But I would say this unto you: if any man desireth a woman to lust after her, he committeth both fornication and adultery in his heart. For the place of woman in life is not unto this end, but that, as an helpmeet, she and the man may be in perfect union. For in such union they are one, as God purposed. The one is not greater than the other, though the woman is the crown of the man. Therefore she should be loved by man as his own Soul."[1]

And some of them brought unto Him one—a poor woman—who had been found committing adultery; and they asked Him what they should do with her since the law of Moses commanded that any woman taken in adultery should be stoned.[2]

And the poor woman knelt in shame before them all.

The Master, when He heard them speak of her sin and of what their law commanded should be done unto her,. looked upon all of them with very sorrow that they could have so bemeaned themselves in their desire to humble the fallen one.[3]

And He stooped to lift up the woman; and as He did so He wrote upon the ground.[4]

78

NOTES.

[1] It deeply grieved the Master to be confronted with such questions. They were not asked in sincerity, but for the purpose of entrapping Him. His whole being revolted against the spirit of traditional Jewry.

What He thought of woman is here succinctly expressed. She was the crown of man, and she was highest in order of manifestation, and the Symbol of the Intuition. The woman represented the Soul, whilst man symbolized the mind. The woman perceived heavenly things, the man reasoned his way to the understanding of them. He was the reflector of the light of the Soul. In perfect union they formed one system ; each was essential to the other.

[2] A law that grew out of a terrible perversion of the truth. It was as unjust as it was untrue. But it has always been the way where the Soul's vision has been perverted. Woman has been put under a different law from man. His failures have been overlooked, but woman has been stoned for hers.

[3] If there is one manifestation of ingratitude more abhorrent than another, it is such as this. Never does a man so bemean himself as when he exposes and gloats over the sin of any one, man or woman. There was absolutely no chivalry present in those who did this iniquitous thing. Many now, as then, into whose power judgment is committed, and who pass judgment, have been themselves the instruments of bringing low the woman who is fallen.

[4] What did the Master write ? He wrote that which those about Him could not endure. He wrote that all of them had been as guilty as she. Then He raised the woman, and they departed : for He addressed the words to them.

DISCIPLESHIP

Then He looked at them again and said: "He who has not sinned, let him cast the first stone."

And each one turned his back upon .Him, and went away in anger.

The Law of Divorce

And unto the woman He said, "Thine accusers have left thee. I do not condemn thee. Thou hast been sorely tried in the way of thy life; but do it no more. Let the healing of God be thine from henceforth."[1]

And some of the disciples asked Him if it were expedient that they should not marry. But He said:

"Unto some it has been given that they should marry, but not unto all. For it is necessary for the sake of the Kingdom that some should stand alone; but this is only given unto the few.[2]

True marriage is beautiful and honourable: it does honour unto both the man and the woman. Yet in seeking the highest estate no concupiscence must rule them. Desire must always be soulie, and of God. In the perfect union, the woman and the man are one."

The Prayers of Two Men

And after the incident of the poor woman taken in adultery, the Master spoke unto those who were present to teach them that only they who were of humble heart and contrite spirit were acceptable unto the Father Mother.

"There were two who went into the Temple to pray: one was of the Pharisees and the other was of the Tax gatherers.

The Pharisee stood in his place and prayed thus—'God, I give thanks to thee that thou hast made me better than others; for I am not of the extortioners, the unjust, the adulterers, nor like yonder sinner. I observe the law of fasting, and tithe all I possess.'[3]

But the Taxgatherer, who had to stand afar off, lifted not up his voice, but smote upon his breast, breathing this prayer—

'Most Blessed One, be propitious to me, for I am a sinful man.'[4]

Which think you went to his home blessed? Every one who exalteth himself shall be humbled; but whosoever is of humble heart shall be exalted."[5]

80

NOTES.

[1] The compassion of the Master was always beautiful. Though He abhorred the evil which He sensed in men and women, yet He always felt deeply for the afflicted ones. He knew because He understood ; and the very love of the Eternal One flowed through His Soul to them.

[2] Some of the disciples were in a state of union. Some of them were indeed in spiritual Christhood. So it was not necessary for that state to remain single. But when a Manifestation was to be given, the vehicle had to be alone. Only the very few were chosen for that, except for the Divine Christhood manifestation celibacy was not essential ; but purity in all cases was.

[3] When a Soul feels deeply, prayer becomes Praise of the Highest, not of the self. When a Soul prays truly, it is not in terms of self-laudation, but in holy yearning for the Blessing of the Highest. When the Soul faces the Presence within the Sanctuary, there is no desire to belittle others.

[4] There is more in this prayer than is apparent. The Soul recognised there was a true forgiveness to be had from the Eternal One, and that He alone was the Propitiation within the Propitiatory of the Soul. The language of the prayer is significant.

Everyone who exalteth the self must learn humility ; but whosoever is of humble spirit shall find exalted life.

PART III.

DISCIPLESHIP

Containing Teachings wherein the disciples are initiated into the deeper meanings of Jesushood, as expressed in the Prayer for the Elect, the doctrine of the Logos, the Birth-Stories, the Witness for the Father-Mother, the Works of the Father Mother accomplished through the Master wherein great Soul-history is unveiled, the Soul in its deeper experiences pursued by elemental spirits and conquering through the power of Christ within, together with stories of the Passion, and the vision of Days of the Regeneration.

DISCIPLESHIP

Within the Secret Place

"*When ye pray, use not the vain repetitions of the priests and pharisees who imagine that they will be heard because of their much speaking.*

But when ye pray, withdraw to your inner room, and there pray to the Father-Mother who dwelleth within the Secret-Place, that He will make Himself manifest unto you.[1]

For within the Secret-Place is the Father-Mother made manifest unto all who seek Him there.

Within the Upper-Room where His Sanctuary is, doth He show Himself openly.[2]

Within the Guest-Chamber of the Soul is He to be found of all who enter that sacred Sanctuary to sup with Him.

There is His Table with its hallowed Bread and Wine, meet food for the life and inspiration of the Soul.

There is the Blessed Fellowship realized by man, even the Fellowship of the Gods.

There is the true Communion of Saints a reality, and the sublime vision of God entered into.

For in the Secret-Place of the Most High the Soul arrives at the Divine Presence, and in the consciousness of that Presence beholds, knows, and realizes all things which are of God.

The Lord's Prayer

And thus do ye pray

'*Our Father-Mother in the Heavens, most hallowed be Thy Name unto us.*

May Thy Kingdom come within us.

Thy will be accomplished by us : even as it is done within Thy Heavens, so be it accomplished upon the Earth.

Give us Thyself the daily portion of the Bread of Life.

Forgive us our sins, and help us as we pass through to forgive others.

Amid the great trial lead us, that evil overtake us not.

For the Kingdom within us is Thine, with its Power and its Glory, even for evermore.

Thou art the Arche and the Amen.[3]' "

NOTES.

[1] The inner room is the upper room of the Soul. The high altar is there. The Presence is there, though yet veiled to most. But unto the Soul who can so enter within the Sanctuary that Presence becomes a blessed reality.

[2] To those who have not yet come into this realization it must appear imaginary. To write of it is difficult, for it is not easy to express in a form of words what the Soul knows and sees. But we may say this much concerning it, that it is not only possible to come into the consciousness of the Presence within, but to witness the blessed manifestation. When a Soul arrives at that vision, it understands who it is and who is its life and glory.

[3] This prayer, called the Lord's Prayer, is a prayer of the Christhood. Its very language and meanings are for the Order of the Christs. None other could understand it in its esoteric significance. All Souls may use it, if they do so reverently, because in all are the potentials latent which, when fully developed, will lead to the blessed realizations implied. But there are few who are able to understand its profound meanings. It is essentially a prayer for those who once were in the high state of Christhood ; Souls who knew the Kingdom of God through most blessed realization ; Souls unto whom the consciousness of the Divine Presence had been a living reality ; Souls in whom the Kingdom of God had come and through whom the Kingdom of the Heavens was revealed. It was a prayer designed to aid them in their return to that consciousness of high life and in their passing through the great tribulation within their Souls throughout the days of the Oblation and the Regeneration.

Its closing cadences are such as only Souls in that high estate could possibly understand.

DISCIPLESHIP

The Doctrine of the Logos

" *From the Arche*[1] *was the Word* ·[2]
The Word was of God :
And God was in the Word.
In the Arche the Word was with God.

By the Word were all things created, and without the Word was there not anything fashioned that had been created.[3]

In the Word was hidden the Life of God, even the heavenly Principle which became the Light of man.[4]

That which hath been from the Beginning, which we have beheld with our inward vision, which we have heard with the ear of the Soul, declare we unto you.[5]

That which we have beheld and heard we make known unto you as the Word of Life, the Life which was made manifest from the Beginning, and hath once more been made manifest in our midst.[6]

For the Word of Life has been again spoken through Him who hath made it manifest, even the Only Begotten One, in the holy estates of Jesus, Christ, and the Lord.[7]

In Him is the Word of Life found dwelling in all Fulness that He should show it forth as the Glory of God the Father-Mother.

He who heareth that Word of Life no longer walketh in the darkness with those whose ways are of the world-mind, nor in the ways of the flesh, nor after the will of man, but in the Light of that Life whose Glory is as the Glory of God.

And he who hath this Word of Life dwelling within him, and who heareth the Voice of the Only Begotten One, purifieth himself even as He is pure.[8]

As children of the Household of the Father-Mother, ye have that Word of Life dwelling within you, even the Life which is the Glory of God.[9]

Therefore love one another as becometh His children who are in the Light of Life.[10]

That Light was once in the world when as yet there was no darkness, the darkness which overtook man when he lost the Light.[11]

NOTES.

[1] The term Arche cannot be adequately translated, though it is most nearly expressed by the word Beginning. It has also been rendered First. It is inconceivable to think of Beginning or end in relation to the Divine ; so it must be postulated only of the commencement of Systems, Suns, and Planetary Worlds.

[2] The Logos : yet the expression conveys more than the idea of the Logos of this world, and is to be understood as the Adonai, the Manifest of the Unmanifest One.

[3] Through the Eternal Son, the Adonai, hath God created and fashioned His Worlds. In Him are all things centered ; from Him do all things go forth and return.

[4] The great magnetic potencies which are to be found in all created Being. These when fully polarised within a human Soul send forth spiritual and even divine radiations. They generate the human aura ; and in Christhood they are revealed. For in that high degree of life the Light of Life is within the Soul, and the Soul knoweth all things.

[5] A clear indication to those disciples who formed the inner group, whence the message came which He had to give them.

[6] The Divine Life that had often been manifested and which was to be revealed again in the Christhood. To the Master it had been once more made manifest. The Presence had been perfectly realized within Him.

[7] Everything of a personal nature must be put away in the interpretation of these Logia. They were not meant personally in any degree whatever, but referred only to the Divine Presence manifesting through the Soul. For the only Begotten One is Adonai who begets within a Soul the Christ-consciousness revealed in the three degrees of Jesus, Christ, and the Lord.

[8] When a Soul hears the Voice of Him within, it seeks unto the finding of the realization. And as the realization is only by the path of purity in everything, the Soul follows that path, seeking to become pure even as He is pure.

[9] The Master impressed upon those who sought the Christhood, the reality of their Divine origin. He led them one by one into ever deepening consciousness of the Divine Powers within them. There was such a Soul intimacy between them and Himself as none could understand who were not privileged to be members of that fellowship.

[10] He discerned the Glory of God in each of them and sought to bring it into manifestation ; but He knew also the difficulties in the way of their return, and that only love would enable them to triumph.

[11] The Light of Life was made manifest through the members of

DISCIPLESHIP

But when the Darkness prevailed, the world knew not the Light ; and when it again shone, man comprehended it not.[1]

That Light was the Light of Life whose Power was within the life of man.

From that Power had all things proceeded.

All the worlds were fashioned by it, and apart from it was nothing fashioned. It was before all things, and by it all things are sustained.

Of that Power did we all receive, even Grace upon Grace,[2] *that we might all arrive at the vision of the Only Begotten One in the fulness of our life, crowned with Grace and Truth from God, even the truth and Grace which are found in the estates of Jesus Christ*

And we have beheld His Glory, Glory such as no man of himself knoweth, which proceedeth from the Ever Blessed Father-Mother whose Radiance it is."[3]

And one asked Him, " When cometh the Kingdom of God within Man ? "

And He answered, " The Kingdom of the Father Mother cometh when the Soul arriveth at the Consciousness of the One Life. But it cometh in varying degrees.

When a Soul arriveth at the consciousness of the One Life, it goeth on to know Him who is that Life.

But to know Him is to realize the Divine Two—the Father-Mother : for God is Divine Duality. And in this realization the Soul has the consciousness of the Holy Trinity, for within it the Son of God is made manifest.

And then its Life is Fourfold ; for the Four Kingdoms are its inheritance.

Thus is it with those in whom the Kingdom of the Father-Mother cometh in fulness. And in that day it is with them even as it is in the Heavens ; for as it is in the Above or overshadowing world, so is it in that which is Beneath, or world overshadowed ; within the Soul are the Sacred Seven. The Holy One is its possession.[4]

NOTES.

The Order of the Christhood, for each was a vehicle revealing in some degree the Glory of the Lord in the way of their going, and the wisdom they were the repositories of, and which they taught the children of the Planet who were advanced enough to be able to receive their ministry.

The Darkness which overtook the world was the loss of that ministry through the descent of the entire household of the Planet into conditions where it could not be revealed.

[1] The Light was restored through the Messengers who were sent to find the Christ-Souls. This Light was revealed anew in the founding of all the Great Religions ; but the world was unable to apprehend it. The descent of the Human Race had brought about an entire change in the power within man by which he could discern spiritual things. Hence the failure of all the Great Religions to accomplish the Redemption and Illumination of the world.

[2] Those of the Ancient Christhood who were with Him had indeed known that Light of Life in great fulness. They had experienced Grace upon Grace, had risen from state to state until they had attained interiorly the vision of Adonai.

[3] The Divine Radiance is the Eternal Life radiating in beautiful fulness within the Soul. It is the Light of His Countenance within the Sanctuary. Such a vision is no dream or vain imagining on the part of those who are in Christhood ; it is a blessed realization.

[4] In this profound saying we may witness the process of the becoming within the Soul of the high estate of Christhood. The process is necessarily slow, for the Soul can only receive as it has power, and realize only in so far as it has grown. From glorious state to glorious state it rises, intensifying in its consciousness, and responding to the ever-increasing vibrations of the Inner Worlds. This covers many ages.

But to those who were once in high Christhood, were the words spoken ; for the inner group of the disciples had been in that state, and they were to realize it once more.

DISCIPLESHIP

The
Shepherds
of
Bethlehem

"*There dwelt upon the planes of the Bethlehem*[1]
Shepherds,[2] *and these watched over their flock during
the long night.*

*For intense darkness had overtaken the Holy City of
Ierusalem,*[3] *and all who dwelt within her borders.*

*And the Shepherds upon the planes were filled with
great anxiety for their flocks lest they should become
lost amid the darkness,*[4] *and be unable to find their
way back to Bethlehem.*

*And the Shepherds sorrowed that the darkness should
so long prevail, and prayed that the Light might soon
break ; for they kept burning upon the altar of their
hearts the Fire of the Holy One.*

*And whilst they prayed, behold the Heavens opened
unto them, and beside them stood the Angel of the
Lord who thus spake unto them :*

'*Behold ! Behold ! Tidings of great Joy to you I bring
And unto all peoples of the land shall it be.
This day there is born unto you in David's city
He who shall become unto you Christ and Lord ;
In Bethlehem shall ye find this One, a Saviour,
And He shall be to you the Light of Life.*'

*And there was with the Angel of the Lord an heavenly
host, who sang this song :*

'*Glory be to God within the Highest
Where He reigneth King over all,
Making manifest His glorious Presence,
In the vision of the Beauty of the Lord ;
And upon the Earth-planes be His Peace,
Through the willinghood of His good pleasure.*'

*And the Shepherds made haste and went up to the
Bethlehem ; and there they found it even as the Angel
of the Lord had said unto them. And great was the
joy within them because of all that had come into
their lives.*"

NOTES.

The Birth Stories which have been the cause of bitter controversy, were stories of the Soul. They had no relation to the event of the birth of the Master, but rather to the event, most sacred to all Souls, of the birth of the Christ consciousness within. One of them—the Shepherds of Bethlehem—embodied most ancient history, being a monograph of an experience which came to the Christ-Souls who were ministering unto the Children of the Planet. It embodied the history of a great epoch and the beginning of a new era. It revealed the nature of the ministry performed by the Shepherds upon the Bethlehem, the conditions which prevailed, and the new experiences that were breaking upon them. For it signified unto them the coming again into their consciousness of the Christ.

But the story was not only meant to give the disciples a glimpse of most ancient history of the Christhood Order, but also to reveal to them their own part in it, and to impress upon them the nature of the ministry unto which He and they were called. For the experience of the Shepherds of Bethlehem was just such as they themselves had been passing through. The coming of Jesus Christ into the world of a human Soul is heralded from the Heavens. The Angel of the Lord announces it, and the Heavenly Hosts sing of its Glory. It matters not in what age or amidst what race, it is ever the same.

[1] The Bethlehem was the lower spiritual planes, the outer or lower House of the Lord.

[2] The Shepherds were the Shepherds of Zion, or teachers of the Christhood Order referred to in the Prophetic Writings.

[3] The Holy City of Ierusalem was this world as a spiritual system.

[4] The Darkness was the loss of the inner Light through the Fall.

DISCIPLESHIP

" Now, the birth of the holy states of Jesus, Christ, and the Lord is after this manner.[1]

he Birth
tory

Maria[2] being great with child, having conceived within the womb of the Soul, and of the Holy One who overshadows her continually,[3] that Life which shall be named Son of God,[4] goes up into Bethlehem that she may bring forth the child begotten within her from the Highest.

And Ioseph[5] also goes with her, being espoused unto her that he may minister unto her in the days of her travail, and companion her. For unto him doth the Angel of the Lord appear to instruct and counsel him what to do in his espousal of Maria, and to inform him of the nature of the holy thing to be born of her.

And they go up to Bethlehem together.[6] And there Maria brings forth her first-born, even Jesus. But he is born in lowly state as becometh one who would love all creatures ; for in the blessing of the new-born Soul-state, all the creatures are to have a share.

For, finding that the Inns whither they go have no room for them,[7] they seek a lodging with the lowly ones, and so make the Manger[8] the cradle of their first-born.

And the child grows and waxes strong, growing in grace and wisdom, and in the fear of the Lord. And he abides at Nazareth with his parents,[9] being subject unto them until the day of the appearing of the Angel of the Lord unto him when he should go forth to make manifest the way of salvation for all peoples, and cause the Light to shine upon the ways of the Gentiles that they may come to know his saving grace."[10]

NOTES.

[1] The three terms were not names given to the Master by His friends. To them He was Ioannes, though they spoke of Him as " the beloved one." The terms represented the three-fold order of the Manifestation through Him, and within and through every Soul who attains to the like high Christhood. The first betokens the saving state within a Soul, of purity—the redeemed and the redeeming life. The second indicates the attainment by means of Soul culture, of the realisation of the Divine Light within, the Light that illumines the Soul and makes the life radiate it. The third signifies the attainment of perfect fulness with the Lord of Being.

[2] Maria was a Mystery term signifying the Soul : but it was applied in a very special sense to One who had at some time reached the Divine Kingdom.

[3] Christ is born within a Soul through the Divine Overshadowing. It could not be otherwise, for only the Eternal One can quicken the spiritual elements within a Soul and cause them to polarise in the conception of so high a life.

[4] The term is to be understood here of the blessed Life ; for the Christhood is the Son of God manifest within a Soul.

[5] Ioseph was also a Mystery term, and like Maria was profound in its meaning. It was originally a Divine name, but came to be associated with a Soul who had a special office. Here it represented the protecting care provided for the Soul in whom Christ was conceived.

[6] To the City of Bethlehem or outer House of the Lord wherein the first degree of the high estate is made manifest. Jesus is born in Bethlehem ; Christ is revealed on the Mount.

[7] The traditional Houses of religious thought. They have no room, nor have they ever had room, for this view of the Christhood. They cannot entertain Maria and Ioseph.

[8] The symbol of lowliness of heart and beautiful compassion, for the creatures find ministry also through the birth of the Jesus life.

[9] The state that is despised. It represents self-denial, purity, aloofness from the world-life, separateness from the traditional and ecclesiastical systems and schools.

[10] When the Soul reaches the full degree of Christhood, it may be said of it that the consciousness begotten within it is no longer subject to Maria and Joseph, but only to the Lord ; for He speaks within the Soul and through it.

DISCIPLESHIP

" *Ever Blessed be the Lord God of Israel, for He hath visited and redeemed His people.*[1]

The Benedictus

He hath raised up a power unto Salvation for us within the House of David,[2]

As He promised unto us through His Holy Messengers who have ministered unto us since this fallen world began ;[3]

That we should be saved from our enemies, and from the power of all that hate us ;[4]

To perform unto us the ministry of our Father-Mother, and to interpret His Holy Covenant ;

That, being delivered from the hand of our enemies, we might continually serve before Him, redeemed from fear, in Holiness, Righteousness and Love ;

That we should again be the children of the Highest, and go before Him to make ready His way ;

To give unto His people the knowledge of Salvation through the healing of their sins.[5]

Through the tender Love of God the Dayspring hath again visited us from on high, to give unto us Light in our darkness, and to take away the shadows of spiritual death, through guiding us into the way of Peace." [6]

NOTES.

[1] This is an ancient Song of Israel. It was named the Benedictus by the Church, and by the writers of the accepted records of the New Testament was associated with their story of the birth of John the Baptist. It was a song of the ancient Christhood, as the language itself reveals, and embodies history none could understand but themselves.

[2] The House of David was a Mystery term signifying the House of Purification. It was in this House of David that a fountain was to be opened whereby all sin and uncleanness could be taken away. The process of purification through the elimination of evil from the life, constituted Salvation—the Salvation which God provides.

[3] The Messengers were those sent to found the Great Religions. In all these this same blessed truth was foretold, though in varying language and under different terms. It had been predicted that the Christhood should once more be restored. But unto Israel alone was it revealed how it was to be accomplished fully; for only the true Israel knew of the projected oblation known in the West as the Sin Offering.

[4] These were no mere national enemies such as the Jews spoke of, but the evil principalities and powers of the Astral realms, powers terribly potent though invisible. These hated the life and the light of Christhood, and their action militated against the upwardness of the Soul, and even the life and ministry of the Christhood.

[5] Here the results of the Oblation are anticipated; for after its accomplishment the Christhood ministry will prove more effective. The forgiveness of Sin is the healing of the life.

[6] This verse was added to the song, for, in its restoration by the Master, the inner group beheld how the Divine Love had once more revealed Himself, and was verily leading them into the Great Peace.

DISCIPLESHIP

" My Soul doth magnify the Lord, and my Spirit hath rejoiced in God my Saviour.[1]

The Magnificat

For He hath regarded my low Estate;[2] *and He who is mighty hath done great things unto me through the Holiness of His Name.*[3]

For His Love is unto His children, even through out all the generations.[4]

He hath made manifest His strength when by His Right Hand He hath scattered the proud who imagined vain things in their hearts.[5]

He hath put down the mighty ones from their high places where they oppressed those who were of lowly estate.[6]

He hath satisfied the hungry with His goodness, and through His richness in Love none need go empty away.

He hath holpen His servants Israel,[7] *through their remembrance of His Love."*

NOTES.

[1] This beautiful ancient Song of the Soul was attributed to the Mother of Jesus. In that respect it is quite true, for it is a song of joy begotten in the Soul through the new consciousness of life conceived within its womb to be born into manifestation in Christhood. But it is far older than the days of the Master, having been known in the times of Ancient Israel. It is true for all time, though its references to the past have a special significance in the history upon this Planet of the Christhood Order.

[2] Not outward estate, but the evil conditions into which the Soul had descended : therefore low in the consciousness of the Blessed Life.

[3] There is a power behind the Name of the Eternal One known only unto those who have realized Christ in themselves. That Name is ever holy and hallowed unto them, and can give a Soul who holds it sacred, the victory.

[4] Not simply the generations of man understood historically, but the individual Soul as it passes through its various generations of lives upon the world. Throughout these, though they cover untold ages, the Divine Love has known no change, whatever the changing conditions may have been.

[5] " Woe unto the pride of Ephraim " said the prophet, wherein is found deeper significance than is apparent ; for Ephraim was the House of ruling Minds, and that House went far astray through pride of heart.

[6] The Rulers of this world who have always oppressed the lowly, with special reference to those rulers who oppressed all who sought to follow the true path in life and worship and serve only the Living God as One whose Life was within them. For this thing has happened in all ages, that those who have sought the pure and lowly way have been oppressed by the rulers in the religious, social and national realms

[7] Another reference to the Ancient Christhood. The term was used to denote the overcoming life, and then the Cross bearers. Israel was the community of Souls who carried the Cross of the Divine Service.

DISCIPLESHIP

The Magi: A Story of Israel

" *There dwelt once, in an ancient City of the East, men who were full of wisdom and who sought out the deep things of God:*[1] *these were interpreters of the Stars, and watchers for the coming of divine events.*[2]

Their ways in life were those of Israel when as yet Israel was unfallen ; for they were pure in their manner of living, eating no flesh, drinking no wine, and desiring only purity and truth.[3]

Now, these three Kings of the East beheld upon the spiritual heavens the arising of a Star, and knowing well its meaning, being interpreters of such wonders, they watched its progress, and followed it as earnest Souls.

And the Star moved towards the Bethlehem, and there it paused.[4] *So they went thither to the place where it had stayed in its course ; for they knew that it was to them the herald of the arising of Christ.*

And the glory of the Star shone upon the place where the Christ had been born: and when they came to the place, they found Ioseph-Maria with the Christ-child.[5]

And these three Kings of the East bowed themselves before the Lord of the heavenly Hosts and worshipped, and were full of joy at what had come to pass. Then they poured out before the Lord of their treasures, Gold, Frankincense and Myrrh.[6]

Now, the Star which the three Kings of the East beheld, and which led them unto the Christ-child in the Bethlehem, whither they went taking their gifts with them, was the arising of the Light within them, even the Light of Christ. For these three were of His Order.

And these found Christ born within the Hostel which sheltered the creatures ; for the Hostel is in Bethlehem, and outside of the Inn. It is in the pure, tender and compassionate one.

Thus is it with everyone within whom the Lord of Life comes to birth."

NOTES.

[1] The East in the Mysteries expressed the idea of the direction of the Divine. A City meant a state such as the Holy City of Zion.

[2] Astrologers, but not such astrologers as history makes us ac quainted with. In the days of Ancient Israel astrology was purely a spiritual science, indeed a Divine Science. The Planetary and Celestial Mysteries were known and understood by such as are here described. And they looked also into the Spiritual Heavens and understood its symbols and signs.

[3] It is impossible to convey to anyone what this world was like prior to the Fall. Many speak of that time, but without realizing what it meant. Israel was unfallen : the Christhood Order with its wonderful ministry, its sweetness and purity in life, interpreted the way of life for the children of this world, and revealed unto those who were sufficiently grown to receive it, the Wisdom of God. All that made for evil was unknown.

[4] A rising Star upon those Heavens foretold the arising of the Christhood. Its shining over the Bethlehem indicated the city or state in which the Christ was born within a Soul.

[5] When the Soul finds Christ born of Maria, it also finds Ioseph-Maria, the Divine Protector and the Soul's own high estate in which it can become the mother of the Lord. This is the sense in which the Virgin Mary is represented as being " The Mother of our Lord." It is the Soul through the high degree of Christhood bringing the Lord consciousness into manifestation.

[6] The gifts laid at the feet of the Christ-child represent the ministry of the three Magians—Gold, Frankincense and Myrrh, symbolise Love, Light and Life—spiritual wealth, spiritual understanding, spiritual devotion ; the Divine Love, the Divine Ministry and the Divine Healing and Saving.

DISCIPLESHIP

The Presentation in the Temple

" *Now, when the days of the Purification were accomplished, Ioseph-Maria went up into the Temple of the Lord to make unto Him the presentation of the one born unto them.*[1]

And for an Oblation they did offer unto the Lord all that they possessed, consecrated upon His Altar for His service.[2]

When this had been accomplished by them, in token that their Oblation was acceptable, there descended the Holy Spirit upon them in the form of two turtle-doves, for these were the emblems of the Life unto which they had attained. And they also laid upon the Altar of the Temple those high gifts in service for their Lord.[3]

There went up to the Temple of the Lord with them a prophetess of the Lord. She was most aged in her Soul and full of heavenly wisdom. She loved the Temple of the Lord, and spent her days in service before Him. When she beheld Ioseph-Maria with the Christ, she lifted up her voice in thanksgiving, and proclaimed the arising in Israel of the Redemption and the coming into manifestation of the Order of the Christhood.[4]

And there was also at the door of the Temple of the Lord, one full of years and good works whose name was Simeon.[5] *Unto him was it revealed of the Spirit that the day of the Lord had come when the Christ should arise and be manifested for the Restoration of Israel, and that Salvation might come unto all peoples. And when he beheld the Glory of the Lord made manifest, he also lifted up his hands in blessing, saying unto Ioseph-Maria :*

' Now know I that the Lord is good, and that He hath not forsaken His children, nor any who put their trust in Him.

He hath restored unto His servant His own Peace, through causing me to behold the Salvation of God ;

For in the Way of Christhood hath He led me to walk, that I might fulfil the Law of the Lord.

NOTES.

[1] The story of the Purification found in the records converts a most beautiful Soul history into a mere Jewish ceremony. It had nothing Jewish in it, and had no relation to the childhood of the Master. It was a story of the experience that takes place in every Soul wherein Christ is born into manifestation. It is when the days of the Purification of Life are accomplished that the great act of consecration takes place.

There was, however, a special reference in it to the Return of the Master, the days of the Purification from the effects of the Oblation or Sin-offering, the entering in of Himself into the consciousness of Christhood, with other matters of great interest and deep moment.

[2] This is always the way of the Soul in whom Christ is born. Life itself is laid upon the altar.

[3] The Spirit in the form of two Doves symbolises the double gift of the Spirit of Love and the Spirit of Wisdom, the two sublime powers always accompanying the manifestation of Christ. And whatever attributes the Soul may possess from the Divine State begotten within her, are consecrated to the one great work of the Christhood.

[4] Symbolising the Intuition. Soul intuition may be said to be most aged, for it is the outcome of thousands of ages of Soul history. It is the Intuition that discerns heavenly things. None but a very old intuitive Soul could recognise Christ with Ioseph-Maria.

This prophetess is named Anna, for the year had come when Christ should be proclaimed as the way, the truth and the life for the Soul, and the arising of Israel to make it manifest for the Redemption.

Concerning the Return of the Master, the arising of the Ancient Order of Christs, the Purification, the Consecration and the Redemption, that same Prophetess has once more spoken.

[5] The Mind purified : not within the innermost Sanctuary, yet related to the Temple, standing at the very door of the Sanctuary. Also very old because burdened with the travail of many ages.

The Nunc Dimittis, as it has been named by the Church, is in its meaning very different from what the Church still imagines.

G—I

DISCIPLESHIP

The Presentation in the Temple

Behold, now am I to see the Salvation Thou dost work out, according to Thy Word ;
For Thou hast prepared the way whereby it may reach unto all peoples.
Unto the Gentiles shall Thy Light now be unveiled, And Thy Glory unto Israel.' "[1]

Gloria in Excelsis

" Glory be unto the Lord in the Highest, who hath made manifest His Loving Kindness unto His Children!

For He hath delivered them by the power of His great Love which had its dwelling in them.

He hath divided the waters ; so are they able to pass through from the thraldom of the Pharaohs, to find a new home amid the planes of Sinai.

There the Lord shall descend that they may again behold His Vision and His Glory.

And unto the stricken Earth hath He had regard :
For He shall yet deliver His once beautiful City Ierusalem from the power of the oppressor, and shall change her wilderness into Green Pastures and her desert into a Garden of Beauty where flow streams full of Life.

He shall give unto all His children within her, the Peace of a New Life, and the Gladness of a true Service ; for He shall send unto them His Servant Jesus to Redeem them out of all their infirmities, and to heal all their wounds which they have received in the House of Bondage."[2]

NOTES.

[1] The Nunc Dimittis had a very special meaning for the Master. It was anticipatory and prophetic. Like the story of the Purification of which it forms a part, it was related to the Oblation or Sin-offering. It portrays the healing of the mind, the restoration of Simon, the burden-bearer, who was to be carried whither he would fain not go. It embodied the healing of the life of the Master during the Purification, and the vision that was to come to Him of the unfailing goodness of the Divine Love in restoring Israel—the Christhood, and accomplishing the Salvation or purification of all who were true seekers after God. To understand its opening words reveals a true discernment of what the Oblation meant to the Master ; for it impoverished Him so greatly that in the last life of the Sin-offering, His trust in the Divine Love and Wisdom was for a time, utterly broken. He believed Himself to be a " Castaway."[2]

[2] This is an Ancient Song of Israel, a Gloria in Excelsis. To all who have understanding, it will speak for itself. It is a song of the Christhood, rich in deep meanings. The Soul's history is in it, its fall and its deliverance. The story of Israel in Egypt is implied, and the awful oppression under the powers of the fallen body—the Egyptians. The dividing of the waters of the Red Sea is referred to, and the passing through of the Soul from that bondage ; for the Red Sea was the Astral World. The planes of Sinai were those spiritual conditions which followed the recovery of the knowledge of the Laws of Life from the Lord upon Mount Sinai, the Mount of spiritual elevation in which such knowledge could be restored.

The second portion of the song refers to the Planet as a spiritual Household, and all her children within her gates. For she was to be restored through a Redeemer when the set-time had come. Through Jesus, the servant of God, was she to be healed, even through the pure and compassionate life of the Jesus-state.

This wonderful song is now to find its perfect fulfilment, for the set-time for Zion (the Order of the Christhood) has come, and with it, the time of the healing of the wounding of Jerusalem.

DISCIPLESHIP

The Children of the Bethlehem

When Herod beheld how the Magians who had beheld the star of the arising of Christ refused to obey his commands to return into his Kingdom, and how they had set out for the East, the land of their nativity, there to pursue their service to their Lord, he was angered and became exceeding wroth.

And he visited his wrath upon the children of the Bethlehem, and in all the regions of it, wheresoever he could reach with his power.

And he slew them ; for thereby he hoped to destroy Christ.

Then was there lamentation in Rama, and the voice of weeping : for Rachel wept for her children, and would not be comforted, because they were lost to her.[1]

The Flight into Egypt

" Behold, the Angel of the Lord appeared into Ioseph and said unto him : 'Take Maria and the child down into Egypt, for Herod desireth to have the child's life.

He feareth that the arising of the Kingdom which He hath been sent to establish will overthrow his regal power and destroy his dominion.

But guard thou him until the word cometh unto thee that thou mayest bring him out of Egypt.'

And Ioseph arose and took Maria and the child with him, and fled into Egypt ; and it became night.

Then when Herod was dead, there appeared unto him once more the Angel of the Lord, and He said unto him : ' Arise, now ; take Maria and the child back into the land of Israel, and there dwell, for Herod is dead.'

And they returned from Egypt, and came unto the City of Nazareth, and abode there."[2]

NOTES.

[1] The story of Herod and the Magians was quite distinct from that of the visit of the Magi. It was a monograph of an episode in most ancient history, history dating back to the ages during which the whole planetary system was gradually descending into conditions which had as their issue the loss to the Planet of all its children. For the children of Bethlehem who were slain were those who had reached the state represented by that term, the elder children of the Planet. For Herod represented the evil power that had come to rule over the middle kingdom. He slew the children in his wrath— symbolising the hatred of evil towards good, and the determination of the powers of evil to stamp out the influence of the Christhood.

The lamentation in Rama and the weeping of Rachel were terms used to express the grief of the Divine Kingdom and the Sorrow of the Heavens over the awful Soul descent, as the result of Herod's treachery.

[2] The Flight into Egypt contains in briefest form the history of the Oblation. Ever since the kingdom spoken of as the Herodian had existence, Herod has sought to lay hold of the Christ and defeat the Kingdom of Christhood. He has always feared the establishment of that Kingdom, because it meant the overthrow of his own. But very specially was this true during the Manifestation and the times that have followed. The purification of the Astral world during the days of the Oblation was the process by which his power was to be broken and his Kingdom overthrown.

The going of Ioseph and Maria with the Christ-child, was the descent of the Master into the states represented by Egypt and the Herodian Kingdom, and carrying the burden of the Oblation in many lives until the power of Herod was broken and his rule dead.

The return from Egypt is now. It meant the return of the Master from the Sin-offering conditions to dwell at Nazareth, where He is said to have made His home. For, to the world, Nazareth is a state to be despised ; but for the Soul it is a condition of life which implies purity and consecration to the service of the Lord.

DISCIPLESHIP

Witnessing of the Father-Mother

There were those who could not understand the deep things of which He spake, and who doubted the source of the light that was in Him. Unto them did He further speak, saying :

" The One who speaketh within me is the Light of the world : whosoever followeth Him shall not remain in darkness, but shall have within him the Light of Life.

" I bear not witness of myself, as ye suppose, but of Him. And the witness I bear of Him is true, for I know Him.

" Yea, my witness of Him is even as I said unto you, for He is with me.[1]

" Ye cannot understand this thing which I tell you, that I am never alone ; for the Father-Mother who is within me, is ever with me.

" I know whence I came ; for I came out from the Father-Mother. I also know whither I have to go."[2]

And when He had so spoken, some marvelled because of the assurance He gave of the Light that was in Him.

But there were others who only questioned what He said ; and these inquired of Him : "Where is the Father-Mother you speak of ? "

But He said : " Had you understood me, ye would have understood of whom I spake.

" Ye are thinking of things upon the earth ; I am thinking and speaking of things from above.[3]

"What I have said unto you has been learnt by me from the Father-Mother in the Heavens.

" There are many such things of which I would fain speak unto you concerning the Father-Mother, and your own need of healing and light from Him. For I have been sent to testify of these things.

" If ye are able to receive this word of truth, and to abide in it, then shall ye come to know the truth in its ulness of meaning ; for truth will make you to be free from the power of this world which enslaveth."[4]

And some who heard these sayings said unto Him ·
" We have never been in bondage to any one. We are

NOTES.

[1] It was not the habit of the Master to witness of Himself. Whatever attributes were His He thought of them as gifts for ministry from the Highest. He never proclaimed Himself, but rather shrank from the thought of anyone associating the message with Himself in any personal sense. The Light within Him was no human knowledge nor occult acquisition ; it was the Light of Adonai. Through that High and Holy Presence did the Divine Sophia come to Him. He knew Adonai, for the consciousness which He represented was present to the Master. He also knew the Father-Mother, for the blessed realization had been His.

[2] But to understand such things was naturally beyond the experience of many. What could the Master mean by saying that He had come out from the Father-Mother ? but this, that in His innermost consciousness that Holy One was always present to Him, and apart from the limitations imposed through the personal mind, that Presence was realized in sublime fulness—the pleroma of His Christhood. He knew His own beginnings, His realisations, and whether He had yet to go. In this last there was a hint of the Sin-offering. It was not simply uttered to emphasize the darkness within those to whom He spake ; for they knew not whence they were nor whither they would go, knowing nothing of the origin of Life, nor the way of the Soul as it progressed from life to life. It was spoken to affirm the purpose of the mission on which He had been sent, in the first place to reveal the Father-Mother and interpret His Way of Love, and then accomplish the Oblation.

[3] The difficulty of getting men and women to think impersonally is great. Their thoughts of the Divine are anthropomorphic. They cannot rise above the limited human personal conception. Where God has His dwelling is not within the radius of their vision. It is beyond their ken : they know Him not, though they have been taught to believe many things about Him. Who is this Father-Mother is a question asked to-day in varying terms ? Even the Churches appear to know little more than those outside their fellowships. With them it is even as it was with Jewry.

DISCIPLESHIP

of the seed of Abraham and so are free.[1] In what sense dost thou mean that we should be made free?"

The Master spake yet again unto them, saying:

" Any one who is bound to sin is not free.

" Any one who is thus bound to sin is unable to abide in the household of the Father-Mother, and so must remain outside as one who is a bondservant.[2]

" Yet, the Son may make the bondservant free. And if the Son make you free, ye shall be free indeed.

" I speak of the Son of God who is within you.[3]

" I know ye claim to be of the seed of Abraham; then the promise of Abraham is unto you, and the blessing of the God of Abraham should be yours.

To inherit that blessing is to come into the possession of all things.[4]

I speak unto you of the blessing of my Father-Mother upon all the seed of Abraham; for from Him have I received it.

And I ask that ye may do the things of which ye have now heard from the Father-Mother through me.

The glory which I bring unto you is that of the Kingdom of God; for it is within you."[5]

Yet, though He thus spake of the Father-Mother, there were present some who would not hear the words He spake, and who sought to confound Him.

These declared that the message which He gave was not from God, and that it was from the evil one.

They even said that He was a Samaritan and was obsessed of the devil.[6]

Unto these the Master spake thus:

" If I had a devil, as ye say I have, I could not speak of God as I have done unto you; for God is true, and the things of which I have spoken are true.

The devil is he who denieth what is true, and who opposeth himself to God.

If ye had known God, ye would also have known that the message which I have given unto you was of Him. For whosoever is of God understandeth the things that be of God.[7]

108

NOTES.

[1] When one knows the truth underlying the Abrahamic idea which in a perverted sense was believed in by the Jews, it is most pathetic to behold the depth of the darkness within the teachers of the people. They knew nothing about the inner sense of the Abrahamic story, nor the high estate of life for the Planet implied in the Divine name. To them it was just a racial descent, and the great blessing only such as races seek of an earthly character ; whereas the descent was purely soulic, and the promise such as only the Soul could realise when it had reached its full estate.

[2] No Soul whilst still in bondage to sin can come into the consciousness implied here.

[3] Only the awakening of Christ within a Soul can deliver it from bondage. He gives to the Soul the liberty of the Children of God.

[4] This hints at a Divine Christhood. To possess all things is to have the seven-fold Spirit.

[5] How instant the Master was in His statements of the real nature of the Kingdom of God. And also how frequently He interpreted its glory as the life of love and devotion.

[6] What is the true test of any statement as to inspiration ? Surely not because any man spoke it, or wrote it, or claimed that it was inspired. For ages, both Christian and pre-Christian, those who follow the way of the schools have decided this grave matter after their traditions. And often have they assigned an evil origin to most high and holy things because they could not understand them. Even of some Seers from the Divine Kingdom have they said that they were of the devil.

The true test of an inspired saying is within itself. The true test of an illumined Soul is its powers to discern and understand.

[7] Only the God within us can understand the deep things of God. Whosoever realises Him is able to say that he knoweth Him and the things of which He speaketh.

DISCIPLESHIP

Witnessing of the Father-Mother

If I should say, I know not God, I should dishonour Him ; for I do know Him, and I seek only His honour.[1]

Though ye may do dishonour unto me, let not your hearts do dishonour unto Him.

Ye call Him your Father ; then honour the Father who is also the Mother of us all.

If ye honour and love Him, and have His word abiding in you, ye shall never taste of death."[2]

Upon hearing these things, those who sought to confound Him were amazed, and said unto Him :

" How can it be so ? Abraham is dead ; so likewise are the prophets. Yet thou sayest that if one honour God, he shall not taste of death ? Art thou one who is greater than Abraham and the prophets ? Whom dost thou make thyself ? "[3]

But He answered :

"Who I am, it matters not. I seek not mine own glory, but the glory of the Father-Mother who sent me. As I said unto you, I speak not of earthly things, but of heavenly. Your father Abraham has rejoiced to see this day, and because of it he is glad."[4]

Not yet perceiving the things of which He spake, they said unto Him :

" Thou art not yet fifty years old, yet thou speakest of Abraham as if thou hadst known him."

But the Master could not further reveal unto them the things of which He spake. Therefore He only replied unto their inquiry by saying :

" Before Abraham, was the I AM."[5]

Verily, verily, he who heareth His message with the understanding to do it, hath Eternal Life abiding in him."[6]

NOTES.

[1] When one has arrived at the consciousness of the God within, he knows Him ; and He may not please anyone by denying that knowledge. To know by realization transcends all other attainments of knowledge through the mind. The experience stands above all else.

[2] The Deathless Life is the life of the Immortals. There is no death, because the Soul lives on and passes through many lives. Yet there is a spiritual death that comes to so many, in the loss of being. The powers of so many are as if they were dead. But those in whom the Son of God has been called forth from the dead, know death no more. They come to live always in the consciousness of the Divine Life.

[3] The revelation of their ignorance of spiritual things is truly appalling. Yet it finds its repetition even in this age and amongst the religious communities. They thought Abraham was dead, because they thought of Him as a man. And they knew that the Prophets re-appeared in different ages with the same message from the Heavens.

[4] The meaning here cannot be fully expressed in a note. It had reference to the Divine Estate of the Planet as a Celestial Being. The Planet Soul rejoiced in the Manifestation through the Master, for it was the forerunner of that other great work which had to be accomplished within the planetary middle Kingdom. For in that work lay the hope of the Redemption of the Planet's children.

[5] Readers will note the difference between this reading and that in the fourth Gospel. What wealth of meaning it contains for those who understand. He is before all things for whom all things be. In all the Celestial systems He is the Arche and the Amen.

[6] To know His word or meaning and to do it, is to attain unto that Life which issues in the consciousness of that Presence within the Soul.

DISCIPLESHIP

Amid the Desert

When the Master looked upon the multitudes He was filled with Compassion towards them, for He beheld them to be like a flock of sheep without a true shepherd.

And He said unto the disciples: "Truly this land is a desert place and one in which no provision is found for the Souls of the people. They languish by the way, for they receive not fit nourishment to sustain them. But the heavenly Father-Mother hath sent His Messenger to break unto them the Bread of Life, that they labour not for meat which perisheth with its use, but for that meat which the Father-Mother giveth unto all whose endurance is unto Life Eternal."

And He asked the disciples to command the people to sit down whilst He spake unto them. And they sat down in rows of hundreds on the grass and listened unto Him as He spake of the Bread that had come down from Heaven.

Feeding the Multitudes

And when they had reached the Sea of Galilee,[1] He took them into a high mountain,[2] and there they sat down with Him. And He spake unto them this allegory:

" A Teacher was sent unto a certain land to show unto the people the true way to the attainment of life.

And they brought unto Him many who had been crippled, maimed, dumb and deaf: these He healed through showing them the way.

And these spake gloriously of the God of Israel.

But the multitudes wandered about like sheep straying for want of shepherding; and towards them he was moved with compassion.

And he spake unto those whom he had healed through showing them the way, and said unto them: 'Upon the multitudes do I have compassion; for they have been wandering about for three days without food, and are perishing from lack.[3] Them we must not send away empty. What bread have ye with you that we may give unto them to eat?'

NOTES.

The story of the feeding of the Multitudes has impressed many, and it has been taken as a striking illustration of His compassion towards men and women, and His power over the elements to change or multiply them at will. But surely any one who understood the elements so well as to be able to multiply their constituent parts at will, and who could so use them, would do so out of compassion for starving multitudes, even though far from the estate of Christhood. Nor would the possession of such power imply Christhood. Great and marvellous things have been wrought by those who know nothing of Christhood.

Compassion, such as the Master's, was not revealed in mere casual acts of pity, but in healing those who were suffering from Soul impoverishment by changing the elemental conditions which brought the suffering to them. His compassion lay in His boundless love which He gave in service to them, and His power was made manifest as the Divine Energy in Him by which the elemental conditions were actually changed so greatly, that it became more possible for the ministry of the Great Love of the Father-Mother to be rendered unto the people.

[1] The Sea of Galilee was a Mystery term, though it was given to the Lake of Tiberius. In other Logia it occurs and will be more fully explained under them. But it signified purity of mind and knowledges of Divine Things.

[2] A high mountain signified exalted state of mind. The Hills were the symbols of Spiritual uplands, and the Mountains the heights of Soul realization.

[3] There is profound meaning here, referring to the three days of the crucifixion and burial, three Naronic Cycles during which the multitudes were perishing from lack.

DISCIPLESHIP

And they said : ' Only seven loaves and a few small fishes.[1] *But what are these ?'*

Feeding the Multitudes

Then He commanded that the seven loaves and the few small fishes be brought to Him.

And He blessed these, breaking them into portions, and distributing through those who were with Him to the multitude.[2]

When all had partaken, there remained much left over ; and He requested that the portions should be gathered. And when they were gathered up they filled seven baskets."[3]

Then did the disciples who were with Him ask the Master if He would interpret the Allegory unto them. And He spake these words :—

" The Teacher is the Son of Man.

Whosoever would come unto Him, and be healed, must learn to sit at the feet of the Lord.[4]

There the deaf come to hear and the dumb to speak ; and the crippled and the maimed to find healing. For it is the Way.

Thither have ye all come.[5] *And ye have received of the Bread of Life through me, even as the Father-Mother gave unto me to give you. Unto your care have been committed the seven sacred loaves and the fishes for use in the day of the return of the Son of Man.*

For, when the Son of Man cometh in the latter days to make manifest the glory of the Father-Mother, and establish the Kingdom of the Heavens in the midst of the nations, wherein truth, equity, righteousness and love shall reign, there will be lack of bread amongst the peoples.

During the three days will they be in a desert land, believing they are following our Way, and listening unto us.[6]

For throughout the three days of the Passover they will suffer hunger ; nor will they know where to find nourishment.[7]

And in those days when the Passover has been fully accomplished, and the Oblation finished, the Bread of the sacred Seven must be broken unto them by the Lord of Life through us all.

NOTES.

[1] The Seven Loaves and small Fishes were symbols of hidden truths. The seven Sacraments of the Church were as seven loaves of bread which should have been broken for the people's nourishment; they should have been interpreted in their esoteric meanings for the benefit of the whole Race. But the most precious nourishing doctrines contained in them have always been shut up in forms of the Church, and the purely exoteric character of the interpretation put upon them. The Soul of the people hungered for the Bread of Heaven, the Church gave them bread which was said to come down from the Heavens, but the people became more and more impoverished and weakened in the way.

In these days of the Return and the Coming again of the Son of Man, the Seven Loaves are being broken and the portions given unto all who can receive. And with these, also the few small fish, the lesser Mysteries.

[2] The way of the Divine ministry to Souls. Through all who truly receive, other Souls are blessed and given a portion.

[3] The multiplication of spiritual things comes with the use of them. Though the Seven Loaves be broken for thousands, yet is there no lessening, the fragments fill each basket and there is plenty for further use. There are seven planes of consciousness for each Soul, and each one of them becomes filled as a basket with the broken portions.

[4] The Son of Man is the Lord in manifestation within the Soul. Whosoever would know Him must learn to sit patiently at His feet. The personal will must needs be superseded by the Divine Will. Maria sits at the feet of her Lord to learn of Him.

[5] How blessed the past was with them! How blessed that day in which restoration had come to them! And what prophecy of coming events in which they would take such an important part! Verily, Verily, the day is upon us, and some of these are thus breaking anew the bread of the Sacred Seven.

[6] The three days of the Oblation : the era of the Church founded in the name of the Master has covered those days or naronic Cycles, in the vain belief that the Way was being followed, with alas! the most sad and impoverished consequences to all Souls.

[7] The spiritual hunger upon Souls is great now, and none know where to find the true nourishment. The Village Inns (The Churches) do not possess it. The people are religiously entertained ; they are rarely fed.

DISCIPLESHIP

Yet will they not be able to receive much at first ; even of the lesser fish only a little portion. For they will be even as children in their understanding unto whom only the child's portion may be given.[1]

And when they have all been ministered unto, there will yet remain over the fulness of the Bread of the Sacred Seven."

Feeding the Multitudes

There came to the Master some of those who were of the sect of the Pharisees, and these complained that He and His followers transgressed against the traditions of the Elders and chief Priests, as they did not observe the ceremonial washings before meat.[2]

But the Master said unto them .

"Why do ye transgress against the Father-Mother in not keeping His commandment ? For your traditions make void the Word spoken by Him through His prophets, and thus ye do dishonour unto Him.

To fail to observe the law of ceremonials defileth no man, nor bringeth dishonour unto the Father-Mother.[3]

It is not that which entereth into a man from without which defileth him, for he must needs receive much that might be called unclean ; but if there should proceed from him things which are unclean, then these defile him.[4]

The Law of Ceremonial

It is from within that there proceed such evils as railings, falsehoods, injustice, fornications, adulteries, and all evil imaginations.

Every tree which has not been planted by the Father-Mother shall be rooted up, aud every tree which is of His planting shall be established.[5]

Remember ye the words of the prophet Isaiah concerning the ways of the leaders of the people—

'This people honoureth me with their lips,
But their heart is far from me.
In vain forms do they seek to worship,
Teaching doctrines which are naught but the precepts of men.'[6]

Let him who heareth, understand."

116

NOTES.

[1] How true this saying is even to-day. Few who hear of the message of the Divine Sophia are more than children in their understanding. They have not yet put away those forms of thought associated with childhood. Many there be who fain would enter the Kingdom unto whom the child's portion must still be given. Hence the degrees of ministry.

[2] The traditions of the Elders and the priestly ceremonials were a burden of sorrow to the Master. He was not of Jewry ; His life and His Teachings were in opposition to their traditions and ceremonial demands. Purity in the personal life was to Him a real experience, for His life was sweet in every way. But the impositions of Jewry He did not recognise, except as unnecessary and useless burdens imposed upon the people.

[3] Ceremonials may be most helpful in many ways, providing their nature and intent are spiritual. Liturgies may be beautiful and uplifting. External acts of adoration and worship may become vehicles through which the Soul expresses itself. But they are not essential, and to some they are a hindrance. It defileth no man to stand aloof from them. Nor does such an one dishonour the Eternal Father-Mother.

[4] Many there have been who have rejoiced in this Saying because of their desires in the way of meats and drinks, and have thought it mattered not what these were. But the discerning Soul who loves purity in all things, will see that even unclean food or drink will defile a man, and that the reference is, like another saying, to what a man sees and hears, and the extent to which he responds to the evil.

[5] The tree is the symbol of Life. Every kind or way of life which is not from the Divine Love and Wisdom, shall be rooted out. The day of the Redemption is to accomplish that. But every way of life which truly leads to Him shall be established. It shall find its adherents, and all who follow will be crowned with the fulness of Life.

[6] When the real teachings of the true Seers and Prophets are separated from the false statements of the chroniclers of Jewry, they will be seen to have been beautiful Soul illuminations and messages from the Spiritual Heavens.

DISCIPLESHIP

Concerning the Works of God

On one occasion when the Master was walking in what was known as Solomon's Porch of the Temple,[1] there drew near unto Him of those who had heard some of the deeper sayings spoken by Him concerning the Father-Mother, and the way of the Soul in its finding of Him.

These inquired of Him as to the source of the things of which He spake, and who He Himself was who made claim to such authority.

Unto these He said ·

"Verily, verily, I say unto you, The Lord is the Good Shepherd of the sheep.[2]

He who entereth not by the door into the sheepfold, but climbeth up some other way, even as the thief would do to rob, may not enter into the sheepfold.[3]

But he who followeth the path through the portals, to him the guardian openeth the door that he may enter into the fold.[4]

Such heareth the voice of the Good Shepherd when He calleth ; for the Shepherd knoweth His own, and calleth them all by name.

He goeth before them to lead them amid the pastures of God."

But they understood not. And the Master said unto the disciples :

"The door into the fold of God is now made known unto you, what it is ; and the path by which it is approached and entered.

He who entereth in shall be safe, for he shall need no more to go out from the pastures of the fold of God.

From the Father-Mother have I come forth ; for He sent me to show unto all who may discern, the true way into life, that entering through the door into the fold of God, they might find Life, even the Life Eternal.

The Good Shepherd, the Lord of Life who is with me, speaketh these things through me.

Those who hear His voice, will follow the way which I go ; and all who follow that way come to know Him.

I know those who are His, even as the Father-

NOTES.

[1] Though this statement would seem to refer to the Temple of the Jews, it had no such meaning. The Porch of the Temple, known as Solomon's, was a high state of Christhood. It means the porch and threshold of the Divine Consciousness, leading to the perfect realisation of that exalted life. The manifestation through Him was disturbing to those who were unable to apprehend its significance. Many felt the power proceeding from the message, though they could not relate or define it.

[2] The Master never related to Himself in any personal way the Divine Message He had been sent to give. The Message always vibrates with the magnetism of Him by whom He was overshadowed. It was utterly unlike Him to speak of Himself as the Good Shepherd. The personal equation was always subservient to that of the Divine.

So in the shepherding of the children of men ; it is the Lord of Love and Life who is the Good Shepherd, and the Soul through whom He speaks and ministers is His servant.

[3] As there is but One Lord and His Name One, who is the Good Shepherd of Souls ; so there is but one door into the Fold of God, even Jesus Christ. Though men and women may try to enter by some other way, some in ignorance and some purposely, yet it cannot be that they pass the threshold.

[4] There is a Guardian at the portals, and the door is closed unto all but those who name the Son of God in their hearts. By the way of the Jesus-life alone may a Soul approach that door and pass through the portals, for the Soul enters the Fold by means of the life purified from evil, and full of love. All who follow the way of Jesus Christ enter in and find Life.

DISCIPLESHIP

Mother gave unto me the power to know them.[1] *And He calleth them through me.*

Concerning the Works of God

And other sheep there are, those of another fold whom I am likewise sent to call, that they also might find the way unto Him.[2]

There is but One who is Shepherd of the fold of God ; and there is but one fold, though many folds within the one.[3]

To find these sheep of the fold of God am I sent into this world from the Father-Mother.[4]

Unto this end am I come ; and my life will I lay down that the sheep of the fold of God may be able to follow the path through the portals, and enter in and find the Eternal Life.[5]

Power has been given me from the Father-Mother to lay down my life and to take it up again.[6]

The work which has been given unto me to do bears witness unto the Love of the Father-Mother who is with me."

When the Master was on His way to the City of Jerusalem, there came to Him to be healed one who was a leper.

The Healing of the Leper

The afflicted one had long desired healing, but knew not how to get it ; for the physicians were powerless to help him.

Then he heard from some kind friend of the beautiful works of the Master, how the afflicted found in Him unfailing compassion and healing, no earnest seeker being turned away without blessing ;

And how that the Master was approaching the City, and would pass near to the place where he dwelt.

Therefore, when the Master drew near to his dwelling-place, the leper came out and entreated Him that He would help him and take away the loathsome disease.

He spake unto the Master, saying unto Him : " If Thou wilt, Thou can'st make me whole."

And the Master approached him, and beholding how greatly the sufferer longed for healing, and how his life was inwardly changed, said unto him : " Be Thou made whole from this hour."

And the leprosy left him, and he was made whole.

NOTES.

[1] The intense power of discernment as to the state of the Soul. The Master had the power to discern the spiritual status of a Soul by drawing near to it. He knew those who were of the Christhood.

[2] This other fold was the House of Ephraim. Originally it was part of the true Israel, and contained the ruling minds. They had as their mission to this Planet the influencing of the children who had to be governed through the mind—for there were such orders. These rulers also had it as part of their service to this Planet, to build up the teachings given through the Christhood, into the philosophies of life, its origin, nature, purpose and possibilities. In this respect they differed from the inner groups of the Christhood, for these latter were the true Mystics. But this other fold, Ephraim, could not be found unto perfect restoration until the Oblation had been accomplished.

[3] This is true even of the Household of this world. This is but one fold : yet within the one there are many. And so within the Christhood there is but one fold, and only one Shepherd—the One who shepherds all ; yet within the fold were also " the Shepherds of Israel."

[4] The purpose of the Manifestation was to arrest the attention of the whole Christhood Order, and draw its members back to the glorious realization.

[5] The Oblation is here referred to ; for by means of it the way was to be prepared for all to pass through the portals into the life and consciousness of Christhood. The redemption of the children of this world depended upon its accomplishment.

[6] " The laying down " was the putting aside of the Christhood, and the giving up of His very Soul to be the vehicle through which the Divine Love would effect the purification of the Astral world— the middle wall or partition.

DISCIPLESHIP

An Event of Great Moment

And when He came into the region of Tyre there met Him a woman of Sidon whose daughter was vexed grievously with a devil; for she had gone down into the land of Syro-phœnicia and become a Canaanite.[1]

And the mother besought the Master to heal her daughter, saying unto Him: "O thou whom the Lord hast favoured, have compassion upon me and my child; for she has been most grievously tormented."

But the Master was strangely silent.[2]

And there were those with Him who said unto Him, not understanding His silence: "Send her away, lest she keep following after us."

And He spake unto them, saying: "Am I not sent to find the lost sheep of the House of Israel?"[3]

Then He turned to the woman and spake thus unto her: "We take the children's bread and give it unto the dogs, why should we not give it unto your daughter?"

And she for answer said: "Yea, the dogs eat of the crumbs which fall from their owner's table."[4]

But the Master said unto her: "Thy daughter is made whole: it is even as thou desirest.

The Lord of Life hath had compassion upon thee and her. Thy faith towards Him is great, daughter of Israel; be it ever so with thee."[5]

A Notable Vision

When the Master was come down to Bethsaida of Galilee, there was brought unto Him one who was blind.[6]

And the Master took him apart from all who were of Bethsaida, and anointed his eyes; and He laid His hand upon him in blessing.[7]

When his eyes were opened, the Master asked him whether he yet discerned the meaning of the things of which He told him, saying unto him, "Canst thou now behold aught of its meaning?"

But he said unto the Master: "I behold the Lord as a tree walking with man; and there are many trees."[8]

Then the Master again laid upon him the hand of blessing, and he saw clearly.

NOTES.

[1] The term represented a low state, one in which the desire body is dominant and the love-principle sacrificed to it. When the state of the Canaanite was reached, the whole love principle became inverted, and the desire degraded. Many have been driven into that awful condition through obsession. Elemental spirits and even the cast-off personalities within the Astral realms have wrought havoc upon many lives in this way.

[2] The Silence of The Master meant much. He was not given to be silent when Souls called for aid. Too full of compassion was He to withhold blessing. Even in the silence blessing was being given. There were diseases that could only be healed through the power that cometh in the silence. The elemental spirit or demon which had obsessed the afflicted one, had to be driven out.

[3] How full of Soul meaning is this Saying ? It is in perfect accord with all that the Logia reveal. He came to find Israel, even those who were most lost.

[4] The dog represented the fallen state of the Canannite ; hence the reference. Even they must have the Children's bread broken to them. How else can they be nourished unto healing ?

[5] She was of Israel, of those who could discern heavenly things whose desire of Soul was unto God. None could have perceived the meaning of the Master but one who had known. Great Faith is great intuitive discernment.

[6] Bethsaida of Galilee represented a state of the higher mind. It was a Mystery term. Here it is to be understood that the Master had been speaking of profound things to the disciples, but had come back to the place spoken of as Bethsaida of Galilee, for there were Souls there who had to be helped up to the higher vision.

[7] Here He found one who was still blind in that he could not discern the meaning. The Master spake to him alone and brought light to his eyes, in that he could now discern.

[8] A most profound revelation. It was a vision of the Passion of the Lord. The tree which symbolises Life here signifies the Cross. The Lord as a Tree (The Sign of the Cross) walked with man ; and there were many crosses. In every life of the Sin-offering Oblation, it was even so.

DISCIPLESHIP

And from that hour he walked with clear vision, and with his understanding illumined so that he saw all things.[1]

The Demons and the Swine

And the Master said unto him : " Now is the Blessing of the Lord upon thee in that He hath given thee to behold the Passion of the Lord and the burden of His cross."[2]

And when He reached the land of the Gerasene, he was met by two who had been obsessed ; for evil spirits had taken up their abode in them, and filled them with pain and anguish.[3]

They had become dwellers amongst the tombs where many others were in captivity and chains ; and these had often broken their bonds and risen out of the tombs, only to be again afflicted and taken back to the tombs in fetters.[4]

As He drew near, the evil spirits cried out because of fear and rage ; and they rent the two whom they had oppressed, throwing them down again into the tombs.

And the two afflicted ones cried out by reason of their affliction, and besought the Lord that He would deliver them from the power of their tormentors.

When they had thus cried for succour, the Master spake unto the obsessing spirits, commanding them in the name of the Lord to come out of the two whom they had afflicted, and to cease to torment Souls.[5]

Then did the afflicted ones give thanks unto God ; and they worshipped.

And the Master said unto the disciples : " The evil spirits who have just departed were of that legion which once obsessed the children of this world, and drew them all down into the tombs that they had fashioned for them when the swine were generated ; for they made all of them rush down the great steep into the depths of the tombs when the human kingdom was left and the swine entered."[6]

124

NOTES.

[1] There is a meaning in this incident which cannot be expressed. The one referred to became a most intimate friend of the Master, and he is now upon these outer planes fulfilling a blessed ministry for His Lord.

[2] It was such a vision as no one could imagine of himself. The Passion of the Lord revealed in it transcends any human conception of the Divine Love in His ministry to this distraught Earth. The Cross of the burden of the Lord was indeed the Tree of Life that suffered, even as one accursed, in every life which the Master lived ; for in those lives He was the vehicle of that One. In and through the Soul of the one whom we speak of as the Master, the Divine Love bore the burden of the Cross.

[3] What controversy has raged around this incident, and what dishonour has been done to the Master by it ! Yet it was the natural outcome of the presentation of the incident given in the synoptic Gospels. The hand of Jewish editorship is most obvious. Swine were obnoxious to the Jews. They were believed to be unclean creatures, and were prohibited by Jewish law. So it was written of the Master by those who composed the form of the accepted records, that He commanded the demons to enter the swine, and that these latter ran down a steep hill into the sea—which, if true, would have been an act of strange injustice to those who owned them, and also a contradiction of His beautiful humaneness and boundless compassion towards all creatures.

[4] The tombs were the low states in which the obsessed ones were detained by the wicked spirits. The chains were the powers exercised over them by the obsessors. The two afflicted ones had at times broken the power of these, and risen out of their low states, but only to be brought back again.

[5] The way of deliverance is through the power of the Highest. There is no power on earth by which Souls thus obsessed can be delivered : to the name of the Lord only are these spirits obedient. Only the Divine One can control them. Such spirits are not to be confounded with those we speak of as elemental spirits : they are far more terrible than these latter.

[6] The tragic history referred to in this passage is more than can ever be recorded ; it contains the awful issues of the planetary fall and the subsequent descent of the whole of the Human Kingdom into the swine or Saurians, a descent terrible in its results for the entire Race. Nay, even the Christhood Order became involved in it, for they went down after the children of the Planet to rescue them and bring them back to the Human Kingdom.

DISCIPLESHIP

When the blessed Master found an hour of quiet with His immediate friends, He spake thus unto them concerning the experiences through which the Soul passes when it is beset with conditions which try it:

The Stilling of the Storm

" The Soul is like a ship upon the open Sea, when all its attributes are out of true harmony ; it is tossed about upon the tempestuous waves, and is in danger of becoming overwhelmed.

The mind[1] of the Soul, which should be always calm and clear like pellucid waters, is then filled with disturbing elements, so that it cannot reflect unto the Soul the Heavens of its Lord.

Even the powers of the mind itself are so troubled that they fill it with the fear of a great dread, and make it cry out like those who are in dire distress.

For, as I have said unto you, the mind of the Soul is the Sea of Galilee;[2] and the sacred little ship upon it is the Soul, the sacred Ark within which the Divine Presence abides."

In order that they might the better remember and understand the significance of the things of which He had spoken, He told them the allegory of the Stilling of the Storm on the Sea of Galilee.

" A great Teacher[3] who was sent from the heavenly Father-Mother entered into a little ship with His disciples, and launched into the Deep.

When in the midst of the Deep, a storm arose, and it grew more and yet more tempestuous, until it was so great as to almost overwhelm the boat ; and fear laid hold of the disciples.[4]

But the Teacher was asleep in the hinder part of the ship.[5]

Then the disciples came unto Him in great distress, and called unto Him to save them.[6]

And when the Teacher was awakened He asked them, saying, 'Why were ye so fearful ? How was it that your spiritual vision was so easily obscured ?'

NOTES.

[1] The mind of the Soul is the spiritual mind or higher reason sometimes called the understanding. It is the mind through which all spiritual knowledges are gathered on the way during the process of the Soul's evolution.

[2] The Sea of Galilee is the mind of the Soul when it has attained a high degree of Life in its experiences. It is the Lake into which flow the streams from the uplands or mountains of Galilee, the spiritual states into which the Soul consciously enters.

[3] Who is the Great Teacher but the Lord of all Being ! And where is His dwelling-place but within the little Ark of the Soul ? And is not the little Ark upon the great Deep, the Soul itself upon the Sea of Life's Mystery ? For the Christ of God is with us. Potentially in all Souls, He is consciously present within those who may be said to be fishers upon the Sea of Galilee, Souls who launch out into the deep, and who become conscious at times of the contrary winds or breaths blowing from the Astral realms, and the storm-spirits seeking to overwhelm them.

[4] Souls who have not yet reached the advanced stage in their evolution when they also will launch out into the Deep, and who therefore have never known such experiences as are recorded here, could not possibly understand the profound meanings implied. The tumultuous seas, the fearful raging of the elemental spirits when besetting a Soul, the tossing to and fro of the sacred Ark of its Being upon the storm-swept waters, fill the Soul with dread unspeakable.

[5] The Lord and His Christ in the Ark of the Soul, apparently asleep because forgotten.

[6] The awakening within them of the memory of His Presence, the coming back into the consciousness of His power. None but He could stay the power of the elementals, and bring the little Ark of the Soul safely out of the tempest.

DISCIPLESHIP

The Peace of the Presence.

' O ye whose faith is not little, wherefore, do ye doubt ? ' [1]
And the Teacher arose and spake unto the storm tossed waters, saying unto them : ' Peace ! Let there be stillness.'
And there was the Great Silence in which the winds and the waves grew calm."[2]

And when they had come as far as the region of Cæsarea Philippi, the Master asked the disciples whether they understood Him in the things which He had spoken concerning the Son of Man.
He said unto them : "Who do ye think the Son of Man is ?"[3]
Thinking that He spake concerning Himself, some of them said they had thought He was Elijah returned to Earth ; others thought that He was another of the Prophets ; some said that He was John the Baptiser , but Simon said : "Nay ; for thou art the Christ, the Son of the Living God."[4]

Coming Events

And unto Simon He turned and said :
"I spake not of myself, but of Him who is with me. And Him hast thou discerned.
No man hath revealed this unto thee, for it is not in man to know of himself who it is who is with me.
But of my Father-Mother in the Heavens hast thou learnt it.[5]
And henceforth is thine understanding illumined from Him, and thy name shall be known as Petros— one whom the Lord has illumined.
It is upon such Petra that He lays the foundations upon which His Church is built."[6]

And He charged them not to speak of Him as the Christ : nor to speak openly of all that they had heard of the Father-Mother from Him.[7]
And He said unto them : "Beware ye of the subtilty of the Scribes and Pharisees ; for they will crucify the Son of Man and cause Him to suffer many things.
They leaven the bread of life and destroy its meaning, so that it is corrupted by them.

128

NOTES.

[1] Spiritual perception and realization are the quintessence of Faith. It is to perceive heavenly things and enter into the realization of them. Faith is the substantial of the things hoped for, and also the evidence through realization of the Unseen.

[2] The Great Silence is through Soul upliftment. To the voice of the Eternal One within us, the winds (the elemental spirits) and the waves (the disturbed conditions of the waters or knowledges of the Soul) are obedient. The spirits are subject to the Christs. At the coming forth into manifestation of the Presence within, all tumult is quelled, and life's sea is changed from tempestuous conditions into one of infinite calm.

[3] In this inquiry may be witnessed the earnest longing of the Master for the full enlightenment of the disciples. It was absolutely essential that they should understand who the Son of Man was ere the more profound teachings were imparted to them.

[4] The inner group of disciples knew the Master as the Beloved One. But there were some who thought of Him as John the Baptiser, and some few as the prophet known by the name Elijah—though the term was a Divine Name.

Peter's discernment must be understood in an impersonal sense. The Master was in a high degree of Christhood, but the Christ overshadowed Him. Peter beheld that vision. Even the vision was not of man, but from the inner realms.

[5] Only from God can anyone arrive at a vision of the Lord.

[6] Had the Church founded in the name of the Master and claiming for its authority the Petros, been truly of Peter, it would have had true Illumination, and would never have written the dark, sad history which its leaders have caused to be engraven upon the pages of historical religion. It has professed to sit in the seat of Petros, and that its teachers were the Petra of the world ; yet it has lamentably failed to understand its own beautiful symbols and signs, and therein has revealed how utterly lacking in Illumination it is.

[7] The Master sought not recognition from any one who was unable to receive His message ; and He knew how important it was that none should be told who He was, and that discretion was absolutely necessary on the part of the disciples concerning the things He taught them.

DISCIPLESHIP

Be ye also subtle, even as the serpent ; but be always harmless as the dove."

cming
vents

And the Master began to unfold to them the things that had to come to pass.

He informed them of all that would be done unto Him by the chief priests and scribes, saying :

" It is part of my work to go into the city of Jerusalem and be tried by the chief priests and scribes and elders ; for they will accuse me of making discord amongst the people, of claiming to be in opposition to the ruling powers and against their chief teachers.[1]

They will acclaim me one who teaches another doctrine than that which they teach, who proclaims a kingdom which is higher than that of Cæsar, and that I make of myself that which belongs only unto the Lord of Life.

And they will think to have accomplished their end when they have me condemned.

But have ye no fear when these things come to pass, for I shall be raised up again and be with you many days. For the work which the Father-Mother hath given me to do must be accomplished before I go hence."[2]

Then Simon took Him aside and said unto Him : " The Lord in His mercy will not suffer such things to be done unto thee. Be it far from Him to permit it."[3]

But the Master said : " Thou perceivest only the things that be of men in this matter, and not those things that be of God."[4]

And Simon said unto Him, " Let not what I have said be a cause of grief to thee, for I would not be to thee as a stumbling block. Rather would I lay down my life for thee than cause thee grief."[5]

" Thou wilt indeed lay down thy life," said the Master unto him ; "and in the laying of it down thou shalt deny even that thou knowest me.[6]

Ere the day break which heralds the accomplishment of the Passover, three times shalt thou so deny me."[7]

NOTES.

[1] Here we see the disciples being prepared for the open persecution of Him by the religious orders. He knew what lay ahead of Him ; for there were those who were indiscreet, and some who were even ready to betray His confidence.

[2] The Master foresaw His condemnation and crucifixion, and counselled His intimate friends what to do. He could not die, though He could have withdrawn. Though the suffering coming to Him would be intense, yet He would be restored.

And it was even so ; for the deeper teachings were given after His crucifixion and restoration.

[3] Even a Peter at that hour could not understand the possibility of such things. He loved the Master greatly, and would not that any hurt should befall Him.

[4] But in moments of impulsiveness he took the limited human view of things, rather than that of the illumined Soul. He perceived the earthly side of it, but not that of the Divine. He yet found it difficult to be always on the plane of an illumined one.

[5] Peter loved much. He was, however, too impetuous and impulsive in his judgment, liable to make great mistakes, though in spirit ready to lay down his life.

[6] He became one who shared in the burden of the Oblation. He had to lay down his life, even his great gift of illumination, to participate in the tragic Sin-offering.

[7] This did actually happen. Peter, who loved the Master with intense devotion, was willing to drink of His Cup and to be baptized with the Baptism which befell the Master. And in the participation of the suffering, he came into a state in three of his lives lived during the Oblation, in which he denied that the Master was in a Divine state of Christhood.

Is it not likewise a remarkable fact that the Western World which has laid special claim to the understanding of the Christhood, and which has likewise claimed to be the inheritor of the power and authority implied in Petros, should also at the same time, and in a great degree, have denied the Christ, and even the Divine Estate of the Soul during the Manifestation ? For three Times or Naronic Cycles has the Western World done so. Its interpretation of the Life of the Christhood has been a denial of the Christhood Estate to the Master.

DISCIPLESHIP

The Master, when speaking unto those friends who were of the innermost group of the disciples concerning all that must happen unto Him when He left them, presented one of the terrible experiences which would come to Him in His Office as Redeemer as He bore the burden of the Ransom, by illustrating it with the story of one who had been healed of an affliction which drew upon the sufferer's life so much that no physician could heal the affliction.

" A certain woman had an affliction for thirty years.'

To try and rid herself of it she spent all that she had possessed ; but no physician could heal her of her infirmity.

But one day she heard of a healer who was passing through the country in which she dwelt, whose wonderful power to heal had become known in many cities.

It had likewise been told her that if only she could touch the hem of his garment, she would find the healing she sought.

So she eagerly set out to find the Healer.

But when she found him, to approach him was most difficult, so hidden was he by the people who thronged about him ; and only by pushing her way through the throng was she able to reach him.

And she kept saying unto herself : ' If only I may but touch the hem of his garment, I shall be healed.

And when she reached him so that the hem of his garment could be touched, the affliction was healed.'

But the healer was conscious amid the throng that he had been specially touched by some one, for there had gone forth from him the power which he possessed.

So he inquired of those immediately about him who it was who had touched him.

But they, perceiving not, neither knowing what manner of woman it was who had pressed through the throng to touch him, wondered that he should inquire.

Then did she who had been so greatly afflicted, and whose touch had not only brought healing to her-

Story
f the
assion

NOTES.

[1] This story is most difficult to interpret here, there is so much that is sad and painful associated with it. In the synoptic records it is changed into a narrative, and represented as a miraculous work of the Master in healing some mysterious ailment in the body of a woman. By this presentation its real and sorrowful meaning for the Master is lost.

It was no ordinary narrative of miraculous healing, but a story of the Passion. The Master Himself told it to the disciples in connection with some other teachings concerning the burden of the Sin-offering. The Woman was Himself during the days of the Oblation, for woman is the symbol of the Soul. It was His Soul that was afflicted. Throughout the years of every life of the Sin-offering, His Soul was poured out ; there issued from Him His very life. Sometimes He was in the form of man, sometimes in the form of woman ; but it was always the same.

Nor could any one help Him. He had to travail alone, for in that travail there were none to understand its meaning and vouchsafe comfort unto Him. No one could heal Him of His affliction. He had to bear His secret sorrow.

But in the last life of the Sin-offering He met the true physician, the Great Healer, even that One who had overshadowed Him during the days of the Manifestation, but who had to withdraw from Him when the Passover took place ; and He then knew that if only He could touch the hem of that healing garment He would be healed. For that One was indeed the Christ of Glory from whom all health flows unto the Soul.

And it may be recorded here, since the last life of the Sin-offering has been lived and its burden fully accomplished in these times in which we live, that it has been even so in the Master's sad experience. But through the awful burden of the past weighing upon His mind, He trembled and feared even to touch the state He once loved so profoundly ; and it is that utter diffidence and fearfulness which was meant in the story by the fear of the woman.

DISCIPLESHIP

Going Through Samaria

self, but impoverishment of power unto him, come to tell him what she had done and how the touching of the hem of his garment had healed her.

And she was troubled and fearful at what she had done. But he said unto her : 'Daughter, be of good cheer ! Thy faith hath saved thee.' "

And when the time had come that He should pass through the land of Samaria, there were sent forth Messengers to prepare the way for His coming.

And they entered into one of the Cities of that land that they might be able to make ready for His passing through.

But the Samaritans would not receive them because they thought they had come from Jerusalem.

But He steadfastly set His face towards Samaria, taking certain of the disciples with Him.[1]

And there were those who hated the Samaritans, and would have had the Lord destroy them because of their evil ways.

But the Master rebuked them, and said : " Ye know not the way of the Spirit, to have such desire. For the Son of Man cometh not to destroy life, but to save it."

The Healing of the Lepers

And it came to pass as the Master passed through Samaria there met Him by the way many lepers ; and these would fain be cured of their leprosy.[2]

They lifted up their voices and cried unto Him saying : " Jesus, Master, have mercy upon us !"[3]

But He counselled them to make prayer unto the Father-Mother in the full assurance that He would heal them.

And, when they had prayed, there fell upon them the power of the Divine Healing so that they were made whole.

Then one who had been sorely afflicted, when he found that he had been healed, turned unto the Lord full of thanksgiving and sacrifice.

And this one had been a Samaritan.

NOTES.

[1] The story of His going through Samaria will be found more fully told in that of the Woman of Samaria. We have put this story amongst the minor teachings, because of its relation to the two which follow. The land of Samaria was once one of pure delight, for it was the spiritual country of those who were Watchers. It was the watch-tower of the Soul. But with the fall it became changed so greatly, that it came to represent a fallen state. It became a land in which the powers of the body were degraded in their uses, an inversion of the generative functions. In the state of the Samaritan the love-principle was changed in its polarity and turned outward to seek satisfaction in promiscuous unions and spiritually unlawful ways.

These have been looked upon as outcasts, especially in the case of women. But all are accounted unclean, and are even hated by many religious people who have more of the spirit of the Pharisee than the Love of God, and who would have the Lord destroy them.

Yet even amid Samaria are many found who were once on the heights of the Watch-tower.

[2] This is another incident of spiritual history, closely bour with the preceding. The leprosy of the Soul is indeed a disease ; and it is no mere accident upon the physical plar spiritual atrophy has prevailed for ages, it reveals i⁺ the outer vehicle. The work accomplished by the the days of the Oblation, has brought condition⸗ those who have been so sadly smitten and afflic⁺ images, magnetic and evil, upon the partit⸱ magnetic circulus, have been destroyed ; magnetism of Souls, imposed terrible wrought evil through them.

[3] This prayer is not only uttered in the Litany of the Churches– They all pray to the man throt given, though He taught them ₁ there is this great truth, that by healing state, the pure life, the li⸱ That state is the saviour of the ₵

DISCIPLESHIP

"*Now it came to pass that a certain man went down through Jericho to Jerusalem to perform a service for his Lord.*[1]

The Good
Samaritan

On the way there met him a band of thieves who beat him sorely, and, having robbed him of the treasures which he carried, left him for dead.

As he lay by the wayside, behold there came a priest of the temple ; but he only looked at him and passed by on the other side.

Then there came a Scribe of the temple, who, when he saw him, also passed by on the other side.

But there likewise journeyed that way a certain Samaritan ; and he, when he beheld how the man had been beaten and robbed, was filled with compassion.

He took him and bound up his wounds, pouring the oil of healing upon them, and set him upon his own Ass and took him to the Inn to be cared for and nourished back to life."

Then the Master said unto them,

"*Truly the foxes have their lairs, the birds of the air their nests, yet the Son of Man hath not where to lay His head.*[2]

Let your hearts be set upon this thing, that the Son of Man may find in you His dwelling.

Let love be within you unto all fulness : blessed is the one who is benign unto a neighbour.

In your ways be ye as the good Samaritan : take into your Soul the burden of the afflicted, and bear it as becometh the children of the Father-Mother.

Thus love ye your Lord with all your Soul, with ll your Heart, with all your Mind, and with all your bstance. In so doing ye will also love others as rself."

NOTES.

[1] This beautiful story was related to the preceding one, and was meant to emphasise the possibilities of high life found amongst those who were accounted fallen and unclean. Of all the lepers healed, it is said that one only gave tangible expression to his deep gratitude, and that he was a Samaritan. So in this story the attitude of the leaders of official religion is revealed. They too often despise those who are not with them in their traditional beliefs, ceremonials, and judgments, looking at them cynically, but passing them by. The Jews, even unto this day, have no dealings with the Samaritans —that is, the authorized traditional religious centres repudiate those who are not of them.

The priest who should have given a true ministry of healing, and the scribe who should have known the Law of the Divine Love towards Souls, were so atrophied in their spiritual life that cynicism and disdain had taken the place of love and its ministry.

But wherein they failed the Samaritan succeeded. The Soul outside the pale of orthodoxy had more true religious feeling and spiritual love than those who were the chief representatives of tradition and ceremonial.

But the story had this further meaning, that it truly represented what was done to the Christhood. The service for the Lord which had to be accomplished in Jerusalem, was the Oblation in the work of which the Soul was robbed of its treasures of Christhood. The priest and the scribe have never befriended that Soul in any of His lives during the Sin-offering. They have passed Him by, or they have condemned Him. Nay, they have always repudiated the vision of Christhood which He gave during the days of the Manifestation, and that vision as He was able to interpret it during the lives of the Sin-offering. Whether they will accept it in its restored form as herein given, remains to be witnessed.

[2] The Foxes are the cunning thoughts and purposes, the Birds the fleeting earthly desires and actions, the Son of Man the Christhood estate. Men and women find shelter in their heart and mind for the earthly, but not for Christ.

DISCIPLESHIP

In the Days of the Re-generation

"*In the days of the Regeneration when the Son of Man shall come again, the tribulation shall be great.*[1]

Nation shall rise against Nation to make war with one another, and many shall be gathered together for battle.

Upon the land desolation shall be found, and amongst the peoples great lamentation.

Want shall be the portion of many, trial and suffering the burden of the multitude.

Fear and dread will sit upon the heart of the peoples; woe will be known in many lands.

For the rulers of the nations shall seek powers and principalities with the sword: Oppression and cruelty shall they reveal in their path; their way will be one of death.

In those days there will be great famine in many lands.

The needy ones will go down before the strong, and the poor perish in the sight of the rich.

Amid the tumults of nations the weak will be downtrodden; and even the strong will be mown like the grass.

For the cup of the peoples will be full with the bitterness of oppression; and the cry of many of them will have reached even unto the heavens.

When ye witness the arising of these things ye may know that the time is at hand.

From out the desolation flee ye unto the mountains, and let prayer be made.

Go ye not down amid the desolating powers, but dwell in the high places.

Make the Lord your refuge; let Zion be the place of your habitation.[2]

Let not him who is upon the hills return into the city of desolation; and let all who are upon the plains around the city flee unto the hills.

Give heed unto these things that no one deceive you; for in those days shall many appear in my name.

For false Christs shall arise and lead many astray by their seeming signs and wonders.[3]

NOTES.

[1] The Regeneration was to be one of the most important epochs in the world's history. It was to be preceded and accompanied by many great changes in the elements of the Planet, and also in the social constitution of nations ; and the conditions were to be of a most trying order.

In those days great events were to transpire. The arising of the Christhood as in the ancient days, was to take place. The Son of Man was to return ; and as He is Adonai, the Eternal Christ, His coming must be through the consciousness and illumination of the ancient Christhood. Only they could endure such a high estate of consciousness and make manifest such a high degree of Life. For the Regeneration very specially concerned them. It was the time of their return into their ancient heritage.

In those days also the Master Himself was to return and bring together those who had been of the inner groups of disciples during the days of the Manifestation ; for the Oblation of the Sin-offering would be accomplished. Yet none but the very few who might discover it would ever know Him as the Master ; for it would not be as such that He would return. But the Teachings which He gave during the days of the manifestation would be restored for all who could receive them. This will become more obvious in some of the later Logia.

In the Regeneration the great Tribulation was to arise. Many were to be involved—individuals, peoples and nations. The judgment of the nations was to take place.

To-day, we are in the midst of these things. Let all who have the understanding perceive.

[2] When the abomination that maketh desolate appeareth, Souls are to flee unto the mountains and hills. These are terms to express the higher spiritual experiences. The hills are the uplands of the Soul ; the mountains exalted realizations. Zion, the Christhood state, is to be the place of the Soul's habitation. Nowhere is there true refuge but in the life which this implies.

[3] Many have appeared in the Master's name : but this is not to be interpreted merely in a personal sense. All the Western religious communities, with their varying tenets and teachings, claim to be of Him. False views of Christ and the Soul's Christhood have been prevalent, leading many astray. Does the West understand Christ and the state of Christhood into which Souls are to enter as a consciousness ? Is not its Christ personal and false, personal, because related solely to the Master, false because misrepresenting its meaning ? The Eternal Christ is not the Master : it is not He who is in every Soul awaiting manifestation, but that One who was perfectly made manifest through Him. He is Adonai · by Him the Master was overshadowed and filled.

DISCIPLESHIP

And it shall be said of them in their appearing : Lo ! he is here whom we have sought ; or, lo ! he is there.

In the Days of the Re-generation

There will be those who will press into cities to find him ; and others who will wander about in the desert places in the hope of meeting him there.

But in neither will He, the Lord, be found ; but only through the Kingdom of God which is within.[1]

Therefore, when ye behold all these things coming upon the world, have no fear, for they must needs be.

Let not your Faith grow dim : keep the Light of your Lamps burning brightly.

Amid the tribulation of those days the Sun shall be darkened, because the light within many shall fail.[2]

The Moon also shall not be able to give her light ; for when the Sun within fails, the mind can have no light.[3]

Even the Stars of the Heavens shall fall when the powers of the world are shaken ; for many will be brought low.[4]

Then shall appear the sign of the Son of Man in the Heavens, and His coming shall be made manifest.

And the nations which have warred against each other shall mourn over their estate ; and the people shall lament that they understood not nor knew Him in His coming.

For upon the clouds of the Heavens shall He come to restore truth and equity, and that righteousness may be established amongst all nations.

And the Angels of Heaven shall gather the elect ones out of the desolation, and send them forth unto the harvest that they may bring together those who acknowledge Him.[5]

And in those days the Angel of the Lord shall proclaim Him with the voice of a trumpet, and show forth unto all nations what is the will of the Father-Mother in the Heavens.

Many who now sleep shall then awake, and come forth into the Life Eternal.[6]

Two shall be grinding corn at the same mill ; one shall be called and the other left.[7]

There shall be two occupying the same room ; one shall be chosen and the other left.[8]

NOTES.

[1] We are in an age of great and grave dangers. The false vision pursues the true that many may be ensnared. There are many false teachings abroad concerning Christ and His coming. In different centres He is expected to appear and make Himself manifest. And many are being deceived. For though the return of the Master is now, He would never so announce Himself ; for the Christ is no man, but the Lord. And though Christ is coming, and to not a few has already come, it is not as a man, but through the Kingdom of God which is within. There is Christ first manifested.

[2] The Lord is the Sun, and the Light given by Him is veiled to most Souls. The Sun is eclipsed, in some partially and in most fully ; and spiritual darkness has prevailed. In not a few within whom the Light should have shone, darkness reigns. They have succumbed to the influences at work, and have fallen amid the great tribulation.

[3] What the moon is now in the solar system, the mind is in the system of the Soul. It receives and reflects the light.

[4] The Stars of the Heavens are Souls and the attributes of Souls who have known Christhood. For as the Sun is the Lord within the Sanctuary of the Soul, and the Moon the Soul's Intuition, so the Stars are its attributes : and when it is in Christhood, it is as the Star given to those who overcome.

[5] The Elect Souls are those who once formed the Ancient Christhood. These are now being gathered out of the world of desolation, and prepared for ministry.

[6] This refers to Souls of the Ancient Order of Christhood who were spiritually asleep, not having yet awakened to the consciousness of their inherent powers. Many of these did not know the Master as such during the days of the Manifestation, though they all knew Him in the days of the Ancient Christhood.

[7] Two grinding the same corn for bread, the same teachings for Soul nourishment, one shall awaken and arise into the consciousness of the Life Eternal, leaving the other still believing without perceiving and realizing.

[8] Two occupying the same room represents two in the like spiritual state, when the Voice of the Angel speaks, one rises into newness of being, whilst the other remains content with things as they are.

DISCIPLESHIP

Of two toiling in the same field, one shall hear and follow the voice of the Angel ; but the other shall remain behind.[1]

In the Days of the Re-generation

Of the coming of those days no man knoweth unless it has been revealed unto him.

Learn ye to read aright the signs of those days, and to understand in what manner the coming of the Son of Man shall be.

The Fig-tree putteth forth her green leaves, and men say that the Summer is nigh ; when those powers (of which the fig-tree is a parable) are made manifest, know that the time is at hand, even at the doors of the nations.[2]

For like lightning breaking in the Eastern Sky shall be the coming.

The Light of the Glory of the Lord shall break within you, and within all those who be of the true Fold ;[3] *and unto you shall appear the sign of the coming again of the Son of Man."*

"And in those days there shall fall upon the earth the woes spoken of by the prophets.

Woe unto those teachers and leaders who will not enter into the Kingdom of the Heavens themselves, and who thereby shut the door of the Kingdom unto those who trust them, and who might enter in.

Woe unto all who devour the substance of the impoverished under the pretence that it is necessary to make long prayers for them in order that they perish not.

The Woes of the Prophets

Woe unto those teachers and leaders who stretch out the arm of power to make upon sea and land, proselytes, accounting as nought the means they make use of to accomplish their end.

Woe unto all who teach that the Temple of God is not of the Spirit that is within, but is to be found in the earthly - houses of man's fashioning ; who are ready always to swear by the temple of their own creation, but deny the Temple of the Spirit of the Lord who is within ; who accord much value to their earthly altars, and gifts laid thereon as sacrifices, yet will not accord value to the altar of the Lord, nor lay their gifts upon that altar for His service.

142

NOTES.

[1] Two toiling in the same service of life, one hears the Voice of the Angel of the Lord and responds, leaving all to follow whither He directs ; the other hears not that voice, neither understands what has happened to the other.

The fulfilment of these sayings in these days must be obvious to whomsoever the Light has come, and who is able to perceive the deep things of God.

[2] The Fig-tree is the symbol of the Divine Wisdom. The Fig-tree of the Church was blighted through the curse of materialism : Wisdom died within it. Nathaniel sat under the Fig-tree as a true son of Israel—one of the Christhood Order. Once more the Fig tree has begun to blossom and show fruit in the recovery by Souls of the Ancient Wisdom, and the blessed recovery of the true Vision of the Christhood and the Teachings which were given by the Master. The meaning of Jesushood, of Christhood crowning it, and of the Lord-Presence crowning the Christhood, is being restored.

The time is at hand ; even now it knocketh at the door of the Nations.

[3] A blessed promise to the disciples, and for all Israel. And it is being fulfilled to-day. This we can verify. To all these the Son of Man is coming. Many have seen His sign in the Heavens of their own being. The appearing is not anything astrological, as many suppose, though we have entered the Sign Aquarius—the Man bearing the Water-pot. It is purely Soullic. For the sign of the Son of Man for the Soul is the sign of the Cross.

[4] The Woes of the Prophets were the warnings uttered by those who were sent. For the Prophets were not of Jewry, but of the true Israel. To the Ancient Christhood, Order they belong ; they had as their mission the proclamation of the Word of the Lord, and the teaching of the people. The Schools of the Prophets were not founded by them to train and create Prophets : that could not be done. The Schools were simply centres of prophetic teaching, wherein the Mysteries were interpreted. But the Prophet was the Servant of the Lord. He was begotten for his office.

DISCIPLESHIP

The Woes of the Prophets

Woe unto those who attribute undue value to the tithing of their material gifts, whose mint, anise and cummin are of perishable things rather than those of the Spirit whose service is unto the Life Eternal; whose tithing is outward and after the ways of all who are not within the Kingdom, and who yet fail in those weightier matters of the Spirit which are made manifest in righteousness, mercy, and enlightenment.

Woe unto those who only make clean the outside of the cup of life, whilst within them the spirit of extortion prevails; who make a garish show of purity and good, whilst their desires are impure and their purposes evil.

Woe unto all who affirm that when the inside of a man is clean it matters not what is the manner of his ways in daily living; who testify that if a man's intention be pure he need not deny himself in the body; who proclaim that the right nourishment of the body is not a part of the way unto the realization of the Kingdom of God.

Unto all these shall come the sorrow of great loss in the days of the Regeneration.

Woe unto those Nations which sell their Soul for power and deem dominion by the sword as something to be sought after, grasped and proudly wielded: by the powers which they employ to accomplish their unrighteousness, shall they fall; in the way of their going shall they perish.

Woe unto the peoples which love not truth and equity, whose leaders and chieftains are those who do unrighteousness, whose great ones oppress the weak and burden the poor, speaking falsehoods for truth and words of deceit for sincerity: unto such shall the judgment of the Great Day come in the which it shall be revealed what they are.

Woe unto the lands wherein God is not known, but in His stead graven images are set up to be worshipped, and served, and accounted the greatest of all things, where the Lord of Glory is continually crucified and put to open shame: upon these shall fall the sorrow of great burden in the days of the purification of the Nations."

144

NOTES.

The Woes uttered by him were warning words against the practice of wrong. He proclaimed the law of righteousness, even the Righteousness of God, and affirmed the consequences to individuals, communities and nations of violating that law.

When the Master spake these Sayings to the disciples, He did not quote the language of the Prophets ; He Himself foresaw the fulfilment of what they had declared. He knew the issues of the terrible betrayal that was coming ; He beheld the arising and the outworking of the awful wickedness. He saw in His vision what would overtake His own Teachings, the false kingdom that would arise in His name, founded ostensibly upon His Teachings, but without an understanding of them. He witnessed a semi-Jewish, semi-Pagan priesthood arising, having the garments and phylacteries and embellishments of a Christhood nomenclature, but which denied the Christhood and kept Souls in spiritual darkness. He beheld it to be a repetition of the Jewish and Pagan priesthood, in the burdens which it imposed upon the children of the Father-Mother. He foresaw its utter failure amongst the nations and the awful spiritual blindness which followed, and this notwithstanding the fact that very real endeavours by Souls sent unto them had been made to bring the Churches into the Light of God. It was shown to Him the nature of the civilization that would result from the false views of life, until He beheld nation in war with nation, and people with people, and all professing to have been taught from the one Divine Source, all proclaiming their allegiance to Himself and the Kingdom of love and wisdom, He had come to establish by means of the Teachings.

To-day we are in the midst of all He foresaw. The Woes are falling upon the earth. The hour of judgment is upon all the Nations. The day of the Purification and Redemption has come. And in that judgment is involved the Kingdom of Churches which has failed so ignominiously and made possible such disasters.

PART IV

THE CHRISTHOOD

Wherein will be found some of the Sayings spoken by the Master to the Inner Group of Disciples concerning the History of the Soul and the Planet, also of the Ancient Christhood Order, together with most profound Teachings on the nature of the burden of the Oblation and Sin-offering; all which were taken away by Paul when he visited the Brethren in Jerusalem, and made use of by him but without the understanding of them, and which thus came to be put into false settings in his Letters to the Churches, and have wrong interpretations given to them; for though they were preserved, they were changed and veiled.

THE CHRISTHOOD

Ye behold of what nature the Life is unto which ye are called.[1]

Those who are the Called or Elect ones

The many who are wise after the ways of the flesh, and the mighty of this world, and those who account themselves noble, are not called to have any part in it.[2]

The things which God hath appointed to be accomplished, are foolishness unto those who are children of this world; for these would account it as shame to pursue them.[3]

The lowly life is one that is despised by those who are the wise, and the mighty, and the lovers of this world; for they account it as naught. In such a way there is no gain for them; it bringeth not the glory which they seek.

Yet God willeth that there shall be no such glorying after the manner of men in those who are the called of Him; but that all who follow the way of Life should glory in the Lord of Life only, who, through the estates of Jesus Christ, becometh our Redemption, Sanctification, Righteousness and Wisdom.

It is the Wisdom of God which we speak unto you that ye may be perfected in Him.

The Wisdom of God hath been hidden for ages, and is as mystery unto all who are unable to understand it. But unto us hath God revealed His wisdom through His Holy Spirit who dwelleth in us; for the Spirit revealeth all things, even the deep things of God. And none knoweth these things save through the Spirit of God who alone can interpret them.

Ye have received the gift of the Holy Spirit that ye may come into the fulness of the knowledge which is in Jesus Christ.

Epistles of Christ

Be ye as epistles for Him, those in whom are the writings of the Law of His Commandments concerning the way of Christ.[4] *For within you are those laws which appertain unto Christ, written by the Spirit, and engraven even upon your body of flesh: not after the manner of the law of ceremonial followed by*

NOTES.

These precious Logia were spoken to the inner group of disciples, and were parts of the Teachings on the nature of Christhood. They were spoken by the Master at different times as occasion presented itself, and they formed part of the Logia of St. John. Some are quite complete in themselves, but others formed a part of Sayings to be given later. They were profound teachings which Paul did not understand when they were shown to him; but nevertheless he took them away with him on the occasion of his visit to the Brethren, and recasting some of them, applied them to himself often, or to Jewish history. Writers have been long conscious of two Pauls in the Epistolary Letters, one the Jew and one the Mystic. And they have also found that some of the mystical parts were beyond understanding, and have wondered what Paul meant. But it is understandable when it is known that the Mystic Teachings were parts of those given by the Master, which Paul had separated from their relation to other teachings, and made use of to build up his own theses of Redemption and the Christhood.

[1] It was the Life of Jesus Christ : the Jesus Life was one of purity in all things—meats, drinks, desires, feelings, ambitions and love ; the Christ-Life was one of glorious illumination from the Divine realms.

[2] Such Life was never sought after by any who loved the things of this world. It did not appeal to the material man whose desires and ambitions found their fulfilment in what this world could provide. It has always been so.

[3] The things of the Soul are foolishness unto those who are accounted the wise of this world. The Wisdom of God does not follow the way of the children of this world, and its way is foolishness unto them. It is unknown to them, like a strange language ; its meanings cannot be apprehended. When men and women despise the things of the Soul, they little understand the precious pearls they are trampling under foot.

[4] To be an epistle is to be an open letter which all may read. An epistle of God is a life in which God is manifested. The disciples were to be such open letters in the sense that Christ was to be revealed in all the way of their going. Within the Soul, the Laws of the Divine are written ; in its very constitution are they engraven. In Christhood these Laws are known and understood, and they are made manifest, even the body of flesh bearing testimony to their nature and power.

K—I

THE CHRISTHOOD

Epistles of Christ

the elders, but after the law of Christ who is within you ; for the law of ceremonial is as the letter which killeth, but the law of Christ giveth Life.

And though for the manifestation of these things as His ministers ye are not sufficient in yourselves, yet in Him ye may have all sufficiency.[1]

In God, the ever Blessed One, is your strength, who, having called you to be partakers of the ministry of Christ, will shed His glory within you and make you to be His manifestors, even as it is said the glory of the Lord shone upon the face of Moses when He made manifest unto Israel.[2]

Through Christ in you will He once more make visible His glory, to be no more veiled by those things which caused it to pass away in the former times, but to increase in power in its ministration through you, growing brighter and stronger until the day of perfect revelation, and rising from glory to glory.[3]

But, if the Truth be veiled so that it cannot be dis cerned, it is veiled from those who have perished, those in whom the gods of this world have taken up their abode, blinding the eyes of the Soul to the Truth lest it should be believed, and the light of the glory of God should shine into the Soul.

When the Lord commandeth the Darkness so that it giveth place unto the Light, then the Soul may behold the glory of God in the face of Jesus Christ.

For in these estates is He imaged, that the Soul may come unto the knowledge of Him.

The Story of Abraham

Ye have heard the story of Abraham and of Isaac his son, and of Sarah the mother of Isaac : how it came to pass that, in the fulness of days, there was born unto them a son who was known as the child of promise, in whom all the nations of the earth were to be blest.

So great was the event in its purpose, that, in the

NOTES.

Herein is set forth the real nature and constitution of the Soul, its essentially spiritual origin, and the reason why it is able to respond to the demands made upon it by the Laws of Being, when these are set before it by the Spirit. And the meaning of Jesus Christ herein is made obvious ; for in the Jesus state, even the body of flesh is pure, so that it becometh a true servant to the Soul for the manifestation of Christ. Its purification is not after any ceremonial laws, but through following the path marked out in the Laws of God. The laws of mere ceremonial have invariably eventuated in killing the Spirit of Truth, changing the living Word into a dead letter.

[1] Who could live the Christ-Life alone ? In that state a Soul must needs be much alone, separated from the world ; but the beautiful realization and manifestation is of God. Even in the lower degrees of Christhood the Soul becomes conscious, in a measure, of the Presence. In the higher degrees that consciousness is intensified : the Soul knows it is never alone ; for with it is the Angel of His Presence.

[2] What was expected of the inner group disciples is here clearly indicated. They were called to rise up into the consciousness of their ancient estate of Christhood. They were to be vehicles of the Divine Manifestation. The glory of God was to shine through them.

The reference to Moses is other in its meaning than it seems. It was not Jewish in any sense. Moses was a Divine Name given to a particular manifestation of the Lord of Being ; and the inner group disciples had beheld that blessed appearing during the days of their sojourn in Upper Egypt. The manifestation was unto Israel ; but the true Israelites were the members of the Christhood Order.

[3] A reference in which the Transcendent Life is fully realized. To rise from glory to glory is to have a consciousness, ever increasing in intensity and expanding in vision, of the Divine Realities.

In this Saying the infinite possibilities of the Soul are revealed. He Himself had risen from sphere to sphere, from kingdom to kingdom, and knew the glory of them. It was a path He had trodden, and it was open to His vision.

151

THE CHRISTHOOD

story, it is recorded that Sarah laughed for very joy, yet wondered how it could be accomplished.

The Story of Abraham

But that was before the days of their going away into Egypt.[1]

When Isaac was born unto them they laid him upon the altar of the Lord in sacrifice for His service whensoever He should require it of him. And Isaac was made consecrate from that time, as he in whom all Souls should find blessing.

And in the story it is recorded that Abraham had an handmaiden named Hagar whom he took into union with himself, and that she bore unto him a son whom they named Ishmael, and how Sarah demanded that Hagar and her son should be put away, until Hagar and Ishmael were sent adrift into the wilderness to suffer many things.

All these things were allegories containing great histories of the Soul. For Abraham and Sarah[2] represented the Divine Realm on the Planet in the days of perfect purity and light, when as yet it was unfallen, and its children had not gone down into the land of darkness.

They were embodiments of the two Divine Principles within the Planet whose operation generated the high and blessed life upon all its planes, the masculine and feminine modes, the centrifugal and centripetal powers in perfect action.

Of them was Isaac, the child of promise, born; for Isaac was the Soul, and it is through the attainment and realization of the Soul, that all peoples are to be made blessed.

And all who are of the seed of Abraham are to be partakers of the inheritance passed on through Isaac;[3] for in that state they are free, knowing not the bondage of those who have been in Egypt, nor the darkness of that bondage.

152

NOTES.

[1] This story of Abraham, found in the Epistles broken and distorted, was told to the inner group by the Master in order to explain to them the going down into bondage of the Planet and all her children, and the sad history which ensued.

Abraham was a Divine Name. It was assigned to this Planet in the ancient Mysteries as these were known to the Hebrews, to designate the Planet in its estate before the Divine World. The term was most sacred, for it signified *that which was of Brahm.* So glorious was the Planet in the ancient unfallen days, that its glory reflected the glory of Brahm. It also represented the Divine Fatherhood, as expressed in the Divine Spirit inherent in the system, the supreme power through which all things were generated within the system.

Abraham was named the Friend of God, for he was a vehicle for the manifestation of the Life of the Infinite and Eternal and ever-Blessed One. He is said to have met the three Kings of the East, Kings or Rulers sent from God ; for the three Divine Elements were in him which these royal Magians represented. He is also said to have met the High Priest of God, Melchizedek, to whom he gave a tenth of all that he possessed for the service of God, wherein lies a mystery which at present we may not here explain.

The expression " Our Father Abraham " may be discovered to possess new meanings, to contain a history profound and glorious, and also a history whose depths of sorrow and anguish no one could fathom.

[2] Now just as Abraham was not any man, but the Divine creative estate, and Spirit inherent in the system, so Sarah was not any woman, but represented the Divine Substances of the system out of which Souls might be fashioned. For Sarah was also representative of Divine things, being a Divine term for the Woman element in the system. She represented the feminine power as Abraham did the masculine. She stood for the Motherhood of God. The two Divine Names therefore represent the Divine Father-Motherhood in the creative life of the Planet. She is the Substance ; he is the Spirit that quickeneth. She is the Mother who beareth and bringeth forth into manifestation ; he is the Father, the begetter of the life to be born.

[3] Of them was the Soul born. For Isaac means the Soul. He is said to have been the child of promise, for the Soul is the end of created things, it being the highest expression of created life when it attains maturity and the Divine Pleroma is found by it.

THE CHRISTHOOD

he Story
f Abraham

Now, the going away of Abraham and Sarah into Egypt, the union with Hagar and the birth of Ishmael, with the consequent conflict between Sarah and the bondwoman and her son, was also an allegory of the going away of this Planet from its divine estate, and its descent into conditions which became unto it a state of bondage.[1]

For Hagar is the embodiment of the state into which the substances of the once glorious Earth went down, to find themselves no longer free, but as a bondwoman subject to the powers that were over her, who could not conceive and bring to the birth a son who was free, but only one who was in bondage; not a child of promise, but one born out of a wrong union.[2]

For Hagar represents not only the conditions of the once beautiful substances of the Planet, but the life which has been begotten of the bondage of all the spiritual elements to the powers who sold her into that state.

And she cannot be other than in a state of conflict until the day of her Redemption come when she will no longer remain bound, and cast out of the higher spiritual relationship and service, but be a free woman, one who can bring into birth children who will not be under the law of bondage, but free in grace, even the grace that cometh in the estates of Jesus Christ.

And in those days Ishmael shall go out no more into the wilderness to languish through lack;[3] for the state of life which he represented in the story will cease, and there will not be any more bond-children.

For the Jerusalem that now is in bondage with all her children, shall once more be free; for the day of her Deliverance and Redemption draweth near in which she will be restored and made beautiful even as in those days when she was in high estate. For she shall again be made like unto the Jerusalem which is above, through the goodness and love of the Father-Mother of us all.

154

NOTES.

Isaac is said to have been demanded of Abraham by the Most High, who commanded him to take Isaac and offer him upon Mount Moriah in sacrifice. For the Soul must be laid upon no man's altar for service, but only upon that of the Divine, which is on Mount Moriah where also His Temple is built. For Isaac as a child of promise is born for the service of God, for through the Soul does God come near to man, and in the approach of Him through the Soul, all life upon the earth is made blessed. In Isaac all the Nations of the Earth were to be blessed, for only through the culture of the spiritual and divine qualities in man could true communal and national life be realized.

[1] When it is said that Abraham with Sarah and Isaac went down into Egypt, what is to be understood first of all is that descent of the Planetary powers for purposes of generation, in which outward forms were fashioned ; for these came after the creation and fashioning of the Soul. For in the Mysteries of the Hebrews, Egypt meant the body, and was thought of as a state of limitation ; and this apart from any association with the Fall. For Egypt, the body, had its pure days prior to the descent which involved the entire system in spiritual darkness.

[2] But the descent into Egypt has also this meaning : it indicated what took place during one of the later periods of Planetary generation, when the Planet moved away from the plane of the Divine Kingdom with most disastrous eventuations. For by-and-bye there issued from it the sad conditions which are represented by Hagar, the bondage of the woman element, the changing of the beautiful substances out of which Life had been perfectly generated. In such a state there could be no child born who was free from bondage to the laws of the fallen elemental world. Hence the birth of Ishmael, one accounted a bond-servant. Hagar and Ishmael therefore represent the fallen state of the Soul, and the life manifested under such conditions, in contrast to Isaac and Sarah. For Isaac was free. Ishmael was not according to promise.

[3] But in the Redemption Ishmael is to be no more as one who is a bond-servant and the son of a bond-woman. He is to be lifted into a state of freedom, even the liberty of the children of God found in the estates of Jesus Christ. For only through these estates or conditions of Soul realization is true liberty to be found. There is no deliverance for the Soul from the thraldom of the elemental world in its fallen state, but by means of the Jesus Life, because that is the way of purity and true love. Jesus is Ishmael's Saviour ; he bringeth to the Soul the salvation which is of God. And when that life is attained, Christ shall give him light so that no more will he be as a child of the darkness.

155

THE CHRISTHOOD

The Story of Abraham

Now, from this allegory learn ye how it came to pass that this world and all her children fell under the law of the powers who fashioned Jerusalem as she now is, and imposed upon all who went down with her, their desires and ordinances.[1]

And from this learn ye to understand all who are in bondage and subject to these desires and ordinances, and how they are to be delivered out of their bondage and brought under the law of the Spirit.

But ye yourselves are not of those who be now in bondage and subjected to the law of this world's ordinances, because ye are again free in Christ. For though ye went away with those who went down into bondage, and suffered much by reason of it through the powers and principalities which have had dominion for many ages; yet have ye always been children of freedom, because ye were by nature Sons of God. And as such the ordinances of this world have had no dominion over you.[2]

Ye are from above, children of Zion, the Holy City of the Lord. Therefore, rejoice in the liberty wherewith ye have been set free for the service of Christ, that, rising up into that liberty in all fulness, ye may be once more the messengers for Jesus Christ, to bring into these holy estates all who now be in bondage.

Unto this end are ye sent forth to be sharers in the burden of the Redemption through the deliverance from bondage of this world, and the gathering together again of the Israel of God, of whom ye yourselves were members, and were in high estate.[3]

Walk ye by the law of the Spirit, and thus fulfil the law of Christ. For ye are of Him, having been born into the consciousness of Him, and are now to be partakers of the sufferings coming to Him, and of the glory that shall follow.[4]

NOTES.

[1] In this connection Jerusalem is also named as being in bondage with all her children, but is promised deliverance and redemption with a glory equalling her former unfallen state. By Jerusalem is meant the Planet as a spiritual household, whose terraces or planes were once remarkable for their glory, and whose dwelling-places were spiritual palaces for all her children. In the day of her perfect redemption her palaces and planes will be restored with all her children within them, and she will be refashioned to bear the likeness once more of the Jerusalem which is above.

[2] A passing glimpse of who the disciples were, what they must have suffered, and the conditions they had to endure. Though they went down with Jerusalem because they loved her children, and had to endure unspeakable things, yet in nature had they always remained true to the inner Light which was theirs as those who had become Sons of God. They were the children of Zion, the members of the Christhood. Zion denoted a high degree of that blessed estate ; the city of Zion—the Holy City—was the community of Christs.

[3] Another hint about the future burden and work in which they were to have so large a share. The burden was the Oblation ; the work was the calling of all the members of that most ancient Household to arise and shine forth the Light of the Glory of the Lord.

[4] In the suffering borne during the days of the Sin-offering they would have a portion, and in the glory to follow the accomplishment of that great work, they would be large partakers.

Most of them are now upon the outer planes ministering ; for they also have awakened with the Master, and are preparing themselves to be the vehicles of blessed Divine ministry.

THE CHRISTHOOD

There are many great events which will be recalled to your remembrance, events which of old time ye knew ; for the time of your dwelling upon the planes of this world hath covered ages upon ages.[1]

Remembering the Divine Graciousness

You will have brought to your remembrance how the Lord delivered His people Israel out of the land of Egypt, and brought about the overthrow of those who had taken them down into bondage ;[2] and how the Angels who left their own Principality that they might minister unto this world, went down from their true estate into the darkness where were the habitations of wickedness, that they might find the children of this world who had gone down and been lost amid these habitations, and how the Lord of Life delivered the Angels through His great judgments ;[3] and also what He accomplished for this world when its children had gone down into the states of Sodom and Gomorrah through the fires which consumed their flesh and filled them with evil imaginings, and had wrought such abominations that the Bow of the Lord which He had set within the heavens of the Planet, fell upon them.[4]

For in those days these children had fallen so low that they desired to defile themselves, having vain dreamings of the lusts of the flesh.

They railed against God and contemned the Most High. They railed against those of the Angels who were sent unto them, and would have none of the ways of the Kingdom of the Heavens lest its dominion should extend to them, and they should behold its glory.

Yet the Lord had compassion towards them, and wrought great things on their behalf ; for He brought them up again out of their low estate wherein they had become as the beasts of the field, even as those that wallow in the mire, and some as creeping things.[5]

They had changed His image within them to become as low as these. But He brought them up once more

158

NOTES.

[1] The members of the Christhood Order who were sent to minister to the children of this world, belonged to another system. They had passed through the various phases of Soul evolution from the inception period up through the different degrees of realization until they reached the Angelic World. Some attained even to Divine estates, and all were Celestials.

The Soul can only recover that which has been known unto it ; and the recovery can come only when the necessary conditions within it are found. The recovery is part of the Regeneration— the days which are now upon us.

[2] The Passage of the Red Sea is here referred to, and the deliverance of the Christhood from the fearful states into which they went down after this world's children. For the Red Sea was the Astral World. With this is connected the mystic story of the standing still of the Sun. The explanation we have given in the " Herald of the Cross,"[3] and is too long to repeat here.

[3] The habitations of wickedness were the fearful creatures which had been generated in the first and second Saurian periods. The history of this Planet in those days cannot even be imagined. Even science fails to find an explanation for the appearing of such creatures.

[4] The cities of Sodom and Gomorrah were states of life into which the children upon the Human Kingdom went down. They had been rescued and brought out of the Saurians, and led up again to the Human Kingdom ; but so terrible were the influences of evil left within them, that they gradually sank into these low states. It covered many long ages during which the whole Planet was convulsed through the magnetic effects of their conduct, with the result that the wonderful magnetic plane spoken of as the Bow in the Heavens, fell upon the Planet. That is the meaning of the Fire being rained from the Heavens upon the Earth. For the Bow was composed of most glorious elements.

[5] It may seem inconceivable to many that such could befall the race ; and to be quite out of harmony with the doctrine of evolution as taught by science, that there should have been such retrograde action. But the like thing may be found even in these days, though in degree it is less. For individuals have fallen so low as to be on a level with the beasts. And in the ages we refer to the conditions became so rampant that the vast majority of the children of this world went down to such levels.

THE CHRISTHOOD

to be human children through the loving ministry of the Angels who had, for their sakes, beforetime gone down from their first estate.[1]

Remembering the Divine Graciousness

For these were they who in the days of the Patriarchs ministered unto the children of this world, and warned them of the events which came to pass in the days of Noah, Sodom and Gomorrah, and in the days of Moses and the Prophets.[2]

Of that ministering host were ye members. For ye have beforetime passed under the Cloud of the Presence of the Lord of Life, and known the blessedness of the overshadowing One.[3]

Yea, ye have all passed through the Sea before the Throne of the Ever Blessed One; for ye have all been baptised into the state of Moses in the Sea and amid the Cloud.[4] Of the spiritual meat of that Divine Estate have ye partaken; and ye have together drunk of the spiritual waters which at that time flowed for your use.

From the Rock of the Ages, even mount Horeb the mountain of the Lord, did the living waters flow unto you; for ye knew the Lord and His Christ, and were partakers of His nature, being ministers unto the children of this world for Him.[5]

Of that same bread do ye now partake; for the things we have said unto you are of the truth which is the Body of the Lord and His Christ.[6]

And the cup of which ye have been drinking is of the like nature; for it contains the wine of God, the Life-stream of the body of the Lord. For in such wise do we participate in the Divine Love and Wisdom, and in the Fellowship of the flesh and blood of the Son of God.

NOTES.

[1] The goodness of the Divine Love to this world is beyond anything that can ever be told, so great and continuous has it been. But for the unfailing ministry of the Divine Kingdom this distraught world could never have been recovered. Indeed, at one epoch in its history, it came near to being utterly lost as a human system. For long ages the Heavens were as if shut up, it being impossible to give any direct ministry. Yet the Divine Love found a way to at last help the children of the Planet, and bring them up out of their low estate.

[2] The Patriarchs were the Ancients or Christs, those who walked with God, and proclaimed His righteousness to mankind.

[3] The disciples of the inner group had this astounding fact impressed upon them from time to time ; for they had to be helped to come at the consciousness of who they were.

To pass under the Cloud of the Presence of the Lord was to come into the consciousness of the overshadowing Presence. They came under the Cloud, out from which the Voice of the Lord of Being spake to them.

[4] To be baptized into the state of Moses was to have had the Divine Baptism of the Spirit. For Moses was a Divine Name, signifying a certain order of manifestation.

[5] Horeb was the Mount of the Lord where the Divine vision of the Soul was attained. The Rock in Horeb, which yielded water for the thirsty when touched by the Rod of Moses, was none other than the Eternal Life found in Christhood. Out of Christ within the Soul flow the living waters.

[6] It was for these Souls that the streams of the Lord of Life flowed, streams of new energy, magnetic currents from the Divine realms to purify, refresh and strengthen them. It was for them the Manna fell, the Angels' Food, their own fit nourishment, the Ambrosia of the Gods, to be their daily portion amid their sojourning in the wilderness. For the Manna was the Wisdom of God, as the streams from Horeb were His Love.

THE CHRISTHOOD

The Mystery of God

For unto this end do we give praise unto the Most High, and make request that ye all may be so filled with the Spirit as to have the knowledge of His will, what it is toward you, that your knowledge may be indeed the heavenly wisdom which He giveth, even the understanding of the Mystery of God.[1]

May ye walk together worthily of the Presence of the Lord who is in you, in every good work bearing your fruit, even the fruit of the Spirit, and ever increasing in the knowledge of the hidden wisdom of God.

And may ye grow in power to interpret His glory, to be patient and long-suffering towards those who cannot behold it, ever giving thanks unto the Father-Mother who hath called you to be partakers of His nature and sharers of the light of His Radiance, even of the inheritance of His Christs.[2]

For it was He who delivered you out of darkness and brought you into the marvellous light of His Son and the Kingdom of His Love who is the express image of the Eternal One, ever Blessed, the first-begotten of all things, through whom ye have had your redemption and the forgiveness of sin.

As ye have received of Him, so walk ye in the ways of Jesus Christ, rooted in Him, and built up in these holy estates.

Unto you is now made known the Mystery[3] *which hath been hidden from generations through the ages, even the Mystery of the Divine purpose to accomplish the deliverance of this world by a Redeemer, to blot out the hand-writings engraven upon the middle kingdom, to overthrow the false principalities and powers which are established there, and to break down the middle wall whose ordinances have been against the Soul; and to accomplish this through the burden of the Cross.*

Beware lest any one despoil you of your inheritance in Him, through a delusive philosophy, or the traditions of men, or the elemental world, which are not according to the Christhood.[4]

Let no one rob you of your inward life and realization of His Presence, by means of the exercise of the

162

NOTES.

[1] To understand the Mystery of God is indeed to reach a high state of consciousness. That Mystery may only be revealed unto those who find their way to the Divine Kingdom. But the correspondence to that realm is within the Soul, and those who find that realm within them come into the consciousness of the Divine Presence. With the deepening and intensification of that realization, the great Mystery unfolds itself, and the Soul comes to know and understand.

The inner group disciples had been there once ; and unto it they were returning.

[2] This is a significant reference to the past and present status of the disciples, for none may or can behold the Radiance of the Eternal One unless they have at some time reached the state of Christhood.

[3] This is the Mystery of the Oblation and Sin-offering. The world was to be delivered by the Divine Love through one whose mission would be that of the Redeemer. From what was the world to be delivered ? Hand-writings upon the Middle Kingdom, with the principalities and powers whose seats of dominion were there. Herein is revealed what was done during the long ages of darkness of which we have already written. The Hand-writings upon the Middle Kingdom were fluidic magnetic images which had been fashioned in the terrible days when the Human Race descended to the level of the beasts of the field, and even worse. These images were evil in nature, because they were the outcome of evil ; and they continued to exercise an evil influence upon the children of men, and even to dominate them to such extent that not infrequently afflicted Humanity wrought over again the very things out of which these fearful graven forms had sprung. And so numerous were these elemental magnetic forms, that they formed a wall in the Middle Kingdom or Astral realm which had to be broken down ere the ministry of the Heavens could be made effectual, and the Redemption of the world be accomplished.

The Sin-offering work was the absorption and transmutation of these elemental evil forms ; and the Oblation was the means by which it was done. In the Oblation the Master laid aside His glorious Christhood, and gave Himself as the instrument of the Divine Love for this great and hazardous and sorrowful work. It was in this way that He came to be an Offering for Sin.

[4] The warning is much required to-day. There are ꓴ mental accomplishments, traditional writings and teachings, and delusive philosophies which are not according to the Christhood : these hinder many 'rom entering the Kingdom.

163

THE CHRISTHOOD

will, or by any false messages purporting to come from the angels.[1]

The Mystery of God

Try the spirits whether they be of God, lest any of them falsify the things that be of Christ, and so deceive you.[2]

And let Christ be made manifest unto you ; for His coming is full of glory, making all things blessed, and, filling all with the great peace.

Beloved and elect ones are ye. Therefore be ye holy, worshipping with the Angels in all humility, Him who is Head over all, even that One who is ever Blessed.

Concerning the gifts of the Spirit it is well that ye understand ; for all gifts are not of the same order, though the uses of all are for the great ministry.

And these gifts are bestowed according to the order of life in the recipient, and the degree unto which the life has attained.

There are diversities of nature, and order, and state ; and according to these so are the gifts bestowed.[3]

The Gifts of the Spirit

And in the administration of the Divine Love and Wisdom there are many stages ; so the uses of the gifts are according to these, in order that all Souls may be ministered unto.

For He who is over all, even the Father-Mother, blessed for evermore, ministers of His Love and Wisdom unto all Souls through those upon whom the Spirit has descended, each endowed one after his and her own order and degree, being His channel.

For the Spirit is manifold in manifestation.

Within one is the Divine Wisdom revealed ; through another is the light of its glory broken as knowledge.

In some the manifestation will be in Faith or the understanding of heavenly secrets ; in some others the power to interpret these.

Through many will the manifestation reveal itself in healing powers ; and in others through the reading of the signs and portents of the Heavens.

In the few the Spirit will make manifest in Revelations, as through Prophets; and in Illuminations, as through Seers.[4]

164

NOTES.

[1] There is a true form of Yogism, and there is a false. Few find the former, but many the latter kind. Much is in these days proclaimed concerning the power of the will, and that there is nothing higher than mind. In the Christhood there is but one will, and that is the Divine. The human is caught up into the realms of the Divine. Through the dominance of the will-power and its wrong uses much hurt lieth upon the world to-day.

[2] And the same may be said of spirit communication. There are many elemental powers, many cast off shades within the Astral realm, and even many Souls who are still in that realm, who give wrong direction and evil influence to those who are open to them or seek guidance there. They still continue to falsify the things that be of the Christhood life. If any confirmation be required of such an indictment it will be found in the non-spiritual growth of the Spiritualistic Movement. It is a form of spiritism without true Spiritualism. In a high sense the spirits are not tried, or there would be a sweeping of the household of the unclean elementals and falsifying powers associated with it. It was meant to fill a much needed ministry for the Soul. Its true purpose was high and holy. But it has missed its way, and failed just where it should have been truly helpful.

[3] Each Soul has its own distinctive nature. The Ego has its own separate individuality. But all Souls belong to one of the seven great orders. The Seven Elohim are the seven creative Divine Powers, and all Souls partake of the nature of Elohim. Each Order partakes of the tincture of one of these. The tinctures are represented in the perfect spectrum. Then, Souls of each Order are in various stages of unfoldment, and these stages are expressed by and revealed in the various states or spiritual experiences.

Thus it may be clearly understood how it is that the gifts of Souls are so varied, and how the same gift may be in manifold degrees.

[4] This does not mean that such power is only bestowed upon a few, though it is always true that the real Prophet and true Seer are rare. But this only means that comparatively few have reached such a high degree of realization.

L—I

THE CHRISTHOOD

The Gifts of the Spirit

And the Office of the Redeemer and the Illuminator does the Spirit fill in and through those whose order of Soul and degree of Life permit such ministrations.[1]

But all are of the One Spirit ; and all are in Christ.

For the gifts of the Spirit are bestowed through Jesus, Christ, and the Lord, according as each one is in the holy estates which these signify.[2]

The baptism of the Spirit is one ; but the measure of it is according to the measure of the stature of Jesus, Christ, and the Lord in each one baptised.[3]

Now, ye all are of the Body of the Lord ; for in you is Jesus Christ made manifest.[4] And unto you has the manifestation come, that ye may know and understand the meaning of these things.[5] Ye are His chosen ones, ordained of Him unto this end, that through you the gift of God may be interpreted, even the Life Eternal which is found in the states of Jesus Christ.[6]

For whatsoever ye have yourselves realized of the Word of Life through the riches of the Spirit who is within you, of that are ye to testify ; for ye are to bear witness to the Son of God who is in you, and to interpret those things that, through me, have been given unto you from the Father-Mother.

Spiritual Discern ment

We speak not unto you with words of enticement fashioned by men, nor born of the wisdom of this world, but in words born within us from the Spirit who understandeth and knoweth all things, even the deep things of God.

For the wisdom of this world is unto God as the language of the child who must needs learn through objective images the meanings of things not beheld —all which wisdom is foolishness when the outward image is mistaken for the inward signification.

But the wisdom of God, which appeareth as foolishness unto those who account themselves wise in this world, maketh the Soul ever rich when it is discerned by the Spirit of the Lord who is within.

Only unto spiritual men and women can spiritual things be interpreted.

NOTES.

[1] This is the highest of all the gifts of the Spirit. To be called to fill the office of the Redeemer is no mean service though it may be one in which the Cross is heavy which has to be borne. Such a ministry is of the very essence of the Divine Love in ministry. And to become the vehicle or reflector of the Divine Wisdom or Illumination, is surely to fill one of the highest and most sacred offices of the Spirit. Yet few believe that these offices now exist apart from the historical Master. Do the religious communities believe that such offices may now be filled ? The Master filled the office of the Illuminator during His Christhood ; throughout all the ages of the Sin-offering, in His Oblation, He has filled the office of the Redeemer.

[2] As these are three states of consciousness and realization with varying degrees of each state, it is to be expected that the order of the gifts will correspond to the state. The gifts of a Jesus are beautiful, but those of Christhood are greater and they are more interior. In the Lord-consciousness they are of the highest and the innermost. To understand the manifoldness of the gifts of the Spirit, they must all be seen from the Inner Realm.

[3] Here also the like holds good. The measure of the Baptism of the Spirit is according to the measure or unfoldment of Christ within the Soul. The cup can receive no more than its measure enables it to contain. Yet the Spirit is freely given unto all.

[4] What a sacred statement this is ! What wealth of meaning it contains. To be of the Body of the Lord drew them into the innermost sanctuary of being. They were of His Substance, and were to be the vehicles of His Manifestation.

[5] The purpose of the Christhood of the Master is here made obvious. Only those who had been in Christhood could possibly understand such a Manifestation. For this same reason very few understood Him.

[6] The inner group were elect ones, chosen to appear at the time of His appearing, that they might form a Brotherhood of Christs. And though that purpose, with the exception of a brief period, was lamentably defeated through the influences of the Astral world, yet the Brotherhood of the Christs will soon be restored.

THE CHRISTHOOD

Love Tran scendent

If any one speak with the tongues of men, and even of angels, but lack in Love, his voice is as the sounding of brass or the clanging cymbal.[1]

Though one may have the prophetic gift so as to foretell events, and have knowledge of the Mysteries and powers from the world beyond, and yet fail in Love, he faileth in all things as if he had nothing.

And though a man give all his goods to feed the poor, and even his body to those who make him to pass through the fires, so that he may be great before men, yet have not Love, these profit him nothing.

Love suffereth long. Love is unfailingly kind. Love envieth not. Love is not puffed up by the praise of men. Love vaunteth not itself. Love never behaveth itself unseemly. Love seeketh not its own. Love is not provoked to evil. Love rejoiceth not in unrighteousness, but only in the truth. Love beareth all things. Love covereth all things with its garments. Lov hopeth amid all things, even when these are most opposed to its way. Love endureth unto the end of all such things.

Love never faileth us. Though the prophecies of all who prophesy come to naught, and the gift of tongues cease ; and though the knowledge of the Mysteries shall have to be taken away : yet Love remaineth.

For the knowledge that cometh from without is only in part, so also is that which cometh through prophecy ; but in the perfect life these are no longer such, for then all things become clear.

When one is a child he thinks as a child, he speaks as a child, and he feels as a child ; but when that one becomes a man, he puts away the states of childhood.

In the states of childhood he sees everything as through a mirror ; but in the perfect life he beholds them with open countenance. He knoweth and understandeth even as he also is known.

And he doeth this through the things that abide, which are Faith, Hope and Love. And the greatest of these three is Love.

NOTES.

[1] In this unfoldment of transcendent Love there are the shadows of coming events. There is a sorrowful anticipation of disaster to the Christhood as a vision of perfect attainment for the Soul. There is the sensing of new conditions which would overwhelm the Christhood vision and raise up another Kingdom and vision in its place ; and there is a covert tender solicitude for the members of the inner group lest they should fail in the day of trial that was coming upon them. Hence the warning in the opening Sayings, and the detailed nature of the action of Love.

The Christhood would pass away, and in its stead would arise another gospel which knew nothing of Christhood. The Brotherhood would pass away, and in its place would arise a Church which contained not the blessed knowledge and vision of Jesus Christ. Like Himself in His passing away, He saw what would overtake the beloved and elect ones unto whom the Manifestation had been given, who had been the witnesses of all that the Master said and did and the sharers of His joys and His sorrows, and the great silence that would fall upon them because of the new opposing elements created by the arising of Paul and his followers.

These beautiful Logia are attributed to Paul in the New Testament records ; yet the founding of the outward kingdom by him and his followers in the face of all that had been told him by the members of the Brotherhood, was directly in opposition to the purpose of the Manifestation and the Teachings of the Master, and a complete violation of the doctrine of the Agape or Divine Love. It is true that Paul made use of these precious Sayings as he did others which he took from the Brotherhood when he visited them, and he added the invariable personal element, an element never absent from any of his letters ; but the beautiful statement concerning the Agape, was given by the Master to help the members of the inner group to keep themselves children of love, that Love, even the Agape of the Soul. All the references to what that Love was, and what it did, and how it triumphed, had this end in view.

Amid all the new and trying conditions, the loss of the vision of Christhood, the withdrawal of the Mysteries in their interior significations during the ages in which the Oblation was being offered and the falsification and misrepresentation of them, the strife of tongues arising out of these things, the wrong uses of occult powers, the mistaken zeal in unworthy causes and the high claims of the new kingdom, they were to retain their Faith, Hope and Love—spiritual perception, the coming again of the Vision, and the Agape. And of these the Agape or Divine Love in them, was the greatest.

169

THE CHRISTHOOD

The Veil of Moses Lifted

Even unto this day, whensoever the Teachings of Moses are read, the people understand them not, a dark veil preventeth them from beholding the truth.[1]

But in Christhood that veil is taken away so that the Soul beholdeth with the Understanding the things which pertain unto the Lord.[2]

For when the Soul turneth unto the Lord, to follow on to know Him as He is made manifest in the holy estates of Jesus and Christ, then is the veil lifted and taken away from before the eyes of the Soul, and the Soul sees unto the understanding of these blessed experiences.

And where the Lord is known, there is liberty of Soul from the thraldom of the world ; for the Lord is the Spirit within the Soul.

And with unveiled vision ye may all reflect the glory of the Lord, even as mirrors reflect the face of those who look into them, as ye are transformed into His Image, and rise from glory unto glory through the Spirit of the Lord who is within you.[3]

The Grace of the Lord

Know ye the Grace of the Lord made manifest in Christ Jesus, who, though He was rich with all the riches of God, yet for our sakes stooped unto our low estate, and knew our impoverishment, that we might become enriched.[4]

And it became Him through whom we all were fashioned, and for whose purpose all the things in the Worlds were made, that, in bringing again unto the state of Salvation all who went down into bondage to the elemental Kingdoms, He should know suffering, even the anguish of the Cross as He bore the burden through us all.[5]

For unto this end is Christ Jesus to be made manifest that He may destroy him who hath the power of spiritual death, even the Devil and Satan, with all his principalities, visible and invisible ; and thus work out the deliverance of all those who fell from their first estate and became subject to the powers of the air, and redeem the members of the House of Israel from the darkness which overtook them, and Judah from the thraldom of her oppressors.[6]

170

NOTES.

[1] This is true even unto this day. Even the Teachers of the people know not. There is a dark veil before them, and it is threefold. There is the veil of Blood fashioned out of their habits of flesh-eating, and the destruction of life to minister to their tastes, their enjoyments, and their health. There is the heavy veil of materialism fashioned by means of the spirit that changes the things of the Soul into the things of sense, rearing an altar of traditionalism and literalism where the mystic altar of the Lord should stand. And there is the veil of idolatry. For it permeates the whole of Christendom and blinds the Intuition to the truth.

[2] In Christhood there is no veil. The field of blood has been left behind ; for a Soul seeking that high estate turns its back upon all these barbaric ways. There is no veil of materialism ; for the Soul that finds the mystic way must indeed cast off the darkening garments of traditionalism and literalism. And the Soul which has risen into Christhood has put away all idolatry, and lives in the consciousness of God, worshipping Him only.

[3] The Soul does actually pass from one state of glory unto another. Its experiences are increasingly transcendent. It is the outcome of the intensification of consciousness.

[4] This Saying refers to Adonai. He stooped unto our estate in that He is present in all Souls, even in their low degrees of realization. The stooping of the Divine Love and Wisdom is beautifully expressed here. If the Eternal One did not lean down to our estate, how could we ever become enriched with the riches of His grace ?

[5] The part played by Adonai in the Redemption is here signified. The Oblation was made by the Master during His lives in which He had to carry the burden of the Sin-offering ; but even He could not possibly have accomplished that work alone. He was alone, utterly in this sense, that He knew not those who had been with Him in the days of the Manifestation ; nor had He the consciousness of Adonai as in the Manifestation. But the Divine Love projected the Oblation and Sin-offering and carried it to completion through Him. But for the Divine sustenance, it could not have been borne by Him.

[6] The great work of Christhood is to overthrow all spirit of denial and evil, to destroy the works of the devil on these planes and within the Astral Kingdom. This is always so, though the Saying refers specially to the great work of the Oblation.

THE CHRISTHOOD

The Earthly and the Heavenly

But there are some who ask how the dead are raised up, and with what kind of body do they come forth.[1]

The glory of earthly things is not as the glory of heavenly things; for the one passeth away with the changing fashions of the things which are of the mortal, but the other continueth, growing ever more and more until the perfect day.[2]

The things which are of the mortal cannot know immortality, nor corruptible things incorruption; for that which is of the Earth is earthly, and that which is of the Heavens is heavenly.

And as the things of the Earth still know decay and corruption, they cannot have immortality; but the things of the Heavens know no decay, having within them the Life which is Immortal and Eternal.[3]

The first things of the Earth were spiritual and were not unnatural, and the natural man was then a living Soul; but now those things accounted natural are not spiritual, and the present natural man discerneth not the things of God.[4]

For the things of God none knoweth, save the Spirit of God who is in man; and none other may interpret them unto him but the Heavenly Counsellor.

For who knoweth the things of God save the Spirit of the Lord? And who could instruct man save the Lord whose Spirit is within him?[5]

But the earthly man whose eyes are holden that he cannot see other than earthly things, discerneth not the things of the Spirit.[6]

The Rising from the Dead

And now is Christ risen within you, as one from the dead, and become the firstfruits of the arising of Christ within all those who through so many ages have slept.[7]

For, as through the betrayal of man came spiritual death, so that all have died; so through the Redemption shall come unto all the resurrection from the dead.

For as in the Adamic Age all died, so in the Christ Age shall all be made alive again.[8]

NOTES.

[1] These Logia, forming one of the most majestic passages in the Pauline Letters and made use of so constantly in the offices of the Churches, have an entirely different meaning from that which has been associated with them. As will be noted in comparing with the text given in the Letter to the Church at Corinth, they were greatly changed by the Pauline editors, so much so as to obscure their original meaning.

[2] The glory of earthly things is truly beautiful where the conditions are pure, but the elements out of which they are built up are not of such fine quality as those of which heavenly or inner things are fashioned. The earthly elements belong to the outer realm of manifestation ; the heavenly elements are of the nature of the inner world. The bodies formed of the earthly elements belong to the phenomenal world ; those formed of the heavenly elements belong to the spiritual world. The lower cannot possibly rise into the higher, except by a very long process of transmutation.

[3] The Mortal was related to the earthly, and to Souls who had not risen above its dominion ; the Immortal stood for the abiding spiritual, and Souls who had risen into high spiritual estate became Immortals.

[4] Before the descent known as " the fall," all things were spiritual. Nothing was unnatural ; even the children of this world who were the Mortals had no unnatural life. The term natural man has been used to designate the fallen nature or personal equation. But in the unfallen days, the personal was not unspiritual.

[5] A profound truth, the understanding of which was never more necessary.

[6] No Soul, however beautiful it may be, can possibly discern the things of the Spirit until it has attained such stages of its evolution when the understanding is opened to receive from the inner world. But it is also true that many Souls who have, long ages ago, reached that stage and passed it, now remain without the inner power of discernment, because they have long been wedded to earthly things.

[7] Christ had come into some degree of manifestation in the disciples, and it was the precursor of the awakening and arising of all the members of the Ancient Order of Christs in the days of the Son of Man.

[8] The age of the descent and that of the new ascent. It was spiritual death that overtook the world ; it is spiritual life that is now coming to it. The Christ-Age is with us.

THE CHRISTHOOD

The Rising from the Dead

For, as all went down into evil in the fall, so through the resurrection shall all come forth into the righteousness of God.[1]

But each in his and her own order. The Christhood Order first; then they who may be able to receive the Christ message when it comes; and then they who are yet afar off, and those at the ends of the earth, shall be delivered from evil and received into the Kingdom of the Father-Mother through the awakening of His Son in them.[2]

For in the day of His manifestation, Christ shall put down all other rule and authority and dominion, having overcome these, and shall, through the deliverance of the Soul, cause it to yield up the Kingdom to the Father-Mother.[3]

But the manifestation of the Son of God through the various orders is different, and is in harmony with the order to which the life belongs.

For even as grain is various, and each kind of grain brings forth after its order; so are all Souls one life in nature, but each order differs from the others in the degree of manifestation of the one life.[4]

The highest fruits are those begotten of the risen Christ within the Soul; yet in these each one will bear according to the order to which the life belongs.

There is a glory which is of the Sun; another of the Moon; and another of the Stars; for each has its own manifestation.

Yet is their glory One, even the Glory of the Highest.

And so is it in the resurrection when the Son of God is made manifest; for each Soul differeth in the glory.

There are those who be Celestial, and those who be Terrestrial; but the glory of the Celestial is one, and the glory of the Terrestrial is another: yet is the glory of each from the One.[5]

And there are spiritual bodies, and there are earthly bodies; and the glory of the spiritual is one, and the glory of the earthly is another: yet is the glory of each from the One.

That which is first is spiritual, and then that which

174

NOTES.

[1] The resurrection here refers to a spiritual experience in which even the body shares. It has nothing to do with any resuscitation of dead elements which have been laid in a grave. In the fall all the children of the Planet descended into non-spiritual conditions and as a result lost what power they had to enable them to function upon the lower Spiritual Heavens—the plains of the Bethlehem where the shepherds are said to have watched their flocks. Because of this they became dead to spiritual things. In the resurrection they were to be quickened and raised from the dead. And this was to take place during the Christ-Age. But, as the following Sayings show, it could only be accomplished after the uprising of the Christhood.

[2] The Christhood Order must come first, because through those who be of that Order the Divine Love and Wisdom makes manifest. Following that first resurrection will be that of the elder children of the Planet, some of whom had almost attained to spiritual Christhood when the fall or Planetary descent took place. Then through the most blessed manifestation of the Christhood by the members of the Ancient Order, and that of true Jesushood by the elder Souls of the Human Race, the younger races will be brought into a spiritual atmosphere in which their life will be resurrected to its original state. Even those who have gone furthest away will be brought nigh to that life.

[3] The reign of Christ is the triumph of the Divine in man. There is no reference to the personal Master : it is of Adonai it speaks. It is the all-conquering power within the Soul who will overthrow all false authorities and evil powers, and lead the Soul into the Kingdom of the Father-Mother. The unfoldment unto blessed manifestation of the Christ within gives to the Soul the triumph over all things.

[4] Souls belong to Orders. These are broken up into Racial groups, Nations, Peoples and Tribal Communities. The Orders represent the tinctures of the Soul. Of these there are seven, and they are according to the Order of the Creative Spirits of Elohim. On the lower or outer Kingdom, these are revealed as the spectrum. According to their order Souls reveal the one Life ; and according to their age and growth is the Life intense or otherwise. To understand Souls, peoples, nations and races in the degrees and aspirations of their manifestation, is to know whence they are, and how far they have come along the path of spiritual evolution, the order to which they belong, and the order of manifestation possible to them.

[5] The Celestials, in this instance, refers to the Christhood ; the Terrestrials to the children of the Planet.

THE CHRISTHOOD

is earthly ; but the earthly is not unnatural, so be that it is spiritual, but is natural even as the spiritual.[1]

The Rising from the Dead

For we are to bear the image in the earthly, even as we are to bear it in the heavenly.[2]

But flesh and blood cannot inherit the Kingdom of God ; and what is mortal cannot attain to be immortal.[3]

Yet is even the body that is mortal changed as the Soul rises into immortality, until it knows the victory over corruption and death.[4]

Thanks be unto God the ever Blessed One, in whom is our Father-Mother, who giveth unto us all this victory through Jesus, Christ, and the Lord.

Now we know that the whole creation of the Divine Love was perfect.

The Imprisoned World

But this world now groaneth and travaileth in pain, waiting for its deliverance from bondage and corruption.[5]

For the Souls of all creatures upon it were made captives, and became subject unto vain ways by reason of him who subjected them.[6]

Their captivity was not brought about by their own willinghood, but through him who had the power of earthly dominion.[7]

For the subjection of all Souls to the powers of the elemental world was not wrought by the Divine Love who fashioned them to bear His image, nor in accordance with His Will, but rather through him who fell from his first estate.[8]

But now is the time of deliverance come for the Souls of all who went down ; for even the creature shall be delivered from the bondage in which it now is, and the elemental kingdoms become subject unto the Sons of God.

I reckon not the sufferings of the coming days as worthy to be compared to the glory that shall follow, and be revealed unto all Souls.

NOTES.

[1] It is a prevalent idea that man began his being in matter as that is understood by physical scientists, and grew up into the spiritual ; that he is the product of inorganic matter, and that the spiritual is developed in him by means of long ages of education. It is quite logical to think, from this point of view, that the first things were material and that the spiritual is the ultimate. But this is a mistaken conception of the beginning of life and even of the elements of the Planet. What is now designated matter, was originally spiritual substance. In the unfallen days that substance was perfect in its magnetism and responsive to the law of its magnetic attraction. It was in those ages that the Human Soul was generated out of the spiritual substances, so that all its elements are spiritual. But since the fall or Planetary descent, no Souls have been generated, though forms are in constant states of generation. Matter, as such, is spiritual substance changed in nature through the loss of its true magnetism. In the Redemption the ultimate will be the restoration of the Planetary substances to their original state.

[2] The Divine Image is also to be radiantly revealed in the personal.

[3] The mere personal consciousness cannot attain unto that of the Christhood, called the Kingdom of God ; but when the life is purified, the personal consciousness can be transfused by the Divine Life-stream which proceeds from within through the vehicles, and receive the glory of radiance within. In high Christhood the personal consciousness becomes at one with the Soul-consciousness.

[4] The mortal body, or rather the body of a Mortal, is changed in its elements as the Soul enters high Christhood to be enrolled one of the Immortals. And one in this latter state could not die, as men and women understand death, for there would be no elements of death or corruption in the body. When the hour for passing away approaches such an one, the more spiritual elements are indrawn by the Soul.

[5] The whole world, from the Planet Soul who has suffered most terrible anguish through the fallen state, to the individual Soul, cries out for purer and happier conditions.

[6] Though so much evil is now wrought by the choice of many, yet the fallen state was not chosen originally. The changing of the elemental world brought it about.

[7] The Planet came under the dominion of influences exercised over it by other fallen ones—the fallen angels, as they have been named. And these influences of fallen spirits together have been spoken of as Satan. He was the angel of the outermost sphere, but fell from his first estate.

[8] Those who have imagined that the fallen conditions of this world are in harmony with the Divine scheme of Creation, have misconceived utterly the nature of the Divine Love and Wisdom.

THE CHRISTHOOD

The Imprisoned World

Though the whole created world groaneth and travaileth in pain together until the Redemption be accomplished, it is the earnest expectation that there shall be a revealing of the Sons of God.[1]

For though the created world was made the subject of vanity, not of its own knowledge, but through him who subjected it ; yet is it borne up by the hope that the day of its deliverance will come in which its bondage will be changed into the liberty whose glory is that of the children of God.[2]

And of this deliverance and glory are ye to be the firstfruits, Sons of the Spirit who know the blessedness of the Redeemed Life, even to the redemption of the body.[3]

And in this is the saving hope for the created world.[4] For we know that all things work together for good towards all who love God and walk according to His purpose ; for they become conformed into the Image of His Son in whose Life they are justified and glorified.

The Divine Conqueror

And in our infirmities will the Spirit help us,[5] even when in our distress we know not how to pray unto the Father-Mother, nor the things for which we should pray.[6]

But with yearnings which cannot be uttered will the Spirit within us make intercession according to the Will of the Father-Mother.

And He who knoweth the Heart and searcheth the Understanding, will interpret the unutterable yearnings of the Spirit.[7]

What then shall we say more concerning these things ? If the Father-Mother be for us, what are the powers that will be against us ?

He who spared not Himself, and who hath given unto all Souls His Love, shall He not in fulness give us all power that we need ?

Who could elect to lay anything to His charge ? Hath He not justified His ways ? And shall He not again justify them ?[8]

178

NOTES.

[1] Where may this remarkable expectation be found ? The heart of what science is pleased to call Nature, does not appear to have any consciousness by which it could live in such a state of hope. But Nature is not what it appears to be, and it as truly shares in the great hope which now fills the Planet Soul, as the body and powers of a human Soul share in the great joy which comes to it.

And it is true indeed, especially so in these days, that all peoples are looking for the appearing of great ones, though they do not quite understand just what they are looking for. The age of the Deliverance and the Redemption has come, and the revealing of the Sons of God is about to take place. Many of them are now with us.

[2] The liberty of the children of God is perfect freedom from the power and dominance of the elemental world. True spiritual liberty is never licence to do what is evil. It is not even that freedom in which men and nations often pride themselves. It is a liberty of sweet bondage to the ways of the Spirit. The glory of it is the glory of God revealed in human lives.

[3] Note again the emphasis on the high calling of the disciples. They were to be the first manifestors in the Christ-age of the Christhood, Sons of the Spirit making manifest the ways of the Spirit in life. They were to interpret the Redeemed Life, and show what it accomplished even for the body.

[4] The hope lying at the heart of the world has had a salutary effect upon life, even when the ages have been very dark. It has been saving in this sense, that it has kept alive the religious aspiration.

[5] Here are some familiar sayings with an entirely new meaning. They belong to the group of the Sin-offering Logia, which had special reference to the burden of the Oblation borne by the Master. They are Sayings in which the travail of His Soul is revealed. He beheld the sufferings of the coming days—the days of the Oblation, and knew what it would bring to Him of sorrow and anguish, yet He thought it was not to be put in comparison with the glory that would follow the great work of changing the middle kingdom by blotting out the evil magnetic images.

[6] Whilst 'He was bearing the burden of the Oblation, He often was so fearfully distracted that He knew not even how to pray.

[7] But for the confidence which this knowledge gave Him, He could not have undertaken a burden so terrible in its nature, so awful in its power to impoverish the Soul. He knew what the Divine Love was to Him, and He had confidence He would bring Him through and accomplish fully the work to be done.

[8] The misconception of the ways of the Divine Love and Wisdom has often caused many to question the goodness of God, and the reality of the Divine Compassion and Love.

THE CHRISTHOOD

The Divine Conqueror

Who is he who would condemn them? Shall not He who hath made manifest Jesus and the Christ, cause them to be raised again from the dead when the Son of Man cometh? [1]

Who shall be able to separate us from His Love? Shall the tribulation, and the anguish, and the persecution, we shall meet in the way? [2]

Nay! Over all these things shall He make us more than conquerors; over the lives we shall have to live, and the death we shall have to die, over the principalities and the powers in the heights and in the depths whither we go. [3]

Experiences of the Sin-offering

But though the Work of Ransom must be accomplished through earthly vessels (bodies), yet will the exceeding greatness of the power within them be of God, and not from ourselves. [4]

We will be pressed by the powers on every side of us, yet not over-straitened in the way of our going.

We will be perplexed by all the conditions into which we must enter, even unto despair; but they will not be permitted to prevail against us. [5]

We will be pursued in our goings by the elementals whose work it has been to enslave the Soul, and afflicted by them; yet will we not be left behind.

By the powers and principalities, both seen and unseen, we will be smitten sorely; yet will they not have the power to destroy us. [6]

Upon our bodies we will have to bear the dying of the Jesus-Life, so that the Ransom of the Soul may be effected, and the Jesus-life again be made manifest by all Souls. [7]

Wherefore should we faint? The Treasure with us is of God.

Though in the outward man the Jesus-life will appear to be perishing, yet within us the Divine Life will be renewed day by day through Him who dwells within, even the Lord.

For though our affliction will be heavy and sore to bear, yet will it seem but light and for a moment when we behold it in the Light of the Eternal; [8]

NOTES.

[1] Who could for one moment imagine that the ways of God could be other than beautiful ? or that He would permit ultimate defeat to come to the one chosen to be His servant through whom the manifestation was given and the Sin-offering was to be accomplished, or that the blessed estates of Jesushood and Christhood should fail to be again raised up ? The Master foresaw that the vision of them would be lost through the ages of the Oblation, but also that the Divine Love would raise them up again in the days of the Regeneration.

[2] There is a pathos attached to these words deeper than any one could realize, for the tribulation, the anguish, and the persecution were unspeakable. In none of the lives of the Oblation did He escape these. And they were of such an order that they sometimes made Him feel as if He were verily an outcast from God and man.

[3] The lives lived had to be magnetically conditioned so as to enable the evil magnetic images to be attracted and transmuted. The death He had to die was that of losing the life of the Christ-consciousness, spiritual death which took Him down to the depths of fallen human experience.

[4] The expression " earthly vessels " in contrast to " the greatness of the power with them," reveals the character of the work to be done. The power within the Soul operating through the earthly vessels or bodies would be of God. Indeed, the work could not otherwise have been accomplished. It is quite true to say that the Divine Love did the work through the Master.

[5] In this great task He was constantly walking through the valley where the Shades or Astral forms cast their shadow. The evil images fought against Him. They overwhelmed Him as they had done other Souls. But in turn they were destroyed through Him.

[6] The Master passed through most awful anguish at the hands of certain occult powers. They had their principalities in the higher Astral world and exercised great power over the minds of men and women. These powers have wrought much havoc in the world's history. They dwelt in the heights whither He had to go. In the Oblation He had to pass through their realm and effect such changes as would result in their overthrow. They persecuted Him without mercy.

[7] The dying of the Jesus-life has a most significant reference to the last incarnation and life of the Regeneration, though it was also true in every life. For the Jesus-life to die is for the Soul who knew Jesushood to descend from that state. Always did the Master desire to live in it, and always did His mission take Him down from it for many years in each life.

THE CHRISTHOOD

For it will work out gloriously, far exceeding the weight of the burden we will carry.[1]

Experi-ences of the Sin-offering

We will look at the things which are not seen, rather than at those seen by us on our way.

For the things which we shall see on our way will be only temporal, but the things then unseen will be of the Eternal.[2]

Blessed be God the Father-Mother of us all, who is full of merciful-kindness and all consolation, and hath made manifest unto us through Him who is our Lord, in the estates of Christ Jesus. He doth promise the comfort of His Love during all our afflictions.

As our tribulation abounds, even so shall His Love abound unto us.

In all our suffering will He suffer, for He is with us; and our affliction is according to His will, and for the salvation of His children.[3]

And of this tribulation are ye also sharers in some measure; and according to the degree of your own suffering, will His comfort be measured unto you.[4]

The Burden of the Sin-offering

Concerning the burden which weighs us down so heavily, we would not have you uncertain; for it is so great that at times it makes us feel as if our life itself would have to be sacrificed.

In carrying the burden, the consciousness of death will be within us; but our trust is in God the Father-Mother who will deliver us from death, and raise us up again through the resurrection of His Son in us.[5]

Only He Himself could deliver us from so great a death, and raise us up again into the image of His Son through His Love and the gift of His Spirit.

And in this thing ye all may be helpers. Let prayer and supplication unto the Father-Mother be made for us by you; and praise for His great gift given on behalf of all His children be rendered unto Him.[6]

182

NOTES.

[8] That is quite true, but only as a Soul is able to look out along the plane of the inner world where all things are beheld in their true perspective.

[1] No one could possibly imagine what lay before the vision of the Master when He uttered these words. The burden of the Oblation was one of awful nature to Him from which He recoiled, as may be gathered from sayings uttered during the Gethsemane ; yet the tragedy of it for Him, however terrible, He recognised to be nothing compared to the glorious results that were to issue. The possibility of a redeemed world, Human and Planetary, through the purification of the middle kingdom far outweighed the sufferings and anguish. The glory that would follow—that was the supreme thought with Him, for He ever sought only the Will of the Father-Mother.

[2] During the days in which the burden lay heavy upon him, He could not see the things that were of the Eternal. But when it lightened for a time, His mind reverted to the spiritual ; and as He rose in each life into Jesushood, the glory of the things that were of the Eternal engaged and captivated Him.

[3] That is one of the most beautiful thoughts, one to be remembered by all Souls in their spiritual experience, but especially by those who were of the Christhood Order. Of course, it had a special meaning in the experience of the Master. For in the way of His going the Passion of our Lord was revealed.

[4] Was it not often told them that they were to be sharers in the sufferings that would overtake the Christhood ? That they would become partakers of the Passion of the Lord ? But only a very few participated in the burden of the Oblation.

[5] What is meant is the return of the Soul into the consciousness of Christhood with all its high and blessed realizations.

[6] Had the Western World which adopted the new religious expression, truly purified its altars and offered the right kind of incense and sacrifice, it would have materially helped the Master, instead of proving almost an insuperable hindrance. The way of the Church has greatly protracted the work of the Redemption, and heaped ignominy upon Him who had to carry the burden. There is no more tragic history to be found written in books or upon the magnetic plane, than that of the Church during the three days or cycles of the Sin-offering, whilst He whom they professed to follow was anguishing under the burden of the Oblation. What might not Christendom speedily have become if true prayer and praise had prevailed within its sanctuaries ?

THE CHRISTHOOD

The Burden of the Sin-offering

Fain would we have forborne to name this thing unto you, and to have caused you to be in a measure partakers of this awful burden with its sorrow; for we would far rather have you filled with the joy of God[1]

But ye have been set apart from the beginning to share this mystery of sorrow, and have part in the fellowship of our suffering.[2] *He who is ever faithful hath called you to be partakers with us in the Passion of our Lord, even as ye were called to be manifestors of His Son through the holy estates of Jesus Christ.*

Unto you His word must be as Yea. For He is the Amen,[3] *whose glory is to be made manifest through our going away. And He will establish us and you once more in Christ, and anoint us, giving anew the seal of His Holy Spirit.*

The Restoration of Israel

Yet could I pray that the awful state of anathema were part of my burden for the sake of all Israel who are my kinsfolk in the Christhood, those who were Israelites indeed, the adopted of God in whom His Glory was manifested, who understood His Covenants, and interpreted His Laws in their service in life, in whom was the promise of the Father-Mother that in them the Christ should be made manifest, even He who is blessed for evermore, God over all.[4]

For my heart's desire and prayer is that Israel may all be restored, though they be but a remnant of all those who fain would be known as Israel.

For there be many who glory as being Israel after the flesh who have known nothing of the true Israel after the spirit:[5] *though these have not now in them the knowledge that is begotten of God in the Soul, yet they also, in their own time, must be saved and brought out of the darkness amid which they dwell, into that Light which is begotten of the Spirit of God.*

But the remnant must first be restored;[6] *as only through their restoration can the others be saved unto the Life Eternal; for they are the Fathers, the Elders of Israel, of whom are God's prophets and seers, the revealers of the Glory of the Lord.*

NOTES.

[1] The Master here not only speaks for Himself, but also for those who were with Him. It is of the very nature of the Divine Love never to impose sorrow upon any one if it can be avoided. The Heavens grieved over the necessity for the burden being borne. It was the mystery of sorrow into which the angels are said to have desired to look.

[2] Having been set apart from the beginning refers to those who were chosen to participate in the burden with the Master when the Sin-offering was first projected, for the Oblation only became a necessity after other means had failed to destroy the images upon the Middle Kingdom. Those who were chosen from the beginning were of the true Israel, and unto them alone was its coming revealed. That is the reason why the religion of the Ancient Hebrews held the Mystery as something to be accomplished when the time for its fulfilment came ; and the literature or sacred writings were full of it. In none of the other Great Religions is this Mystery to be found.

[3] When the Divine Love and Wisdom asks of any of the members of the Christhood Order some great sacrifice, unto such is the word of the Lord, Yea. For whatever mystery there may be in it to remain unveiled until the work be accomplished, He is the Amen. As He is the Arche of all great things, so is He the Amen or consummation.

[4] Of this it is most trying for us to write, so tragically sad and sorrowful is the statement. Was the Master ever anathema ? Surely not. Yet it is said of Him that He was made accursed. Though He was never in such a state before the Divine Love, verily He felt, alas ! too frequently, as if He were, and anguished over it.

[5] It was a great misfortune for the Ancient Mysteries when they passed into the possession of the Jews ; for these latter laid claim to the title of Israel and materialized everyone of the Hebrew Mysteries. Israel was but a remnant of those who took the name. Of Israel many were lost long ages before the founding of the Ancient Hebrew Religion. The lost Tribes of Israel have a deeper significance than has yet been discovered by those who look for their restoration.

[6] The remnant to be the first restored was the inner group of the Christhood Order. That is what is now taking place, to be followed by the more general rising and redemption.

THE CHRISTHOOD

he estoration f Israel

O the depth of the Wisdom of God, and the riches of His Love which we know! How unfathomable are His judgments, and how unsearchable are His ways![1] The mind of the Lord, who knoweth? And unto whom is His counsel revealed?[2] Who hath come into the perfect knowledge of His Love and Wisdom, and received as His recompense the great peace?

He who speaketh these things unto you, and doth testify for the Father-Mother, knoweth that the day hasteneth in the which all Israel shall be redeemed and restored to her ancient glory. And through her shall the Wisdom and Love of the Father-Mother be revealed, even unto the ends of the Earth.[3]

Unto this end do ye present yourselves as living sacrifices : in all the ways of your going be holy, making manifest in your life the way that is acceptable unto the Lord, and the reasonableness of your high service.

And be not fashioned after the manner of this world ; but be ye transformed in all things. Let your mind be so renewed, and your body be so purified, that ye may be able to interpret the life that is good, and acceptable, and according to the will of the Father Mother—even the perfect way.[4]

Unto Him who alone can now establish you in the powers of the Life of Jesus Christ, according to the working of the Divine Mystery within you, which is in the secret-place and is unknown unto this world ;

But is now made manifest unto you, even as fore-told in the scriptures of the Prophets, according to the will of the Ever Blessed One, and for the guidance of those who be seeking unto the path of obedience ;—

Unto God only wise, be glory through Jesus Christ.

186

NOTES.

[1] No one could possibly gauge the feelings of the Master in such moments of exalted realization, unless that one had also been in that state, or in one in which the Master could be understood and the Divine stream that flowed through Him, deeply felt. O the depths of the Wisdom of God which He knew and the wealth of His Love towards all Souls upon this world, which He had witnessed and realized ! The history of the Planet and all its children lay before Him, its Golden Age when youth and beauty clothed all Souls, and the music of the Heavens was repeated in the rhythm of all its planes ; the great descent which issued in the fall of all the children of Judah—the Planet Soul, and the going away of the Tribes of Israel into bondage as they sought out the children of Judah ; the tragic history which was written during the untold ages which covered the immense periods of the Deluge, the Ice Age, the later Ice Age or glacial epoch, and the Volcanic ; the rise and fall of all the great Religions owing to the conditions that prevailed within the Middle Kingdom as the result of the gross living of the Planet's children ; the failure of His own mission to establish the Christhood as a permanent Fellowship because of all that would be done to the Teachings He had come to give in the manifestation of the estates of Jesus Christ, and the meaning of the Passion of the Lord of Glory. These things He knew. But He beheld also the Divine outworking, the way of the Divine Love, the wisdom of the Divine Judgments ; for the issue was the approaching arising of all Israel into the ancient Christhood Fellowship and Service, and through Israel the return and redemption of all the children of Judah because of the great work to be accomplished by means of the Oblation.

[2] None knoweth the mind of the Divine Love and Wisdom except it be revealed by the Spirit. It never has come through traditional channels, though these have claimed to be the true venues through which the Eternal Spirit speaks. Nor can the true knowledge of the mind of the Lord come through any philosophy, though in a pure state philosophy may interpret the Divine Love and Wisdom. But to know the mind of the Lord the Soul must be at one with His purpose, Love and Spirit.

[3] A rift in the clouds of sorrow in which a glimpse is given of the consummate glory.

[4] When a Soul seeks Christhood it makes a living sacrifice unto the Lord. It purifies its vehicles to make itself worthy. As it seeks to think and act nobly, it puts away everything that is wrong. It comes to understand that the eating and drinking of things which are pure, are as essential to its sacrificial service as pure thinking and feeling. It will come to know that the lives of the creatures are sacred, and not to be made use of for unnecessary ends, such as food, clothing, pleasure or healing.

187

PART V.

THE CHRISTHOOD

Containing further Logia setting forth the true meaning of the Marriage of the Soul to the Lord which is consummated in Christhood, and the high and holy Fellowship of the Soul with the Lord wherein she becomes conscious of the Indwelling Presence ministering unto it of the Bread and Wine of God, and is taken up into the Mount of Transfiguration where she has the Vision of the Lord.

THE CHRISTHOOD

The Marriage in Cana of Galilee

This allegory did the blessed Master speak unto all who were in the House of Mary[1] ·—

"There was a Marriage in Cana of Galilee[2] unto which a Divine Teacher and His disciples were asked. And the Mother of the Teacher was also there.[3]

The Marriage festival was celebrated with great rejoicing for many days, and all were filled with gladness.

But when the festival had continued its appointed time, the wine provided by the Lord of the festival was all consumed.[4]

And many of the guests were troubled because there was no more wine to drink.

But the Mother of the Divine Teacher came to Him and asked that He would provide more wine, and He told her that His hour had not yet come.[5]

Then did she, in anticipation of what He would do, advise all who served, to do His bidding when He commanded them.[6]

And when His hour was come, the Divine Teacher asked that all the vessels containing the waters for the purpose of purification, might be filled. And those who served, obeyed His command.[7]

And when those who served drew the new Wine and gave it unto the Lord of the Festival, he recognised that the wine was changed, and that it was better than the wine of which they had partaken ; and he said that at such festivals the best wine was first served, and then that which was less good, but that this wine was the best, though it came last.

In this way was the Glory of the Divine Teacher made manifest unto all who drank of the new wine ; it was also His first manifested work.[8]

The Day of the Manifestation is now come for you all, when the Lord should show forth His Glory.

His Hour is come when He should turn the Water into Wine, even the Waters of Purification into the Wine of Christhood.

The Marriage Festival has run its appointed time, and the Wine has been well drunk of by you all since

190

NOTES.

[1] The House of Mary was the state of Christhood. It is the state in which the Soul becomes Maria.

[2] It is the Marriage of the Soul, its union with the Lord ; and it takes place in Cana of Galilee, that state in which the higher mind is perfectly at one with the Lord. It is the place of union, the mind one with the Soul, even as the inner will is one with the Lord.

[3] The Divine Teacher is none other than the Lord Presence, the Christ of God within the House of Maria, the Soul who has attained so high a degree of spiritual realization.

The Mother of the Divine Teacher is the Soul ; for she alone is the Mother of her Lord, because she conceives, bears and brings forth into manifestation Him who is Christ and Lord.

[4] The first Wine is the joy of the new blessed realizations of which the whole being drinks deeply. But by and bye that Wine becomes exhausted, and no more of it is provided, for the Soul must pass upward to other realizations.

[5] The Soul longs for constant realization of Divine things, and often is impatient that they do not come more quickly. But though the Christ-consciousness be present, the hour of manifestation may not have arrived.

[6] But such a Soul would take time by the forelock and prepare those concerned to obey the Christ-command, that is, all the guests or attributes of Soul, mind, heart and body to be brought into the path of perfect service.

[7] In the perfect union of the Soul, the Christ within changes all the waters of spiritual knowledges which were for purification, into the Wine of Inspired Life—wine that refreshes, strengthens, exhilarates and inspires the whole being. The new Wine surpasses the first wine of joy born of the new relationship, for it transfuses the entire being with the power of Christhood, and bears it forward into the path of an inspired and illumined service.

[8] The Glory of the Lord within the Soul is revealed in Christhood, and the first work of manifestation is to transmute the waters which are for purification into the Wine of God.

THE CHRISTHOOD

you found a place within the House of Maria wherein the celebration has taken place.

The Marriage in Cana of Galilee

And the Wine of the Festival having run short, Maria saith unto her Son : 'They have no wine.'

And unto all who serve at the Marriage does she say · 'Whatsoever He commandeth you to do, see ye do it.'

And they, having obeyed His behests, draw forth the Waters which were for the Purification, and behold they are turned into new Wine, even the Wine of Christhood.

And now the Glory of Christhood is made manifest unto all who have been within the House of Maria wherein the celebration has been accomplished.[1]

The Cup of God is now given you that ye may drink : it is the Cup bearing the Wine of the Christhood, even that Wine which He giveth unto all who have drunk of the Wine of the Marriage Feast unto fulness.

Behold ! it is the Wine that sparkles with the inspiring Love of God, whose exhilarating power within the Soul is great, filling her with new life, even the life of His Christ.

Drink ye of it, therefore, that ye may be filled with the beautiful buoyancy of spiritual youthfulness, and know only the agedness which the Wisdom of God crowns ; for it is the Wine of Divine Inspiration.

How blessed is that Love which hath called us unto such an hour ! How Holy and Good is the Wine which through the Christhood He giveth us to drink ! Who ever dreamed of such power coming upon the Soul, even the power of His Love who hath begotten us and fashioned us to be the vessels of His Glory ?

'O Wine of God, whose power changeth our life from one of weakness and sorrow into one of joy and strength, and whose inspiring elements change our vision so that we behold in the Creator's Light and come to understand the deep mysteries of God and the Soul, of thee have we drunk, for thou camest

NOTES.

[1] The purpose of the allegory is here revealed. The inner groups of the disciples had gradually risen into the Christhood state ; having found Jesus and followed in the way, they had reached the threshold of the House of Maria—the House of the Lord, and found a place within it. The joy of the new life had been theirs. They rejoiced much in the fellowship which they had entered into with the Master. They had drunk deeply of the wine of the new teachings—not new altogether, though new once more to their understanding. They thought much of the Kingdom of the Heavens, of the gladness and blessedness which the Kingdom brought. Of that Kingdom they were a part, having become citizens. Now they must realize perfect citizenship. The Lord was their King, and He sought perfect union with all who were of His Kingdom. The day had arrived when they must enter into the consciousness of that union. The marriage or perfect union of the Soul with its Lord must take place. The hour for the manifestation of the Christ within had come. They must drink of the new wine, the wine of Christhood. They must enter into yet higher realizations, and reveal the glorious life within them in service. His Christ within them must now work the works of God, and bring forth into manifestation the hidden Divine Power ; and all those who serve—the various attributes, must be obedient unto His gracious behests. Whatsoever He commandeth they must do.

The Cup of the Wine of God ! That is what the Master brought into this world, and held to the lips of all who were able to drink of it. He came to aid Souls to reach and cross the threshold of the House of Maria, and enter into perfect union with the Lord. Through Him the Lord revealed His Christ that the glory might be made manifest unto all who belonged to that House.

THE CHRISTHOOD

The Marriage in Cana of Galilee

unto us as sent from Him whose Life thou art! But we would yet drink more and more of this Cup that our inspiration may be perfect, and our whole being lit up with the Glory of the Illumination given from thee unto all who drink deeply of thy power!

So pray ye the Father-Mother that the Cup of Life may be given unto you to drink, even the Cup of Life which He filleth through His Christ." [1]

Behold how good and how pleasant a thing it is to dwell in Unity!

When Life is One before the Vision of the Soul, none being greatest and none least, but the greatest and the least all members of the one Household, the least true brethren even as the greatest, the outermost in true harmony with the innermost, then is there Unity. [2]

The Perfect Union and Unity

When the Soul dwells in Unity, there is harmony in all its life. From the outermost sphere of its experience to the innermost sphere, harmony reigns.

Within the Soul there is the Peace which passeth all human understanding, and the Joy which is full of the Glory of Love Divine.

When all within the Spiritual Household are in a state of Unity, then is the Peace of the Divine Love in their midst. Zion is glad and Jerusalem is comforted. The dews of Hermon descend, rich with the blessing of the Lord, and full of refreshing for all the Brethren according to their needs. [3]

Pray ye, therefore, for the restoration unto Unity of Zion; and for all who dwell in the City of Jerusalem, that Peace may be within their Gates. For through the restoration of the Soul is the Holy City of Zion built up, when all who love her enter within her Gates and restore her bulwarks of love, making of her Sanctuaries Temples of Praise; and through the rebuilding of Zion as the Holy City of the Lord, and the restoration of all her Sanctuaries for His Praise, shall Jerusalem become once more the City of the Lord, beautiful in her situation or Estate, and the joy of all the children within her Gates. [4]

194

NOTES.

[1] There is more in this counsel than is apparent. Like most of His Sayings, this contains depths which only the few could possibly fathom. He yearned over them, and longed to see the manifestation of the deeper realizations in them. He sensed even early in His ministry what lay ahead, and He knew that the more deeply they drank of the cup of the Wine of God, the greater would the power in them be to take up the burden which it would be their lot to bear during the three cycles of the Oblation. Whilst the Christ of Glory was crucified between the two thieves of materialism and superstition there could be no manifestation ; and they themselves would suffer impoverishment when the Mysteries were gathered up and withdrawn because of the conditions. When they reappeared and sought for the realization within them of the blessedness of Christhood, they would have to suffer and know oppression and persecution at the hands of those who would crucify Christ and put Him to open shame.

So were they to drink deep draughts of the Wine of God that they might be made strong to endure unto the end of the Oblation as the Sons of God ; and, when it was accomplished, to arise and enter the Holy City of the Christ estate once more that through them the risen Lord might be made manifest.

[2] True unity is not uniformity ; it is not a likeness ; but it is oneness of love and purpose amid infinite diversity. In the Kingdom of the Heavens all are as one. In degree of life some are great and some are less, but the greatest is at one with the least.

So are all the attributes of the Soul within that kingdom in a state of unity. Those in the least degree serving in the outer must be cherished and never accounted as of no degree and value, because, as servants, they are one with those of the innermost.

[3] There are two households named here, Zion of the Christhood and Jerusalem of the spiritual household of the Planet. The Holy City of Zion was within the city of Jerusalem ; and within it, and upon Mount Moriah, was the Temple of the Lord built—that is, Christhood.

Hermon was the high realization within the Soul where the Peace of God is found, and the descending Spirit was realized as the dews of the Heavens.

[4] The restoration of the Order of the Christs is here meant. It was the ancient Zion whose children were to arise out of the dust of their humiliation and put on their beautiful garments. And as a result of this restoration, Jerusalem will be restored, her children redeemed, the gates into the city of holiness rebuilt, and the life of Unity entered into.

THE CHRISTHOOD

And when six days had passed the Master took Peter, James and John apart ; and they went up on to the Mount of the Lord to commune.[1]

The Mount of the Trans figuration

And as He prayed, behold there appeared in the Heavens a Vision of the Lord transfigured.[2]

His Face did shine like the noonday Sun, so glorious was His Countenance ; and His raiment was whiter than any fuller's soap could make them, and they glistened with the Light that streamed from the Radiance of His Countenance.

And there appeared in the Glory with Him the form of one like unto Moses, and the form of one like unto Elijah ; and these spake unto the Master concerning the Decease which He was to accomplish at Jerusalem.[3]

Whilst they yet were speaking unto Him, there descended upon them the Cloud of the Lord ; and there came a voice from out the Cloud which said unto the three disciples : "This is the Beloved One with whom I am well pleased : hear ye Him."[4]

Then were the disciples bowed to the Earth, and the fear of the Divine Awe came upon them ; for it was such that none could hear without fear, for its vibrations shook them to their foundations.[5]

But when the Cloud of the Lord had ascended, Peter spake thus : "Lord, it is good for us to be here. Let us now make three tents to dwell in, one for Thee, one for Moses, and one for Elijah."

For he wist not yet what it was that was spoken of on the Mount.[6]

And when the Vision had passed from them, they beheld no one but the Master.

When they had come down from the Mount He said unto them : "See that ye tell no one of this Vision until the Son of Man be risen again from the dead."[7]

But amongst themselves they questioned what could be the meaning of the Son of Man rising from the dead. And they wondered, and were sore troubled.

And when the Master saw how perplexed they were, He spake unto them, and said : "Why are ye troubled ?

196

NOTES.

[1] There is a profound significance in these opening words which is not obvious to everyone. The Mount of the Lord is a high estate of spiritual realization whereon the vision of Adonai becomes possible to the Soul. It also represents the seventh plane. It was after six days that the innermost initiates were taken up to the Mount, which was a covert expression denoting the rising from the sixth plane or state of spiritual Christhood, on to the seventh or plane of Divine Christhood. Though the disciples could not remain there, they were able to rise for a time to look upon the glorious vision.

Peter, James and John represent the three innermost powers of the Soul—the Divine Light, Life and Love, as well as three disciples.

[2] They were all transfigured: and the vision beheld was the Lord in transfiguration or a form which they could recognise.

[3] But the vision became threefold. There appeared two other forms, one like the form of Moses and one like Elijah. And the disciples knew them. They were with the Lord, and were two other forms of Adonai which the disciples had known in past ages. And they represented the Laws of Life from God, the energy of Life from God, and the glory of Being from God—the Light, the Life and the Love principles within the Soul.

The Decease to be accomplished was the Passing-over from Christhood to the lives of the Oblation.

[4] Whosoever may be lifted up to hear that voice will know that the one in whom God is ever well pleased, is the Christ within when He is brought into manifestation. It is the Lord who speaks through His Christ.

[5] And whosoever is privileged to hear the voice that speaks out from the Cloud over the Sanctuary, will henceforth be filled with the Spirit of the Divine Awe.

[6] It is quite true, though the vision was glorious, yet was the Understanding, Peter, unable to grasp the deep significance of what had been said. The Mount was indeed a place to tabernacle in, but the Oblation had to be accomplished. So the vision with its glory passed, and the disciples so privileged once more found themselves again upon the lower plane. And the Master was with them.

[7] This injunction notwithstanding, the vision was recorded by St. Matthew, and embodied in the first record to which we have elsewhere referred ; but not its meaning. That was not told. And only now when the arising of the Son of Man is taking place may it be told with all its sacred meanings for the Soul. Only now is the meaning of the Decease which was to be accomplished by the Master, being revealed.

N—I

THE CHRISTHOOD

The Mount of the Trans figuration

The Son of Man will be delivered into the hands of sinful men to suffer many things.[1] He will be betrayed and crucified by the chief priests, scribes and rulers; but after three days He will rise again from the dead."

Then the disciples asked Him what was meant by the Son of Man being crucified and rising again from the dead;[2] and when He had told them what would happen to the Christhood Teachings they said unto Him: " Why then do the Scriptures say that Elijah must first come to restore all things?"[3]

He spake again unto them saying: " Elijah will indeed come to restore all things. Know ye not that Elijah has come already and done those things which he listed to do?"

Then did they understand that He spake unto them of Himself as John the Baptizer.[4]

The Manna of Life

"The heavenly Father-Mother hath given unto His Son to have Life in Himself, that He might give that Life unto all who are able to hear His voice and receive His word.

For the Son of the Father-Mother is the Bread of Life, the Blessed Word whose Flesh is given unto all Souls as they are able to receive Him.

Whosoever eateth of His Flesh hath Life in himself; for His Flesh is meat, indeed, unto the Soul.

This is the Bread of Life which cometh down from the Heavens, the which if a man eat he shall hunger no more.

This is the Manna which was rained down from the Heavens when Moses led the children of Israel through the Wilderness of Sin unto the Land of Promise.

For the Angels' Food which the fathers gathered in the Wilderness was this Manna of the Heavens, the Flesh of the Son of God broken for all Souls.

For it was not any man who gave that Bread unto the Children of Israel, but the Father-Mother who is in the Heavens.

And He it is who ever giveth the true Bread of Life unto the Soul."[5]

NOTES.

[1] The reference is to the betrayal of the Christ-vision. How that most blessed vision was betrayed, and all that befell it, together with the ignominy heaped upon the head of the Master through whom it was given, and upon the name of the ever Blessed One who manifested through Him, those who have not reached the spiritual state in which that high experience can be entered upon, will not understand. But those who have attained that state and who beheld that vision or another like it in earlier ages, will understand. To them it will be obvious what has been done to that holy vision of life, and the fearful things wrought in its name during the development through the era of historical Christianity, by the chief priests of the various systems—ecclesiastical, scientific, social and national.

[2] The inner groups of disciples found it difficult to realize that such a betrayal could take place, and a few of them had not fully grasped the meaning of the term the Son of Man.

[3] They had not yet been fully informed of those inner meanings which were imparted to them later ; hence the question.

[4] Not even here are they informed who Elijah was, and what was meant by His coming. But the statement that He had come and done what He listed to do, led most of them to associate Him with the personal Master in His ministry as John the Baptizer. By and by other light broke within them as to the nature and office of Elijah.

[5] The Bread of Life is no word of man, though man may be used by the Eternal Father-Mother as the instrument of blessing. The heavenly Manna which the true Israel gathered amid the Wilderness, which had to be partaken of for nourishment as it was gathered, but not to be gathered merely to hold in possession, an ephah of which was preserved in the Ark of the Lord, along with the two Tables of the Law of the Lord and the Rod of miraculous Power by which the Red Sea was divided and the waters from Horeb brought forth, is no other than the Divine Love and Wisdom broken for the Soul as the Word of Life. It is not to be confounded with that other Bread of the Sanctuary, the Shew Bread of which it is said that only the priests partook. For the Manna is more than it. The Shew Bread is the Word of Life for those who are in the states represented by the first degrees of the Christ-life : the Manna is that Bread given unto all who reach the Altar which is within the Sanctuary. Unto Israel it could be given, for they were of the Christhood.

THE CHRISTHOOD

The Lord
the Bread
of Life

" ' I am the Bread $_{of}$ Life,' saith the Lord.

' The bread $_{of}$ this world perisheth in the use $_{of}$ it, but the Bread which I give unto men, even the Wisdom $_{of}$ God, preserveth and enricheth those who eat $_{of}$ it.' [1]

The Bread $_{of}$ the Wisdom $_{of}$ God is given from the Father-Mother unto all who have attained to the realization $_{of}$ His Son in them.[2]

These are they who have come into the state in which they have the right to the Tree $_{of}$ Life, having passed through the Gates and entered into the Holy City.[3]

The Bread $_{of}$ the Wisdom $_{of}$ God which the Lord giveth is Life indeed ; to the one who partakes $_{of}$ it there is imparted the power to ascend into the Heavens to see and understand those things which are $_{of}$ the Mystery $_{of}$ Godliness.[4]

Whosoever eateth $_{of}$ that Bread so that he liveth by it, shall become a citizen $_{of}$ the Heavens and a Son $_{of}$ the Father-Mother.

Within those who seek that Bread unto the nourishment $_{of}$ their lives, the Kingdom $_{of}$ the Father-Mother is come."

The Lord as
the Vine

" ' I am the true Vine,' saith the Lord ; the Father-Mother is the Husbandman.

All ye are Branches from Me ; for ye derive your Life from the Vine.[5]

All who abide in Me, have Life in abundance ; but they who do not abide in the Life $_{of}$ the Vine can have no Life in themselves, but become as withered branches.

Abide ye in Me that My Life may abide in you, and that ye may be purified through My Word unto the bearing $_{of}$ much fruit.

For whosoever abideth in the Vine, the same bringeth forth good fruit.'

Ye are now members $_{of}$ one another, even as the branches are members $_{of}$ one another ; and all ye are brethren $_{of}$ the Lord, even as all the branches are members $_{of}$ the Vine.

Love ye one another.

NOTES.

[1] The change here from the personal Master to the Divine Lord who spake through Him will be appreciated by those who understand. As the Lord is never a man, so no messenger of His could ever call attention to himself, and lay claim to those attributes which belong only unto Him. That was a sad day for the Western World in which the Master was represented as affirming Himself to be the Light of the World, the Bread of Life, the True Vine, and the Life of Men. Had those who so represented Him only known Him as He was, surely they could never have done such a cruel thing to Him and the Souls who ought to have been able to understand and follow the Way. It was so utterly alien to His word and spirit, and, of course, impossible in a state of Christhood. In all His Sayings it was always the Lord of Life who overshadowed Him, and the Father-Mother who spake within Him.

[2] The Bread of Life is not only nourishment, it is also enrichment. For the heavenly Wisdom is more than spiritual knowledge ; it is Realization. It is an enrichment of the inner consciousness, so that the Soul knows direct from God who is within its sanctuary. And there is only one way by which such blessedness can become the heritage of a Soul, namely, through the awakening of God's Son within.

[3] The Holy City is the Christhood estate, and the Gates are the Labours of the Soul. For none can enter into Christhood except by means of the Gates of Initiation by the Spirit.

[4] The Soul may rise above all the states represented by the lower planes so as to be able to transcend them. It is possible for such to rise into the Heavens even whilst it is ministering upon these outer planes. The Angelic Kingdom may be reached, and even the Divine World. The Mystery of God can only be revealed unto such Souls.

[5] In the ancient Mysteries, the Vine was used as a symbol of the Divine Presence. It was specially associated with the Divine Love in its life-giving and inspiring power. The bacchanalian festivals originated in the utter degradation of the sublime idea, and the sensualizing of its meaning. But the relation of the Soul to the true Vine of Love and the celebration of its festival, were of a high spiritual order, and always beautiful. The Lord of all Being is the Vine ; of Him we have the substance of the Eternal Life-stream, the precious Blood of the Lamb of God, the perfect Love.

THE CHRISTHOOD

The
Beatitudes
of the
Immortals

Herein is the Father-Mother glorified, that ye are one in Him who hath made the Father-Mother manifest : for the full fruit of the Vine is to be one in Him, to make manifest the Love wherewith the Father-Mother hath loved the world, and to abide for ever in that Love.

If ye do His commandments ye will abide in His Love ; and His commandments are not grievous unto those who abide in that Love."

" O ye Immortals, ye whom this world hath made poor : blessed are ye ! For your portion is in the Kingdom of the Father-Mother.[1]

O ye Immortals, ye whose mourning hath been long : blessed are ye ! With the Comfort of God shall ye be comforted.[2]

O ye Immortals, ye who have been meek and lowly upon the earth : blessed are ye ! Your inheritance in the Kingdom of the Father-Mother is your portion for ever.[3]

O ye Immortals, ye who ever hunger and thirst for the revealing of the Father-Mother : blessed are ye ! With the righteousness of God shall ye be filled.[4]

O ye Immortals, ye who alone have been truly merciful upon this world : blessed are ye ! Within you the Love of Adonai hath prevailed to make manifest His mercy.[5]

O ye Immortals, ye whose hearts have ever been pure : blessed are ye ! Unto you is the vision of Adonai known.[6]

O ye Immortals, ye whose mission to earth was for the restoration of harmony within all its kingdoms blessed are ye ! Rejoice, for the day of the return draweth near.[7]

O ye Immortals, ye who have been the harbingers of peace unto men : blessed are ye ! For so do ye make manifest that ye are the children of God.[8]

O ye Immortals, ye whom this world hath persecuted when ye have come as the Prophets and Seers of your Lord : blessed are ye ! Though men revile and persecute you, and speak, after their manner, false things concerning you, yet have ye cause to rejoice

NOTES.

[1] The Beatitudes found in the first and third records of the New Testament, however beautiful they may seem in their present form, are only fragments of the Beatitudes of the Immortals spoken by the Master to the inner group of friends. And it will be obvious to all who are able to discern inner things, how profoundly inward their meanings were.

The Immortals were those Souls who had attained to the life of the Son of God in them, and who had come into the inheritance of the consciousness of the Divine Presence. They were not of this Planetary system, for none of the children of this earth had transcended the Mortal and reached the Immortal state, though some were approaching it when the descent or fall took place. The Immortals were of the Christhood group of Souls who had been sent to this earth to aid the children in their spiritual evolution.

Through their long ministry upon this Planet, they had all been greatly impoverished. They had been shorn of their Christhood. That had been their portion in the Kingdom of the Father-Mother ; and it was to be restored unto them.

[2] A reference to the long ages of their sojourn upon the earth, and the manifold sorrow which had overtaken them. The Comfort of God was the restoration of the inward Presence.

[3] Ever were they in strange contrast to those who sought earthly ambitions, powers and dominions. True, the House of Ephraim was lost through pride of nature and place ; but the innermost groups were always meek and lowly of heart. They were of humble mind and spirit.

[4] Distinguished always from the lovers of ecclesiasticism in any form, the traditionalists and literalists in all ages, they have been those Souls who in the midst of the religious desert have kept the flame of true religion burning, and have longed with deep yearnings for the perfect realization.

[5] Who are the truly merciful ? Does the Church in any of its manifold divisions teach true mercy ? Behold the holocaust of creatures whose involuntary sacrifice is daily demanded by all who constitute the religious communities ; and see how scientists, whose high priests the Church shelters, teach mercy in their schools and manifest it in their laboratories ! But the Immortals have never been of these ; for they have loved mercy for man and creature.

[6] That is, in their intention they have always been pure of heart, even when amid the maelstrom of the world's impurity.

[7] The reference is to the arising of the Christhood for a ministry of redemption and manifestation as the first fruits of the Oblation.

[8] Upon all planes of life and in their various orders of ministry, they are children of the Great Peace.

THE CHRISTHOOD

greatly that ye have been accounted worthy to be the messengers of the Father-Mother.[1]

The Beatitudes of the Immortals

O ye Immortals, ye whose way has been one full of blessing to men ; who when reviled, reviled not again, and when made accursed by the despite of all who hated your way, blessed only with the blessing of God : blessed are ye ! For in your way ye reveal the perfect love which is of God.[2]

O ye Immortals, ye who have been as preserving salt upon this Earth after it had lost its own savour : blessed are ye ! Though men have cast you out as worthless, and in their ways have trodden you down ; yet have ye been preserved by the Father-Mother unto this day.[3]

O ye Immortals, ye who have been as shining lights in a world of darkness : blessed are ye ! Now is your light to shine forth unto all who are able to behold it : for it is come.[4]

When the Son of Man hath come again to you in glorious fulness, and the Angel of His Presence is come unto you with Him, then shall His reign within you be glorious.[5]

The Return of the Presence

And in those days shall ye also come with Him to judge and purify the nations.

For these shall be gathered before Him that with the light of His truth they may be judged, that the evil found in their ways may be separated from the good.[6]

And in those days shall ye sit upon the thrones of the twelve Tribes of Israel to give judgment as between the righteous and the unrighteous.[7]

For your Lord and King will once more have spoken within you, and His voice ye will have recognised and understood. And He shall say,

' Come, ye Blessed Ones of the Father-Mother, inherit the kingdom which was yours before the founding of this cosmos ;

When my servant was an hungered, ye did give Him to eat ;

When He was athirst, ye gave unto Him wherewith to drink ,

NOTES.

[1] The true Seers and Prophets of the Lord have always been members of the ancient Order of Israel. These were the Cross-bearers, the inner groups of the Christhood. Of them were the Messengers of the Lord. Though they brought nothing but good to the race, yet for doing so and disturbing the conditions amid which so many of the professed leaders and teachers were satisfied, they were betrayed, persecuted, and often suffered the loss of their life. On the surface it does seem strange that those very institutions and peoples who professed to desire illumination, guidance and redemption, should have been the instruments of oppression and persecution unto those who were divinely sent. Yet such has it been through all the ages unto this day.

Yet though oppressed and rejected, the office of the Seer and the Prophet is blessed.

[2] The religious world believes this is the true way of Love ; but where is to be found the ecclesiastical community whose members exhibit that Love in their ways ? Is not the present religious world just like the non-religious world in this matter ? Were it not so, the civic courts would have little to do.

To bless those who would make us accursed, that is the blessed way. It is the way of the Cross. There is a non-resistance that is the true resistance. To refuse to retaliate is to resist evil ; even the devil is said to flee from those who so resist him.

[3] The reference here to the loss by the Earth of its own inherent preserving power is indeed profound in its meanings, the full inter-pretation of which must await another work. But it implies the sad conditions which prevailed for thousands of ages upon the Earth as the result of the changes wrought within the elemental kingdoms through the great Planetary descent, and the way which the Human Race took.

[4] The coming consciousness of Christhood. Though it could not be fully entered into until these days, yet the heritage had come back to them ; and after the three Naronic Days or cycles of the Oblation or Sin-offering, and the return of the Son of Man, the Light within them would shine in fulness.

[5] The beauty of this Saying will now be seen separated from the false environment in which it is found so broken and mixed in the first Gospel Record. It is so obvious what was meant by the coming of the Son of Man and the Angel of the Presence of God, and in perfect accord with all the other Sayings of the Master.

[6] The Divine Judgment of the nations is here closely identified with the coming of the Son of Man. That Judgment is now proceed-ing. For what is the Judgment of the Great Day, but the application of truth to life by which every form of evil is overthrown and every good thing established ?

THE CHRISTHOOD

When He was sorely afflicted, and grew sick in His sorrow and anguish, ye ministered unto Him ;

The Return of the Presence

When He was cast out by men, and oppressed, ye took Him in and sheltered Him ,

When He was cast into the prison-houses where He anguished with the pains and sorrows of those who were bound, ye did visit Him and give Him comfort ;

When ye found Him with His raiment rent and red-dyed as one who has been treading the wine vat, whilst in pain He travailed for the deliverance of all creatures and all Souls, ye did clothe His nakedness with such raiment as ye had ;

For on behalf of all His Brethren did my servant endure and suffer, even for the least ; and in ministering unto Him ye ministered unto them.''[1]

O ye Immortals, the night which is about to come will be dark indeed for you all.[2]

But the dawn will break when the night hath been spent, and the glory shall be even as the night shall have been.[3]

The Night and the Dawn

Then shall ye have cause to rejoice that ye were not of the children of the darkness, but were the Sons of the Light.[4]

And in that day shall ye say, ' Blessed be the Lord, the God of Israel, who hath called us again into the inheritance of His Christs.' ''[5]

And one said unto Him, " When shall we be able to do the Greater Works ? ''[6]

And He answered, " When ye have come into the realization of the Father-Mother."

That disciple said, " Show us the Father-Mother that we may be sufficed."

But He said unto him, " Have I been so long with you, Philip, and yet dost thou not comprehend ? The Father-Mother is not seen, though He dwelleth within me and doeth His work. No one can come unto the vision of Him except through the Only Begotten, who is ever in the bosom of the Father-Mother, and He dwelleth within you.

Henceforth ye shall know Him : and in that day ye shall understand how it is that the Father-Mother is in me and I am in Him."

NOTES.

[7] The Thrones of the Twelve Tribes of Israel represent high states of Soul consciousness. They embody the twelve attributes of Christhood, each Tribe representing very specially one attribute in the power to serve. These are the 144,000 in the Apocalypse.

[1] This passage on the coming of the Son of Man is a very remarkable one. It is remarkable for the description which it gives of the states passed through during the Oblation and the intense loneliness and suffering of the Soul during the passing through. In the use made of it in the first Gospel Record this meaning is lost ; and it is unfortunately so mixed up with Divine Judgments, pre-eminently Jewish in their conception, that this latter idea dominates the passage, whereas originally it contained nothing of a condemnatory character, but purely an indication to the inner group of experiences that would come to them.

But in addition to this meaning which is so obvious, there was likewise one that was more general in its application. Only the inner group disciples were to play a part with the Master in the Oblation; but the larger group, together with many of the Christhood Order who were not then on the outer planes, in a very real sense did minister unto the suffering Divine Love that was so sadly betrayed in the betrayal of the Christ-vision ; for they were the only Souls to regard the true Mystic Life with favour, and seek unto its realization. They ministered unto and sheltered the Christ ideal and love.

[2] The coming night was the betrayal of the Christ-vision with the consequent loss of the Christ-light. The night was dark indeed, as the Master foresaw, and as the development of historical Christianity has testified to.

[3] The dawn is with us. The night is far spent and the darkness passeth away. The glory of the day shall be exceedingly great, even as the darkness of the night hath been. The Oblation hath been fully accomplished, and the end of the Travail has come. It is the hour of the arising for the whole of the Order of the Christhood.

[4] This had special reference to the power within them to recognise the Divine Light when it shone for them. The Sons of the Light learn from no man, but only through the Spirit of the Lord who is in them. They follow no man ; only the Lord of Life and Glory do they follow.

[5] The Saying is finding fulfilment to-day. Israel is being restored. Souls are awakening to the consciousness of their ancient heritage, and are entering in.

[6] " The Greater Works " are those of the Christhood. It is not to be interpreted as having relation to miracles, after the evangelical idea, but rather as appertaining to Manifestation and Revelation. For the Greater Works are not of the nature of the things wrought upon the lower and outer planes, but belong entirely to the spheres where the Divine is in Manifestation. They are of the Soul.

PART VI.

THE GREAT OBLATION

*Containing Logia wherein the nature of the Passover
is revealed, the Anguish of Gethsemane and how
it was brought about, the broken utterances of
the Master in His sorrow and anguish with their
veiled prophetic meanings of all that was
to overtake Him in the lives He would
have to live during the Oblation,
the nature and duration of it, the
pathetic last hours with the
disciples and the prophecy
of the Coming again of
the Christhood in the
Regeneration when
they should
once more
meet*

THE CHRISTHOOD

When they were come to Bethany where Mary had her dwelling, they made unto Him a feast ere He took His journey into Jerusalem.

And the sister of Mary, Martha who loved to serve, was there.

In the House of Mary

And in the preparation of the feast, Martha became too anxious and troubled over many things, whilst Mary sought only to sit at His feet and learn of all that was about to take place.

But Martha, becoming perplexed and cumbered in her service, made request that Mary should serve with her, and said unto the Master : " Carest thou not that my sister hath left me to perform this service alone ? Bid her serve with me."

But He said unto her : " Martha, why art thou perplexed and troubled about many things in thy service ? Only one thing is needful. And Mary hath chosen a good service which shall not be taken away from her."[1]

The Anointing by Mary

And during the feast, Mary, perceiving the meaning of what was about to be accomplished in the passing away of the Master from the Christhood, and how necessary it was for the future of the world that the Passion of the Lord should be borne on behalf of all Souls, took down an alabaster cruse filled with most precious ointment and poured out the costly unguent upon Him.

She anointed His head with it, and then His feet , for she perceived the nature of the work to be accom plished as He bore the burden of the Lord's Passover.

And she wiped His feet with her hair and kissed them in token of her great love, and as a testimony to the understanding by her of the sacred mission appointed unto Him.[2] *And the fragrance of the precious unguent filled the room.*

There were present some who could not understand what she had done, and these questioned amongst them selves as to the wisdom of it, and thought it to be a great waste of the precious spikenard.

And these would fain have restrained her.[3]

NOTES.

[1] The Logia spoken at Bethany contain great depths of meaning. The incidents which called them forth were spiritual allegories concerning the way of the Soul. Bethany was the House of ripe Figs, and therefore the House of Divine Wisdom. It was in Bethany that the Lord loved to dwell, or make His home ; and it was there that Maria and her sister Martha dwelt.

It was thus in Bethany that the Feast was prepared for Christ and His disciples, and that Maria and Martha were present, for the Supper of the Lord is there provided and partaken of : it is the communion of the Christ state. At the Feast, Maria sat at the feet of her Lord ; but Martha was full of activity in her service. At the feet of the Lord alone is the Divine Wisdom learnt by the Soul; and to sit there with great desire to understand the Divine Will expressed through the Divine Love and Wisdom, is the supreme thing which will never be taken away : the service of Martha was beautiful, for it also was of the Christhood ; but it was the inner service broken upon the plane of the mind, and it is in such a service that the Soul, even at Bethany, is apt to forget itself.

Maria and Martha thus represent the two modes of the same Soul in its service to its Lord.

[2] The Anointing by Maria is even more profound. It also was at Bethany : it could not have taken place elsewhere. Only in Christhood could such a vision have come to Maria as to the true meaning of the Oblation, and only in such a consciousness could any Soul pour out of its being the love that is represented by the costly spikenard.

It was a symbolical act, absolutely spiritual in its nature, though it had its correspondence on the outer plane. There was a Maria, a Soul who greatly loved the message and work of the Master, who did accomplish such an anointing. The personal work, however, was only meant symbolically ; for that which the hand did with the precious unguent, the heart did with its store of love. What lay behind it was a mystery which even some who beheld the outer act failed to apprehend.

[3] Could there have been anything more tragic in such an hour than the misinterpretation of such a love? And that it should be the result of misapprehension on the part of some who had reached the Bethany in their experience ? Yet it has had its reflection even in these days of the return. It cast a long shadow before it, and only now can that shadow be put away.

211

THE CHRISTHOOD

Then the Master, perceiving their opposition to Mary, said unto them ·

Mary's Good Work

"Why trouble ye that Mary hath wrought this work upon me?[1]

Perceive ye not yet the meaning of the things which I have spoken unto you concerning the coming Passover, how expedient it is that I go away, and that the Passion of the Lord be borne by me?[2]

Mary hath wrought upon me a good work, for she hath anointed me unto my burial throughout the days of the Passover; herein hath she revealed her love, and made manifest her depth of understanding of the work to be accomplished through me.[3]

The hour is come when I must be offered up that the name of the Father-Mother may be glorified.

Now is my Soul sorely vexed, and fain would I pray unto the Father-Mother that He would save me from the coming hour: yet for this end came I unto this hour.

O my Father-Mother, may Thy name be glorified by me, and through the work which Thou hast appointed unto me to do."[4]

Then did a voice speak through Him, saying: "I have glorified My name, and I will glorify it again."

And those present at the feast heard the voice, and its sound was as that of an angel.

Yet once more it spake through Him, saying: "If My name be lifted up out of the earth, I will draw all Souls unto Myself.

Now cometh the hour in which judgment shall be made manifest, and the prince of the powers of the air be thrown down."[5]

The Gethsemane

Then cometh He into the state of the Gethsemane— the garden of sorrow which lay at the foot of the Mount of Olives.

And there He sought to be alone, for the sorrow upon Him was great.

212

NOTES.

[1] The Master was deeply moved that any such service rendered unto the work which He had come to accomplish should have been misinterpreted, and blame attached to the beautiful Soul who wrought the work of love—nothing gave Him greater grief than misjudgment on the part of those who were so near to Him, and so greatly thought for and loved.

[2] Herein is evidence that He attached very deep importance to the discovery made by Maria regarding the nature and work of the Oblation. Some of the group had failed to grasp its full meaning. Though He had uttered strange Sayings about its nature and significance for the world, the hour had not come in which He could speak in terms quite unveiled. But it was at hand. Yet only those of the very innermost circle were able at the time to apprehend its awful and sorrowful nature, and what He meant by it being expedient that He should go the way of the Oblation.

[3] There are meanings in the anointing which are beyond any form of translation. What Maria perceived could not be more beautifully expressed than in her gracious act. It was the expression of a profound love, though it was unspeakably sad in its meaning, for it recognised the long separation during the ages of the three Naronic Cycles, the deep descent of the Master from the Christhood state, with the consequent sorrow and anguish. He was consecrated in all the powers of His thought and service to the accomplishment of the Divine Will, however great the burden of the Cross might be, and Maria revealed her perception of this when she anointed His head and then His feet.

[4] Though the willinghood of the Master was perfect in that He had no will but that of the Divine One who was with Him, and longed to bear the Cross appointed unto Him, yet the nature of the burden filled Him with grave misgivings at times lest He should fail in the way and become utterly lost, and that the Divine Name and Glory should suffer. As the hour drew near in which He was to enter into the consciousness of the burden, He became more and more deeply troubled.

[5] To the rationalistic mind such a thing will seem impossible. To the superstitious it will not prove unacceptable, though it will gather around it the air of inexplicable mystery. To the lover of spiritual phenomena it may have the appearance of a form of higher obsession. Yet none of these could account for it. When a Soul is in high Christhood the Divine Presence is always within the Sanctuary, and at times thus speaks from within the Temple. There are those now upon this Earth who have heard once more that Voice.

O—I

THE CHRISTHOOD

The Geth semane

But there were those of the disciples who went with Him into the Garden ; and of these were Peter, James and John.[1]

These beheld how great the sorrow was that sat upon Him, and would fain have comforted Him.

It became as night when the heavens are darkest, for His Light was veiled within Him.[2]

And He said unto those who were with Him : "Watch with me, for my Soul is exceeding sorrowful, even unto death."[3]

And it came to pass that as He prayed He agonised and uttered strange cries unto the Father-Mother, and was distraught as one greatly bereaved.[4]

Upon His face there sat the look of dread as if some awful horror had come upon Him.[5]

He wept tears wrung from His very Soul by the fearful visions He beheld.

The Soul's Anguish

In His anguish, in tears and groanings, He cried unto Him who was able to keep Him from falling, that the burden might pass from Him.

And thus did He cry in His anguish :—

"Oh my Father-Mother in the Heavens, if it be possible to accomplish Thy Holy Will without the drinking of this cup by me, may it be done ; but if not without my drinking of this cup, Thy Holy Will be done by me."

And He yet agonised more and more, and cried unto the Father-Mother to deliver Him in His sorrow, and to sustain Him in His work ; for He feared lest, in the accomplishment of that work, He Himself should become even as the castaway.

Now when His anguish was passed away, He was ministered unto by Angels ; and these accompanied Him unto the hour of His Passover when He entered upon the work of Ransoming which the Father-Mother had given Him to do.

214

NOTES.

[1] The Garden of the Gethsemane was a Soul state. It was the Garden of Sorrow, and it lay at the foot of, or beneath, the Mount of Olives. This latter lay over against Bethany. From the House of the Christhood to the Mount of Olives or state in which the past and the future alike open out to the vision, was only a brief journey. It was from the Mount of Olives that it is said the Master beheld the City of Jerusalem and wept over it; for Jerusalem was the Planet with all the burden of the awful history through which it had passed; and it was upon Mount Olivet His feet were to stand in the day of the return, for in that day the vision would be restored.

Now, the Garden of Gethsemane was at the foot of the Mount, for the vision which came to the Master there filled Him with the most intense sorrow and anguish. The vision oppressed His Soul so greatly that He sought to be alone. Even the companionship of those who were nearest to Him was more than He could bear. But it is said that three of His intimate friends went into the Garden with Him, and that these were Peter, James and John. In this statement there is a symbolical meaning, for these three represented the innermost attributes of Christhood. And these attributes were also the three Divine Principles within the Soul, for they were typical of the Light, the Life, and the Love of the Eternal One. And in a very special manner the Love-principle, the Life-principle, and the Light-principle, suffered through the bearing of the burden fore-shadowed in the sorrow and anguish of the Gethsemane.

[2] It was the veiling of the Divine Light within Him. In state He had to descend to the plane where what was about to come to Him could be seen. The light within Him could not manifest upon that plane, and hence the darkness within the Heavens of His own being.

[3] Spiritual death is occasioned through the loss of the Light of the indwelling Spirit, and as He descended He felt this loss coming upon Him. It is utterly impossible to convey to the reader what the Master felt in that hour. He could not bear to be spoken to or have His awful sorrow intruded upon; and yet so utterly alone did He feel as He sensed the depths into which He would, by and bye, have to descend, that He wanted His dearest ones to be near at hand.

[4] Some of these most strange utterances will be found in the pages that follow.

[5] It was caused by some of the visions which He beheld.

THE CHRISTHOOD

Whilst the anguish of the Gethsemane Vision was upon Him, the Master spake many things whose meanings were veiled to those who overheard them. He prayed as one would who was undergoing terrible privation, suffering and wrong at the hands of unseen enemies. For in His anguish He spake these words :—

" O my Father-Mother, forgive them : they know not what they do." [1]

" Of me shall it be said,—He saved others ; Himself He cannot save."
" Let Him cry unto the God in whom He trusts, and see whether He will deliver Him out of our hands." [2]

" Maria ! Behold Thy Son ! "
In answer to this cry, a voice spake within Him and through Him, saying,
" My Son, behold Thy Maria." [3]

" I thirst. My whole being is languishing ; and they only give me gall to drink." [4]

" Eli ! Eli ! Lama Sa Bach Thani." [5]

" It is Finished : I am now alone.
Yet am I not alone ; for He who hath sent me, the same said unto me, Lo ! I am with thee, even unto the end of the æon of the consummation, and unto the æons upon æons." [6]

" O my Father-Mother, into Thy hands I resign my spirit." [7]
And when He had so spoken, He yielded up the Presence of the Holy Ghost who had been with Him from the beginning.

NOTES.

[1] In the vision the Master beheld those who had come to betray the Christ-vision, misrepresenting it. It was shown to Him what would befall the Christhood vision and all the Teachings associated with it. And it was what He saw issuing from that fearful betrayal that led Him to pray that they might find healing.

[2] This was literally true during His Crucifixion throughout the days of the Oblation. It was so spoken concerning Him. Whilst His burden-bearing was for the salvation of others, He could not save Himself from the effects of the burden.

[3] The effects upon Him of such a terrible betrayal of all that He held so sacred, His own crucifixion before the world at the hands of the betrayers, and what was more to Him, the crucifixion of the glorious Christhood were such that He languished and was as one distraught. The burden was so heavy upon Him that He was moved to the depths of His being; and there stole upon Him a strange fearfulness. Hence His cry to Maria. For was not Maria the Divine Soul from whom had been born into manifestation the glorious Christhood? He was addressing the one who was within Him.

The answer may appear strange to any one who cannot understand such a Christhood; and unto such no explanation would suffice. But the initiated will understand; for they will know that the Soul may be addressed directly from the Divine Realm and that the Voice may speak through her. In Christhood she is one with Maria.

[4] The thirst was of the Soul. It is quite inconceivable unless one has gone through a like experience in some degree. He was sensing acutely the awful spiritual conditions amid which He would have to bear the burden of the Oblation.

The gall given Him to drink was the Wine of Christhood changed and mingled with the vinegar of perverted truth. It was gall to His Soul.

[5] Occasioned through the withdrawal of the Angel of His Presence, and the passing of His inward Light.

"My Lord! My Lord! Thy Light is extinguished within my Spirit: it is death to me."

[6] The Gethsemane Vision had ended. At first He felt as if utterly alone, so intense were the experiences through which He had passed. Then He knew He was not alone, but still guarded and guided from Him who had sent Him to accomplish His will.

[7] To yield up the Holy Ghost was not to pass away, as it is stated in the records; for He was with the friends for some time after this event. It was His perfect resignation in yielding up the consciousness of the Holy One who overshadowed Him.

THE CHRISTHOOD

Fragments from the Soul's Garden of Sorrow

"*O my Father-Mother, my Soul is overwhelmed within me. My whole being languisheth for Thee. I am burdened with sorrow because of the path which I must take.*

Send unto me the succour which I need in this hour.

My heart is heavy within me ; it is full of pain. My mind also is filled with the terror which flieth at noon-day, and through the fear of the going down of my Sun ; the anguish of the reproach that will be mine is now upon me.

And none can help me : only Thou Thyself canst take away the terror and remove the burden; but it is my portion now to bear these with Thee.

O my Father-Mother, my Soul is even as a cup which is full to overflowing, so full am I with grief that the path which I must tread in bearing this burden, will take me away from Thee. So dark and deep is the way that I am filled with dread lest no more shall I be able to come unto Thee.

Do Thou Thyself cause me to be enfolded in Thy Love, and upheld by the strength of its bonds.

When my Being languisheth amid the wilderness for the Streams of Life, wilt Thou have regard unto my prayer ?

When my Soul anguisheth amid the hells where Thou mayest not be known, will Thy Spirit find me there and comfort me ?

When my Spirit yearns to come unto Thee that my life may be healed of its afflictions and sorrows, wilt Thou give unto me indeed from Thy Mercy and Goodness that my Soul may be made whole ?

When the darkness has overtaken me so that my path is unseen, and I am as one who is a wanderer and a fugitive from Thee, will Thy Holy Spirit shine within me again that I may behold the way wherein to walk ?

NOTES.

The Gethsemane in all its tragic reality cannot be portrayed. It is impossible to do more than indicate some of the experiences passed through. These are implied in the broken fragments of His Soul's yearnings and dread in the days of extreme sorrow and anguish.

The Gethsemane covered a considerable period; not a few brief hours, but many months. It broke upon the vision of the Master long after the crucifixion by the Roman powers, and was the beginning of the crucifixion of the Christ within Him. The chief parts of the more profound Logia were given after the Gethsemane. Many of the Sayings could not have been spoken prior to the passing through of the Master represented by the Gethsemane; for these were related to the various states into which He had to enter during the days of the Oblation, and the work to be accomplished by means of them.

The Master has been often referred to as the Man of Sorrows. But in His Christhood there was ever present to Him the Divine Joy. He shared that state with all the other most blessed experiences associated with such a Christhood. The state of the Man of Sorrows came later in His ministry, and its approach was with the Gethsemane. And when that hour came, His sorrow was so great that no measure of human sorrow could express it; it could not be gauged. The Gethsemane brought unto Him such sorrow that it seemed as if it could never be healed. Yet it was only the beginning of His work as the Man of Sorrows. For in every life through which He passed carrying His burden of the Oblation as a Sin-offering, He also passed through the conditions of the Man of Sorrows. None knew Him in those lives, not even His own most intimate ones; and His strange sorrow was beyond the understanding of all who beheld it.

Nor was the Gethsemane confined to the days of the Manifestation. It had its repetition in every one of the lives of the Oblation, in that, whensoever the hour of the Soul's awakening came, and its consequent arising out of the low state into which it had to descend to perform the work of purification upon the Astral realms, the most awful anguish broke over it, and its sorrow became overwhelmingly great. So in every life there was a very real Gethsemane, though no vision of the future was permitted as in the Gethsemane of the Manifestation. And in the last life of the Oblation, Gethsemane culminated; for not only had the Master to again endure the burden of sorrow and anguish caused in the awakening and arising, but the full burden of all the Gethsemanes had to be borne as the whole of the past was recovered and retrodden.

Now, the real cause of the Gethsemane during the days of the Manifestation was the opening out to Him, in panoramic pictures, of the nature of the work that lay ahead of Him. That work was to

THE CHRISTHOOD

Fragments from the Soul's Garden of Sorrow

When my Heart is torn with anguish, my Mind rent in twain, and my flesh crieth out unto Thee for such healing as no man giveth ; surely then shall the path be made plain unto me, that the Love with which Thou dost ever love me shall not leave me to perish where the awful darkness reigns ; for Thy Love will find me even amid the darkness, and will bear me back into Thy Light.

In the days of my sorrow when I make request unto Thee that Thou wouldest heal me of my pain which those have given unto me who were even as my brethren ; then may Thy great Love minister unto me of its healing balm, to make whole the bonds which the enemy hath broken !

In the day of dire anguish when my Soul is torn asunder, and languisheth for a pity none giveth unto me because no man regardeth my crying ; then let Thy Pity heal my anguish, and Thy Compassion my wounded life.

In the day of my awful going away into the land of sorrow, and my passing hence to be no more as Thy child full of Thine own Life and Love ; then let Thy Heavens encompass me, that my feet fail not to keep the way which my Soul must take.

In the day of my transgression against Thy pure and Holy Love, when my way takes me through the valleys and pits of impurity, and my whole being seemeth turned away from Thee ; then may Thy Love find me to bear me home again !

In the day of my setting out from Thee to pass through the land of the fallen, and to see only the loss to my life of its purity before Thee ; then may Thy Holy Spirit again find me amid the Valley of the Slain, and raise me up upon my feet, and lift me unto the Mount of God, and kindle within me Thine own pure Light.

NOTES.

be accomplished in a series of lives with vehicles so constituted magnetically that they would attract to them the fearful evil images which had been fashioned upon the Astral realms of the Planet during the long ages in which the human race had descended beneath the Human Kingdom. The images were magnetic and composed of elements of the Planet, so that they were fluidic. They were of a most evil order, and they influenced the Planet's human children to repeat in their bodies the wickedness out from which they had been originally generated. Whilst these evil images persisted there could be no redemption accomplished for the Human Race. So greatly did they militate against the Soul that few Souls ever rose above their dominion ; and those who were for a time able to do so, were mostly drawn down again and laid low by these images.

The work to be accomplished by the Sin-offering was the blotting out of these. And it was to be wrought by a process of magnetic attraction, absorption and transmutation in the various lives which He would have to live. In the Gethsemane these lives arose before Him one by one. He beheld and He sensed the nature of the life in the case of each which He would be compelled to live for some years. He beheld the awful forms upon the Astral realms, and sensed their conditions with unspeakable horrór. He passed into the consciousness of all that awaited Him when He descended from the Christhood estate, and so terrible were the conditions that, notwithstanding His great love for Souls and the perfect surrender of Himself for the service of the Divine Love and Wisdom, He would fain have drawn back. It was not the heaviness of the Cross He would have to bear, but the awful nature of the states He would have to carry upon Him. It was His delight to yield up all in the doing of the Divine Will ; but to descend into states of hell of the lowest order, to become as one in the outer darkness, to know in His Soul the spiritual state of the magdalene, to drink of the cup of iniquity in its most awful forms—these were the things He shrank from. His pure and beautiful Soul recoiled from the vision. The experience that accompanies anticipation is often more intense than that passed through when the event is met and entered into. But that could not be said of this burden. No imaginings could possibly exceed the reality. And He knew it. Is it any wonder that He inquired whether it were not possible to let the cup of such anguish pass from Him ? Whether it could not be possible to find some other means by which to accomplish the Divine purpose ?

There has been a great silence over the Gethsemane, which is eloquent. But little connected with it was recorded, for it could not be told ; and what was given was soon veiled. Without understanding it in the slightest degree, the Church has believed it took

THE CHRISTHOOD

In the day of my deepest woe that I have become even as the fallen, with my garments all blood-stained in the warfare with sin ; then let Thy Holy, Holy, Holy Love and Light shield and enlighten me.

When my heart fainteth within me, and my flesh faileth me in the day of trial ; wilt Thou send me succour from Thy Sanctuary that my faith fail not ?

When my Soul is cast down within me by those who will reproach and condemn me because of the way that my Angel leadeth me in service unto Thee ; may Thy Grace be unto me my meat and Thy Love my drink.

When my love would fain wax cold, and my light burns only like some dim star in a darkened sky, because of the oppression wherewith my Soul hath been oppressed ; may Thy Great Love be unto me even as a garment which shieldeth from the cold, and a light which burneth brightly.

When my love unto Thee seemeth to die amid the awful darkness where abideth no love like Thine, because such darkness desireth only those things which Thy Love knoweth not ; may Thy Purity become again known unto me, that Thy beautiful Love may be restored unto my Soul.

When my love hath again been purified from the slain put upon it through languishing amid the hells ; may Thy Grace be unto me my meat in season, that my Soul may again rejoice in Thee.

When my whole Being crieth out unto Thee amid the sinful wilderness wherein is no refreshing for my life, or strength for my days ; then be Thou unto me both refreshment and strength, that my burden may be borne even when it seemeth too great for me.

When the burden of the Cross unto which Thou hast called me seemeth to be greater than that which one beareth alone, and its pain maketh my whole being cry out against its load ; then do Thou Thyself enfold me, lest in the path my life be crushed utterly beneath its load.

When my Soul overfloweth in its anguish before Thee, O my Father-Mother, and my way is that of

Fragments from the Soul's Garden of Sorrow

NOTES.

place. It has accepted the fact of a deep mysterious anguish breaking over Him, but related it to the dread of the outward crucifixion. It knows there was the experience of dire extremity, but what was the cause of it is beyond its ken. Little has it dreamed that whilst it spread out its wares that others might trade with it, the Gethsemane was being repeated ; and that throughout all the ages of the Era during which it has sought kingdoms and dominions, the mysterious sorrow has been heavy within the Soul of the Master. In its high Mass, its Holy Eucharist, its Supper of the Lord, its inner Communion, it has professed to apprehend the mind of the Master at that time ; but it has shown by the utter failure of its manifold sacramentarianism that its interpretation of the Gethsemane is completely at fault, and that the spiritual darkness in which the Church was founded, continues with it until this day. It has no true understanding of the nature of the Gethsemane; and the Oblation which it professes to believe in, remains unto it a spiritual problem whose solution it cannot find. So the silence in which the Gethsemane has been shrouded throughout the ages, has its reflection in the silence within the Church as to its true mystic meaning. The day, however, is hastening when that silence will be broken, in the full interpretation being given through those whose understanding has been and is illumined. There has been darkness over the earth from the sixth to the ninth hour ; but the ninth hour is also past and the tenth has chimed upon the world. The Christhood rises out of the desolation wrought upon Calvary. The Golgotha is fully accomplished, and they are set free. And these Souls will re-interpret for the Church and the world the meaning of Gethsemane. Nay, the great silence has been broken through Him who went down into the unspeakable sorrow ; for the passing through of the accumulated Gethsemanes of all the lives of the Oblation, has also been accomplished.

The broken utterances of the Master in the Gethsemane are only detached fragments. They were spoken by Him in hours of great sorrow. His mind often became distraught and filled with a sense of great dread. The prospect before Him was overwhelmingly sad. Something lay ahead of Him which filled Him with a horror He could not shake off. And in the fragments this may be discerned. There is reference to it many times under different conditions. The recurrence of this thought makes the Sayings of extreme sorrow and anguish appear to overlap one another. The experience most obviously feared was the ultimate loss to Himself of the Divine Spirit, through the descent into depths so terrible as those foreseen by Him. He feared lest He should become a Castaway—utterly lost. And what this must have meant to Him none could imagine unless they had tasted of the glory of God in Christhood. The cup

223

THE CHRISTHOOD

deep darkness where Thy Vision is not beheld because of its awful Purity; wilt Thou sustain me in Thy tenderness and lead me by Thy Love?

Fragments from the Soul's Garden of Sorrow

When my Heart overfloweth in its sorrow because of what has befallen me through going down into the darkness that taketh me away from Thee, and my prayers and tears are before Thee as offerings of my great grief; then let Thy tenderness and Love minister unto me, that my sorrow may be healed.

When I am full of grief at the thought of my betrayal of Thy Holiness, and I make my prayer unto Thee for that healing which Thy Love alone can give unto the Soul when evil hath made its garments even as the darkness; then let Thy Purity find me again, and do Thou restore me unto the Ancient Estate.

When I am full of terrible pain, and my life is shadowed by evil so that my way is no more that of those who have thought of me as their brother; wilt Thou let Thy great Love be unto me even as a shield in the day when the arrow flieth, to protect my love for them from being hurt or slain?

When my Heart is torn with the anguish born out of their loss unto me, and my faith in Thy Goodness and Love is broken by all that has happened to me; then let Thy Love in its tenderness flow into my Heart again to blot out the memory of mine anguish, and to heal all my unspeakable pain.

When my Being is riven in the agony of my sorrow through the loss of Thy Vision so pure, and my nights give place to weeping and my days to anguish and fear, because Thy Vision no more may I behold until that day when the Children of the Kingdom shall all see it too; then let the Heavens themselves sphere me, and Thy beautiful Love enfold me, to heal me with the healing which proceedeth alone from Thee.

O my Father-Mother in the Heavens, thus do Thou lean down to mine estate, though so lowly and sorrowful, and draw me up to Thyself again to dwell with Thee."

NOTES.

of which He had to drink, and the baptism with which He had to be baptized, were of an order which no man of himself could understand.

Is there any more any wonder that He agonized amid His sorrow and appeared to recoil before the vision that broke upon Him ? Can it yet appear strange that He who was in Christhood should shrink from the burden of the Cross laid upon Him, and even pray that it might be taken away ? Do any still marvel that He could anguish so greatly ? Let such understand the Gethsemane, taste the contents of His bitter cup, know the consuming fires with which He was baptized, enter from the full glory of spiritual day when the Eternal Light shines within the Soul, into the most intense Soul darkness where the realization of the Divine is impossible, descend from the blessedness of the innermost Heavens into the horrors of the deepest hells, then they too will know something of His sorrow and anguish.

O Gethsemane ! Gethsemane ! Who is able to fathom all the meaning which thou dost express ? Who has ever known thy secret, the deep mystery of the travail that came with thee to the Soul ? Who could penetrate the vail that unshrouded all thy story of the deep anguish and sore travail of Him who bore the burden of the Cross ?

It was said that angels desired to look into thy mystery, to witness the process by which the Divine Love and Wisdom accomplished the Great Work through the Soul and the lives of the Master. Many are they who have stood outside thy gates and wondered what the mysterious sorrow could mean that was pouring itself forth within thee. Many have approached thee with bated breath, full of great sympathy and tender love for the One who was sorrowing so, mysteriously, and have tried to hear that sorrow, or even the echo of it, and to catch something of its real meaning and purpose.

But none have known : for thy gates have been closed all through the ages that have passed since the days of the Manifestation until now. None have witnessed the burdened anguish of the Soul, except the three who were permitted to enter the Garden with Him ; and even these slept so long that they also missed the mystery expressed in the sore travail.

May the mystery of this sorrow draw all who can approach such a Garden with reverent steps and feelings and desires to behold anew the exceeding graciousness of that Love who called all Souls into Being, even the Love of the Father-Mother. And may all who so draw near, lift up the heart in true Praise unto that Most Blessed and Eternal One who hath wrought such marvellous things for His children to make them glad, beautiful and glorious in all their ways.

And let the whole Earth Bless His Holy Name !

THE CHRISTHOOD

The Burden of the Ransom

Now, when the days of the Gethsemane had been accomplished, and He found Himself equal to conversing again with the disciples who formed the inner group, He spake unto them many things concerning His coming Passover and all that it would mean for the world, for them, and for Himself.

" Unto this end came I into this world that I might lay down my life.[1]

I lay it down on behalf of the sheep of the Fold of God.[2]

No one taketh it from me. Of myself lay I it down, for the Father-Mother hath given me power to lay it down, and power to take it up again.[3]

And though the Temple which has been built up, be pulled down and destroyed through my going, yet after three days it shall be restored again.[4]

For the Son of Man goeth, as it was written of Him ; but woe unto the one through whom He goeth.[5]

For the Son of Man goeth down into the city of Jerusalem to suffer many things at the hands of sinful men and women ; for these will betray Him.

And the chief priests, scribes and elders will crucify Him, and put Him to death.[6]

And in those days shall he, through whom the Son of Man goeth, feel that it had been better not to have been born than to have to bear the burden of the going away of the Son of Man.[7]

For, were it not that the Son of Man must needs go down even unto the land of the Samaritans and the country of the Gadarenes, that He may know of those things whose existence is there, verily, He would not have imposed such shame and degradation, anguish and woe, upon that one.[8]

But unto whom it is given to bear the burden of the Ransom, shall much be given when the Redemption is accomplished ; for unto whom much is given to bear in the day of the travail of the Son of Man, shall there be given of the Love and Glory of the Father-Mother in the days of the Regeneration.[9]

226

NOTES.

[1] There never was any uncertainty in the mind of the Master as to the twofold purpose of His mission, that of the Manifestation of Christhood followed by the Redemption as the result of the Oblation. He came into this world or order of things for that sublime and supreme end. The Kingdom out from which He came was not of the nature of the kingdoms of this world. He knew it well, and He was aware of all that it would cost Him. He came to lay down His life, to lay aside the Glory of the Kingdom of the Father-Mother, to sacrifice all that He most valued in order to accomplish the will of the Father-Mother.

[2] The Christhood Order : they had to come first in the Redemption, and through them the whole world. They had been designated the Sheep of the Fold of God, because they had once had the inward knowledge and realization of Him.

[3] All service on and from the Divine Kingdom is voluntary. It is also true to say that it is appointed. Each one is chosen for the office that is to be filled, and each one knows interiorly when and how that work is to be accomplished.

[4] The Temple of the Christhood which had been reared. He had foreseen what would be done unto it. He beheld it, in vision, being destroyed ; then He beheld it being restored.

[5] The vehicle had to carry a heavy burden of woe.

[6] Not simply those of Jewry. They accomplished the crucifixion of the Master ; but the Son of Man (Adonai and the blessed Manifestation of Christhood), the priests and schools of the hierarchies in all the ages of this Era have betrayed and crucified. They have indeed done the Christhood to death. In robes which are a mockery of Christhood, they have arrayed Him.

[7] Just what that one did feel. Every life of the Master was of a like order as regards the consciousness of woe ; in the last life in which the burden was borne it was appalling.

[8] This is an indication of some of the states into which He would have to enter. What they were will be explained elsewhere.

[9] Here the reference is not to the Master so much as to those few who were called upon in each of the lives to share the conditions.

THE CHRISTHOOD

In His going down into the city, the Son of Man shall also suffer much from the rulers of this world.[1]

He shall be rejected and despised of men, even of the priests and scribes and all who have been taught to follow them.

These will fail to behold Him as the Son of God, the true witness of the Highest, the Testimony of the Lord, the Manifestation of the Father-Mother.[2]

Even unto His own shall He come, and they shall not receive Him; for their eyes will be holden because of the power which this world's rulers have had upon them.[3]

But the Son of Man came into this world, not to be ministered unto, but to minister in the giving of Himself to ransom many; for in the ransoming of this world it must needs be that He goeth that way.

The hour cometh when the Son of Man shall go hence, and I shall be no more with the Father-Mother.[4]

Then shall it come to pass that He whom the Father-Mother loveth shall be led of His Holy Spirit to go into the wilderness of Judah to be there tempted of the wild beasts whose habitations are there.[5]

He must needs go down to endure many things at the hands of the Tempter; for the Prince of this World, who found nothing in Him to tempt, is coming, and he shall cause Him to be buffeted when He maketh of Himself an offering for sin.[6]

Beloved, the going of the Son of Man and the coming of the days in which He whom the Father-Mother loveth shall be no more with Him, is that the Prince of this world may be cast out from his dominion in the high places where his seat is, and all his works overthrown; for the principalities and powers of the mighty ones in the high places must be overthrown and themselves cast down.[7]

Then shall the Souls who have been kept in low degree and shut out from the Kingdom of the Heavens, be exalted; for when He shall have made of Himself an offering for Sin, the powers of wickedness in the high places will be broken.

NOTES.

[1] This will be obvious to all who understand the inner meaning of this sublime expression. Pilate has followed the judgment of Caiaphas through all the ages. Nominally the rulers of the world are Christians, in practice they are crucifiers of the Christhood. At the hands of these persons the Master Himself suffered much during the lives of the Oblation ; but what was most tragic were the things done to the Name of the Most High and His Christ.

[2] Where is the true vision of Christhood to be found ? Not in the Schools where the vision is academic and personal ; not within the hierarchies where it is presented arrayed in garments foreign to its nature. They accept the vision of the personal Master, such as has come to them through the records, and confound that vision with that of the impersonal Son of God. The real Christ vision they reject, though it is the living testimony of the indwelling Lord.

[3] This has been sadly true throughout the era ; and it is true of many to-day, though more and more of those here spoken of are coming to recognise the true meaning of life and enter into the Christhood state, thus receiving Him who is Christ in us.

[4] Herein is the great tragedy clearly indicated. The Son of Man —the Blessed Adonai who overshadowed the Master—was to go hence. He was to ascend. The Master was to be, as it were, left. The direct overshadowing was to cease for a time, for the Oblation could not be performed with such a consciousness as that overshadowing gave to Him. Through the withdrawal of it He would be no more with the Father-Mother. This does not mean that He would be left absolutely alone. Had it been so, He could not have borne the burden of the Oblation. There was a very special provision made for Him, so that the states could be entered whilst He was sphered and controlled from the Divine World.

[5] The wilderness of Judah was in a very special sense the Astral realm. The wild beasts were the magnetic images to destroy which the Oblation had to be borne.

[6] He offered Himself as the vehicle of the Divine ministry to be buffeted or affected by these images, that in the process they might be destroyed.

[7] Here there is reference to other powers also, powers whose dominion was the outcome of pure occultism changed into black magic.

P—I

229

THE CHRISTHOOD

And in those days when He shall be led of the Spirit to go into the wilderness of Judah there to be tried by the devil :[1]

The Temptations in the Wilderness

For forty days shall He be with the wild beasts ; and He shall subdue and overcome them.[2]

And throughout those days shall He fast and become as one who is an hungered ; for there He shall not have wherewith to satisfy His hunger for the Bread of Life which is now His portion.[3]

And when He hungers, the tempter will try Him · 'If Thou be a Son of the Gods, speak the word of command to the stones in this wilderness that they become bread.'

But He must needs answer :—'The Bread by which alone one can live is the Word of God ; and that proceedeth from the Father-Mother.'

And the tempter will also take Him unto the Pinnacle of the Temple of God to try Him.[4] *Unto Him shall he speak the words: 'If Thou art a Son of the Gods, cast Thyself down unto the Earth ; for hath it not been written concerning Thee that His Angels shall bear Thee up lest Thou dash Thyself upon the Earth ?'*

But unto the tempter shall He reply : 'Is it not evil to so think of the ministry of the Heavens vouchsafed from the Lord ? And hath it not been said, Thou shalt not tempt the Lord Thy God ?'

Then shall the devil likewise take Him unto an exceeding high mountain of the Earth, and from it show Him all its kingdoms and the glory of them, and tempt Him to worship these.[5] *And the tempter shall say unto Him: 'All these kingdoms and the glory of them shall I give Thee for a possession, if only Thou wilt fall down and worship me.'*

But He will put the temptation away from Him, and will say unto the tempter : 'Get thee hence, Satan ; thou savourest not the things that be of God, but regardest only the things that be of men. Is it not also written of man, Thou must worship only the Lord thy God, and Him only must thou serve ?'

And when the forty days have been accomplished, the tempter will leave Him ; and the Angels of God shall minister unto Him."

NOTES.

[1] The story of the Temptations was a parable. Its meaning was infinitely deeper than any mere narrative of outward events could convey. It was not anything incidental to the life of the Manifestation, but covered the whole ground of the Oblation. If the Western World had understood such a Christhood as that of the Manifestation, it would also have known how utterly impossible it was for one in such a state to be tempted and tried as man is. To feel temptation there must be something in the individual that responds in some measure, otherwise there is no temptation. As there was nothing in the Master to respond to any form of evil, it must be obvious that He could not thus be tempted. Yet the temptations amid the wild beasts in the wilderness were most real, as He came to know to His unspeakable sorrow in the days of the Oblation.

[2] The forty days or periods were forty lives. In each life He had to contend with these evil forms and powers, and blot out the portion assigned to that life. In this way He overcame them.

[3] This was no mere physical hunger, but Soul yearning. He was no stranger to outward impoverishment, for He passed through great tribulation in that respect. But it was spiritual hunger that filled Him with great desire to turn the stones of the wilderness into bread : for what were the stones but the truths which had been degraded until all their spiritual power was gone, and they had become religious fossils, the petrified remnants of things that once were full of life ? These are the stones He was tempted to turn into spiritual bread, to become satisfied with the conditions as they were.

[4] The Pinnacle of the Temple represented a high spiritual state. It was really a temptation to descend in state, not only for actual ministry to the world, but in desire ; to presume upon the Divine protection afforded Him. And this temptation did come to Him more than once. The tempter was most subtle and the temptation very fascinating and alluring. It came to Him in the midst of extreme weakness, when He was overwrought with the carrying of His all-too heavy burden.

[5] The High Mountain from which the kingdoms of the world were viewed was none other than the Papal See ; for that has not only sought world dominion, but has laid claim to it as a right. The Master passed that way also, being tempted to give up His very Soul to that power. In one life He was offered the Pontificate.

THE CHRISTHOOD

An Echo of the Sin-offering

On one occasion when the Master had been speaking unto the inner group concerning the burden of the Passover, which in His redemptive mission He would have to bear, one who loved Him greatly and who was fearful for Him in the laying down of His Christhood, said unto Him:[1]

'Go not down into Jerusalem, for Herod will seek to destroy Thee.'[2]

But He said: 'Nay, I must go hence. Though Herod have the cunning of the fox, yet shall I be able to accomplish the work which the Father-Mother hath given me to do.

I shall be able to work to-day, the morrow, and the day that will follow, casting out the devils and changing the causes of many sicknesses, overthrowing the works of Herod and those who be of him in high places.[3]

Then will the work of God in Jerusalem be perfected through His prophets.'[4]

The Great Lament

"O Jerusalem! Jerusalem![5] thou that killest the prophets sent unto thee! How often would He from whom they came forth have gathered thy children together for thee! But thou wouldst not.

And thou wert left without one spiritual guide, because they had all been betrayed to death within thee. For he whom thou didst listen to, whose message brought ruin unto thy beautiful house, destroyed thy children within thee.[6]

Nay, he assumed to be thy lord, and even reigned over all thy beautiful terraces, and made them such as he desired.

Yea, he became thy king, and his power is still over thee;

For he had taken up the reins of thy household, and shown himself within its Sanctuary.[7]

Of old time he sought out all the Children of Zion that he might destroy them along with The Bethlehem.[8]

He fashioned for thee the worst things, and made of them graves for all thy children along with the Children of Zion.[9]

232

NOTES.

[1] This disciple was not alone in his fearfulness for the Master. After the terrible Gethsemane, the strange words they had heard Him speak in His sorrow, the description He had given to them of the appalling conditions of the Astral realm and the work to be accomplished through His going, the inner group was filled with fear for Him. So this disciple only expressed what others felt.

[2] Jerusalem was the spiritual Household of the Planet, and its conditions were such that they not only failed to sustain and nourish the Soul, but depleted it of its inherent spiritual vitality. For Herod ruled in Galilee. He was tetrarch there ; and this meant that the mind or magnetic plane of the Planet was ruled over by the sensual and sensualizing powers for which Herod stood. For the magnetic plane or reflective (mind) circulus of the Planet was and is part of the middle kingdom known as the Astral, and spoken of as the Partition or Middle Wall between these lower planes and the real spiritual world. The Partition was not a wall, but its conditions had made it such, and that was the wall with the Hand-writings that had to be broken down by means of the Oblation.

[3] To-day, to-morrow, and the day that will follow during which the Divine World of purification was to be accomplished, the devilish things cast down from their seats of power and the evil hand-writings blotted out, were the three days of the Oblation, the three Naronic Cycles during which He descended (in state) into the Hells. Herod with his emissaries is at last overthrown, though the effects of his long reign and evil dominion are yet great for evil. But even these will be blotted out also, and Galilee freed of them all, and Jerusalem saved.

[4] The work of the Redemption is meant. That is now proceeding. The Christhood is being restored, the Prophets of God are at work, and through the accomplishment of the Oblation, their work will have permanent results.

[5] The Planet as a Human Spiritual Household.

[6] The great betrayer and the terrible betrayal of the Planet.

[7] The materializing of every spiritual quality and quantity in the doing of which the Soul itself was brought down to seek fulfilment by means of the material, until its very Sanctuary was trodden down by the oppressive powers.

[8] The children of Zion were the Christ Souls who ministered upon the Bethlehem unto the Planet's children.

[9] The reference is to the evil forms into which they all were drawn down.

THE CHRISTHOOD

The Great Lament

He destroyed thy beautiful palaces within thee, and laid bare all thy planes.[1]

Thus did he accomplish for thee the evil thing which he desired to do before the Lord.[2]

And now thy planes are the dwelling-places of all manner of evil things; for he hath turned thy substances into waste, and thy beautiful possessions into things of evil.[3]

He hath laid thee bare, that all who pass by may laugh at thee; for, when he sought thee out to deceive thee, he brought with him those who had been seeking an habitation to dwell in, such as he accomplished in thee.[4]

And now that his hand is heavy upon thee, he turneth thy bared planes into all manner of abiding places for those whom he brought with him; for thy planes in their condition are no more those of the ways to Zion, but the paths to spiritual death.

Until thy planes are ways to Zion, the Divine Wisdom can no more shine forth from thee.[5]

To be as thou wert in the days of old, thou must be redeemed. Behold and see! For the Divine Love shall at last accomplish thy ransom from bondage, through the strength of a Redeemer.

And in that day thou shalt say once more, ' Blessed is He who cometh in the Name of the Lord.' "

The Exceeding Sorrow

" How greatly have I feared the passing over, lest I should not return any more.[6]

For, though with great desire did I come unto this in order that, as a result of the work to be accomplished by it, we might be all once more with the Father-Mother in the Kingdom of the Divine, and that even he who went out from us to find another kingdom might likewise be with us again in the Regeneration when the Son of Man shall awaken from His long sleep within the grave—yet do I fear.

For the gross darkness of Jerusalem is terrible unto me even now whilst my Soul has yet its light.

And if that darkness be now so great ere the light within me is veiled, how awful must the darkness

234

NOTES.

[1] The Great Lament is a pathetic composition. It is a parable; and yet it is a review of ages of the Planet's history. It is a parable in that the language is veiled; it is a review because it epitomizes the disasters which overtook the Planet after the great descent known as the Fall. It is but an echo of that Great Lament uttered by the Divine Kingdom when the Planetary Angel decided to move away from the Plane of the Divine Kingdom, to thereby accomplish the evolution of the created life upon the Planet the more speedily, as the Angel thought. For it brought great grief to Ramah, and ended in Rachel weeping for her children because they were not.

The Palaces were the dwelling places of the children, and the Planes were the once beautiful terraces: really the spiritual house or states, the many Planetary mansions, wherein the children were; and the various planes of consciousness for the children in which they walked, but also the actual planes of the Planet which were brought down and destroyed.

[2] The mystery implied here must not yet be unfolded.

[3] The false step which took the Planet away from the plane of the Divine Kingdom brought about such elemental changes that the very substances of the Planet were changed, and wrong orders of life generated.

[4] The entire Household of the Planet suffered, the spiritual evolution of the children was intercepted, evil habitations were formed out of the substances, and woe upon woe followed as a result.

[5] It is this that passes before the vision of the Master. He was looking on the Planet's long past and mourning over it. He saw all that it had meant and what it still meant of suffering and sorrow ere the Redemption could come. He beheld all that had yet to come, and the heavy burden which He Himself would have to carry during the Oblation. Is there any wonder at His Great Lament? Yet He also beheld the ultimate issue. He knew the Redeemer had come in the Divine Burden-bearing about to take place, and that in the Regeneration the end would be glorious.

[6] These Logia are burdened with an unspeakable sorrow. To many it will seem strange that it could ever have been with the Master as is here indicated. Yet those who were with Him when they were spoken will understand them, as will also the inner groups of the Christhood Order—the real Israel.

235

THE CHRISTHOOD

be where there is no light within the Soul?

Surely when the light within Jerusalem is now even as gross darkness unto my Soul, how great will that darkness be when my light is altogether veiled within me?[1]

The Exceeding Sorrow

If my Soul is exceeding sorrowful, even unto death, whilst the light still burns within me; how terrible must the agony be when my Soul awakens from its long sad history, written in language which no man knoweth, to discover all that has overtaken me through my absence from Him whom we know to be the Light of our Life?[2]

It must needs be that none perish amid the awful darkness which overtook the Soul who went away from the Kingdom of the Divine, otherwise it would not find that my Soul would go down into it.

But lest there should perish utterly one of those little children of the Father-Mother who went down into it, it must needs be that my Passover in Jerusalem be accomplished.[3]

If the light which is in men be darkness, how great must the darkness be unto which the Son of Man goeth!

For if, when the light be with them shining in a dark place, to give light unto all who will follow the path unto the Divine Love and Life, and in order that none may walk in darkness but find the Light of Life, they find themselves in the darkness so that they know not the way; then how awful must that darkness be where no light shineth to guide the wayfarer even should he seek out a city to dwell in where no darkness is, and where the night draweth not nigh!

Walk in the light that is now shining upon the path, that ye may behold the way unto the Father-Mother who is now making Himself manifest, lest the darkness overtake you also, and the night overwhelm you in the path.

For whilst the light is in you, ye are the children of the Light; but if the Light become extinguished through the darkness, then verily will ye become as the children of the darkness."[4]

NOTES.

[1] To the reader who can sense the atmosphere of plaintive sorrow surrounding these Sayings there will come a consciousness of what the passing over meant to Him. He was so borne down by the consciousness of all that awaited Him, that, however much He would have had it otherwise for the sake of those who were witnesses of His sorrow, He could not rise above the awful things which He sensed and the grief with which they filled Him.

Is it any wonder that He dreaded His passing over ? For was not this passing over the passing away, not merely from life upon this Planet, which would have brought no sorrow, but only joy, to Him, but the passing away of His consciousness of high Christhood ? For in the loss of that blessed experience, the Divine Light within Him would have to be withdrawn and veiled.

The strange fearfulness of the future which oppressed His Soul never left Him ; and, sad to relate, it pursued Him through all the lives of the Oblation, and in the last it haunted Him as an oppressing shadow, notwithstanding that the Divine Presence was ever near Him and His Light was in great part restored.

[2] To any one who has never known the glory of Christhood, nor has yet risen to that high spiritual experience, such Logia will appear to be enigmatical. For such an one there can be no clear meaning shown. Unto such there are Mysteries of the Kingdom which cannot be revealed. For the Soul can only intuitively apprehend that which of old time she hath known. But all who once were in Christhood and have known the glory of the Divine Overshadowing and the Light of that Glory shining within the Sanctuary of the Soul, will understand all that the darkness of the world meant. But the anguish of the Soul, in its awakening at the closing acts of the Oblation, none could fathom, so deep and intense was it. So the Master rightly gauged the future, and sensed what would accompany His awakening, and the recovery of the path of the Oblation in the days of the Regeneration—the days in which we live.

[3] Herein once more is expressed the absolute necessity of the Oblation, as without the accomplishment of the purification of the Middle Kingdom the Redemption of Jerusalem and all her children could not be effected.

[4] It was most important that they should understand the dangerous conditions amid which they would have their lot cast during the Oblation, and how essential it was they should direct their thoughts to the holy purpose of keeping the Light of the Spirit burning within them. For the darkness that would obtain and prevail throughout the days of the Oblation might overtake them also, unless they lived the life and walked in the Light. The intensity of their struggle to find and keep that Light may be witnessed in the strange and profound experiences of those who have been regarded as the Saints during the three Nari.

237

THE CHRISTHOOD

The Recoveries of the Logia Anticipated

" *These things have I spoken unto you that ye may not stumble by the way; for ye will be cast out by the children of this world from their Sanctuaries and their Fellowships, because ye have believed in the message which the Father-Mother gave me to declare.[1]*

Yea, the time will come in which ye shall be persecuted and afflicted by those who will profess to do service to God, even by those who know not the Father-Mother, nor His Son whom He sent to make Him manifest.[2]

Of these things have I spoken unto you that, when that hour is come upon you, ye may remember; yea, that ye may recall to remembrance all the things of which I have spoken unto you.[3]

For the Paraclete, even the Holy Spirit who proceedeth from the Father-Mother, shall teach you all things when He is come, and bring all things to your remembrance, even whatsoever things ye have known of old time.[4]

And when He is come, He will reveal unto you the nature of the Sin of this world, the Righteousness of the Divine Love, and the Judgment of that Love upon the world.[5]

He shall not speak of Himself; but He shall speak of the Father-Mother, and of Him through whom the Father-Mother maketh Himself manifest, even of the Only Begotten One whose dwelling is in the bosom of the Father-Mother.

He shall take of those things which belong unto the Father-Mother and declare their meaning unto you, for He must glorify the Father-Mother.

A little while and ye will no more see me until the days of the Regeneration, because it is expedient that I go away from you.

But by and bye we will all be brought together again, when the work of the Father-Mother given us to do, is accomplished.[6]

And in that day will our sorrow be turned into joy, for the Father-Mother will Himself be made manifest unto us, and all our requests will be fulfilled by Him.

238

NOTES.

[1] Who could gainsay this ? Has it not been true in every age that the illumined ones sent forth from the Father-Mother have had to cross the Rubicon of the Church, and seek another sphere for their activities ? Men and women may eat flesh and drink wine, and indulge in those embellishments which invariably accompany such things, and yet remain in the Church and be as its leaders, teachers and apostles ; but when Souls arise out of the darkness into the consciousness of that Light which lighteth every one who riseth up out of the life of the world, the Church eschews and crucifies them. It has been so throughout all the ages ; it is so even until this day.

[2] All forms of the Inquisition, protestant and catholic, have been done in the name of the Most Adorable One, and ostensibly for the good of Souls.

[3] A prophecy of events now coming to pass. We are in the Age of the Recovery. The Vision has come to some. There are upon these planes now those who have recovered visions of the Master as He was in the days of the Manifestation. These have again beheld some of the events in His life. And in these Logia they recognise those things of which He spake unto them.

[4] The Holy Paraclete is the Remembrancer. He is the Presence within the Soul and the Light of its Lamp. When the Soul rises into that state of consciousness, it has the past brought before it in so far as it is able to receive it. This is what is meant by its recovery. Though it is of the Soul, yet it is of no man, but of the Lord within the Sanctuary.

The reference is not to be understood in any mere occult sense— what is meant is not the reading of the records upon the present magnetic plane of the Planet. It is something far more spiritual, much more interior, that which can be entered upon only through following the way of the Spirit.

[5] The Revelation is to be accomplished through the arising of the Son of Man within the consciousness of all who once knew Christhood ; for in this day of the recovery they are to be the manifestors of the Divine Love, the revealers of the Divine Righteousness, and the interpreters of the Divine Ways.

[6] After the Oblation the re-union of those who had been with Him. Though it could not be other than sad, yet it was to be blessed.

239

THE CHRISTHOOD

The Recoveries of the Logia Anticipated

Many things have I had to speak of unto you in allegory ; but in that hour ye will no more need to be spoken unto in allegory, for ye shall understand all things, because the Father-Mother abideth with you and shall be in you." [1]

And one who had been much perplexed concerning the meaning of many things spoken of by the Master, said unto Him—

" Now know we that Thou knowest all things, and requirest not that any one should tell Thee."

" Do ye indeed believe this ? Behold the hour cometh when ye will be scattered, and each one left alone, even as I will be left alone ; may ye in that day believe that the Father-Mother hath sent me. [2]

And in that day when I shall come back to you, having accomplished the work which the Father-Mother hath given me to do, may ye then also believe that the Father-Mother sent me." [3]

Preparing the Guest Chamber

"And in the days of the Feast of Unleavened Bread, [4] when the Son of Man [5] shall come again, God will send His Messengers [6] before Him to prepare the way for His coming.

He will send Peter and John [7] that they may make ready the Guest-Chamber for the Lord. For these two disciples will tarry upon the Earth until He is come.

They will behold the sign of the Son of Man in the Heavens, [8] the Water-carrier, and know that the days of His return unto the Earth are come.

And, in those days, they will behold a man [9] who bears the sign of the Water-carrier upon him ; and he will direct them to the Upper Room where the Lord celebrated His Passover, and where He would consummate the Holy Supper.

They will find in the House of that man the Guest-Chamber within which the Lord's Passover was accomplished ;

And they will make it ready for the Lord that He may again celebrate the Holy Supper with the Twelve. [10]

For in the House of that man would the Lord commemorate His Passing Over." [11]

NOTES.

[1] Some of the allegories referred to will be found in another section. It was necessary at the time to veil His meanings concerning some things connected with the Oblation and the part which He would take in it ; and also the future that lay ahead of them. And the reference to the full recovery and understanding of all things by them through the consciousness of the indwelling Presence of the Father-Mother, is to the age of the Regeneration.

[2] He beheld what was coming, the trials that awaited them as they reappeared from time to time to take their part, how hard they would find it to believe in Him as now they did ; for He knew what would be done to the Teachings and what the ecclesiastical systems would accomplish. The members of the group would be scattered and each would be alone ; for they would not know one another again until the Oblation was finished.

[3] To express all that is hidden in this expression of hope is indeed impossible. The tender solicitude and wonder in what He said was indeed great ; and it found its repetition within Him in the days of the awakening.

[4] The days in which the true spiritual interpretation of the Soul and the Christhood would be found again. These days are now.

[5] An ancient Mystery term signifying the Adonai. His coming again meant the awakening of the Christhood Order to realize His overshadowing Presence.

[6] All the redeeming and purifying powers set in motion from the Heavens to make clean the ways of men and women in all societies, peoples and nations.

[7] These were two of the most intimate friends of the Master, and disciples of the innermost group, whose initiate names represented the two Divine Principles of the Soul known as the Understanding or Intuition, and the Love-principle. The two who were to be sent on this special mission were to represent these principles in the work they would have to accomplish.

[8] In the Celestial Heavens, the Sign of Aquarius into which the Planet would then enter in its Celestial revolution. In 1881 the New Age began. The new cycle then opened for the Planet, though astronomically we only entered Aquarius in 1914.

[9] This refers, not to Aquarius, but to the Soul who bore the burden of the Sin-offering, for He had been a Water-carrier or Truth-bearer. It was He in whom the burden or travail of the Lord's Passion had taken place, the Master Himself at the close of the Sin-offering days.

[10] This refers to the restoration of the Soul to the Christhood estate, the blessed realization of the Presence within.

[11] " The passing through " of that Soul in the recovery of what it

THE CHRISTHOOD

The Eucharistic Supper

On the eve of the Passover of the Lord when the Beloved Master and the disciples were gathered together, and the Master made known unto them fully the meaning of the Passover, He spake also these words :—

" I have received of the Lord this Testament, and I give it unto you that ye may know and understand the meaning of this Passing Over which must needs be accomplished by me.[1]

It is the body of the Lord that is broken for the life of the World : for that Body is the Bread of Life let down from the Heavens to nourish all Souls.[2]

It is the Life of the Lord that is poured forth for a Ransom unto the Redemption of all Souls, even the Blood shed unto the remission of Sin ; for the Blood of the Lamb of God is the Life-stream of the Soul which floweth unto remission of all Sin.[3]

Eat ye of this Bread, and drink ye of this Cup ; for His Body is meat indeed, and His Blood is drink indeed unto the Soul.

It is the seal of the Lord's Testament, the Bread and the Wine of the New Covenant.[4]

When ye eat of this Bread, and drink of this Cup, ye show forth the coming of the Lord.[5]

Therefore, partake ye of this Bread, and of this Cup drink ye all, even until He come ;

For, in partaking of this Bread, and in drinking of this Cup, ye shall be the inheritors of the Glory of the Lord whose coming within you shall be unto the Revelation of His righteous judgments, and the condemnation of all that is unrighteous and unholy.

And though the condemnation of the world be meted out to you because ye eat of this Bread and drink of this Cup, yet unto you shall it be as Maranatha.

But I shall no more drink of this Cup until I drink of it anew with you in the Kingdom." [6]

NOTES.

had endured in the burden of the Sin-offering, and all that it meant for the world. The commemoration or celebration of the Passover was the Recovery of the passing over from the Christhood, and the intense Soul-travail endured throughout the ages of this era.

And all these things have come to pass in these days.

[1] With this portion of the Logia there were most tender and sacred associations, and even unto this day something of the spiritual intimacy and sacredness of them have been retained. Whether the form used has been that found in the synoptic records or the Pauline letters, a hallowedness has been attached to the words which even the profane have felt. And this has happened notwithstanding the fact that in neither form are the Logia correctly given. What then should be the effect of the Logia of the Eucharist as they were spoken by the Master ?

It will be seen how the words attributed to Paul could not have been received by him as a special message from the Lord, since they were known unto the disciples, and were spoken by the Master to them. They were embodied in the original Logia of St. John and were amongst those taken away by Paul when he visited the Brethren.

[2] The hour was one of the most sacred fellowship. It was in very deed the Supper of the Lord : they had broken to them the Bread of the Innermost. It was an hour of the blessed Eucharist when they realized what could never be expressed to any of them. It was the most blessed Sacrament in which the few entered into perfect union with the Lord.

[3] The Cup of God given unto the Soul to drink, contained the Blood of the Lamb. Amongst all the sacred Logia of the Master, none has been so grossly materialized as this. It has become a mere shibboleth of orthodoxy. It is thought of and spoken of as having reference to the body of the Master whose blood is believed to have been shed. But its meaning belongs to those things which are of the Divine Kingdom; for the Lamb of God is the Divine Love in its sacrificial capacity, and the Blood of the Lamb is the Life stream of that Love which flows to nourish, to heal, to perfect. To partake of it in such a manner and in such an hour, was verily to enter into the consciousness of its power.

[4] The seal of the New Covenant or Testimony is not to be found in symbols, but in the realities.

[5] To eat of the hidden Manna and to drink of the Cup of the Gods, is to reveal the coming of the Soul into the high estate of the most Blessed Union.

[6] It was the Last Supper indeed until the accomplishment of the Oblation. What depth of meaning there is implied in this Saying of the Master. He would drink no more of this Fruit of the Vine until all was accomplished.

243

THE CHRISTHOOD

The Eve of the Passover

" *How greatly am I straitened in my desires !* [1]

With much longing have I desired the approach of this hour that I might accomplish this Passover with you ; yet is my sorrow great to leave you for a time.

But it is expedient for you that I go away ; for if I go not away, the Paraclete will not come. [2]

Therefore I do not leave you comfortless, for He will come to you to bring to your remembrance all the things which I have told you.

Behold, a woman when she is in travail hath pain and sorrow until the hour of her deliverance is come, then hath she joy in that she hath brought life into the world.

And so shall our travail be. We shall have pain and sorrow until the hour of the fulfilment of our travail hath come, then will our sorrow give place to joy. [3]

But now, the hand of him who betrayeth me is stretched out towards me ; and he will take the sop that I shall give him, and put it in my cup that he may do the things which he hath purposed to do against me.

And may he do what he hath purposed, quickly, that the work given me to do be accomplished. [4]

But, let not your hearts be troubled : believe ye in the Father-Mother, and in the message which I have given unto you.

In the Household of the Father-Mother there are many dwelling-places, even as I have told you. [5]

And though I now go away from you, I will come back again to you and receive you to myself when the place whither I go has been prepared. [6]

For whither I go ye now know ; and the way of my going know ye also. [7]

I will no more be able to talk with you, for the prince of this world cometh that I may go hence. [8]

But let not your hearts be troubled ; neither be ye fearful for me."

NOTES.

[1] It is impossible to convey to the reader what all this implied for the Master. To carry out the Divine Will was ever His supreme joy. As far as the doing of that Will was concerned, He never faltered. But the Gethsemane Vision had revealed to Him states of experience which were so utterly outside the pale of what He had anticipated as His burden, that He became unspeakably oppressed, and most straitened in His desires. He had longed to do the Divine Will; for that end He came into this world. But the nature of the burden made Him wish it had been otherwise.

[2] The Paraclete had come in a measure to those of the inner group, but He was to come in fulness to them and all the members of the Order of the Christhood. But for such a realization it was expedient, nay, it was absolutely essential, that He should carry the burden.

[3] A beautiful anticipation: yet He has been the Man of sorrows ever since that hour. Though glints and gleamings of coming joy have at times broken upon Him, the shadow of the Cross has been deep and long.

[4] Oh, it is too tragic to think that any one who was a member of the inner group could ever have so betrayed the Master, as presented in the accepted records. Nor was it so. It is true many betrayed Him, though not in that way. The real betrayal was by the Astral powers. The betrayer referred to is the personification of those powers.

The sop was given by the Master to the betrayer when He offered His very Soul to be burdened and afflicted by all the terrible Astral conditions. And it was put into the cup of the Master's lives.

[5] The reference is not to be limited in its interpretation to the celestial systems and planetary worlds, for it has also another meaning. The various states of Soul experience as represented by the celestial signs, are dwelling-places in which each one abides for a time.

[6] The place whither He went was the Astral Realm. By the work of the Oblation He went to prepare that place to enable the Heavens to perform their full ministry to the children of the Planet.

[7] All had now been made known to them concerning the Oblation in so far as it might be revealed, and they were able to receive its Mystery.

[8] The hour was drawing near when He must needs leave them. The coming of the Prince of this world was the coming of Astral dominion over His lives.

THE CHRISTHOOD

The Humiliation and Condemnation of Christ

"*Now Herod was set over Galilee to rule, having been appointed by Cæsar to act as adjudicator ; and he was most desirous of beholding Him through whom the manifestation was made, and commanding Him to do some mighty work for the pleasure of his court.*

He therefore sent out his emissaries to bring Him ; but these found Him already accused by Caiaphas of threatening to destroy the Temple of Herod and claiming to be a son of the Gods, and bound before Pilate for these things and because He professed to have a Kingdom which was higher than Cæsar's : and He was led to the Herodian court.[1]

When Herod saw Him bound captive, suffering from the cruel treatment meted out to Him by Caiaphas and Pilate, he mocked Him as one unable to perform any mighty work.

And in mockery he arrayed Him in the robes of his own court, put into His right hand a false sceptre, and placed upon His head a crown of thorns.

And he smote Him with cruel buffetings, and commanded Him to prophecy concerning the destruction of the Temple of Herod and the coming of the New Kingdom.

The Crucifixion of Christ

Then did they lead Him away to be crucified. And they laid the Cross upon Him and took Him unto Golgotha,[2] *and there crucified Him.*

And between two thieves did they place Him, one on the right hand and the other on the left.[3]

And there were those who railed at Him, saying—' If Thou be the Son of God, come down from the Cross.'

But there spake a voice unto those who railed at Him, saying : ' He saved others, Himself He cannot save.'[4]

And there was darkness over the land from the sixth hour until the ninth ; the Sun was veiled, the Moon turned into blood, and the Stars from the Heavens fell.[5]

And when the ninth hour had come, there was a great shaking of the Earth, and many of the Saints who slept were awakened ; and these came forth from the graves in which they had lain, and went forth into the Holy City, appearing unto many."[6]

246

NOTES.

[1] Though this seems narrative and a description of the trial of the Master before the Herodian Court, followed by the Roman Crucifixion, yet it is allegory. It is an allegorical portrayal of the things which befell the Master during the days of the Oblation at the hands of Herod and his court, but more especially the events that issued from the betrayal of the Christhood vision. When Caiaphas, the high priest of ecclesiasticism, had that sublime vision before his court, he repudiated it and had the Christhood bound in ecclesiastical chains, the dogmas of his schools. He called in the world-power—Pilate—to accomplish his purpose against such a Life ; and though Pilate joined him, he did so under protest, for he saw no fault in the captive. But Herod crowned the betrayal and condemnation with humiliation, insult and mockery. He had Him arrayed in garments of his own court ; he put into His hand a false sceptre, and smote Him in hailing Him as King ; afterwards he crowned Him with the thorns of every cruelty. For Herod the tetrarch of Galilee, is the Astral Kingdom in its fallen state ! And the Temple of Herod which was supposed to be reared upon the foundations of the Temple of Solomon, is that false religious expression known as ecclesiastical Christianity which stands where the Temple of Solomon—the high Christhood—ought to have stood.

With the coming again of the Christhood, it shall be overthrown.

[2] That part of the circulus of the middle kingdom where death reigned. It was the part infested with the images that had to be blotted out. It was true of the Master and the Christ vision : they were both taken to Golgotha, and there crucified.

[3] The thieves were not two poor criminals, but two evil systems. The spirit of Negation in its manifold ways in which it denies and crucifies the spiritual, robbing the Soul of its heritage of beautiful aspiration and desire ; and the spirit that surrounds what is spiritual with a false atmosphere, and makes superstition prevail over the Soul, so that realization within of spiritual and Divine things becomes impossible. These are the two thieves between whom the Christ vision and all the Teachings of the Master were crucified.

[4] This is ever true of the Divine Love. That Love has suffered ever since the betrayal of this Planet. And it was true of the Master. He could not save Himself though He ministered to and for others.

[5] The three hours of intense darkness during which the Sun is said to have been veiled, were the three Naronic Cycles. The Light of the Christhood was veiled ; the mind was directed to conflict ; the Souls who should have been as Stars in the firmament, fell. Those who have eyes to see may behold it in ecclesiastical history

[6] The ninth hour is past and the tenth is with us. The spiritual earthquake is making the whole earth tremble ; the Saints are arising and entering the Holy City of Christhood.

THE CHRISTHOOD

And when those disciples were gathered together, who had not been informed of what had taken place when the Master was thought to expire on the Cross, He came into their midst. For they had gathered in the house of Mary His mother.[1]

After Ten Days

And He, being again restored, made Himself known unto them as one risen from the dead.

But they were all amazed and filled with fear, thinking it was a vision.

But He spake thus unto them : " Peace, the great Peace, be with you all."

Yet were they still troubled, doubts arising in their hearts concerning what they saw and heard.

Then He said unto them : " Behold my hands and my feet ; for ye may handle them and see that I am not insubstantial as ye suppose, but yet in my body of flesh."

And they were filled with wonder that He was alive ; and joy welled up in their hearts to hear His voice again.

Upon the same day, but towards the eventide when the doors were closed, the Master came into the midst of His own most intimate ones.

And there was gladness in their hearts as He communed with them.

The Power by which Sin is Retained or Remitted

Unto them did He thus speak : " Peace, even the Peace of the Father-Mother, be within you. My Father-Mother hath sent me into this world to accomplish His will, that the sins of the children of this world may be remitted unto them, even those sins which they have been compelled to retain throughout all the ages since the days when the Breath of the Holy One ceased to be inbreathed by them.

And whosoever willeth to have their sin remitted, it shall even be so unto them ; but whosoever willeth not to have remission of their sin, it shall be retained by them.[2]

As He hath sent me into this world for the restoration of all Israel, and that the remission of sin may be accomplished that all Souls may come to know Him

NOTES.

[1] The crucifixion of the Master must ever be distinguished from the crucifixion of the Christhood. The one took place before the manifestation was fully accomplished ; the other after the passing away of the Master.

In the crucifixion the Master is supposed to have died. But if the laws of being were understood by those who believe so, together with the true nature of His Christhood, they would also understand that it was not possible for Him to be holden of death, nor to die in the sense in which people understand death. His body was not like the bodies of others. It was so beautiful in its nature that it may be said that, though opaque and dense, it was nevertheless spiritual and ethereal. There were no elements of death in it.

But in such a body He was capable of suffering most intensely. And the crucifixion caused Him to suffer very greatly. He knew what was coming to Him and informed those nearest to Him what would happen, and how they should act. But it had to be kept secret ; so very few knew what was to take place.

[2] These Logia were spoken in connection with others of which they formed a part. We have placed them here because they were given by the Master to the few intimate ones who came to meet Him and have fellowship on that first day of re-union after the Roman Crucifixion. It will be observed that they contain a direct intimation of the purpose of the Oblation, and also the fact that whilst the Divine Love is ever blessing His children and healing them of their diseases and evils, yet the effects of some sins had been retained throughout long ages, sins which could not be healed until the Oblation was accomplished. For the true forgiveness of sin is the healing of life. It is the blotting out of sin's effects and the changing of desire.

In this process a Soul must have the willinghood to be thus forgiven, for there can be no true forgiveness apart from the consent of the Soul. And it can be accomplished only through purification. If anyone does not desire in the inward parts to be pure, there can be no true healing, and the effect of sin is retained.

Those who are familiar with the ecclesiastical interpretation of these Logia as recorded in the gospels and the uses to which they have been put, and likewise with the revival of the gifts of healing, will surely recognise how sad have been the effects upon the whole Western World of their misinterpretation and abuse.

THE CHRISTHOOD

*through the salvation He hath wrought out for them,
even so are ye sent by Him also unto the arising of
Israel, His messengers to go before Him proclaiming
the way of the return unto those who may be able to
receive it, and likewise to be sharers in the sufferings
of the way, partakers of the Passion of the Lord, having
tasted of the cup of which I must drink, and the
baptism with which I must be baptized."* [1]

*But there was one of the inner group of His intimate
ones not present when He made Himself known as one
risen from the dead, and when he heard of the things
that had taken place, he said he could not receive them,
nor would he believe unless he saw the wounds caused
at the crucifixion.*

*So it came to pass that when they gathered together
again, Thomas came with them.*

*And when the doors were shut for fear of interruption,
and that the authorities might not know that the Master
was still with them, the Master came into their midst
and thus spake unto them :*

*" Peace, even the Peace of the Father-Mother, be
within you."*

*Unto Thomas He thus spake : " Thomas, be not
unbelieving.*

*Reach hither thy hand and behold my wounds, and
understand the things that have happened unto me."*

*And Thomas bowed his head worshipfully before the
gathering, and he exclaimed : " O my Lord ! O my
God ! Thou hast humbled me in this great thing which
Thou hast wrought on behalf of our Beloved One."*

*And when the hour had come when He knew that
He must needs be alone, He turned to those who had
remained with Him to the last and said unto them :*

" The hour is come when I must needs leave you. [2]

*My Soul is exceeding sorrowful : Yet unto this
hour came I into this world.*

*I go hence because the Will of the Father-Mother
must be accomplished.*

250

NOTES.

[1] In connection with the work of the Redemption referred to above through the purification to be made possible as a blessed result of the Oblation, there was the arising and restoration of Israel. The Master closely associated the two. Indeed He made the full realization of the one contingent upon the other. The relationship between the Order of the Christhood and the Master was intimate. He was of them : the members of the Ancient Order were His brethren. Their mission to this Planet was the same. If His had to take a special form for the purpose of the Manifestation and the Oblation, yet their work was identical. Its purpose was the interpretation and manifestation of the Divine Love through a Christ ministry, and the redemption of the children of this Planet through the path of purification.

Without the arising and full restoration of the Ancient Christhood there could be little hope of the Redemption being effected ; for only they could understand Christhood and make it manifest. Only they could bring to the children of the Planet a true vision of the Redeemed Life. They had been the teachers, prophets and seers through all the æons of ages, and they had to fill those offices again under conditions more favourable.

This arising was to be the first effects of the Oblation ; and then would come to them the Regeneration, and through their ministry the Redemption.

And of this Order the intimate friends of the Master were all members. Nay, most of them belonged to the inner degrees of the Christhood. And some of these had been chosen to partake in some measure of the Passion. It is to this the Master here refers.

[2] The hour was approaching for His withdrawal. The Passover had been accomplished in the degree that He had descended from the Christhood estate, through the gradual withdrawal of the Overshadowing Presence. The Light within Him had become more and more veiled.

This took place long after the events associated with His crucifixion. It was the closing scene. But though He left the friends to whom He spake the last allegory in order to be alone, it was some time before He was withdrawn. He knew no death in the ordinary sense. The spiritual elements in His body were indrawn. Only the delicate and wearied frame was left behind.

THE CHRISTHOOD

The Closing Scene

Ye shall not see me any more until it is accomplished ; but when His Will hath been wrought upon the place whither I go, then I will come to you again.

For you a place hath been prepared in the work to be accomplished in my going hence.

The Father-Mother hath appointed you to be sharers in the preparation of the place whither I go ; and when the time cometh ye will understand what I have said unto you.[1]

And now I must leave you ; and in doing so I would say this farewell word concerning the events that are coming, that ye may understand.[2]

The Last Allegory

There was once a teacher sent from the Heavens to teach the Way unto the Father-Mother ; and he gathered around him some who loved that way and followed it.

And when he had accomplished part of the work for which he had been sent, he told them that it was expedient for him to leave them for a time, as he must needs take up the burden of other work given him to do.

Now, as these loved ones of the teacher were fishers,[3] he counselled them to take their vessel and launch out into the deep. And they did as he requested.

But he withdrew to a hill-side, and was there alone.[4]

And he prayed for those whom he so loved and who so loved him, that they might be guarded against all evil, and succoured in the day of trial from the Father-Mother.

And for himself he also prayed that he might be strengthened and upheld in the work to which he had been appointed.

And he laboured in his prayer, and the Angel of the Lord strengthened him for his work. And when the night fell upon him, he went forth to accomplish it.[5]

Now when his devoted and loved ones went forth in their vessel upon the sea, very soon a storm arose, and the waters were turbulent, so much so that they became sore distressed.[6]

All through the night the storm continued, tossing

NOTES.

[1] The place whither He went was the Astral realm. That was the place which had to be prepared for the Redemption. As we have indicated, it was in a state of terrible disharmony, and crowded with evil magnetic images. The blotting out of these images, the changing, purifying and transmutation of the elements, was the work assigned to Him. And He had to attain the desired end by means of the Oblation.

In this work a part was assigned to the very few who formed the innermost group. They were to accompany Him in some of His lives, though not to know Him nor He them ; for this was necessary for what had to be done. They were to share in the travail in aiding Him in different ways to accomplish the work. But the real meaning of the part they were to take would not come to them until all things had been done in regard to the Oblation.

[2] This allegory is to be found in the accepted records in the form of an incident on the Sea of Galilee in which the Master is said to have appeared to the disciples walking on the waters. Its meaning is more profound.

[3] They were all Fishers, seekers for the Divine Things, not content with the hay, wood and stubble of material existence, seekers after realizations as well as spiritual knowledge. To launch out unto the deep was to go forth on the mission of Divine Quest and Ministry.

[4] Here we have a vista of the last hours. He must needs be alone. For the Teacher was the Master Himself. The prayer given as the intercessory prayer in the fourth record was part of what He spake, though it likewise suffered at the hands of those who compiled these records.

[5] It is utterly impossible to give even the faintest idea of what took place. The Angel of the Lord strengthened Him to carry the burden as it came out from the darkness to Him. When the darkness fell, the Light within Him was completely veiled.

[6] The stormy conditions which overtook them, the troubling of the waters and the turbulent elemental results, made their share in the work harder to understand and endure. It began soon after the closing scene, and it continued all through the era until these days. They could not reach the land whither they went, though they toiled all through the long night, for the land was the Christhood. The conditions were made difficult for them. When they were again born into the Western World, all things were changed. The precious Logia had been broken up and so mixed amid false settings that they found it difficult to arrive at the true Vision for which they sought. The Temple of the Christhood had been pulled down, and its vision destroyed.

The travail of all of the inner Christhood group, during the days of the Oblation, has been great.

THE CHRISTHOOD

them to and fro ; and they toiled in rowing, but could not reach the land.

The Last Allegory

Then about the fourth watch of the night, just as the grey dawn was breaking, they beheld one walking upon the troubled waters and drawing nigh to them.[1]

But so changed was his form that they did not know him ; and when he spake they were troubled, and wondered who it could be.

Yet with his coming there fell upon them, even amid the troubled waters, a great calm.

And when he had entered into the vessel with them, he said : ' Be not afraid. It is well.'

And soon they came to the land whither they went."[2]

Then did the disciples know that He spake unto them of things which were coming to pass, and they were sorrowful and heavy of heart.

And He lifted up His hands and blessed them in the name of the Father-Mother, saying unto them : " Peace, the Great Peace of my Father-Mother, be upon you all.

Let us arise, for now I must go hence."

And He went out from them to be alone.

His Prayer for them

" O my Father-Mother! the hour is come in which I am to pass hence and be no more with Thee, until Thy Holy Will be accomplished through me.

Thou hast made manifest Thy Glory that all may behold it, and glorified Thy Son that all may know Him.

Unto Him didst Thou give the dominion of all Souls, that, unto as many as could receive it, He should give the Life Eternal.

And in this is the Life Eternal made manifest, even in the perfect knowledge of Thee through the blessed estates of Jesus, Christ, and the Lord.

The work which Thou gavest me to do upon the Earth I must now finish, having revealed Thy Glory unto those who have heard the message which Thou gavest unto me to declare.

Thine these were ; for they knew of Thee, and that I had come out from Thee.

254

NOTES.

[1] The fourth watch of the night was the fourth day or the fourth cycle of the Naros, which was to usher in the days of the Regeneration and the appearing again of the Son of Man. The three days which were as night, were the first, second and third Naronic Cycles since the Passing-over. They have been dark indeed for all Souls.

But the fourth watch has come, and with it the coming again of the Son of Man. For Christ is indeed risen, and the Divine Avatâr encompasses the earth. Nay, even the Master has come back from His long sojourn in Edom, the land of forgetfulness, the land whither He went to accomplish the Divine Purpose, and prepare it for the coming of the Redemption.

It is only yet the grey dawn : the noontide hasteneth.

[2] In the return of the Master it had to be as in all the lives of the Oblation. His presence upon these planes has had to be veiled. His visage was marred in all the lives of the Oblation, and it could not be other than more deeply marred in the last of them. No one could penetrate that visage unless they had power given them to do so.

That it should be so, is well. The personal must never again be worshipped in place of the Divine, nor obtrude itself in any way. The Church, with its personal worship of Him, and its attributing to Him work which only the Divine Father-Mother could accomplish, has added to the deep sorrow which has been laid upon Him. For Him to hear the praise accorded to Him which should only be ascribed to the Most High and ever Most Blessed One, poured forth from the various Churches of all degrees and orders, has filled His Soul with anguish. The liturgies, hymnaries and theologies of the Churches have added to His burden and made more poignant His grief.

The Dawn has come. Once more has He been in the midst of the troubled waters, walking towards those who launched out into the deep, who amid the turbulent conditions have toiled in rowing throughout the three Naronic Cycles without reaching the land whither they went, the Christhood estate. His coming to them was as the coming of one risen from the dead. And with His coming they found the land whither they went.

THE CHRISTHOOD

The Great Request of the Master

The message concerning Thy purpose which Thou didst give unto me to declare, they received ; for their understanding was open, and they discerned that the message was from Thee.

O my Father-Mother, I would make request for them : I would pray that when I am no more with them, Thou wouldst preserve them as they sojourn in the world, that whilst yet in the world they may not be of it : for they are Thine.

May they abide in the Oneness which is in Thee through Thy dwelling within them, even the Oneness which I have known with Thee through Thy dwelling within me.

When I am no more with them, may they keep sacred the things of which I have spoken unto them concerning Thee, that nothing may be lost through the son of perdition, of all that Thou gavest unto me.

May they all have within them the fulfilment of these sacred things in the Divine Joy, that when I come back to Thee we may all be one in Thee.

O Father-Mother, may Thy truth illumine and sanctify them, even Thy truth as declared through Him who is the Image of Thee, the Word of God.

They are not of this world even as I am not of this world ; and I pray that they may consecrate themselves to accomplish Thy holy will, even as I now consecrate myself to fulfil Thy holy will, and thus prepare themselves to be sent for the fulfilment of Thy purpose.

And I would pray that we all may be guarded in the way to be taken by us, from being overwhelmed by the evil in this world, and that we may return to be again with Thee, to behold Thy Glory even as we beheld it before the foundations of this world.

O most righteous Father-Mother, this world hath not known Thee in Thy Love and Wisdom : but I have known Thee and Thy Love for all Souls, and have made manifest that the Love wherewith Thou lovest me may also be in them, even unto the knowing of Thee."

NOTES.

The Intercessory Prayer is like no other prayer that ever was composed or offered by man. There are depths of Mystery in it which none but the Elect Ones could possibly understand. It could only have been uttered by a Soul who knew the Divine ; its mystic references are profound. There runs through it from beginning to end one beautiful strain of intimate knowledge of the Divine. It is the deep minor key that is struck, yet the strain contains rich major tones.

Now, one of the most striking things in it is the constant reference to those who had been with Him ; and in these references He claims for them the like intimate relationship with the Father-Mother that He claims for Himself. They also knew the Father-Mother. They also were from the Divine realm and knew that He had come forth from the Father-Mother. From the Father-Mother had they been sent to receive His message and pass it on to others ; for they could understand it.

The burden of much of the Prayer is for them, that they might be preserved from the evils in the world, and at last come into perfect Oneness again with the Father-Mother. He was anxious for them. He knew what awaited the Teachings by the materializing powers. He knew what awaited Himself at the hands of those who dominated the Astral realm. He knew the kind of history that would be written by the great ecclesiastical institution reared in His name. He knew that for the period of the Oblation they would be scattered abroad, and that they would know deep Soul travail. So His love, even in this hour of His own sorrow and loss, bore them up before the Divine. He prayed for their preservation ; and He yearned over them. He prayed for His reunion with them in the days of the Regeneration when all should come once more into the consciousness of the Overshadowing One and the realization of the Divine Indwelling, and that they together might behold the glory of the Father-Mother even as in the ancient days ere this world had fallen into its present state.

They were not of this world even as He was not : they were not children of this Planet. They were children of the Sun, of the Ancient Christhood Orders.

PART VII.

THE CHRISTHOOD.

VISTAS OF EVENTS TO COME *wherein the nature and duration of the Oblation is further set forth, and the effects of the same upon the Master as He bore the Burden, and accomplished the Work which it involved ; the manner in which the Western World received the Christhood which it invited to be a Guest in its house, and the recognition by the Soul of the Master who was represented by the Woman who was a sinner in the House of Simon, of the true nature of the Christhood, and the false concept of it entertained by Simon or the Western Mind ; the great sorrow that overtook Him in this discovery, and the process of Purification; the Anguish of the Master in His awakening to the consciousness that the Lord Presence had been taken away from Him, followed by the Joy of the Renewed Vision of the Lord, and the Blessed Work to be done.*

VISTAS OF EVENTS TO COME

When the days of the Garden of Gethsemane were fully accomplished, and the dire, anguish of them had abated, the Master spake under allegory of many things concerning events to come ; and amongst these were the following Sayings :

1. *Going through the Land of Samaria.*
2. *The Christ in the House of Simon.*
3. *The Seven Fishermen of Galilee.*
4. *The Mysterious Soliloquy.*
5. *The Teacher who washed the Feet of his Disciples.*
6. *The Sickness, Death and Resurrection of Lazarus.*
7. *Maria Magdalene seeking the Lord, and the Recovery of the Soul's Vision.*

THE CHRISTHOOD

Vistas of events to come

" *In His going hence the Son of Man must needs pass through Samaria.*[1] *As the way is trod through the wilderness of Judah,*[2] *He cometh into the way of the Samaritans.*[3]

There He cometh into the city of Sychar which was built upon the parcel of land which the Patriarch gave unto his son Joseph, and where the Well of Jacob was situated which the Patriarch gave for the use of all the Household that they might find in it waters of refreshment.[4]

And He through whom the Son of Man goeth sitteth by the well to rest Himself, for a great weariness overtaketh Him because of His journeying through that land.

Going through Samaria

As He sitteth by the Well, a longing for rest from all His labour overtaketh Him, and His Soul is filled with sorrow.[5]

To Himself He thus speaketh: ' I am full of weariness even to the laying down of my burden; and I would fain find a place of rest.[6]

And until the sixth hour did He remain there, weary and alone, for the disciples had gone their way into the villages to find provision there.[7]

When the sixth hour had fully come, there drew nigh unto the Well, a woman, a dweller in Samaria, for she had come hither to draw water.[8]

And of her did He request a drink, for the thirst upon Him was great.

But the woman was filled with astonishment that He should ask her to give Him drink, and said unto Him: ' Thou art a stranger in these parts: how is it that thou askest a drink from one with whom Thou hast no dealings?'

Then did He say unto her: ' If thou knewest the gift of God, and who it is who asketh drink of thee, thou wouldst have given to Him what thou hast, and unto thee God would have bestowed the living water For the water which He giveth is from the Well of Life.'

And the woman said unto Him: ' This well is deep, and I perceive not whence cometh the water

262

NOTES.

[1] " He must needs pass through Samaria " has a far deeper significance than any itinerary through a portion of the land of Palestine. Samaria was once the watch-tower, a state of spiritual experience within the Soul, and also that part of the Astral Circulus where the watchmen abode who were sent forth to herald to those upon the lower planes the approach of the Messengers of the Lord. But in the days of the Manifestation Samaria was in a fallen state, and the Samaritans were accounted as outcasts.

[2] Another reference to the conditions upon the Planet ; for the Planet was the sphere of Judah, the Planet-Soul.

[3] That meant that there would be a descent to the state represented by the Samaritans.

[4] Here there is reference to a Planetary Mystery which elsewhere we have interpreted. Suffice it to now say here that the Well of Jacob was the ministry given to Souls from the Angelic World, the spiritual nourishing of life as the Soul unfolded in the ages of its true evolution. There have been many Jacobs in spiritual history, but only one Patriarch known by that name ; for Jacob is the Angel of the lower spiritual heavens of the Planet, and is therefore one of the Planetary Gods or Directors. The House of Jacob was and is the spiritual state the name represents. The Well which the Patriarch gave in the land of Samaria was the fountain of spiritual teaching to the Soul who had reached that state. And even that Well was deep, though its waters did not bring to the Soul the conscious realization of the Life Eternal. To find that the Soul in the House of Jacob must pass to the House of Israel.

[5] No one could ever understand the sorrow that constantly filled the Soul of the Master as He performed His painful and sad ministry. It was even as it is here expressed.

[6] This may appear to some impossible in the case of one like the Master ; yet it was such a ministry as no other could understand unless they had passed that way. And it was such a burden that, whilst ever anxious to do the Divine Will, He continued to fear it, even unto the end. And He longed to find rest from it.

[7] Those who accompanied Him on this journey were able to find satisfactory portions of spiritual food in various centres. And they would fain have had Him partake of the same. In the Return this was very specially so.

[8] The Woman or Intuition even in Him during the days of the burden of the Oblation, was in a state of bondage.

THE CHRISTHOOD

of which Thou dost speak. Thou hast ⁓nothing to draw with. Whence does the Water of Life flow? Art Thou greater than the Patriarch who gave us this well that Thou canst draw Waters of Life from its depths?'[1]

But He said unto her: 'The water which thou drawest from this well, refreshes the thirsty ones; but these thirst again. But the water which God giveth from the Well of Life unto all who are athirst, assuageth the thirst for ever; for it becomes in those who drink of it, the gift of God unto the Life Eternal.'[2]

Then did she make request of Him: 'Give unto me this living Water that I may know thirst no more, neither have to come hither to draw water.'[3]

And He said unto her: 'Go, call thy husband hither that I may speak with him also.'

But she replied in great sadness: 'I have now no one to husband me.'

'Thou hast truly said that now thou hast no one to husband thee; though thou hast had five husbands, he whom thou now hast is no husband unto thee.'[4]

And the woman was filled with wonder that He should have discerned so much, and said unto Him: 'In this thing hast Thou spoken truly. I perceive that Thou art a prophet, and more than a prophet, for Thou hast discerned the things hidden in my heart. It hath been said that when Christ cometh He revealeth all things: I perceive it must be He who speaketh with me.'[5]

'When Christ cometh, He truly revealeth all things. And He is come; for it is He through whom God giveth the Living Waters.'

And the woman said unto Him: 'Our fathers worshipped God in this land upon mount Gerizim; and they said it was the true place in which to worship Him. But others have said that the true place in which to worship was Jerusalem. But Thou wilt know.'

And He said unto her: 'The hour is now drawing

NOTES.

[1] The Woman of Samaria represents the Soul on its intuitional side, approaching a consciousness of spiritual things represented by the Well of Jacob and the water found in its depths. It is said to have been the sixth hour, and towards the close of the Master's journey through that land. She longed for new things, the higher things of life, but perceived not how they were to be found. Even a Soul in the state of the Samaritan can have deep religious feelings and noble desires and endeavours.

The Master in His return when the Oblation was almost accomplished, passed through the very experiences represented by the Woman. He sat by the Well of Jacob until the sixth hour, and it was whilst He sat there sorrowfully, weary and longing for the inward rest that never came, that the new consciousness broke upon Him of the Presence which was once His constant heritage. That which the Well of Jacob could not give Him, Christ could. For Him there could be no rest but in the sublime consciousness that comes in Christhood.

[2] This is always true for all Souls. The gift of God is Eternal Life through the holy estates of Jesus, Christ and the Lord. And in the case of the Master the Overshadowing One had to remind Him that His rest would be found, that the deep yearnings of His being would be satisfied, that the great spiritual thirst within Him would find assuagement, but only when the return to Christhood had been accomplished.

[3] When once a Soul who has known Christhood in past ages has returned as far as the conditions of life represented as the parcel of land wherein was placed the Well of Jacob, not even the waters of that Well can give permanent assuagement. For the Soul returns to the Well from time to time to find refreshment, yet never finds the results permanent. The living water of the Christhood must be found.

[4] The five who husband the Soul are the senses. These latter are not merely physical as is commonly supposed, but actual powers of the Soul, and are spiritual. But when degraded, they become taskmasters. The sixth, who was no true husband, was the state of the Samaritan, or illicit intercourse of the Soul with matter.

[5] When Christ cometh He revealeth all things, even the Soul's own past. And the Soul comes to discern this, and to distinguish the Overshadowing Presence from all else, even from the high estate of Prophet and Seer.

THE CHRISTHOOD

The Woman Discovering Christ

near, and it even is now come, when not only in this land and upon Gerizim, but everywhere the true worshipper will worship the Father-Mother in the Spirit: for the Spirit is of God.'[1]

Then the woman left her water pot at the Well and went into the city of Sychar, proclaiming unto all the dwellers there that the Christ had come; for she said to them: ' Come, see a man who hath told me all things; is not this the Christ? '[2]

And many who heard the message of the woman left the City of Sychar, and came out unto Him that they might learn for themselves concerning the coming of Christ into their midst.[3]

Then it came to pass that the disciples who had gone away into the villages to find food for themselves, returned; and when they heard of what had been done, and how Christ had been revealed unto the woman, they were filled with wonder. And they marvelled that He should condescend to again make Himself manifest unto one who had been a dweller in Samaria.[4]

Then the disciples brought of the provisions which they had secured in the villages, and they drew near unto the Well of Jacob and found Him whom they sought still there, sitting amid great weariness, and sorrowful.

And they pressed Him to eat of the provisions which they had brought.[5]

But He refused them all, and said unto them: ' I have meat to eat that ye know not of. My meat is to do the will of Him who sent me, and to accomplish the work which He hath given me to do. For I came not to do mine own will; I came to do the will of my Father-Mother who sent me. And He giveth unto me my meat and my drink, even the Flesh and the Blood of the Son of God.'[6]

But they questioned amongst themselves in what manner He could be thus nourished, and marvelled that it should be thus with Him; for they now knew that no man gave unto Him.'

NOTES.

[1] Mount Gerizim, which was in Samaria, was the Mount of Prayer. It was the Watch-tower where the watchers who were upon the Planetary Heavens dwelt. The statement is, therefore, full of beautiful spiritual significance. In the pure days, worship was a sublime experience there, just as in Jerusalem—the spiritual household of the Human Family—it was essential to the growth and unfoldment of the Soul. The Soul must needs worship; it is of man's very innermost being that he seek to realize the Divine Love and Wisdom perfectly. For this is the end of all true worship. It is not the laudation of God such as men give to one another ; rather is it the adoration of the Supreme Being who is within our Sanctuary, and who filleth all things. When the Soul realizes that Presence it becomes filled with the Divine Awe.

[2] An allegorical form of statement, indicating that when the Soul who has known Christhood of old time has once more awakened and risen out of the grave of matter, the Christ within it speaks, and the Presence brings all things to the Soul's remembrance.

[3] Through the awakened intuition of the Soul many are influenced to leave the City of Sychar—intoxication of the Soul through the sense-life—and come out and up to the Well of Jacob to there find Christ.

[4] This has been sadly true in the experience of the Soul in its return. Even those who should have understood, have not been slow to express their surprise that such wonderful things as are contained in the new interpretation of Jesushood, the Christhood, and the high estate of the Lord-consciousness, should have been given to any one outcast from the traditional centres. Even some of those disciples who belonged to the outer group, have wondered and questioned in their heart. For the Woman of Samaria was the Master's own intuitional Soul power, questioning and perceiving heavenly things, yet terribly conscious of the burden which it had been His lot to carry.

[5] They pressed Him to accept of the food which they had found by the way, food found in the communities of Samaria ; really, various orders of teaching concerning life. In the Return in the last life of the Oblation, this actually took place on the part of some who were even of the inner group.

[6] As in the crucifixion they gave Him gall to drink which He refused, so was it in the Return. Yet no food or teaching of any one ever gave Him nourishment ; and He had to learn constantly to live upon the Flesh and Blood of the Son of God within Him, and to do the Will of the Father-Mother in all things, even at the expense of Himself in the days of great hunger and weariness.

267

THE CHRISTHOOD

In the Days of the Son of Man

" *And He said unto them : Hath it not been said unto you that when four times have been accomplished, then cometh the harvest ? Behold, I have seen the harvest as if it had already come. He who gathereth, reapeth unto Life Eternal. One soweth ; another reapeth. Some are sent to reap that upon which no labour was bestowed by them. Others have laboured, and these have entered into the fruits of that labour. But they who have laboured, and they who have gathered in the fruits of that labour, shall rejoice together in that day.*"[1]

This further allegory did the Master speak unto the inner group of disciples concerning the return of the Son of Man :—

" *In those days, when the Son of Man cometh again to restore unto His own the Kingdom of the Father Mother, shall He find Faith upon the Earth ?*[2]

Nay, Faith shall not be found ; for the vision of the Soul will be veiled.

Like little children meeting in the market place for play, will men and women come together to rejoice in that they can buy and sell, and get gain thereby.[3]

And unto those who do not go in their way nor belong to their generation, will they say, ' Behold, though we did call unto you that ye might join us, yet did ye not respond ; though we have played and rejoiced, yet have ye not joined us in the dance ; and when we have wailed over those who have gone out from us, ye did not come to wail with us.'[4]

Behold, when the messenger of the Lord cometh he will neither eat nor drink after the manner of that generation, and of him will they say that he hath a devil.[5]

The Wisdom of this world will justify the ways of its children ; for it shall be spoken of the Lord Himself that He came eating and drinking after the manner of themselves, as if He could be one with the gluttonous and the winebibber.[6]

NOTES.

[1] It had been presented to the vision of the Master what would be the final issue of the work of the Oblation. He foresaw what would happen to Himself on the way along which the Oblation would take Him. He beheld the conditions that were likely to prevail during the age of His return. For three times would the path of the Oblation or Sin-offering have to be followed ; but after the return in the fourth time or Naronic Cycle would the blessed result be gathered in. During this fourth cycle upon which the Planet has entered since the beginning of the Oblation, the ripening unto harvest will proceed. Even now it may be witnessed in the new consciousness that is breaking upon so many Souls. They who now are gathering into their life from the outpourings of the Heavens, are preparing themselves to reap the consciousness of the Life Eternal—the consciousness of the Presence within the Soul, and the Divine Power which such a blessed realization brings.

[2] In the return of the Christhood to those who were once in that most blessed state, the Son of Man, Adonai, returns to earth for manifestation. The Kingdom of the Father-Mother to be restored is this Christ-consciousness. The return is now. The Son of Man is coming : to the few, He is already come. Can it be said that there is Faith upon the earth ? Do even the religious communities perceive true heavenly secrets ?

[3] Could the state of the world to-day, especially the Western world, be more pertinently described ? Are not all its aims and activities rounded by the mercantile spirit ? It is the supreme joy of men and women to buy and sell and get gain, so much so that they imagine the world could not fulfil its destiny without their form of contribution to its activities. It is a delusion that has ensnared and made captive the Race, and very specially, the Western Nations.

[4] Life for the Soul who would climb the steep ascent to the Christhood, is quite distinct and separate from that life which finds its consummation in earthly things.

[5] This has actually been said of more than one Messenger in these latter days ; and even of the Master Himself hath it been said in His return.

[6] The reference is to the Master during the days of the Manifestation who is represented in the records as being the Lord Himself, and as having so lived that men and women could so speak of Him. The betrayal of His Teachings was foreseen.

269

THE CHRISTHOOD

Christ in
the House
of Simon

When the Son of Man cometh again it shall be even as we have said. The Christ will be invited to dine in the house of one Simon the pharisee and leper.[1]

And when He goeth into his house, behold, there is no water provided in the waterpots for purification, so that He has no one to wash His feet; nor is there the kiss of welcome given by a host to his distinguished guest; nor does Simon anoint Him with any precious unguent as becometh a host.[2]

For Simon will have none of these things.

But in the midst of the feast there entereth the house one who has been accounted a sinner, and she crosseth the threshold and cometh where the Christ is.

And she is filled with great sorrow; and she stands behind Him weeping.

And as she weeps in her strange sorrow, she stoopeth and kneeleth at His feet and batheth them with her tears.

Then she taketh her own hair for towel and wipeth them after they are cleansed; and she kisseth them much.

Afterwards she taketh a precious cruse of unguent and poureth its contents upon them; and thus she maketh manifest how much she loveth Him.[3]

But Simon is filled with amazement that such things should be done in his house, and that one who professeth to be Christ should permit the woman to work such things upon Him.[4]

Now, the thoughts of Simon were not hidden from his guest, so he saith unto him: ' Simon, I have somewhat to speak of unto thee.

There were two who were indebted to the same master.

One owed to him five hundred pence, and the other fifty pence.

When the master to whom they owed the money heard that they were so impoverished that they could not pay, he freely cancelled their indebtedness and forgave them both.

NOTES.

[1] Who could Simon be who invited the Christhood to cross his threshold and dine with him, and who was so utterly lacking in love for the Christ that he refused the things essential to the expression of love and devotion ?

Where has the Christ ostensibly been entertained and served ? Surely in the Western World ! For Simon means the mind on its outward aspect, the Reason upon the objective side of its activities. Though spiritually leprous and materialistic, it has been religious, that is, it has been ecclesiastically religious, and has pharisee-like tithed of its own anise, mint and cummin.

[2] Saddest of all sad things in its history, it has served the Christhood just as Simon is represented as having done. It has entertained a guest with feet unwashen, for the Christ it has entertained was not pure, humane and divinely loving in all His ways. He ate the flesh of the sub-human creatures, He drank the wine that intoxicated and destroyed, and He poured forth anger and judgment upon those who persecuted Him, except on the Cross. To the real Christ no good welcome was given. The utter failure of historical Christianity is the obvious testimony to its truth.

[3] The Master Himself in His return ; for the woman is the Soul who was as a Sin-bearer, in whose awakening consciousness to all that she had been in the days of the blessed Manifestation, came the most pathetic of sorrows. That Soul intuitively recognised the true nature of Christ, and of the Christhood which was made manifest. For the Master knew and understood as none other could, even in the days of the return, what the Christhood of the Manifestation was. So the Woman represents Himself in the days following the accomplishment of the Oblation, washing the feet of the Christ in tears and sorrow, kissing them when washed in token of the glad welcome of the restored vision to the Soul, and pouring out the fulness of His Soul's being, the precious unguent of love, in ministry of anointing or enlightenment for others to see and understand.

In sorrow and mind anguish, in great fearfulness and devotion to the Will of the Father-Mother, has the Soul of the Master done for the Christhood that which Simon refused to do.

[4] The amazement of Simon is obvious to all who are able to perceive and understand.

THE CHRISTHOOD

Which of these two debtors would most love the one who forgave them?'

Simon answereth: 'I suppose he unto whom most was forgiven.'

And his guest saith: 'Simon, thou hast rightly answered. Yet is it not always the way where forgiveness of much is experienced.

In the Kingdom of the Heavens we are taught to forgive until seventy times seven; nay, even unto the uttermost.[1]

The Kingdom of the Heavens is like a king who had two servants attending upon his treasury; and when he sought an account of their transactions, he found that one owed to him ten thousand talents of gold.

But the unfaithful servant who owed so much, fell down at the feet of the king and entreated forgiveness.

And the king was moved with compassion and forgave him the great debt.

But that same servant had a fellow servant who owed to him one hundred pence; and he had not wherewith to pay him, but entreated to be forgiven.

But the greater debtor, though he had been forgiven so much, would not forgive his fellowservant who owed him so little, but had him cast into prison and beaten.

Now, what shall be done unto those who, being debtors, have had much forgiven them by the Father-Mother, yet fail to forgive the trespasses of their fellow debtors?

They will be handed over to those who are appointed over the prison-houses, that they may go into these habitations until they have accomplished their purification from unjust judgment, and have learnt the way of forgiveness.'[2]

But Simon saith unto Him: 'If that be so, who then can be saved?'[3]

And He saith unto Simon: 'If these things appear to be impossible unto men, yet are they possible unto all who be of God. The kings and rulers of this earth exercise authority over men and women, and oppress

he Way
f the
ebtors

272

NOTES.

[1] The way of the Kingdom of the Heavens is not as the way of men. All Souls must needs tread the path of forgiveness, for all have much of which to be healed. Some have gone farther afield in their history than others ; they have gone far from the way of the Divine Love and Wisdom in their desires, feelings, motives and actions, and in this way have accumulated great debts, Karmic burdens that have to be carried and worked out until healing come. Under the conditions which have prevailed upon this Planet for long ages, it has been impossible for any Soul to pay off that debt fully in the sense of working it out. But that which the Soul cannot do for itself, the Divine Love does. Unto the uttermost is it forgiven or healed when it seeks the Divine Life. The Karmic effects of the way the race took in the last great descent from the Human Kingdom, had to be blotted out for all Souls by the Divine Love through the process associated with the Oblation and Sin-offering. And in this connection it cannot be truly said that those who have had most forgiven them love most ; for those of the children of this world who wrought such dire wickedness upon its planes and made the Oblation a necessity, have not been those who have made manifest the deepest sorrow and the noblest love. And it is this thing that is intended to be illustrated.

[2] But there is another aspect of the Law of Forgiveness, and it is here set forth. Forgiveness is not a commercial cancelling of moral and spiritual obligation ; it is a healing of the life. The life is to be healed of the influences of the past upon it. Now, when any Soul has been conscious of the operation of the Divine Love in healing it, naturally that Soul longs to make manifest to others that which it has received. For the Law of Forgiveness has its objective as well as its subjective side. In the measure with which we are forgiven, so must forgiveness be shown forth in our lives.

What a commentary the parable is upon the ways of men and women the world over. But for the failure of the Law of Forgiveness, the great legal systems could never have arisen. And they prevail most where the doctrine of the Divine Forgiveness is most believed in and taught, namely, amongst the Western peoples.

The judgment upon the unfaithful, unforgiving servant, is just. It is the Divine way of purification ; for the Soul must needs learn to love in the path of trial and suffering, and, in returning to earth, enter habitations of bodies and conditions where such healing can be effected.

[3] Simon still questions concerning this great truth, for the Western mind repudiates such Law of Forgiveness.

THE CHRISTHOOD

them at will; but it is not so in the Kingdom of the Heavens.

The Woman in the House of Simon

In that Kingdom all debts are forgiven to those who are impoverished, for the Son of Man cometh that He may save those who be lost.[1]

And in that Kingdom those who have had much forgiven them, the same love much.[2]

Thou seest this woman and dost in thine heart misjudge her; for thou reasonest with thyself that because of her state she was unworthy to enter thy house, and that she could have no true love to express in her ways, no pure devotion to make manifest for Christ, no noble service to render unto her Lord.[3]

When I entered thy house to be thy guest, thou didst not provide water to bathe My feet, My brow thou didst not kiss in token of the welcome thou gavest to Me; nor didst thou pour out the precious ointment for the anointing.[4]

But this woman, when she entered thy house, beheld wherein thou didst lack, and she hath washed My feet with her tears and wiped them with the hair of her head; she hath bestowed upon Me the kiss of welcome, and made manifest her own humiliation; and she hath broken upon Me the cruse of most precious unguent unto My anointing.'[5]

And looking upon the woman, and laying His hand of blessing upon her, Christ said, 'Woman, why weepest thou so greatly? Why doth thy sorrow lack healing? Thou hast indeed loved much, even unto the giving of all thou hadst. Thy passing through hath been accomplished; thy Faith is saved unto thee, enter now into the Great Peace.' "[6]

NOTES.

[1] The impossible to man is possible with God ; the Divine Kingdom can effect that which is beyond the powers of the Human Kingdom. The Law of Karma is not hard and fast as it has often been represented to be. God's thoughts are not as man's thoughts, nor are His ways those of man. The interpretation put upon the outworking of His Laws is not according to His thoughts and ways. The doctrine of commutation finds no place upon the Heavens. That doctrine was begotten on the Astral Kingdom, and is perpetuated from there. The way of the Divine Love is not oppressive. It is not to demand so much Karmic burden for so much wrong. Had that been so, not one of the children of this Planet could be saved. The Son of Man, the manifestation of the Christhood, cometh to forgive, to heal Souls, to restore harmony. Christ healeth—the Christ Love and Light within : that is His mission. Through that Love and Light Karma can be changed.

[2] All who arrive within the Kingdom of Christhood love and sorrow much. They love Christhood ; they sorrow that they are not more worthy.

[3] It is most sad that within the Household of the West the woman element in the Soul should have been regarded as one unworthy to be trusted and loved. Has not the West, which so obviously makes it known to the world that Christ is upon its threshold as its guest, repudiated the Intuition as the highest spiritual faculty— the faculty by which alone Christ can be discerned ; the faculty through which God has spoken in His Prophets and Seers ? What place has that Divine Attribute of the Soul had in the House of Simon ? Is it not true that it has not been a guest in the house, but one who has had to steal upon his threshold ? He has despised the woman whom he has helped to degrade by his cynicism, his traditionalism, and his ecclesiastical religion.

[4] Yet it is the despised one in every pure Soul who recognises the Christ-vision. And in relation to the Master we have to state that in the lives lived by Him in the West, the treatment meted out to the woman in the allegory was just what Simon felt towards Him ; and this is very specially true of the last life of the Oblation, and the awakening and return. For He was as an outcast in the House of Simon ; yet it was on that threshold that he had to perform the work of devotion made manifest in the sorrowful cleansing of the feet of the Christhood and the anointing.

[5] See " The Life and Teachings of the Master " by us, for a full interpretation of this action.

[6] No living Soul could ever understand the awful sorrow that filled the Master during the life of which we write.

275

THE CHRISTHOOD

The Seven Fishermen of Galilee

The blessed Master, ere He passed from the midst of His disciples, spake also this allegory unto those of them who were of the innermost circle :—

" There were once seven disciples of the Lord of Life who were overtaken with great loss.

Of such a nature was their loss that it brought unto them much sorrow.

So deep was their sorrow that they became blind to everything but the sense of their loss.

It was as if the night had fallen upon them and they could not see.[1]

These seven, being Fishers upon the Waters of Galilee, seekers for the deep things of God, launched out into the Deep to seek for the meaning of the great sorrow which had overtaken them.

But all through the long night of their sorrow did they toil in vain, for they could catch nothing that would interpret the Mystery for them.[2]

Then in the fourth watch of the night, just as the dawn was breaking, in looking Eastwards they beheld the Lord walking upon the shores of the Sea of Galilee.[3]

And He spake unto them, saying : ' Children, have ye naught to eat that ye sorrow so ? '

But they replied unto the Lord : ' We have been toiling all the night, and have taken nothing.'

And the Lord commanded that they should let down their nets upon the right side, for there they would find ; so they cast their nets on the Eastward side, and behold their nets filled so much that they could scarcely drag them to land.[4]

Now one of the seven, when He knew that it was the Lord, threw himself into the sea that he might come to the shore first.[5]

But when the waters began to close about him he was filled with great fear, and called out unto the Lord to save him lest amid the waters he should perish.

And the Lord stretched forth His right hand and upheld him, and drew him to the land.

Then was that disciple overwhelmed with sorrow,

276

NOTES.

[1] It is an allegory of the experiences about to overtake the few who were of the innermost circle, though the number seven has a mystical meaning. These friends of the Master were all to be sharers in the mystery of the Divine Passion which was so very specially to be made manifest through the Master. Though much had been said to them concerning all that had to come to pass, yet they found it difficult to fully realize its nearness and all that it would mean of travail even to them. And the Night was drawing near when, upon the seven planes of their being, they would be sorely smitten. for the darkness would prevail until the fourth watch. Oh, the sorrow of those who knew the Master best, that such a fellowship as theirs could ever be disbanded, and that such apparent disaster should overtake all of them! Only those who knew that blessed fellowship could realize how great the sacrifice was, and how poignant the sorrow in the making of it.

[2] They were Fishers or Truth-seekers. · Amid the Waters of the Sea of Galilee or the knowledges of the spiritual mind, the knowledges brought forth from the Intuition, they sought for the meaning of the Mystery of the Passion. It was Simon Peter who led the way—the spiritual Understanding. And all through the long night of the Oblation did these saints of God toil to discover the meaning of the way the Master took and the Passion of the Lord. But they could not find it ; they caught nothing to fully explain the Mystery.

[3] The Fourth Watch in which the dawn came and the day broke is now. It is the fourth Naronic Cycle on which the Planet has entered since those days. Unto them has the Lord of Life appeared, for they have seen His Vision and heard His Voice in the blessed truth that has been given to them.

[4] To find the Truth, the Soul must look Eastward ; that is the direction of the Divine, and none but the Divine can reveal through the Intuition this Mystery. It is the Mystery that has been hidden for ages. From the outward aspects of things the Understanding cannot arrive at the interior knowledges, even though it toil long and earnestly. That is the wrong side on which to fish or seek for such understanding of the Divine Mystery. So the Soul must seek on the right side, the Eastward side, the direction in which Light comes and the glory of the Day is shed.

[5] Simon Peter, the Understanding itself, when looking Eastward and so illumined and perceiving the Lord's Presence within. When the vision comes, the understanding passes through this very experience. It seems anxious to know all, yet becomes overwhelmed with the greatness of it all.

S—I

THE CHRISTHOOD

and saith unto the Lord : ' Depart no more from me O my Lord, for I am a sinful Soul.'[1]

But the Lord rebuked him not. And He said unto him : ' Why were ye so fearful ? Have ye now no trust ? Has your faith grown dim ? '

And he girt his fisherman's coat about him and once more threw himself into the sea.[2]

When all the seven had reached the shore they found the Lord awaiting them there.[3]

And they beheld a fire upon the shore, and there was a Fish laid thereon.[4]

And the Lord said unto them : ' Bring ye of the things which ye have caught.' So they emptied their nets and found that they had taken 153, so deep had been the draught.[5]

And the Lord invited them to come and dine with Him ; for He said, ' Come and dine with Me.'

And He broke unto them the Bread of Life, and gave unto them of the Fish from the Fire that they might eat of the Divine Mystery of Love.

Then, when they had dined, the Lord revealed unto them the depth of the Divine Love as it had been made manifest in the life of the Christhood, and interpreted in the lives of the Ransomer."

And when He had spoken of these many things that were to come to pass when the Son of Man cometh again, the Master desired to be alone.

But those who were nearest to Him heard Him uttering strange sayings, and speaking as if to some one present with Him. And He spake these words :—

" Simon Iona, Satan hath desired to possess thee that he may sift thee as wheat, and crush thee ; but prayer is made for thee that thy Faith fail thee not, and when it hath been accomplished, thou shalt be once more restored unto thy brethren."

" O, most wretched man that I shall be ! When I shall wish to do the good thing, evil shall prevail to prevent me, so that the good I would fain do I shall be unable to do, and the evil which now I abhor that will I have to do.

278

NOTES.

[1] However conscious of sin a Soul may be, when it learns the true way and turns unto the Lord, it has no more any desire that that Holy Presence should depart from it. It may feel unworthy ; it is sure so to feel : but even so, great will be its desire that the Lord Presence should abide with it. Such an experience is true always of the Soul whose understanding is illumined. And the Master, in His return, passed through this experience also, and that in a most profound way.

[2] The Fisherman's coat is significant. It was the garment the true Mystic must wear, the raiment of the Seeker after the Divine Love and Wisdom, as distinguished from mere occult knowledges.

[3] The Eastern shore of Galilee, the spiritual mind, is the threshold of the Lord Presence. When the Soul reaches that land it finds the Lord awaiting it. He is ever there for the Soul.

[4] It is also upon that shore, that inward land, that the Flame of the Spirit burns. For the Spirit is of God, and the Flame is that Sacred Fire which energizes and illumines, but without consuming. And the Fish, not one of those caught by the Fishermen, but one provided by the Lord of Being—was the Sacred Mystery of the Divine Love as revealed in and interpreted by the Oblation.

[5] Herein is revealed what the true seeker finds in the depths of the Waters of Galilee. For what was the draught of great Fish which numbered 153 ? The sum is nine, which in mystical numbers represents Jesushood realized, for the Fish provided by the Lord was related to the Mystery of high Christhood. But nine stated as 153 contains three most precious realizations.

The first number represents the One Life ; and in Jesushood this blessed experience breaks upon the Soul, and the Soul sees it, feels it, and makes it concrete in all its actions.

The second number represents the five senses of the Soul, the power of the Divine Life within by which the Soul senses all things upon every plane ; for the senses are not physical, but spiritual.

The third number represents the yet deeper consciousness which eventuates from the cognition and realizations of the One Life and the true operation of the five senses—namely, the consciousness of the triune nature of the Life given us, the One Life in its twofold modes making manifest the Son of God who is within the Soul's system.

THE CHRISTHOOD

For the messengers of Satan will buffet me in the way of my going, and only through the Grace of my Lord shall I be prevented from becoming a castaway."[1]

A Sorrowful Soliloquy

"Simon Iona,[2] *when thou wast young, thou didst gird thyself, and didst go whithersoever thou hadst desire to go; and now when thy days have been crowned with age, others are to take thee, and bind thee, and carry thee whithersoever thou wouldest fain not go.*[3]

And when thou dost come back again from the places whithersoever thou art to be carried by others, how shall it then be with thee? Wilt thou be able to once more strengthen thy brethren, and make manifest unto them what the Lord Himself hath wrought for them?

In that day when the Lord requireth of thee the love wherewith thou hast loved Him, what will thine answer be?

When He saith to thee: ' Simon Iona, lovest thou Me more than these thy brethren?' what wilt thou have to answer Him?[4]

Shall it indeed be that thou wilt make answer. ' Yea, Lord, Thou knowest that I love Thee.' Will it be remembered then how thy love has been tried whilst thou hast borne the burden in order that the sheep of the fold might be brought back to Him?

When the Lord inquireth of thee yet again whether thou lovest Him whilst in the depths whither thou shalt have gone in the return, and thou dost yet make answer: ' Lord, thou knowest that I love Thee,' will He remember that the love wherewith thou wouldst fain love Him, has suffered through the burden-bearing on behalf of the lambs of the fold?

And when He inquireth of thee for a third time and thou art hurt and grieved that thy love should be doubted though it has suffered such loss in the way whither thou hadst to go, and the oppression with which it has been oppressed, shall it be spoken again unto thee by thy Lord as He spake it in the days of thy coming hither unto this hour: ' Feed My sheep?'"

"O my Lord, Thou knowest all things, and Thou knowest that I love Thee."

NOTES.

[1] A new meaning will now be found lighting up these Sayings, and here they will be seen in their true relationship. The first was applied to a disciple by the writer of the first Gospel Record and continued by those who wrote the accepted Gospels ; the second was taken by Paul, and those who sent out the Epistolary Letters in his name applied it to him. Yet they had a more profound meaning than any experience that came to either Simon Peter or Paul. And the depth of Soul experience for the Master which they reveal testifies once more to the reality of the Oblation, the exceeding greatness of the burden borne, the sorrow and anguish which were the portion of the Soul in the path that had to be pursued, and the awful dread that lay upon the mind of the Master as He foresaw all that awaited Him. To stoop from the sublime experiences of the Christ-consciousness in such fulness to the levels of the hell states, was part of His blessed mission ; but to pass through these awful experiences during many lives, covering the three days of the Naronic Cycles, filled His whole being with the horror of the states and an unspeakable dread lest He should fail at last to rise out of them and ascend once more into the blessed Life of the Christhood.

[2] Who was Simon Iona ? The Mind of the Master, and the beautiful spiritual condition in which it was at one time when the sad soliloquy was spoken. Simon Peter was the mind illumined, and, therefore, an enlightened Understanding. Simon Iona was the mind in a state of Divine Love. So full of love was the mind of the Master that He loved all Souls, even those who were in their attitude enemies to the message He had to give ; and His love revealed itself in the yielding up of all He had, even to the loss of His Christhood attributes.

In a mystic sense the term Simon Iona may, therefore, be spoken concerning any one whose mind is in a state of Love.

[3] This refers to the gradual ascension of the Soul, through desiring the Highest, into Christhood of high degree. Those were the days when the Soul performed its evolution, the ages of its growth towards the perfect fulfilment of its being in Christhood, ages in which it may be said of it that it was young.

There is no age in the sense in which we speak of old age, where spiritual life is concerned, for the Spirit is ever young. But the Soul is spoken of as crowned with Age in Christhood. Hence the reference here to past ages and the then present conditions as crowned with Age.

The Mind was to be put under such sad limitations that it would be bound, and carried by the terrible conditions of the burden to be borne whithersoever it would fain not go.

[4] In this sad soliloquy two terms were made use of to express Love —Agapeo and Phileo. The Master was in the state expressed by Agapeo, and he dreaded lest He should lose the power to so love.

281

THE CHRISTHOOD

Now, when the Passover drew near, the Master was deeply moved because so soon would He have to leave those whom He had greatly loved;[1] and He prayed that His love for them might continue with Him unto the end.[2]

And Iscariot was preparing for His betrayal even unto the devil with whom he was in league, and he was ready to receive the sop which the Master would give him.[3]

Unto the friends who were with Him to the last, He spake this allegory .

" There dwelt in an ancient city one whose office it was to instruct Souls concerning the Kingdom of the Heavens, and to lead them into a knowledge of the way of the Divine Love and Wisdom.[4]

And some of those who had gathered around him desired to reach unto the perfect realization of the Divine Love, Radiance, and Life.

But as they could not attain that high degree of life owing to the conditions by which they were environed, he had to descend from his high position and reach the plane where they were, in order to aid them in the accomplishment of the exaltation of their spiritual life through their regeneration.

Those who had become seekers after the realization of the Divine, were Souls who had come up on to the Heavens from the various planetary systems, and accomplished the purification necessary in the Soul who would find the Divine Kingdom ; but these had been sent out on a mission to this world, and, whilst fulfilling their ministry, had gone down into the conditions which had overtaken all whom they were to teach.

Now, the Teacher, in order to be able to effectually aid them, found it necessary to descend into the conditions by which they found themselves oppressed and hindered ; but to accomplish this he had to divest himself of many attributes, those which had been acquired by him as he himself rose to the Divine Kingdom, and those which had been given to him for his ministry.

The Teacher who Washed the Feet His Disciples

NOTES.

[1] The Passover was the act of passing over from the high Christhood state to enter one in which the light within would be veiled ; for only in that way could He possibly descend into the conditions amid which the burden of the Oblation must needs be borne. It is in this sense that the Christhood was laid aside, all its attributes suspended, its Holy Flame withheld, the consciousness of the Presence withdrawn. From the state in which these Divine realizations were continuous to states in which they could not be realized, He passed over, and became as even the least of His brethren.

But here the actual leaving of the outer planes, or passing over of the Master to take up the Oblation work, is also referred to. The hour was drawing near when He must go away from them.

[2] Another reference to His own inherent dread lest He should lose His love through the sufferings that would be His portion. For some of those who had been with Him would have a part to play in providing some of the conditions necessary for the work to be accomplished.

[3] As explained earlier, Iscariot was no disciple of the Master, nor indeed any man, but the betraying materializing power of the Astral realm. It is quite true that power acts through men and women, and accomplishes the Soul's betrayal for material gain. But here it is to be understood in an impersonal way, for the Sop offered by the Master was the Soul born into lives in which Iscariot would have the betraying power. Yet, through these very lives, the power of Iscariot was to be broken and the Herodean kingdom (the Astral realm) was to be overthrown.

[4] The story of the Feet-washing found in the fourth Gospel Record is only a part of the original allegory spoken by the Master. It will be seen how full of meaning the allegory was for the disciples, and the ages of Soul history which were implied in its references to the past. And it reveals the intimate relationships existing between the Master and themselves. For they are those Souls who had accomplished their evolution upon other planetary systems and risen into the Christhood consciousness, and had been banded together as a community of Christs for Divine ministry, of which the Master Himself was a member. He had been their helper and Teacher, and had been sent to them amid the difficult ministry they had to perform upon this Planet.

They were ministering upon this Planet when the descent or fall took place, and had become involved in the changed conditions which had arisen as the result. So much had they all been affected, that many were unable to rise out of the conditions into the Christhood state.

THE CHRISTHOOD

Washing the Feet of Simon Peter

But this divestment was not an easy task for the Teacher, and involved him in extreme sorrow ; yet it was necessary for the work he had to do.

And he unrobed himself, laying aside his high attributes, one by one, until he was even as the least of those who had gone down into the evil conditions from the high estate.[1]

Now, the Teacher had taught those disciples who had gathered around him, many things concerning the conditions amid which they found themselves, and what would be required of him in the work he had to do in order to change them.

But the disciples did not understand all that he meant, for he spake words unto them whose depth was difficult to reach in the state of their understanding.

Having laid aside his garments, he girt himself with a towel ; and, taking a sacred vessel, he poured water out from it into a basin, and stooping down he began to wash the feet of the disciples.

And as he proceeded in the washing of them, he came unto one who did not approve of what he was doing, and that one withstood him in the doing of it, saying : ' Thou shalt not wash my feet.'

But the Teacher said unto him : ' Unless I wash thy feet, thou canst have no part in the work to be accomplished.'

Then that one, when he had come into a right attitude of mind, said unto him : ' Then, wash not only my feet, but also my head and my hands.'

And the Teacher said unto him : ' Nay, for if I wash thy feet thou art clean in every whit ; he who would be cleansed needeth only to make clean his feet.'

And the Master spake again, saying : " Do ye understand the things of which I have now spoken unto you, and those things which have to be accomplished in the going down of the Son of Man ?

Behold, He who is yet with us goeth, and I must leave you for a time so that this purification may be accomplished.

284

NOTES.

[1] Divestment is a most trying experience. When a Soul has once attained a high degree of Life such as is implied in Christhood, it more and more longs for yet higher realizations, more complete fulfilment of its innermost yearnings for the perfect consciousness of the Divine. To attain Christhood means long æonial evolution upon the spiritual planes, on the part of the Soul. The cedars of Lebanon which have witnessed the passing of a thousand years, are but as yesterday compared to the age of a Soul who has reached the Human Kingdom ; and the younger children of this system who are now upon the Human Kingdom, though they have been thousands of ages on the path of spiritual evolution, are indeed but young in contrast to a Soul who has acquired the attributes of Christhood.

The attributes acquired by a Soul who reaches the Divine Kingdom are of a nature difficult to explain in any terms at our command, but they are not to be confounded with those powers usually associated with Christhood. They are not of the same nature as those powers attributed to great Yogoi and Occultists who can perform magical acts and work material wonders ; for they are of the Soul, whereas the powers of the Yogoi and Occultists are of the mind. The attributes of a Christ work along spiritual lines ; those of the Yogoi and Occultist have the elemental and upper elemental or astral spheres for their realm of action. The Soul in Christhood seeks only that through the attributes the Will of the Father-Mother may be done ; the path of Occultism has not led to the accomplishment of that Will.

This much we must needs say concerning the inwardness of the meaning of Christhood, and the nature of the attributes acquired in that state of Soul realization. For it is essential that things so different should not be mixed up and confounded. The Priesthood of the Soul in Christhood and the service wherein its attributes are made manifest, are entirely of the Divine Realm. It is the Priesthood of the Rosy Cross. Its ministry is of that Cross. For the Christs are Divine Alchemists : they know nothing of occultism and magic.

For a Soul in such Priesthood to divest, laying aside the attributes attained, so as to enable that one to descend into lowly conditions of life, is a process most painful, difficult to understand, except where in the ministry of life it has had to be experienced. The story of the Teacher is the story of the Master.

THE CHRISTHOOD

A Story
of the
Oblation

The servant is not greater than his Lord ; nor is He who is sent, greater than He who sent Him.

The Lord of Life stoopeth to minister unto all, and he who would be His minister must so stoop.

He who loveth most, giveth most ; and he who giveth most is likest the Lord of Love."

Then they asked Him if the allegory might be more fully interpreted to them.[1]

And He explained to them how it had reference to the work which He must now go to accomplish.

" The water has to be poured out from the chalice of life into the basin as an Oblation for the purification of the Middle Kingdom, and the blotting out of the graven images upon it.

In order to be able to accomplish this, the robes of Christhood must be laid aside, and the reins must be girt about with the garment of one who is a bond-servant.

Unto this end came I to be the servant of the Lord, that through me He might perform this great work.

And in this service He will purify the mind of this world, and of her children within her.

And in this ministry which calls me hither, the feet of all who would follow on to know the Lord of Life, must be cleansed.

But the last to be washed and made pure is the mind known as Simon Peter ; and that mind will reason with itself that it requires no such cleansing, and will question the wisdom of the Lord in essaying to perform that work upon it.

Yet it must needs be that the feet of Simon Peter be likewise purified, and then will the Oblation be accomplished.

" Now, understand ye what it is that must needs be wrought by the Lord of Love through me ?"

And the Master said unto them : ' What I do now, ye know not ; but ye shall understand by and bye.' "

286

NOTES.

[1] The allegory, as is made obvious in the interpretation given to the disciples, was a picture of the descent of the Soul through whom the blessed manifestation had been given, from the consciousness of that high life in which the Soul is one with the Divine. It is a picture of the real descent from the Cross ; for it is the descent from the state in which the Soul is one with Him who is the Luminous Cross, to take up the burden of the Cross that is accounted accursed. For what was the unrobing but the laying aside of the most beautiful attributes af the Christhood in order to perform the office appointed unto Him ? And what was the meaning of being girt about the loins with a towel, but the symbol of the manner in which He was to be bound and limited for the work to be done ? And what was the sacred vessel with the water, but His own Soul-life that was poured forth unto the death of the Luminous Cross within Him, so that the Radiance was veiled and the blessed consciousness of the Presence lost ? And what was the stooping to the ground in order to accomplish the oblation, but the great humiliation of the Soul in the service undertaken in order to effect the restoration of the whole Christhood, and thus prepare the way for the redemption of the world ? Nay, what was the washing of the feet of the disciples, who when they were so cleansed were clean every whit, if it was not the purification of the way of the Soul and the understanding in the days of the return ? For the feet symbolize the path trod in the life. And is it not an astonishing fact that the last to be so purified is Simon Peter ? In these days of the Redemption and the Regeneration, the mind of all who ought to have followed the true way in life, has had to be shown what it means. For there are many who profess to be following the Christ and entering into the Christhood consciousness, who vainly imagine that such a high and blessed state may be attained without regard to what they eat and drink, or to the true manifestation of Divine Love, which embraces all Souls and all Creatures. And is it not likewise true that in the last days of the Oblation—those in which we ourselves have been living—the chief opposition to the process of such purification, and even resentment to the Teaching that it is necessary, have come from those who would fain be accounted the followers of Christhood ?

THE CHRISTHOOD

The Story of Lazarus: his sleep and his wakening

" *In the city of Bethany there dwelt Mary and Martha ; and their home was that which the Lord loved to enter.[1]*

Now their brother Lazarus fell sick, being smitten with the fever ; and the sickness deepened unto death.[2]

When this took place the Lord was not present, for He had withdrawn beyond Jordan.[3]

And in her deep distress Mary sent unto the Lord, saying : ' My Lord, he whom Thou lovest is sick, and nigh unto death.'[4]

But the Blessed One sent this message in reply : ' This sickness is not unto death, but for the Glory of God ; and in this sickness shall the Son of Man be glorified.'[5]

But Lazarus only grew the more sick of the fever until the deepening shades of death fell upon him.

When this took place, Mary and Martha were filled with great sorrow, and were sore distressed that the Lord had not been with them ; and they sent yet another message unto Him, saying :

' The sickness of our brother has issued in death ; but hadst Thou been here our brother would not have died.'[6]

Then the Lord met them in their sorrowful journey and was deeply touched by their poignant grief and pain ; and He said unto them ·

' Fear not ; I, the Lord, am the Resurrection and the Life. Whosoever is in Me cannot die. Receive ye this ? '[7]

For answer they said unto Him : ' Yea, Lord ! but he whom Thou lovest has been dead and buried, and this is the morning of the fourth day since he left us.'[8]

For their grief was so deep that they were without hope.

And they came to the place where he had been laid as dead ; and in the sepulchre he lay bound hands and feet, with grave clothes wound around him.

And the Lord groaned within Himself because of what He beheld ; for it filled Him with grief to behold in such low estate the one whom He so greatly loved.

288

NOTES.

[1] The allegory is another illustration of the process, effects and duration of the Sin-offering. As a story of ordinary human experience it has always awakened deep sympathy, for it has appealed to the sorrowing. But if the pathos in it be so great when thus interpreted, how much more profound it is when related to the Soul during the three cycles of the Oblation.

Bethany was the House of Christhood, the city in which Mary and Martha had their home—the Soul in its two modes of service, the contemplative wherein the Divine Wisdom is learnt, and the active wherein the service of life is rendered to the Lord. As such it was the home in which the Lord was ever welcome, and where the Lord loved to be—that is, within the Soul in the state of Christhood.

[2] Lazarus, of whom nothing is heard until this event, was the brother of Mary and Martha, or the mind in a state of great suffering and impoverishment, as the word means. But though the allegory in part hides the meaning, as was necessary, Lazarus was none other than the Master Himself after the attributes of the Christhood had been laid aside, and He became impoverished.

[3] The Lord or Presence was veiled, and so withdrawn from His consciousness. For the Jordan is the river of the Spirit that divides the outer consciousness from the innermost. The Overshadowing One had thus left Him.

[4] The Soul realizing the meaning of the loss that has come upon it, through the sickening of the mind owing to the impoverished life, and calling unto the Lord of Love for aid. For was not the Master known as the Beloved One ? His name meant it.

[5] The sickness verily was unto spiritual death, but not unto ultimate loss, for in it the Christ would be glorified.

[6] Quite true : where the consciousness of the Presence is, Life only is found.

[7] Those who be in Him in that high degree have power to lay down the life if it be required of them, and power to take it up again. For the Lord within them is the Life for them.

[8] The allegory anticipated the times that are now with us. It is the fourth day or Naronic Cycle since the Oblation began. It is the morning of the fourth cycle, and the resurrection has taken place ; for the Master has been raised up again, and many of the Souls who knew Him in those days of the Manifestation, have been awakened.

THE CHRISTHOOD

Then He commanded Lazarus to come back to life ; and he who had been dead arose and came forth from the tomb.

The Resurrection of the Soul

And to those who were with Him the Lord gave instructions to unbind his hands and his feet, and to loosen the garments in which he had been bound.

And these unbound the grave-clothes that were about him, and gave back unto him his own ; and with the Lord he went forth."[1]

" And in those days it shall come to pass that early in the morning, before the breaking of the day, cometh Mary Magdalene, and she findeth the stone rolled away from the sepulchre.[2]

But she could not find the Lord ; for it was as yet very dark.[3]

She stooped and entered the sepulchre and beheld the garments in which He had been buried ; but Him she could not see.

Then, within the sepulchre, two shining ones made themselves known unto her.[4]

But Mary wept sorely ; and the shining ones said unto her : ' Woman, why weepest thou ? '

The Sorrow of Maria Magdalene

And unto them she replied : ' My Lord has been taken away, and I know not where to find Him.'[5]

And though they spake many things unto her, her sorrow would not be comforted.

When she turned away from the sepulchre there was one who stood by her, but in the darkness and the intensity of her sorrow, she was unable to discern who it was.[6]

And supposing that one to be the guardian of the sepulchre, she said unto him : ' Sir, if thou hast taken away my Lord, tell me where thou hast borne Him that I may go unto Him.'

Then the Presence drew near and spake unto her, saying : ' Maria ! '[7]

And she trembled and bowed herself to the earth. And when she would have taken hold of Him, He said unto her :

290

NOTES.

[1] Oh, that it ever had to be so done unto one who always loved the Lord, and never ceased to long throughout the long weary days of His travail for the coming again of the Presence to Him! For so weakened was He in the way, so impoverished was He in His strength, that even when called back into the higher consciousness, He was still bound in His feet and hands and about His head; for the effects of His travail were great upon Him. And He had to be aided in the unbinding by those who were present at His awakening. They had this special work allotted to them. And when they had done their part, there were restored unto Him the garments which He had had to lay aside, even the raiment associated with the Christhood. And with the Lord Presence He went forth.

[2] In the story of Maria Magdalene there is presented a most remarkable picture of what happened to the Master after the rising from the grave and the unbinding of Him. For he was Maria who had been Magdalene in His travail; and in the awakening He sought in vain for the Lord vision.

[3] The day had not broken. It was very dark all around, and the darkness within was yet great. The veil was not yet taken away.

[4] Who those were who were appointed to meet Him upon the threshold of the sepulchre, cannot be told; though they may be discovered. They were the Lord's messengers.

[5] The Soul in its intense sorrow could not recover the vision of the Lord; He found it most difficult to realize the Overshadowing Presence with Him. In great grief the vision is dimmed; and it was thus with Maria, the Soul of the Master.

[6] Even the Lord Presence was mistaken for another. This was literally so in the case of the Master during the Return. The intensity of the Soul's grief dimmed the vision to such an extent, that discernment of the Presence was difficult. That which was the outcome of His own Soul-travail, He thought might be the work of the One with Him. He thought that the one with Him had purposely hidden the vision of the Lord.

To make this experience of the Master clear to the understanding of everyone, is impossible; to the perceiving ones it will be obvious.

[7] It is indeed beautiful, the coming of the Presence to any Soul; for it means a high state of consciousness and the most blessed realizations. How much it would mean for the Master to hear that voice once more and become conscious of the drawing near of the Presence!

THE CHRISTHOOD

'*Touch me not yet; but ascend unto the Father-Mother in thine estate.*' *And go unto those who may hear thee, and say unto them,*

The Lord hath risen indeed, and called us all to ascend unto the Father-Mother in our estate, that all may come to be at One in Him.'

And Mary Magdalene bore the message of the Lord unto all who were able to bear it.

And it came to pass that those who followed the Lord from Galilee went to the grave wherein they had laid Him, taking with them precious spices and unguents with which to anoint Him.[2]

But they found the stone had been rolled away from the sepulchre.[3] *And they questioned amongst themselves what it could mean.*

But whilst they gazed into the sepulchre and wondered, two angels appeared unto them to proclaim that the Lord had risen again, and that He would show Himself unto them upon a high mountain in Galilee, even as He had said unto them while He was yet with them.[4]

And unto these did the Angels say : ' Why seek ye the Living One amongst the dead ? Behold, He is not here, but is risen again even as it was foretold you.'[5]

And Maria and Joseph accompanied these ; and they told of all the wonderful things which the Lord had wrought.

But their message was only received as an idle tale, even by many of those who had come down to the grave to find the Lord."[6]

The Soul's Vision of the Lord Recovered

292

NOTES.

[1] The command not to touch Him yet must seem strange in the light of the sorrow and longing ; yet it had its deep significance for the world as well as for Maria, the Master. In His return He was to dwell at Nazareth—the pure consecrate life, but one that was despised ; and that has been true in the Master's experience. Until the effects of the return were fully accomplished He was not to rise into that high consciousness spoken of as touching the Lord-state, and abiding there. Yet was He to ascend from time to time unto the Father-Mother, that He might receive of the Divine Love and Wisdom and thus be fitted and strengthened to appear before His brethren with the Living Word of the Lord concerning the Ascension Life unto which all were called.

[2] Who were those who followed the Lord from Galilee ? Galilee signified the higher or Soul-mind. These are distinguished from the intuitional Souls in this that they follow the Lord through the preceptions of the mind, and require the presentation of the Gnosis from that plane of vision ; whereas the Intuitional Souls perceive by means of the Soul's own vision, knowing interiorly from themselves, the Gnosis. Here the reference is to those who were in the state of Galilee.

[3] These spiritual minds found, in the last days, the stone rolled away from the sepulchre ; for the Angel of the Lord had descended to roll it away. That meant that the power, the seal, the guard which the Astral realm had exercised was broken and overwhelmed. No longer was that realm able to prevent the Soul from arriving at the consciousness of the Lord Presence ; for the resurrection of the Lord is the arising of the Soul once more into that most blessed realization. Here the effects of the Oblation are manifest.

[4] The High Mountain of Galilee shown unto them, where the Lord would make Himself known, was that most blessed spiritual condition of the mind when it may be said that it is in high altitudes, and can look upon the glory of the Divine World.

[5] The Heavens are so speaking unto the Soul of all who may be able to hear, asking this very question, and directing to the only true place in which the vision is to be come at. For the Lord is not found in any Astral realm, nor in Astral knowledges, or occult powers, nor in philosophies : He is discovered and known within the Soul in its highest experiences.

[6] The Resurrection is upon the world : the Lord has risen as one from the dead, and Maria Ioseph has proclaimed what hath been done for all Souls through the Lord of Love.

THE AFTERMATH

O my Lord, in Thee only is my hope; in Thee only is to be found the comfort that my Soul needeth.[1]

The Prayer of the Aftermath

If Thou shouldest fail to help me, truly I shall be helpless; for without the strength that cometh from Thy Holy Presence, I can do no good thing.

Unto Thee have I cried for help against all those that be enemy unto my Soul; but no one seemed to regard my crying, and no help was vouchsafed unto me.

My innermost being has wept in the secret, and cried unto Thee in its anguish: " Hast Thou cast me off for ever, O my Lord? Are all Thy tender mercies withdrawn from me?

Wilt Thou be gracious no more? Can it be that Thou hast turned me from Thee as a castaway, and one whom Thou can'st no longer love?"

All my days hath my prayer been unto Thee. In all seasons hath my spirit yearned for the glory of Thy Countenance; and throughout the long Night my Soul hath wept sorely for very sorrow that Thou didst hide Thy face from me.

Amid my weariness and pain have I cried unto Thee to take away my life; and in order that I might forget the bitterness of my sorrow, and have no more any anguish, I have longed for Thee to take from me even my power to remember, so great have my sorrows and anguish been.

In its love hath my Soul been smitten; for in the degree that my love hath been unto Thee, so have my sufferings been.

Thou hast made of my love a power for sorrow, it hath been so rewarded as to fill me with dismay.[2]

Thou bestowest Thy compassion everywhere; many are they who are filled with Thy great goodness : but upon me chastisements of sorrow and anguish seem to fall, as if these were my only portion.

I wonder at Thy dealings with me, and am at times overwhelmed as one whose Temple has been for-

NOTES.

[1] We wonder how many of our readers will be able to receive with the understanding necessary to the true perception of the inner meaning of the allusions, this remarkable outpouring of the Soul of the Master at the close of the days of the Oblation. It must seem almost inconceivable that one who had been in such a high estate of Christhood, and was the chosen vehicle of the blessed Manifestation, could ever have come into the heritage of such sorrow and anguish as may be discovered in the Heart-stirring and Soul-moving appeal of this Aftermath prayer. It may indeed be asked how it came to pass that He who had been appointed from the Divine Kingdom to carry a burden so awful in its nature, and bear a Cross whose anguish no man could fathom, in order that the Divine Purpose towards this world and all its children might be accomplished, could in the last life of the Oblation, and towards the end of the burden-bearing, be so forsaken, apparently bereft of all that He most loved, and even denied the heavenly succour for which His whole being cried with unutterable yearnings.

Yet all that is expressed of sorrow and anguish, all the deep pain and consciousness of loss, the feeling that He was forsaken by the Divine Father-Mother, that the Heavens were silent amid His anguishing and refused the succour He so sorely needed and asked for, the awful dread of being a castaway—were the results of the nature of the Cross which was laid upon Him. Whilst for the Planet the resultant of the Oblation was the changing of its Middle Kingdom, and for the Planet's children the possibility of rising out of all earthliness through the better spiritual conditions brought to bear upon them as the effect of the change within the Middle Kingdom, yet for Him the resultant was the awakening to a consciousness of the most unspeakable sorrow and pain accompanied by frequent hours of great anguish. For the burden which He bore in all the lives of the Oblation was felt by Him during His recovery of all the past.

This Prayer of the Aftermath is included with the Logia, in order that those who read it may come into some small degree of understanding of all that the Oblation meant.

[2] This is most difficult to explain for reasons which will not be obvious to our readers. But it was one of the strangest contradictions of the law of consequences, that where He most loved and trusted, He was often most sadly betrayed. His love verily was a power for sorrow, for it brought Him anguish unspeakable.

THE AFTERMATH

saken, and is become the sport of evil things; for Thou didst once dwell within me, and the consciousness of Thy Holy Presence was sweet unto me.[1]

The Prayer of the Aftermath

Out of my anguish have I cried unto Thee as one who wishes he had never been born, and who longeth for the hour of forgetfulness; yet have I sorrowed to sin so against Thee, and have grieved that my power to endure for Thee has been so weakened in the way.[2]

That Thou hast purpose in all Thy doings my Soul knoweth right well, for Thy ways are ever in righteousness; but Thou concealest from me the reason for all my anguish, and the meaning of my suffering.[3]

So blinded with sorrow have I been, that mine eyes have been unable to behold Thy Holy purpose in my suffering, or any testimony of Thy compassion in my anguish.

The ways of my going have been turned into waters of bitterness, and no branch of healing hast Thou sent to sweeten them; of the waters of Marah hast Thou made me to drink deeply, even whilst my Soul has cried out for the springs of Elim.[4]

Out of Horeb hast Thou made living waters to flow by the Rod of Thy Power, that the thirsty may drink thereof and live for evermore : but me Thou only rebukest, and dost humble me as one who has lifted himself up.[5]

In the sight of the people Thou hast abased me, even in the hour when I sought to proclaim unto them Thy great goodness; and so hast Thou taken my power from me, and brought me low.

With great loneliness hast Thou filled my days and made me as one forsaken; the bitterness of death was in the cup of which Thou didst give unto me to drink.

Gall was I given to drink in the day of my deep thirst for Thee; wormwood instead of the wells of joy has been my portion.[6]

296

NOTES.

[1] In the Recovery, so intensified were the conditions that He did feel Himself to be the sport of things essentially evil. There were hours when He was so terribly afflicted as the adumbrations of the past fell upon Him, that He wondered much whether the God within His Temple had departed, and in the Divine stead there had entered into His Sanctuary the powers He had come to dread and loath. Sometimes these hours extended through many weeks.

[2] If this should seem strange to our readers, we can assure them that it is not more so than it was to Him. In His Soul-consciousness He knew why the burden had to be borne, and that it was not His own burden ; yet whilst the burden lay upon Him He felt it as His own, and in the lower consciousness looked upon it as sin in Himself. So He continually sorrowed over it as such.

And He longed for oblivion during the Recovery, and not infrequently wondered whether such would come to Him.

[3] In the personal consciousness, to Himself even His own anguish was mysterious. The meaning of His suffering He could not understand, it differed so much from any sorrow He beheld in others. There seemed no sorrow like His. And it was even so. And the Divine Love concealed from Him the reason for it, because it was necessary for a time.

[4] Marah and Elim were terms familiar to ancient Israel. Marah was the state in which the experience was bitter and sorrowful ; when Deep called unto Deep within the Soul at the Voice, or Thunder, of Divine Articulation within it. It represented the Sea of Bitterness, that bitterness which comes through Iniquity, Transgression and Sin.

Elim signified the Healing of Life through the Branch, the Christ-Presence. For only God can heal the Soul, and bring Elim into the life.

[5] This did seem literally true. Even into the last life was the tragedy carried ; and He was crushed and humbled in the sight of men by the conduct of those who could not understand Him, some of whom forsook Him amid His dire extremity, after they had professed fealty to Him.

For the years of the Recovery were even as bitter as those of the lives of the Oblation.

[6] Who hath measured the portion that came into the cup of His life as He bore the burden of the Accursed Cross ? Who hath dreamt of the meaning of the gall He was given to drink, and the intensity of its bitterness ?

Soon after He had awakened to the high consciousness of Jesus-hood followed by spiritual Christhood, and when He was filled with the joy of these blessed states, the past broke upon Him and brought into His life the most unspeakable sorrow and anguish.

THE AFTERMATH

The Prayer of the Aftermath

In my dire extremity have I cried aloud, Eli ! Eli ! Lama Sa Bach Thani ! and unto Thee have I yielded up my Spirit : for I am Thine.[1] Thou gavest me my life, and it was Thine to take for Thy service. I am no more mine own, but Thine ; Thine to live Thy life, and to serve as Thou willest."

In Thy loving-kindness cause the sword which has pierced my Soul to be withdrawn, and with the precious ointment of Thy Love heal my wounding ; for not anywhere can I find healing but in Thee : Thou art the Balm of Gilead and the true Physician.[2]

Command now that Thy Countenance be unto me, so that Thy glory may shed its radiance within ; for in the light of Thy Countenance the Night is no more, Thy Radiance is as the glory of Thy Day.

Thus Thou dost confirm the righteousness of Thy doings, and the ways which Thou didst appoint unto me to walk in ; for the Wisdom of Thy judgment is made manifest, and Thy Love glorious as the radiant noonday.

NOTES.

[1] During the days of the Recovery of all the past, in hours of deepest anguish, these very words were again spoken just as they were uttered during the Gethsemane in the closing days of the Manifestation. And once more were they uttered in the direst agony. There were those who heard the agonising cry, though at the time they could not relate it, nor understand the reason for the agony. Indeed, at the time, He Himself could not realize all that it meant, though He was fully conscious of the awful burden. Again He went through the experience of yielding up His Spirit—an experience impossible to describe. But it is not to be associated with the experience spoken of as death. When Souls pass over in that sense they are withdrawn from the outermost planes only, and do not in any degree yield up the Spirit. For this latter is a spiritual process. It involves great anguish and sense of loss. It fills the consciousness with an unutterable feeling of having been forsaken of God. For it is the willing surrender of the consciousness of the Divine Presence in Divine Fulness, for some Divine Purpose. It will therefore be apparent that any one who had not attained to such Christhood could not undergo such an experience, and that only one who had been in that most blessed estate could pass down into the experience expressed in the pathetic outburst of the Soul—Eli! Eli! Lama Sa Bach Thani. For when Christ died, it was the dying of the Christ-Light in Him.

[2] In the crucifixion story it is said that a Roman soldier pierced the side of the Master. It is quite true that He was wounded in His side. But that was only a small matter compared to the sword that pierced His very Soul. It made Him feel as if His Being were riven in twain. And for this wounding He could find no true healing anywhere. The things that brought comfort and aid to others, contained none for Him. He comforted and healed others, but He could not come at healing for Himself. During the celebration of the Passing Over and the work of the Oblation, He was utterly broken in His Spirit. And He knew that only one could heal Him, the Divine Physician, and that only that One, even the Father-Mother, could pour into His wounded Life the Balm of the Mountains of Gilead.

The significance of this prayer of The Aftermath will be perceived by all who have been able to discern the true nature and path of the Oblation.

PART VIII.

THE APOCALYPTIC VISIONS.

*A series of Visions beheld by the Master concerning the
Ancient Christhood Order and Ministry; the Ancient
Gnosis held by them; the Initiation of the Soul to the
Divine Kingdom; the Descent of the Planet, its Fall
and the calamities that overtook it; the fearful
anguish of all Souls, especially those of the
Christhood, amid the tragic Travail; the arising
of the conditions known as the Dragon, the
Beast, the false Lamb, the false Prophet; the
claims of the Church and her betrayal of
Christ; the coming of the Redemption
through the Oblation, and the Resur
rection of the Christhood; the
overthrow of evil and the
triumph of Righteousness
and Love; the restored
Planet and the Age of
the Redemption with
the regnancy of
Christhood*

THE APOCALYPSE.

SECTION I.

*The Message to the Seer ; the unveiling of the Mystery
of the Ancient Church ; a glorious Vision of
Adonai ; the several messages from Him unto
the Seven Churches of Asia, wherein is
revealed their past history on this
Planet, and what befell them
during their ministry ; also
how they are to return
unto their ancient
estate of the
Christhood.*

THE APOCALYPSE

The
Overthrow
of the
Great City

When I was in the Isle of Patmos receiving the word of testimony, the Word of the Lord came unto me,[1] saying :

" Son of Man, prophesy unto the whole of the Tribes of Israel[2] concerning their return from the Great City[3] whose abominations have made drunken the Souls of all who love to dwell therein ;

For their sorrows have come up before the Lord and His Anointed ;[4]

He hath heard the crying of the oppressed of His children, and the groaning of all who were bound in the prison-houses ;[5]

The prayers of His Saints slain within the Great City, have ascended unto Him as the sweet incense of heavenly sacrifice ,

From beneath the Altar,[6] where His Holy Presence is, have they cried unto Him that He would once more make manifest His power in the Highest to accomplish the Redemption of all His children, and the overthrow of all those powers of the false Prophet, the Dragon and the Beast,[7] by which they have been afflicted and oppressed ;

For the hour is now come when the Great City which hath deceived the Nations shall be overthrown, and the powers of the false Prophet, the Dragon and the Beast, destroyed."

NOTES.

[1] The Word of the Lord is the Logos. When the Logos comes into a Soul, it is by the process of coming into the consciousness as the Presence bringing the fullest illumination. In the Light of that Presence all things are made clear, and the Soul can see upon the plane of the Divine Kingdom. If it is to proclaim what it sees and hears, it is informed through the mighty stream of magnetism called Inspiration, which flows from the Presence.

The term Isle of Patmos had once an Esoteric significance, just like the several terms applied to the Churches. " The Isles wait for Him," the coming of the Christ-consciousness ; and the Isle of Patmos was adjacent to the Divine Kingdom.

[2] Who were the Tribes of Israel ? Many are they who have professed to understand who Israel were. In recent ages much has been written concerning the lost Tribes of Israel. And these have associated them with the Jewish Race. They have presented as forming one of the Jewish Kingdoms, and that the larger of the two.

But these Tribes of Israel were not tribes of Jewry, though they sent out from their midst into the heart of Jewry, Prophets and Seers. They were the children of the Radiance of the Lord : Issa-Ra-El—those in whom were the Holy Spirit and Glory of Ra. They were the Orders of the Ancient Christhood. These tribes were lost amid the nations built up of the elder children of this system.

[3] The Astral Realm in its impure conditions. It is and has been for untold ages, the City of Desolation, making desolate the life of the Soul. But the Great City also implied those materialistic systems begotten and sustained out of the astral conditions. Amid these the Christhood members suffered greatly ; and the prophecy is concerning their return to the High Estate.

[4] The Eternal Christ. He is the Lord in manifestation within the Soul ; and He is latently and potentially within all Souls.

[5] An indication of the nature of the sufferings borne by them amid the awful conditions which have prevailed upon the Planet. They were great Souls ; and to them it was indeed as the bondage and limitation of the prison-house when their powers were impoverished and their inner Light veiled.

[6] The Shechinah of the Soul : -the Altar of the Innermost.

[7] The great materialistic systems which have prevailed, Scientific, Social and Ecclesiastical, by which the Soul has been persecuted.

The False Prophet—the false vision and interpretation of Life.

The Dragon—the oppressive sense-powers in the individual, the community and the nation.

The Beast—the false and cruel systems, scientific, social and religious, whose mark has been left upon all the Nations :— Impurity, Inhumanity, and the Inquisition.

THE APOCALYPSE

The Unveiling of the Mystery of the Ancient Church

" *The Revelation of the Lord Christ,*[1] *which God commanded Him to show forth unto His servants concerning many things that are coming to pass; and by His servant John hath He sent them, for His Angel hath signified of them unto Him.*[2]

Of these things doth He bear witness, even the testimony of the Word of God, as He hath been revealed in Jesus Christ.

John the servant of God,[3] *to the seven Churches which were in Asia:*[4] *unto you Grace and Peace from Him who was, and is, and who is again about to come; and from the Seven Breaths which proceed from His throne; and from His faithful and true witness Jesus Christ who has been begotten again as the first fruits of the Seven Breaths, to reign within the Kingdoms of the Earth.*[5]

Unto Him who hath loved us and brought us unto Himself in the blood most precious, to make of us a Kingdom of Mediators for Him in the making manifest of God the Father-Mother, be the glory and the dominion throughout all ages.[6]

Amen:[7] *Behold He cometh with the coming of the clouds upon the Heavens.*

Then every eye shall perceive Him, even they who have pierced Him; and all nations shall yet mourn over Him because of the piercing. Even so shall it be.

Amen: thus saith He: ' I am the Alpha and the Omega, the God, the Lord, who was, and who is, and who is about to come, even the Almighty One.'

I, John, am your brother in the Kingdom, partaker with you in the tribulation, and a sharer with you of the patience of the Lord.

In the day of the Lord I was dwelling in an isle called Patmos, having been carried thither by the Spirit.

There spake unto me the Voice, and the sound was like a great trumpet, saying: ' What thou seest, send

NOTES.

[1] The unveiling of the vision, which is Revelation, wherein the Lord is known as the Eternal Christ. This Revealing of the Lord Christ had relation to the Mystery of the Soul and the vision of the Christ as the Beloved Son of God.

[2] When a Soul comes into the consciousness of that vision, it is informed from the sublime Presence within its sanctuary, even the Angel of His Presence.

[3] The Master. He was Iôannês the Seer.

[4] The seven Communities of the Christs ministering upon the seven planes—by which is meant the seven orders of the Christ ministry; as is revealed in the several addresses to these Communities, they were Souls who once were in a very high spiritual state and understood the Heavenly Arcana.

They were once in Asia, the land of the Holy Spirit; for this term originally meant that, though in latter ages it was also applied to the country where these Souls performed their special ministry.

[5] The Seven Breaths represent the action of the Elohim upon all the planes of the Soul. The inbreathing of the Holy Life-stream which flows from the Throne of the Eternal One proceeds with ever-increasing intensity from plane to plane as the Soul is initiated into the Sevenfold Mystery of Being. Where the Soul is truly seeking for the Divine Realization, it rises from sphere to sphere and from one plane to another, until it attains that state of Christhood which culminates in the possession of the Divine Pleroma or fulness of the Spirit.

Out of the operation of the Seven Breaths within all who are able to respond to them, a Divine Christhood is once more to issue and reign or prevail in influence and teaching within the kingdoms of the Earth.

[6] He who hath loved all Souls is the Most Blessed One. He and He alone is the Saviour and Redeemer of His children. And the vision of His Love must nevermore be obscured and confounded with the Soul who becomes His Messenger and the channel of His redeeming ministry.

The Orders of the Christhood were His Mediators. They were a Kingdom of Priests, but their hierarchy was not ecclesiastical; and some of them were after the Order of Melchizedek.

[7] AMEN : an ancient Divine Name. It implied what we may not express here, beyond saying that the Name represented the Divine Consummation in Creation, and, therefore, is the term to signify the Presence of the Eternal One with the Soul when it attains the fulness of Being possible unto it.

AMEN is the perfect Realization of the ARCHE—the Divine Principle within us.

307

THE APOCALYPSE

A Glorious Vision of Adonai

unto the seven Churches that once were in Asia; unto Ephesus and Smyrna, unto Pergamos and Thyatira, unto Sardis and Philadelphia, and even unto Laodicea:

And I looked whence the Voice proceeded;[1] and lo, seven golden Candlesticks,[2] and in the midst of them One who was the Son of Man.[3]

He was clothed in a garment of glorious Light which covered His feet, and it was girdled at the breast with a golden cord.

His head and His hair were white light, light white as snow; and His eyes burned like two flames of fire.

His feet were resplendent, reflecting the glory of the Light proceeding from Him, even as brass that has been purified and burnished reflects the glory of the Sun.

And His Voice in its sounding was as the voice of many waters.

Within His right hand He held seven Stars, and from out His mouth proceeded a flame like a sword double edged.

The glory of His countenance was even like the Sun shining in his power.[4]

When I beheld who it was who had spoken unto me, I fell before Him worshipfully.

And He said unto me: 'I am the Alpha and the Omega, the Living One, who was, and who is, and who is about to come.[5]

The keys of death and hades are with me; fear not · ' and He laid upon me the hand of Blessing.[6]

Then He gave me commandment to bear His message unto the seven Churches that were once in Asia, concerning the things that were, and which are, and which are about to come to pass.

And the Voice spake unto me, saying: 'Tell the mystery of the seven Stars beheld in the right hand, and also the mystery of the seven golden Candlesticks.

For the seven Stars are the seven Angels of the seven spheres;[7] and the Candlesticks are the seven Churches upon these spheres.'

308

NOTES.

[1] The Voice is the sound which the breaking upon the Soul of the Glory of the Presence, makes : sound and colour are one upon two planes of manifestation. The idea of sound has thus to be understood in relation to the Divine Presence. That Presence does not speak as one with human articulation : when He addresses the Soul, the order of vision maketh the sound. Thus are His thoughts voiced to and within the Soul. This may appear difficult to understand on the part of any who may never have heard that Voice within them ; and it can only be fully understood by those who have had such realization of the Presence. Yet its truth may be sensed by many who are on the Path to that sublime realization.

[2] The seven golden Candlesticks were the seven Communities or Churches of the Christhood. They were Candlesticks in which the Candle of the Lord burned. They were all Lamps wherein the Light of the Holy Spirit burned to give the Light of the Lord unto those to whom they were appointed to minister.

[3] The Logos as the Eternal Christ. As the term is often made use of to express Planetary as well as Solar Deities, we make use of the more beautiful and more truly expressive term, Adonai. He walked amid the seven golden Candlesticks, for those who comprised these Christhood Communities knew Him. They had, long ages before, arrived at the consciousness of His Presence within them.

The Vision pictures them as they were when they were in the Asian state—in the Life and Light and Love of the Father-Mother.

They were then seven—the perfect number ; and they were golden Light-bearers, for they were children of the perfect Love.

[4] Who is able to understand what such a vision within the Soul implies ? Who has been there to behold with open countenance the Lord of Glory ? None of the children of this Planet have as yet been upon that Mountain of Glory, though prior to the great Planetary descent some of them were crossing the threshold of spiritual Christhood. But the inner groups of the Christhood Order had been upon that Mountain where the glorious Vision is beheld. So they had known it, and could recognise it again when presented to them.

[5] The Beginning and the End of all Being. *He always is.* But within the system of the Christhood as individuals and communities, He was present as a consciousness, and it became lost ; He was restored through the consciousness of Him in the Master ; and He was to become once more within the Soul of all who once knew Him.

[6] This is spoken to the Master concerning His own passage through spiritual death and Hades or the realm of the shades. Adonai had the key ; no other power could overwhelm Him there : He was not to fear.

[7] The Seven Elohim. They are the seven Stars or Rays of the Light.

THE APOCALYPSE

The Beloved of the Father-Mother in whom are the seven Spirits of Elohim,[1] who holdeth the seven Stars[2] in His right hand and walketh amid the Spheres,[3] unto the Church in Ephesus[4] :—

*The Heavenly Father-Mother knoweth thy works of love, thy patience in labour, and how thou hast abhorred **the evil by which thou wast overtaken in the day when there came unto thee those who claimed to have been** sent forth from the Kingdom of the Divine Love, and who betrayed thee unto the going array from the ministry unto which the Heavenly Father-Mother appointed thee.[5]*

The trials which befell thee in that false Kingdom,[6] the grievous burdens that thou hast had to carry for the name which thou didst bear, have all been known unto Him ; for in thine affliction the Lord Himself was afflicted.

In grief wast thou regarded when thou didst leave the former estate, the Kingdom thou didst love ; and in grief wast thou counselled to return lest the Light of thy Lamp[7] should become extinguished amid the darkness.

*The Heavenly Father-Mother has sought thee sorrowfully that He might restore unto thee the Kingdom from which thou wentest out, and the Tree of Life which is in the midst of the Paradise of the Divine **Love and Wisdom**.[8]*

Those who have the ear to hear, let them understand what the Spirit saith unto all who are of this Church.

NOTES.

[1] The seven Spirits or Elohim are the seven creative principles by which the Eternal One bringeth all things into Being and Existence. On the outer planes their presence may be perceived in manifold ways in the manifestation of Life. They are the seven Holy Breaths whose inbreathing fills the Soul in all its planes with the Divine vibrations, each in turn breathing upon and within the Soul until the innermost is reached, and the Soul becomes conscious of God as an overshadowing and indwelling Presence.

[2] The sevenfold Light of the Spirit. The Angel of each sphere or plane represents one of the sevenfold rays which form the Spectrum of the Holy Spirit. In Adonai are all the Gods or Spirits or Rays. He Himself is clothed in glorious White Light, the Ineffable Light; and in His right hand or creative power, He holds the seven Stars or Rays.

[3] The action of Adonai upon all the planes of Being—from the innermost to the outermost of the Planet and the Soul.

[4] This Society, has been confounded by interpreters with the people of the City of Ephesus who worshipped Diana in an idolatrous and sensual way, which worship and conduct were the direct inversion of all that the Ephesian community of the Priesthood stood for. The Ancient Community of Souls who were on the plane represented by Ephesus, was one in which the Divine Love was radiated Divinely.

[5] But long ages after the Planetary descent these Souls also felt the materializing influences of the changed elemental conditions, and became involved in them. They left their high estate thinking they could the more effectually minister unto those children of the Planet who were their special care. They were betrayed by others, who also purported to have been sent forth from the Divine Kingdom.

[6] The false systems which arose within the changed order. Their kingdom was not of this world: they were from above. The kingdom established upon this world was astral, and it filled their lives with great bitterness.

[7] The Heavens grieved over them and feared lest the influences of the awful spiritual ignorance and degradation should eventuate in the loss to them of the Divine Light within their Lamp.

[8] This message was and is the call to these Souls to return unto their high estate, even to possess the Kingdom of the Father-Mother and the Cross of Adonai found amid the Radiance of the Divine Love and Wisdom—the Cross of God at the heart of the true Agapé and Sophia.

THE APOCALYPSE

The Beloved of the Father-Mother, the First in manifestation and the Last to be known,[1] who now speakest unto all who were dead but who have become alive again,[2] unto the Church in Smyrna[3]:—

The Blessing of the Heavenly Father-Mother be ever thine Heritage.

Thy works have all been known, and thy deep tribulation and impoverishment through thy ministry unto all who claimed it, even unto those who came unto thee professing to be of Israel and willing to learn, yet meant it not, for they were of the synagogue of Baal.[4]

But none of these sufferings hurt thy love for the Kingdom of the Father-Mother; even when the evil overwhelmed thee and thou wert cast into the prison houses didst thou remain faithful even unto the death of all thy most beautiful hopes,[5] and the loss of thy Crown of Life[6] which Adonai gave unto Thee.

For thy return the Heavenly Father-Mother waiteth He calleth unto thee to return, and must needs grieve whilst thou art absent.

Return to again possess the Crown of Life over which the second death hath no power.[7]

They who have the ear to hear, let them understand what the Spirit saith unto all who are of this Church.

NOTES.

[1] Adonai, whether spoken of in relation to the great Cosmic Order, or a Planetary World, or the individual Soul, is always the first in manifestation. He is the Head of all Things, the first formulate of the Unformulated, the visible expression upon the Divine Kingdom of the Invisible One, the Incomprehensible made comprehensible upon that Kingdom.

[2] The Christhood Orders had died out upon this world, owing to the conditions which prevailed ; they were as the dead. But the hour drew nigh for their arising, and some had already awakened and arisen.

[3] As the Ephesians of most ancient times interpreted the Divine Love from the innermost realm, so the community in Smyrna interpreted the Divine Wisdom from the innermost realm. The Church was the channel of Divine Illumination for those Souls who were on the threshold of the House of Mary, or spiritual Christhood.

[4] The members also passed through deep tribulation and suffered impoverishment ; and they were also betrayed. To them came Ioudeans who professed to be anxious to be of Israel—children in whom is the Radiance of the Lord ; but who were not pure in desire and purpose, for they were worshippers at the shrine which they had set up unto Mammon, who valued the earthly things above all spiritual and divine.

[5] The result was disastrous : there is reference here to one of the cataclysms which overtook the Human Race, and caused unspeakable sufferings to the Christhood.

They lost the consciousness of the Christhood estate—an estate given by Adonai, since when realized it is through the Overshadowing Presence. For the Crown of Life is this most blessed attainment. Though it fadeth not away, it may nevertheless be darkly veiled. The blessed consciousness may be suspended. Conditions may affect it. The conditions and environment of the Soul's ministry may impose great limitations, even to the extent of making the blessed realization impossible. But though a Soul may pass through experiences of this kind, yet it can return again into the high degree of Life, whensoever the conditions are changed and the limitations overcome.

[7] When the Soul once more triumphs over the elemental powers it shall know spiritual death no more. There will be no death for it ; it will have conquered all things ; for the kingdom with its powers, from which came death, shall be itself overthrown.

THE APOCALYPSE

The Beloved $_{of}$ the Father-Mother unto the Church in Pergamos [1] —

The Church in Pergamos

The Word $_{of}$ the Lord thus speaketh unto thee, even the Adonai who is the divider between good and evil, the two-edged sword $_{of}$ the Divine Love and Divine Wisdom.

I have known thy work accomplished where thou once didst dwell, even upon the planes where Saturn [2] had his power, and how thou didst hold fast to the Divine Name even in the days when the Faithful [3] were brought low, and my Servant [4] was put to death and the power $_{of}$ Saturn was broken. [5]

But there was grief in the heavenly Kingdom when thou didst go down into the conditions fashioned by Baal [6] who cast in the way $_{of}$ all the House $_{of}$ Israel [7] such a stumbling block, and taught the Children $_{of}$ Judah to commit evil and make $_{of}$ themselves sacrifices unto graven images. [8]

Be again zealous to do the first works [9] and return unto the Divine Love, and the Adonai will cause His Word to part asunder the evil, that all which thou hast loved may once more be thine.

To thee again will be given the Hidden Manna [10] that thou mayest eat $_{of}$ it and become strong in thy ministry before the Lord, and the precious White Stone [11] with the hidden name upon it which none knoweth but those unto whom it is given.

They who have the ear to hear, let them understand what the Spirit saith unto all who are $_{of}$ this Church.

NOTES.

[1] Pergamos was a community of Souls who dwelt upon the Higher Mind plane and ministered there to those who were approaching that state of spiritual consciousness represented by the fifth plane. As the communities in the states represented by Ephesus and Smyrna were of the innermost planes in their ministry, Souls whose vision was directly from the Divine Realm, and were, therefore, the Mystics of the Ancient days ; so those in Pergamos were the interpreters of the Mystic Teachings upon the plane of the Higher Reason.

It is unto them that Adonai as the Word, speaks, that Word which divides, and is the sword of the Lord.

[2] One of the Elohim. It must not be confounded with the Planetary System now known by that name.

[3] The Faithful being brought low means the bringing down into hurtful conditions those of the Mystic Orders. This community of Souls, long after the Mystic communities were scattered and lost, held on to the Divine Name as a knowledge of the Reason. But there was no inner vision. The knowledge was philosophical, for the work of those in Pergamos was to teach through a pure Philosophy.

[4] Who was the Lord's Servant meant here ? Surely His Servant the Mystic Christhood, the consciousness of which was lost, having been done to death by the appalling conditions which arose.

[5] Through that calamity Christhood became extinct in the land, and the power of Saturn, the Elohe, was broken ; for as there was no Christhood consciousness, there was no higher illumination of the Mind. The true office of Pergamos was to reflect the interior things.

[6] The materialistic systems personified.

[7] The whole of the Christhood Orders : children of the Radiance.

[8] The Planet's children who fell into great depths, and at last were the sport and victims of the fluidic images which they had themselves engraven upon the astral realm.

[9] The first works were services of pure devotion in all their philosophy to the Highest, making it the handmaiden of the Mystic Vision to lead Souls into the life by which the most blessed realizations were entered into.

[10] In the return of the Soul to the first Works, the Hidden Manna would once more be given the Mind, the Mystic meaning of all things, to nourish and strengthen it for ministry.

[11] The Philosopher's Stone—pure Divine Reason in which the Name of the Most Blessed is paramount.

THE APOCALYPSE

The Beloved $_{of}$ the Father-Mother who is also Son $_{of}$ God, whose eyes are like the Seven Sacred Fires[1] before the Throne $_{of}$ the Eternal One, and whose feet are like pure gold,[2] unto the Church in Thyatira[3] ·—

The Church in Thyatira

The Blessing $_{of}$ the Father-Mother be unto thee always : He knoweth thy works $_{of}$ love, and thy patient service even unto the last $_{of}$ all thy works.

But it grieved the Divine Father-Mother that thou didst fall into the snare $_{of}$ that evil way known as Jezebel[5] by which the prophets and prophetesses have been slain, and the altars $_{of}$ the Lord thrown down , for the way has been one $_{of}$ defilement wherein the people have wrought evil thinking it was good, and have taken the flesh $_{of}$ creatures after sacrificing them upon the false altars $_{of}$ the land wherein they dwelt.

The Divine Father-Mother thus calleth thee, and all those who have forsaken the doctrines and ways $_{of}$ Baal and his priests, to hold fast to every good and pure way in the full assurance $_{of}$ overcoming all things, and rising up until again crowned as the bright and morning Star.[6]

They who have the ear to hear, let them understand what the Spirit saith unto all who are $_{of}$ this Church.

NOTES.

[1] The seven sacred Fires or Lamps of the Eternal Sanctuary, whose Flame is the energizing power of God upon all the planes of Being. The eyes of Adonai are as these, for in Him reside all the Spirits who are the energizing Fires of God. From Adonai proceed these creative powers, for in Him are all things of God contained. From these sacred Fires proceed the seven Rays whose creative spirit and purpose are to be found in the seven orders of Souls. For the seven Rays are the seven tinctures of the Eternal Light, and each order of Soul has one of these.

[2] Pure Gold is the emblem of perfect Love, and the Feet the symbol of the Path of Life. Understanding these things, the meaning is at once beautiful and obvious. The ways of Adonai are always full of Love.

[3] A Community of Souls whose service was sacrificially beautiful. As the Church in Pergamos interpreted through a pure and true philosophy, the Mystic Wisdom given through the Church in Smyrna, so those in Thyatira interpreted the Mystic Love revealed through the Ephesian; and they did this by means of a most beautiful priestly ministry, whose hierarchy was spiritual and non-ecclesiastical.

[4] Theirs was a direct ministry of blessing. They had always sought spiritual priesthood and sacrificial service. And the last work they performed was the giving of themselves to share in the burden of the Divine Cross. For in their love they travailed sorely on behalf of the children who were approaching the state of experience to which their ministry called the Soul.

[5] Jezebel represented the monstrous perversions of the Divine Love expressed in the religious systems where the Altars reared in the Name of the God of Israel are defiled by the sacrificial systems in vogue amongst them, wherein the beautiful creatures are slain upon the altars of the desires and tastes of the people, as a true way and a devout way in which to render life beautiful.

So these children of beautiful Love fell under the spell of Jezebel. They too became tainted with the awful thing, and polluted their altars.

[6] The Morning Star—the Sun as the Lord whose arising giveth back the glory of day unto the Soul. So would they once more be children of the Radiance of Love.

317

THE APOCALYPSE

The Beloved of the Father-Mother in whom are to be found the seven Spirits of God, and the inheritor of the seven Stars upon His Kingdom, unto the Church in Sardis [1] ·—

Behold, it hath been said of thee that thou hast a name as one alive, but that thou art as one who is dead.[2]

Strengthen, therefore, the love that is in thee lest it should die,[3] that thy remaining works may be even perfect before the Lord.[4]

Remember how thou hast been blest from the Lord, the love thou hast received, the glorious things which thou hast heard and seen upon His Heavens and through the Light proceeding from His Spirit within thee, and return again unto thy first Estate.[5]

Thou shalt then be of those who walk in white before the Lord, who do not defile their garments, but ever seek to be His Saints to serve before Him in perfect service continually.[6]

Thy name shall again be written as one who is of the Lamb [7]; and it shall be again confessed before the Heavenly Father-Mother as worthy, because thou didst live even as the Angels who minister before the Lord.[8]

They who have the ear to hear, let them understand what the Spirit saith unto all who are of this Church.

NOTES.

[1] The Community of Christs represented by the Church in the state of Sardis, were originally the embodiments and interpreters of the Joy of God. They were full of the Joy of Life; the Divine Joy had found its fulfilment in them. It was their life-ministry to interpret Life in its mystery to those upon the plane where they ministered, and lead those children step by step from all earthly joys to those which were higher and abiding, even until they came to taste of the Joy of God.

[2] They were dead so far that the high consciousness of their former Christ-state was no longer their inheritance. The conditions had changed them. They were still children of Joy, but it was more the joy of existence than the Joy of Being.

[3] Love must be cherished, for it is the true solvent. By it power is attained to rise out of the love of mere existence into that of true Being.

[4] And by means of Love (Agapê) and Love alone, can the perfect work of God be wrought, the Soul taught the true way of attainment, and the fulness of Joy in Life be found.

[5] The First Estate means the first in degree, greatness or height. It was the inheritance to which they had attained in Christhood. To return into that was indeed to recall the past, to remember the Divine Graciousness, the Blessing of the Sevenfold, the outpouring of the Joy of God, the Illumination of the Spirit whose dwelling was within their Sanctuary. And the remembrance of these things would aid them in the return.

[6] The white garments refer not only to the purity of life to be found in all who are of the Christhood, but also to the radiation of the Light through the magnetic streams of the life. These Souls are Healers. Their service before the Lord is now unto the healing of the lives of those who have defiled their garments amid the maelstrom of the world's evil.

[7] Here the reference is to the Divine Love in its sacrificial capacity. That Love in its ministry is the Lamb that has been slain. To have the name written as of the Lamb, is to be accorded a place in that Divine Priestly service. It is the imaging through and within the Soul, of the Divine Love, so that the service of the Soul is actually the ministry of the Eternal Love.

[8] The ministry of this Church was of the nature of the Angelic World; the Joy was Angelic; the Garments were Angelic. To be confessed as of those who are worthy to so minister for God, is indeed to know the Joy of God.

THE APOCALYPSE

The Beloved of the Father-Mother who is also known as the Holy and True One who hath the key into the Kingdom of God,[1] who openeth the door of the Kingdom unto all Souls and shutteth it not to anyone,[2] unto the Church in Philadelphia[3]:—

Thy works have come up unto the Heavens as those who have passed through the opened door, and as those whose strength has been spent in service unto the Lord even when others were led to forget His name.[4]

Behold, the worshippers within the Synagogue of Baal shall come to worship at the altars where thy service hath been, and to know that thou hast been greatly beloved.[5]

Because thou hast kept pure the Word of the Lord in the day of great trial, and been patient when burdens too heavy to bear were laid upon thee, the Divine Love hath been thy shield against the evils which came upon thee.[6]

Behold, the Lord cometh! Thy Crown no one shall take away from thee. In overcoming thou shalt be once more a pillar within the Temple of the Lord upon which the Divine Name is written, and an inhabitant of the Holy City of the Lord when the new Jerusalem hath been established through the Divine Love.[7]

They who have the ear to hear, let them understand what the Spirit saith unto all who are of this Church.

NOTES.

[1] The vision of the Adonai within the Soul is the way unto the realization of the Father-Mother. And that vision comes in various degrees according to the state of the Soul's attainment. If it be given upon the Angelic Heavens it appeareth as a Sun, for the Lord is our Sun who illumineth, nourisheth and enricheth the life. This is the Divine Love upon those Heavens. If it be given upon the plane known as Celestial in the Solar world, it cometh as the Word of the Lord breaking the bread of the Divine Wisdom. After that it cometh upon the Divine Kingdom as Elohim, in the Sevenfold Ray of the Spirit whose spectrum or rainbow is beheld around the Throne of the Eternal One.

[2] Adonai, by means of the Oblation, hath opened the door of the various Heavens for all who can enter, and who desire to enter therein.

[3] The Community of Souls whose ministry had for its burden the teaching of the impersonal love, the love of all Souls and all creatures. For love is first personal, then family, afterwards tribal, then racial, in its manifestations ; and Souls have to be shown the way of the greater love ere they can attain unto the realization of that Presence whose love is unto and for all.

[4] A beautiful testimony to the power of Love to survive outward disasters.

[5] Another reference to the awful sacrificial systems which have always negatived such a love, degraded it and inverted it, counting as nought the lives of the Human children and the creatures. Out of these awful systems shall many come to learn the Love which this Church will again teach. They will find the Path to the Redemption of Life.

[6] The trials spoken of, the patient burden-bearing, have profound meanings in the history of the whole of the Christhood communities. They followed this world's children into great depths of sadness and sorrow ; and the Souls in the state here represented retained their love amid the fearful conditions.

[7] The Lord is indeed come ; and these Souls, with those of the other communities, are being gathered together. Their Crown is their Love, and in the Divine Temple such Love is a Pillar. Without it, the Temple would be incomplete.

THE APOCALYPSE

The Beloved of the Father-Mother, the Amen[1] upon the Divine Kingdom who is ever the faithful and true witness[2] of the Most High One unto His Saints, and the Arche of the creation of the Divine, unto the Church at Laodicea[3] ·—

Thou art known now upon the Heavens as one who has become neither warm nor cold, having lost thy zeal in the ways of the Divine Love.[4]

Thou thinkest thyself increased with the goods of the kingdom with which thou wast enriched, and seemest not to know that thou art impoverished, darkened, unclothed, and exposed to the evil which floweth in upon thee.[5]

Thou art, therefore, counselled to seek the purified gold that thou mayest be henceforth rich, and the white raiment wherewith thy nakedness may be clothed, and the anointing which openeth the eyes to behold and see.[6]

Be zealous once more, and return unto thy first Estate. The chastening of the Lord is not grievous, and in love doth He seek Thee.

Behold, He waiteth at the door! If thou hear His knocking and open unto Him, behold how He cometh even as a guest who suppeth with a friend.[7]

Unto the Soul in its return will He give the power to serve within the Kingdom of the Divine Love and Wisdom, and to be enthroned with Him.[8]

Whosoever heareth, let that one understand what the Spirit saith unto this Church.

NOTES.

[1] Adonai is the Amen in this respect, that all creation is gathered up into Him. He is the Arche or heavenly principle out of which the Soul is begotten, and the Amen in that the consummation or fulness of Life for the Soul is the realization of Adonai within its Sanctuary.

[2] He alone is the Faithful One and True Witness to the Soul. All other witness is limited, even though true. When the Soul knows Adonai, it is the inheritor of all things.

[3] The community in the state of Laodicea were indeed meritorious workers. They were teachers of the Divine Righteousness, administrators of Justice weighed in the balances of the Divine Love and Wisdom.

[4] That they lost their true vision of the meaning of the Divine Righteousness is not to be wondered at, when the conditions amid which they had to labour are understood ; but they also lost their love for the work which they had had appointed unto them.

They belonged to the House of Minds in the Christhood Order. Alas ! they lost their humbleness and meekness also ; and with these they lost all. But they continued to fill an office which they claimed to be that of true administration. So they had the appearance of zealousness and enrichment, even whilst they were cold in their love and lukewarm in their service.

[5] They had lost the Radiance, the Love, and the Life of Righteousness, and knew not the meaning of the loss to them, nor the tragedy of the evil that flowed in upon them.

[6] This threefold appeal reveals how great their loss was. It shows their impoverishment, even as it reveals their ancient powers and dignity.

[7] These Souls had indeed gone far afield, for they had become as strangers to Adonai. " Behold ! He waiteth at the door ! " shows that He was without.

[8] To be enthroned with Him is once more to reign. Were they Souls who were enthroned upon the earth and who in their kingly and queenly state had enriched themselves with earthly things to the impoverishment of the Divine Things ?

In this is it revealed who they were. For they were to become once more enthroned with Him, that is, they were to reign in Righteousness, and administer in Love, and with true Vision.

THE APOCALYPSE.

SECTION II.

Visions of the Divine Kingdom; the operations of Elohim within the Four Kingdoms in their perfect states; the Mystery of the Planet's History in the Sealed Book, its glorious beginning, its descent, its overwhelming loss of spiritual power until even spiritual death reigned, the Travail of the Christhood community of Souls who had gone down with all the Planet's children, and the Great Tribulation of them all, with a vision of their Passing Through once more to realize the Redemption, followed by the Regeneration.

THE APOCALYPSE

The Throne of the Eternal One

After these things a door within the Heavens was opened, and I was taken up by the Spirit to the innermost realm.[1]

And there I saw a Throne and the One who sat upon it. To look at Him was as if one were looking upon a Jasper and Sardius stone;[2] and around the Throne was a marvellous rainbow that had the appearance also of an Emerald.[3]

And round about the Throne there were twenty and four other thrones whereon sat four and twenty Elders; and these were arrayed in white raiment and wore crowns of gold.[4]

And out of the Throne in the midst of the thrones there proceeded great radiations, and these were as lightnings in their action, and in their proceeding the seven Thunders made their voices heard through the Heavens.[5]

Before the Throne which was in the midst of the thrones, there burned seven Lamps whose flame was kindled from the seven Spirits of God;[6] and there was also a great Sea which looked like crystal, and it was before the Throne and round about it;[7] and also before the Throne were four Living Creatures, and these had eyes with which to look into the four dimensions.[8]

And the four Living Ones had each six wings; with twain they covered their heads, with twain they covered their feet, and with twain they did fly.[9]

These rest not, but continually cry unto Him who sitteth upon the Throne: 'Holy, holy, holy, is the Lord God, the Omnipotent One, who was, who is, and who is about to come.'

And they give glory and honour and praise unto Him, and worship Him evermore, and lay down at His feet the crowns with which they are crowned; and the four and twenty Elders also lay down their crowns and worship; and they make this ascription unto Him :—

'Worthy art Thou, O Lord our God, to receive the glory and the honour and the power : for Thou didst create all things, and through Thy Will Thou hast created them.'

326

NOTES.

[1] This does not mean that the preceding vision of Adonai was not from the Divine Kingdom, for He could only be so beheld upon that realm. But in this vision there is greater fulness of realization of the Presence.

This vision commences the second portion of the Revelation. The first was Adonai in the form of the Son of Man speaking unto the Christhood communities ; this vision is also of Adonai and the supreme creative forces of the Eternal One.

[2] Such a vision is indescribable. The Divine Presence cannot be portrayed as we would write of a man. But the two precious stones suggest the intensity of the Appearance. Like one of the glorious Suns whose colour seems to change as we behold it, so with the vision of the Eternal : they represent the glorious Love and Power.

[3] The Bow took its reflections from the Presence, and shed around it the Great Peace.

[4] These Elders were the Ancients and represented the Divine Christhood Estate—the twelve Divine Attributes, each twofold, having its negative and positive mode. They are arrayed in the Divine Purity and crowned with Love.

[5] Of the seven Thunders we will write later. The great radiations are magnetic streams.

[6] The perfect Light upon the seven spheres of the innermost realm. A Divine Christhood is not one, but seven. Herein lies a mystery that has to be understood through realization.

[7] The Great Sea, pure and transparent as crystal, is the pure auric Light and Creative Substance proceeding from the Eternal. Out from this Sea have all things issued.

It is the Great Sea out of whose waters or substances Souls are born. When a Soul attains to Christhood, it realizes within itself the meaning of that Sea, and becomes of it, and so is Maria—one with the Divine Presence, begotten of the Divine Substance.

[8] The Four Living Creatures have been described as a Lion, an Ox, a Man and an Eagle. But it is utterly impossible to define in correct form what was beheld. They represented the creative powers operating upon the four kingdoms and extending into the four dimensions. They therefore represent the Omnipresence of the Eternal One who is in All things created from and by Him.

The Wings signify power—the power to soar, the power to serve, and the power to remain passive. And in all is the Mystery of the Divine Operation. It is hidden from the vulgar gaze, and can be known only through the Soul.

THE APOCALYPSE

The Book that was Sealed

Then I beheld in the hand of Him who sitteth upon the Throne, a Book that was written within and without ; and it was closed with seven seals.[1]

And I heard one of the Angels of the Spheres inquire, 'Who is able to open the book and to interpret the seals?'

But none of the Angels in the Heavens, nor any one upon the Earth-spheres, was able to open the Book or interpret the seals.[2]

And I sorrowed much that no one was able to open the Book, or interpret the Seals, or to look therein.

Then one said unto me : 'Sorrow not at this, for there is One who is able to open the Book and to interpret the seals ; for the Lion of the household of Judah hath been overcome by the House of David, and He who hath overcome is able to open the Book and unloose the seals thereof.'[3]

And I beheld upon the Throne which was in the midst of the four Living Creatures and the four and twenty Elders, a Lamb standing as though it had been slain ; it had seven Horns and seven Eyes, for it possessed the powers of the seven Spirits of God.[4]

And the Lamb rose and took the Book out of the right hand of Him who sitteth upon the Throne ; and when He had taken it, the four Living Creatures and the four and twenty Elders fell down before the Lamb, and worshipped : each one had a harp of praise, and a golden orb full of incense, the prayers of the Saints.[5]

And they sang anew the song, saying : ' Worthy art Thou to take the Book and to unloosen the seals of it ; for Thou wast slain, and didst give Thyself to redeem by Thy blood most precious, and bring to know God of every tribe and nation, out of all peoples and tongues, to establish His Kingdom in the midst of them, and make of them a royal Priesthood.'[6]

Then I saw around the Throne with the four Living Creatures and the four and twenty Elders, a great company of Angels ; and the number of them was ten thousand times ten thousand, even thousands upon thousands.

NOTES.

[1] What could this Book be that was sealed with seven Seals ? In relation to the Individual Soul it is the whole human Life, the seals being its seven planes whose Mystery is sealed unto all but the Divine. That Book is written within and without ; for the history of the Soul is written within it, and upon all its planes and vehicles.

But here the Book so sealed is not the history of any individual Soul, but that of the Planet. And the opening of the seven seals is the revelation of the history written within it. That which is true of the Macrocosm is likewise true in some degree of the Microcosm, for the Soul's history is of that written on the Planet.

The mystery of the Soul individual is held sacred. It is veiled to all but the Divine Realm ; and none can know it even upon the Heavens unless it be given unto them to do so from the Divine. And this is likewise true concerning Planetary history. Science can guess at much through observation of the phenomena upon the physical planes, and Occultism read much upon the magnetic plane in what is known as the Akashic Records ; but the Planet's real inner history cannot be unveiled from these scientific and occult readings. The history of this distraught world is known only upon the Divine Kingdom.

[3] The One able to open the Book and interpret the Seals is Adonai Himself. He opens the Book of the Soul and interprets its Seals through the Angel of His Presence within the Soul's Sanctuary. And He it is who is said to have overcome the Lion of the household of Judah, for the Lion of Judah is the Astral realm whose condition for thousands of ages has been inimical to the true growth and unfoldment of the Soul. And He has changed the Lion sphere in Judah by means of the House of David—the House of merciful purification. Here there is reference to the Oblation and its resultant.

[4] The Lamb is always the symbol of the Divine ; and the Divine as Love and Wisdom had been slain upon the various planes of the Planet. The seven Horns represent Powers, and the seven Eyes, Vision upon all the planes. For they are the all-seeing administrative powers of the Eternal Spirit.

[5] When the Divine Love and Wisdom opens the Book, the Kingdoms of the Heavens and the Earth reveal His Praise. For notwithstanding the awful history written upon the Soul of this world, the Divine Ministry has always been beautiful. The Saints have known this ; hence the allusion to their prayers.

[6] Such is the Song of the Christhood Order : they also join in the Creative Powers of the Eternal, and Praise. For they alone can understand. And they are the Souls who form the Royal Priesthood.

329

THE APOCALYPSE

he pening f the even Seals

And I heard these saying: ' Worthy is the Lamb who hath been slain, to receive the Power, and the Riches, and the Wisdom, and the Might, and the Honour, and the Glory, and the Blessing!' [1]

Then I beheld how every created one who was in the Heavens, on the Earth, and on the great Sea, came to give praise unto Him who was upon the Throne with the Lamb ; and I heard them saying : ' Unto Him who sitteth upon the Throne with the Lamb, be the Blessing, and the Honour, and the Dominion, and the Glory, evermore.' [2]

And the four Living Ones and the four and twenty Elders bowed in worship before the Amen.

And as I looked, I beheld the Lamb open one of the seals ; and the Voice spake unto me again saying : ' Come and see :' and it was as if the Seven Thunders had spoken.

Then I beheld a white horse, and he who sat upon it had a bow in his hand ; and he went forth crowned as one who is to conquer. [3]

When the Lamb opened the second seal I beheld another horse come forth ; but it was red : and to him who sat thereon was the power given to take the hope of peace from the Earth, for there was given unto him a great sword wherewith to slay, and to cause to be slain. [4]

Then the third seal was opened, and at its opening a third horse issued and went forth. The horse was black, and he who sat upon it carried in his hand a balance, and unto him was it given to destroy, and fill the Earth with famine.

And a voice was heard in the midst of the four Living Creatures, crying : ' No measure of wheat for the buying, nor can three measures of barley be found, but the oil and the wine remain unhurt.' [5]

And when the Lamb opened the fourth seal, I beheld yet another horse, and its colour was of the paleness of death ; the name of him who sat upon it was Death. In his train Hades followed.

330

NOTES.

[1] This is true glory to God in the Highest. It is beautiful acknowledgment by the whole Heavens of the Love of the Eternal One. In the Heavens there is no pride of heart such as men know and value ; all Praise is acclaimed to Him in whom all live, and from whom all have their being. God is All !

[2] In this ascription we have given us a glimpse of the ultimate issue of the Divine Ministry, when the stricken Earth shall be even as the Heavens in its acknowledgment of the Eternal Love and Wisdom. For a redeemed Earth is to be the glorious resultant.

[3] The Horse was used as a hieroglyph, and its cryptic meaning had relation to the Mind and the state in which it was. The White Horse therefore denoted purity of intellect, and so of knowledge. He who rode upon the Horse was crowned as one who is to conquer ; that signifies one whose mind is pure and whose knowledge is true spiritual power.

Now this was the state of the Mind of the Planet in its unfallen days. The power operating at its heart and in its children was prophetic of victory—the attainment by all its children of the perfectionment of Life. Unto that end did the Divine Thought go forth. All things created were perfect, each after its kind and according to its degree. The steep ascents had to be conquered ere the fulness of life could come ; but there was no evil. The Horse (the Mind) had to be controlled and guided from the Divine Realm, but the runner took the path to conquest.

[4] The opening of the second seal revealed a momentous change. The White Horse is succeeded by a Red Horse whose rider, by means of his sword, takes peace from the Earth.

Red when pure and transparent is the symbol of intense Life. But when it is impure it is the symbol of passion of an evil order. The Red Horse therefore symbolized the Mind filled with thought begotten of such passion.

It is a vision of what took place upon the Planet through the great descent when its elemental kingdoms were changed ; for through that event the Mind or magnetic circulus of the Planet was filled with wrong directions which eventuated in the filling of the mind of the children with intense desire which became evil, whose manifestation drove peace from the earth.

The rider rode his Horse to the goal of strife and conflict.

[5] The opening of the third seal revealed a yet deeper state of descent. The Horse was Black and he who rode upon it led the earth and all its children to famine.

Black is negation. The Black Horse was the negation of the White Horse. It brought utter spiritual famine to the earth. All the children were affected. Only the oil for the Lamps and the

THE APOCALYPSE

And he had the power to kill by means of the sword, and famine, and by the wild beasts upon the Earth.[1]

The Travail of the Christhood Orders

Then with the opening of the fifth seal I beheld this most wonderful event. Underneath the altar of God within the Temple I saw the Souls of those who had been slain because of their testimony to the Word of God whom they knew ; and these Souls cried aloud with one voice, saying : ' How long, O Lord the holy and true One, how long ere Thou dost come in Thy just judgment to make manifest Thy righteousness unto those who be upon the Earth ? '[2]

And unto each of them there was given the white robe of the Saints of God ; and unto them came the message from above the altar that they should yet rest awhile until their fellow servants who were of the brethren should have fulfilled the work given them to do.[3]

And when the sixth seal was opened by the Lamb, a great earthquake shook the Earth to its foundations , and the Sun was veiled until it became as dark as the blackness of sackcloth, and the Moon was turned into the appearance of blood : then the Stars of the Heavens fell upon the Earth even as the Figtree shaken by the earthquake casteth her young Figs.

The Sinking of Atlantis

Then were the Heavens rolled up as one rolls a scroll ; and the islands, hills and mountains were all moved out of the places where they had been.

But the rulers of the Earth with their princes, and the military tribunes with the enriched and the powerful, and all who were not freemen, but were bondsmen to these, hid themselves within the caverns which they had hewn out for themselves, for they would not listen to the voices from the mountains which proclaimed the coming of the Lamb of God, and the judgment of the Most High.[4]

Then I beheld four Angels standing upon the four dimensions of the Earth, and these held in their power the fourfold Breath whose breathing giveth life unto the Earth. And by them the fourfold Breath had to

NOTES.

Wine for the Life of the Christhood, remained unhurt. For the oil was the anointing or illumining power, and the Wine the Divine Love that nourished and inspired.

[1] With the opening of the fourth seal there was a yet more tragic descent, and this was symbolized by a Pale Horse ridden by one whose name was Death. In his train Hades followed.

The goal of the rider was not simply the conflict of passion and the famine of spiritual impoverishment, but also that of spiritual death. That is, the state of mind induced by the misdirected passional nature and consequent spiritual impoverishment, issued in spiritual death. Men and women lost the power to live as spiritual Beings, and they descended into the forms of the wild beasts whose existence was due to the changed elemental conditions.

The period covered by the first four seals was countless ages, during which the Human Race left the Human Kingdom more than once, and were only saved through the beautiful ministry of the Christhood Orders who were the channels of the Divine Salvation from the fearful and even degraded states into which they sank. The history of these will be dealt with in a later work on the Planet.

[2] These were the Souls who had been in Christhood, and had arrived at the consciousness of God. They too had been slain by the conditions and had been made to pass through the hells of the wild beast forms. This is the vision of the yearning of them all for the great Realization once more and the triumph of righteousness on the earth. They were underneath the altar, for they had been sacrificed in ministry.

[3] The White Robes, the garments of the Saints, is the restored purity of the Christ Life ; and the waiting for future manifestation is that great changes had to be wrought in the middle kingdom of the Planet ere such manifestation could be given.

[4] The revelation of Planetary History in the opening of the Sixth Seal covers a period which was so terrible that the wonder is that any Souls were able to survive it. The physical changes wrought were so tremendous that the poor distraught Planet was verily shaken to its foundations. It was a catastrophe, material and spiritual, of indescribable magnitude. Atlantis sank, and the surface as well as the interior of the outer planes was changed. The Sun refused its light in the sense that it was unable to penetrate the dense conditions. The Moon being so near, when it was visible, looked like blood. Meteoric stars fell upon the earth. But, worse than all these outward disasters, it came to pass that the Sun—the inner vision—was completely veiled ; the Moon—the Mind—was brought down into conflict of the worst kind, for black magic had prevailed ; the Stars that yet shone in the spiritual heavens of the Planet's life —the Christ-Souls—were thrown down.

THE APOCALYPSE

be withheld because of the conditions which had been brought upon the Earth by the ways of man.[1]

The Loosening of the Four Breaths

And another Angel ascended with the rising of the Sun, and he cried unto the four Angels who guarded the kingdoms of the four dimensions of the Earth: 'This is the seal of the living God sent unto you by His Angel, that ye now cause the fourfold Breath to be breathed, and that the healing of the hurt of the Earth, with the sea also, and all the trees, be accomplished.'[2]

For the day is nigh for the sealing of all the servants of God upon their foreheads; and the number of these is one hundred and forty and four thousands out of the Household of Israel, from each tribe twelve thousand.'[3]

Then I saw a great multitude: it had been gathered out of all the nations and tribes and tongues; and the peoples stood before the Throne whereon was seated the Lord with the Lamb of God.

And the peoples were arrayed in white raiment from the Lord, and wore crowns fashioned from refined gold, and in their hands they carried branches of the Tree of Life.

The Hosts of the Tribulation

With a great voice did these cry: 'Salvation is of God;' and the angels who encircled the Throne whereon the Lord was seated with the Lamb, and the four and twenty Elders, and the four Living Creatures, bowed before the throne and worshipped, saying: 'O Amen! The Blessing and the Glory, the Wisdom and the Power, the Thanksgiving and the Might, with the Honour of all these, are Thine for ever and ever, O God of our life and the Amen.'

And when I looked upon the great multitude I discerned that the peoples were those who had come up out of the great tribulation, having washed their robes in the Blood of the Lamb; and now they are ever before the Throne of God.

And whithersoever the Lamb goeth, they follow; and they sing the song which Moses taught them concerning the Lord and the Lamb in the midst of the Throne:

334

NOTES.

The Planetary Heavens were destroyed through the conduct of the Atlanteans. And though terrible sufferings befell all upon these Heavens and upon the outer planes of the Planet, yet those who had brought about the disaster remained in their evil states or caverns, ignoring the messages sent unto them from the Divine.

[1] The Four Breaths are the Divine magnetic currents which flow through the Four Atmospheres, and replenish the Life of all things upon the Four Kingdoms.

The Four Angels of the Four Dimensions are the Planetary Angels, the channels through which the Breath is given.

The reason for the withholding of the fourfold Breath, was the state of the Planet's Kingdoms. These latter had become so dangerously evil, that the Breath had to be withheld until the conditions were changed.

These Divine Streams of magnetic power must not be confounded with the various atmospheric currents known as the winds, for they were of a spiritual order.

[2] Though the period covered by the description here, was great, yet the Divine Love preserved the world and the race until the Breath could again be given. And now the Breath may be felt within each Atmosphere and upon each Kingdom. For the Angel of the Lord, who is also the Angel or Archangel of the Sun, Gabriel, hath commanded in the Name of the Lord that they should again flow.

[3] This sealing of the Household of Israel is taking place now, though there was also another event in which, in part, it likewise took place. The true Israel is known by this Seal. What is it ? The Elohim likeness. They bear within themselves the likeness or image of the Eternal Christ, themselves being His Christs in ministry. They are Issa-Ra-El—*the children of the Sun in whom is the Holy Spirit and Radiance of the Lord.*

The meaning of their number is mystical. They are said to be 144,000, from each tribe 12,000. The twelve tribes of Israel must not be confounded with the tribes of Judah ; they do not belong to the same Race. The tribes of Judah are of the Planet's Children ; the tribes of Israel were and are the Christhood Orders. The 144,000 is the square of twelve without the cyphers. And in progressional numbers, they make nine. Nine is the Jesus state, the purified Life, the Heart of Love, the cosmic consciousness of Oneness with all Souls upon this Planet. Twelve signifies the attributes of Christhood, the Life that has come into the Anointing or Illumination from the Lord. Whilst twelve times twelve signifies the all-entrancing ministry of the Order.

These are the Souls who chiefly pass through the great Tribulation,

335

THE APOCALYPSE

The Song
of the
Redeemed

' *Worthy art Thou, O Lord, to receive the Glory of the Heavens, the worship of all Thy Saints, and the service of Thy children.*

Thou, in Thy power, hast redeemed us out of every nation and tribe and tongue known amongst men, and hast brought us through the Blood of the Lamb into the land which Thou didst promise unto us.

Hunger know we no more, for the Living Bread have we found in Thee: thirst know we no longer, for we have found assuagement in the Living Waters which flow from Thee: sigh we no more for the coming of the Light, for Thy countenance Thou hast again unveiled to us, and Thy Radiance falls upon us: and we mourn no more without comfort, as those in a strange land, for Thou hast given unto us the Holy One in whom is Thy Peace.

Thou art our Shepherd, we shall lack no more. Thou wipest away all our tears, and leadest us whither we would fain go, even unto the Living Fountains where are the Waters of Life.

We praise Thee, O Most Holy One! '

After this I beheld the Lamb open the seventh seal; and there was silence in the Heavens for half a time.[1]

Then the seven Angels of the innermost spheres who minister for God before His Throne, had given unto them the seven Trumpets of God; and with these were they to proclaim His will upon the Earth.[2]

The
Seraphim
with the
Golden
Censer

And one of the Seraphim came and stood at the golden altar which was before the Throne, and he carried a golden censer; and unto him was given much incense, and this he added unto the incense of the prayers of the Saints, and laid it upon the golden Altar.[3]

And the cloud of the incense of the prayers of the Saints arose before God.

And when he had taken up the golden censer again, and filled it from the fire which burned upon the Altar of pure gold, he poured it out upon the Earth: and there followed the voices of the seven Thunders; and there were lightnings, and there was the shaking of the foundations of the Earth.[4]

NOTES.

though the elder children of the Planet do also suffer intensely, and sorrow much under the world-burdens imposed upon them. But the Tribulation is the Passing through of the Soul on the Path of Purification and the Regeneration.

[1] What could this Silence mean ? It is said in relation to Creation, that after six days' labour, God rested and was silent upon the seventh. Is Heaven ever silent or inactive in the way understood of men ? No ; for even amid the Silence there are operative great potencies. It is said of the Eternal One that when the prophet who bore the message of the Lord to Israel, stood upon Mount Horeb, that the Presence passed by, first as an Earthquake, then as a Whirlwind, afterwards as a Chariot of Fire, and that though these were so great in their manifestation, the Prophet failed to discern the Presence, and it was not until there came the Voice of the Great Stillness or Silence that he perceived.

In a human Soul's evolution the six days are passed through ere the seventh is reached. And though the Soul passes through many divisions having seven as the number, during the six creative days of its perfect fashioning ; yet it is only when it reaches the seventh or innermost that it meets with the Great Stillness or Silence. It is the creative Day of Nirvana, the attaining to the consciousness of the Presence whose voice is heard amid the Silence.

The Silence here referred to must not, therefore, be taken to imply inactivity ; for the Divine Operations never cease. But there was a long silence whilst the work of the Oblation was being accomplished. And when it was about to be fully accomplished, the Silence was broken, and the Heavens spake again. We are now in those days.

[2] And those who spake for God were the Angels of the Innermost Spheres. Unto them were given the Seven Trumpets or Voices of the Eternal One that they might proclaim His will unto His Christs, how it should be accomplished upon the Earth.

The messages these Angels give are from the Divine Realm. They are given unto those who, upon the outer planes, are to act as the Messengers of the Most High. And the teachings of these messages are accommodated to the Soul upon the different planes.

[3] The Seraphim is the Presence overshadowing the Altar of the Soul, wherein is the Ark of the Spirit. For within the Soul it is even as it is in the Heavens.

[4] The seven Thunders are the effects of the Fire of God. They are the Seven Creative Agencies revealing the holy purpose of the Most Blessed One. Through the purifying processes, the redeeming potencies, the aspirations of the saints, the seven Thunders speak, and the Earth is shaken to its foundations, spiritually, and there is great enlightenment and illumination.

THE APOCALYPSE.

SECTION III.

The Utterance of the Seven Trumpets and the Changes effected by them; Lucifer's Fall; the conflicts amid the Hell States, and between them and the Heavens; the Temple and the two Witnesses; the Glory and the Sufferings of Christhood; the Purifying Fires of God; the Beast, the Dragon, and the False Prophet; the Pseudo-Lamb representing the Church Historic ally; the Sealing of Israel and the Harvest; the Ecclesiastical Babylon whose Mystery deceived the Earth; its Fall and final overthrow of its False Systems through the Power of Adonai; the Binding of Satan and the First Resurrection.

THE APOCALYPSE

And the seven Angels who had the seven Trumpets, prepared themselves to proclaim the will of Him who was seated upon the Throne.

The Voices of the Seven Trumpets

When the first Angel sounded forth the message of the Eternal One, there descended upon the Earth a hail of fire which was scattered from the Altar of Fire which was before the Throne ; and the hail of fire was mingled with the Blood of the Lamb : these were cast upon the Earth to consume away its evil, to destroy the evil plants which had been planted, and the false pastures whereon the dwellers of the Earth were nourished.[1]

At the sounding forth of the message of the second Angel, there was let down a Mountain around which lightnings played, and it went into the sea ; and it changed the waters of the sea from a state of blood in which so many had died, and drove out of them those things which had killed all the life within them ; and the ships that had traded in these waters were likewise destroyed. For the mountain had power given unto it to change all things.[2]

When the message of the third Angel was sounded forth, a great Star went down from the Heavens, and it fell upon the Earth, and when it reached the Earth it was as a burning torch. By it were the rivers flowing from the fountains to the sea, changed ; for their waters were bitter as wormwood, and their bitterness had killed many. And the name of that Star no man knoweth.[3]

At the sounding forth of the message by the fourth Angel, I perceived the Sun, the Moon and the Stars as if the light of them had in part been veiled, and that their light did not shine fully upon the Earth ; but, with the sounding of the Trumpet, the veil was taken away so that their light could shine in fulness.[4]

And I beheld an Angel flying in the Heavens, and heard a great voice saying unto the dwellers on the Earth : ' Woe, woe, woe, unto those who hear not to observe the message of the Angel which he beareth from the Throne of the Eternal One ! For the Day of God

340

NOTES.

[1] The Hail of Fire from off the Altar around the Throne, symbolizes the Eternal Love as Energy manifested for the purpose of transmutation, changing the conditions upon the various planes of the Planet by means of the purification of all the elements. By this process the evil is said to be consumed away, the evil plants or growths destroyed, and the false pastures changed.

As the Hail of Fire represents spiritual elements rained from the Divine Kingdom upon the Earth, so the work these accomplish is spiritual. The evil plants are false systems planted and rooted in the soil of the nations and peoples, with equally false pastures cultivated as the right kind of food for the nourishing of peoples, nations and races—just such things as may be found now in every national ideal.

The Fire of God is the most potent purifying force. It is the Alembic in which all things are separated, the Crucible in which the true is disintegrated from the false, and the dross consumed. It enshrines and illumines every Tree of Life of the Divine planting, but burns up those that are not from the Divine.

And the Blood of the Lamb, the most Sacred Life stream from the Divine Realm, was likewise poured out as rain upon the earth, unto the healing of its wounds, the rejuvenating of all its spiritual elements, the redemption of all its children and all its kingdoms.

[2] The Great Mountain is the new and blessed vision of Life sent through the Christhood. Around the heights of the Christhood state the Lightnings of the Lord play—the great illumining powers.

The Sea whose waters were made bitter is, first, the Astral in the Planet and the Soul ; then the waters of the Soul's thought. How bitter life has been for the Soul upon this world for many thousands of ages, the history of the race and the Planet reveal. The waters of life have been full of bloodshed, human and creature ; and even the Life-stream of the Soul has been made bitter.

The introduction of the Christ-love and the Christ-life and ministry, through the true Christ-vision and realization, turn Marah into Elim, the bitterness of sorrow and despair into the sweetness of waters of Life.

[3] Who was this Star ? It was named by one, Wormwood. But the Stars of God are full of Blessing. They nourish, illumine, direct and redeem. They are Logoi of God. In the stellar Heavens they are Divine Systems ; in the Spiritual Heavens they are His Sons, the Immortals, the Christs of God.

That Star was a Soul let down from the Heavens. When it was on the earth it was as a lighted torch. Upon the Earth it fell in the lives of the Oblation, and through its fall the streams of thought that fed the Sea (the Astral world) were purified.

[4] The unveiling, for purposes of manifestation of the Lord vision within the Soul, the Light of the Mind, and the glory of the twelve

Y—I
341

THE APOCALYPSE

is upon them in which the wickedness of the wicked shall be overthrown, and the dominion of the Beast who opposeth God shall be cast out for ever, and the Beast slain.' [1]

When the fifth Angel sounded forth the message of the Highest, I beheld a Star of the Heavens, but one which had fallen upon the Earth : it was Lucifer, once the Star of the Morning. [2]

And he held the key of the abyss wherein the mystery of iniquity had its dwelling ; and with the key he unlocked the pit of the abyss.

And there issued from it clouds of smoke like that which proceedeth from a great furnace ; and it filled the air and darkened it, and obscured the light of the Sun.

Then out of the smoke came forms like great locusts and scorpions, having power to sting and hurt ; and these went forth to give torment unto all the dwellers upon the Earth, but they had not the power to hurt and destroy the pastures and trees of those who had not the mark of the Beast upon them ; only those who were not sealed of God were they able to torment, for they struck them as the scorpion striketh.

And many of the forms were like horses prepared for battle ; and these wore crowns which looked like gold, but were not, and they had the faces of men. And they took the adornment of women, and their glory ; for they had power like a lion. [3]

There was one who reigned over them all, even the Star of the Morning which had fallen upon the Earth, Lucifer ; but they named him Abaddon, for he was the Destroyer.

At the sounding forth of the message of the sixth Angel, I heard a Voice speaking from between the Horns of the Golden Altar where God was seated, and it said : 'Unloose the four Angels who are bound by the great river Euphrates.'

And the four Angels were unloosed, for they had been kept in waiting unto the hour of that day in which

NOTES.

Stars or Christhood attributes with which in Christhood the Soul is crowned.

[1] This is the Messenger—not one of the seven Angels of the Innermost Sphere, but one nevertheless sent with a message from the Throne of the Eternal One. Such a messenger is one who is overshadowed from the Divine Realm. He flies amid the Heavens ; that is, he has his dwelling there. Though on the Earth-planes, he rises into the Heavens for all His visions that are to be interpreted. Such a messenger has appeared, and the message is being promulgated. And woe unto those who hear not to observe the message, for upon them the times will bring woe. For the message is one unto purification of life, the birth of God in the Soul, and the service begotten of His Love and Radiance within.

For those who cannot or will not respond to purity, love and wisdom—the Divine Life, Love and Light—but who persist in following the beast of materiality, shall find life overthrown for them. For the day of God is upon this world in which all wickedness shall be consumed in the furnace of purification.

[2] Who was Lucifer, once Star of the morning, bright and beautiful star ? O the sad history which he has caused to be written since the day when he went out from the Presence of the Lord to found another kingdom ! It was a day of mourning in the Heavens when he went away, falling from his high estate. He was the once glorious mind of the Planet, the reflector or light-bearer. His place was in the high Heavens (Planetary). " O Lucifer ! How thou art fallen," exclaimed the Prophet, " behold how thou whose office once was within the Heavens, hast descended into the state of Hell (darkness)!"

He was also the Angel of the outermost spheres, because his ministry was amongst those. In his fallen state he is Abaddon the Destroyer, because through the change in him the outer and middle spheres were also changed. The peace upon the earth was destroyed, for magnetic antagonisms ensued, followed by conflicts the most unimaginable, so terrible were they.

The abyss was the new state generated upon the middle kingdom now known as the Astral. It became the seat of most awful powers and principalities. Lucifer had the key, for it was the mind that fashioned all of them, and it is the mind who lets them loose. The mystery of the world's iniquity has been hidden within its realm.

[3] The opening of the pit of the abyss, or the unloosening of the evil magnetic potencies gathered there, led to the most fearful conditions upon the outer planes. The clouds of smoke are the dense vapours, the spiritual mists whose miasmic elements not only poisoned the thoughts, desires and feelings of the people who were subject to them, but caused the obscuration of all spiritual light.

The forms said to issue from the smoke represent the most evil

343

THE APOCALYPSE

the sign *of* the Day *of* God should appear, and the year *of* the Redeemed should come.[1]

The Conflict between the Heavens and the Hells

And when the four Angels were loosed, I beheld great armies *of* horsemen, ten thousand times ten thousand, going forth to battle with those forms which had come out *of* the smoke that ascended from the pit *of* the abyss ; and these had upon them breastplates the colour *of* hyacinth, and they appeared as *if* they were emitting fire.[2]

From their mouths proceeded a flame *of* fire, and it scorched those who loved to do wickedness ; for they fought against those forms which had issued from the pit and which stung like scorpions and destroyed as locusts ; and they drove them down again into the abyss to overwhelm them that they may have no more power for ever.[3]

Then I beheld a great Angel descending from the innermost sphere in a cloud ; upon his head a rainbow rested. His face was as the Sun for brightness, and his feet were resting upon pillars *of* fire.[4]

And the Angel descended until he reached the sea *of* the Earth, and he stood with his right foot upon it, and he spake in a great voice ; and when he spake, the seven Thunders gave utterance, but their utterance was sealed up for a time.[5]

And the Angel raised his right hand to the Heavens and spake the Word *of* Him who liveth for evermore, the Creator *of* all the worlds and the Nourisher *of* all Life upon them ; and the word which he spake was that the end *of* the time had come, and that its reign should be no longer.[6]

And the Angel carried in his right hand a Book, and it contained the Mystery *of* God spoken *of* by His Prophets and Seers, the Good Tidings concerning the finding again *of* Israel and the Redemption *of* Judah, and the Restoration *of* Ierusalem with the restitution *of* all things.

And I was commanded to receive the Book from the Angel who held it in his right hand, and as I took

344

NOTES.

things, thought forms of low desire, the perverted passional nature, pride, dominion with oppression. With the sting of the Scorpion they smote, tormenting and destroying the people.

And in these days the results may be witnessed upon the outer planes. The very forms and powers and conduct are significant.

[1] The great river Euphrates symbolizes the Spirit. Of the four rivers in the Garden of Eden, the four flowing from one central fountain, it flowed Eastwards. That meant towards the Divine. It was not the river that divided the innermost from the outermost, like the Jordan ; but it was the river or Divine Stream within the Soul.

Beside that river in the interior of man's spiritual being, and also in that of the Planet Soul, the four Angels or Potencies of the four-fold Kingdom and the Life of it, had been bound. So fettered were they that they could not perform their ministry and bring to the Soul and the World the Life of the Spirit. For these Angels were and are the four Divine Elements whose polarization constitute the man a living Soul, and whose ministry accomplishes Divinity in him : and in the Planet they are those finest elements which are begotten of its Divine Status.

[2] The multitude of horsemen represent the marvellous effect of the loosening of the four Divine Elements within the Soul and the Planetary life ; for the great multitude is composed of purified minds, minds whose colour is as hyacinth, a pure electric blue, the symbol of devotion to the Highest. And they were so charged with magnetic auric power, that it appeared as if they were emitting fire. For the Horse is hieroglyph of the Mind, the Breastplate the emblem of Divine Guardianship.

[3] These heavenly armies of purified lives and Divine Potencies had issuing from them a Flame of Fire, symbolizing the utterance of the Spirit. And they made battle against the powers that issued from the abyss, and extinguished them.

This mighty conflict now proceeds apace. The Hosts of the Lord are upon the upper planes of the Planet, valiantly contending against the evil powers let loose, and driving them down to that state in which they will be overwhelmed and blotted out.

[4] One in whom were the Elohim. He reflected the glory of all the Elohim, for He was crowned with the Spectrum of the Divine Kingdom in the form of a Rainbow. He was also glorious as the Sun, and He rested upon two pillars of Fire, indicating what His mission was. For He was and is Adonai, the Lord of Glory, whose Presence overshadows the Soul. His feet stand on the two pillars of the Divine Mystery contained in the Divine Love and Divine Wisdom.

[5] At His Voice the seven Voices (Elohim) utter the Word. They are the Messengers in the Heavens, of the Mysteries of the Father-Mother. The sealing up of these is the withholding of their inner-

345

THE APOCALYPSE

it from him, he said unto me : ' Truly it shall be most sweet unto thee to eat of, but when thou hast eaten it, bitterness shall it bring into thy life ,' and it was so, even as the Angel said.[1]

Then He who sat upon the Throne with the Lamb said unto me : ' Thou must yet prophesy concerning many things, and proclaim them unto peoples and nations. Arise and measure the Temple of God, the Altar, and they who worship within it. And the court that is without and which has been trodden down by the Gentiles also measure, for it must not be left unmeasured, though the nations who have laid waste the Holy City have polluted it.'

And the Rod of the measure of God was given unto me with which to measure the Temple, and its Altar, and all who worship therein.[2]

Then the Voice of Him who sat upon the Throne heard I saying : ' Behold, my two witnesses whom I sent to prophesy for me, and to make known unto the nations the Living Way ! For forty and two months did they prophesy, clothed in the garments which those wear who mourn.'

These were the two Olive Branches witnessing upon the Earth for the Lord, the two Light-bearers testifying of Him.

And as they testified, there came a beast up from the abyss, and it persecuted them and made war upon them and killed them ; and they lay in the great city which is spiritually known as Sodom and Egypt, the great city wherein the Lord Himself was crucified.

And the peoples and tribes and nations of all tongues did look upon their dead bodies for the three days and a portion of a day, during which the Oblation for the sins of these peoples was being made ; but after the three days and the portion of a day had been accomplished, and the Oblation for sin made, then by the Holy Breath of the Most High One these two witnesses of God rose upon their feet to renew their testimony. And from within the Temple they prophesied concerning the Mystery of God and its unveiling.[3]

The Measuring **of the** Temple of God

The Two Witnesses for God

346

NOTES.

most significance until the day when they may be unveiled.

The right foot of the Angel standing upon the sea of the Earth denotes power manifested upon the Astral or Middle Kingdom. This is in harmony with the tremendous Divine Agencies operating upon that realm to drive out and overthrow the evil and wicked powers whose habitations are there.

[6] The end of the era. The old is passing away, the new era has come. The reign or dominion of the Astral Principalities is coming to an end. And the Mystery of God is being unveiled now.

[1] The Book of the Mystery of God given to any Soul to eat, represents within that Soul the process of recovery by which the Divine Mystery of Life in the Soul and the Planet, not to name other systems, is unveiled so that it is revealed. No one can give such a Book to the Soul but the Angel of His Presence, for it is from Adonai alone that the Mystery of Being can be unveiled and revealed through the Logos within.

Now this Book contained the Mystery which had been hidden throughout long ages in which the history of this world as a spiritual or Soul system was to be found. In it were comprised the histories of the Kingdoms of Israel (the Christhood Order) and Judah (this world), and the process of finding and redeeming them both.

Though it is indeed sweet to be the servant of the Most High and to receive from the hand of His Angel that great multiple Mystery, yet the Book was so full of sorrow and the things concerning the sorrow, that its contents were Marah to the Soul—full of bitterness. For the contents of the Book filled the whole being of the Master— Iôannês—with intense anguish. For it also contained in its hidden depths the Mystery of the Oblation.

[2] The Temple of God is the Soul, Planetary and Individual. And in the use of the expression here, it is the Temple of Solomon that is alluded to. For that Temple was not any earthly house, but the Soul in Christhood of a high order. The Altar was the Ark overshadowed by the Shechinah or Presence. The outer court which was trodden down of the Gentiles, was the body in its functions and attributes ; for these had been dethroned and subjugated by the outward powers, put to unlawful uses, and so desecrated.

The whole Temple was to be measured even to the outer court. And it was to be measured with the Rod of the measure of God. This meant that the Realization of God by the Soul was and is the true measure or fulness of Life. It is Zôê in beautiful fulness, and is the measure of Christhood or the full-grown man.

[3] Who were the two witnesses ? Many have witnessed for God during the three Naronic Cycles which have passed since the days of the Manifestation, but few have witnessed as His special Messengers ; for few have been ready to hear with the understanding

347

THE APOCALYPSE

Then came the sounding forth of the message of the seventh Angel; and when he had proclaimed it, a great Voice within the Temple said: 'Now is the hour when the Kingdoms of this world shall become again the Kingdom of God and His Christ, and His shall be the regnancy for evermore.' [1]

The Voice within the Temple

And at the sound of this Voice the four and twenty Elders which sit upon the thrones around the Throne of the Eternal One, bowed down before Him worshipfully, saying

'We give Thee thanks, O Lord God Omnipotent, who was, and is, and is now about to come; for Thou art the King Eternal, Immortal and Glorious, doing wonders for all Thy children, enriching Thy servants whose awe of Thee within them is blessed, redeeming Thy oppressed children, and overthrowing the works of those who do iniquity and hurt the Earth.' [2]

Then the Heavens were opened that the Temple of God could be beheld; and within the Temple there was to be seen the Ark of His Covenant. And there were heard the voices of the seven Thunders, and these were followed by glorious radiations as when it lighteneth. And the Earth was shaken to its foundations. [3]

The Woman Clothed with the Sun

After these things I saw upon the Heavens a most wonderful sign: it was that of a Woman standing in light as if she were clothed with the Sun. Upon the Moon her feet did rest; and she was crowned with twelve Stars. [4]

The Woman was as one who travailed in great pain and longed to be delivered, for she was to bring forth a Man-child, who was to make manifest that Divine One who was about to come to govern the people with the Rod of His Power. [5]

But there also appeared this other wonder: there arose a Dragon which took upon itself to persecute the Woman and destroy the Man-child which she was bringing forth.

The Dragon had seven heads and ten horns, and was crowned with seven crowns; and it made war

348

NOTES.

what they would have had to say. Even now after the three days and portion of a day have passed, and the two Messengers have been raised up from the dead to bear witness for God, few are willing to follow that witness into the full Light.

On the Mystic planes the two witnesses are the Intuition purified and the Understanding illumined. On the outer planes these two are manifested through all those who are true Messengers.

[1] This is the message of the Angel of the innermost sphere. The Crown of all things, in both Planet and Soul, is the coming of the Kingdom of God : for the Soul it is the realizing of the Christhood in those who once knew it ; for the Planet it is the Kingdom of God and the Heavens coming into the life of all the children. For the Kingdom of the Heavens is the atmosphere generated from the ways of love and purity. It is the regnancy of God as righteousness, truth and goodness. In this Elohistic message we see the prophecy of the days in which the Planet would be perfectly restored. And the coming of that pristine glory is hastening, for now is the hour in which His Christs are being awakened, to become once more the vehicles of a glorious manifestation.

[2] If there is one thought more than any other specially emphasized in all the Logia spoken by the Master, it is this. To Him it was ever the Supreme One, the Father-Mother, who accomplished all things in and through His children. There was always absent the personal and even the individual Soul equation. The Most Blessed One was All in All. And in the Apocalyptic vision this is specially evident in the Visions relating to the innermost spheres.

[3] It is the opening of the Heavens of the Soul also wherein the Temple of God is, and the manifestation of the Glory of that sacred Ark, the hearing within of the Sevenfold Voice of Elohim, the beholding of the Radiance of the Lord Presence within. When this takes place for a Soul, the earthly elements are shaken to their foundations ; and through the ministry of such Souls, the foundations of the whole Earth are moved.

[4] This is a Vision of Divine Christhood. Woman is a symbol of the Soul. She is the Intuition. Clothed with the Sun she is fully illumined from the Lord Presence. The Radiance is within her, and she is transfigured. The Moon upon which her feet rest is the Soul's higher mind or reason. Both Moon and Feet represent the Understanding ; but the Feet also symbolize the ways of life, and here signify that these are the ways of an illumined Understanding. The Stars are the Twelve Christhood Attributes.

[5] This refers to a high manifestation of Christhood, the revelation in life, in concrete form, of the Divine Man. It is through all Souls who are able to rise into such a high degree of consciousness that the Divine Presence is to be manifested and the Rod of His Power

THE APOCALYPSE

with the woman, and drew down unto his kingdom many of the Stars of the Heavens.[1]

And the Eternal One caught up into the Heavens of His dwelling the Man-child born unto the woman until the day of the manifestation should come when he should again appear.[2]

And the Woman was preserved by the Eternal One within the wilderness[3] whither she fled because of the persecution of the Dragon, until the Dragon was cast out of the Heavens ; for Michael and the Angels overthrew its power and all its works within the Heavens.

And the great Dragon was cast down, the old serpent who is named the Devil, and Satan, the Deceiver of the whole world, he was cast down out of the Heavens of the Earth ; and with him his angels were also cast out.[4]

Then spake the great Voice from between the four Living Ones, and it said :

' Now is come the Salvation and the Power in the Kingdom of our God and His Christ ; for He hath put down the authority and dominion of the adversary of His children, even of him who accused the Brethren and persecuted them, turning their day of manifestation into a night of sorrow.

But through the Blood of the Lamb have they overcome him ; and in the day of their testimony they loved not their lives, but gave them even unto the death of all they most loved.[5]

Rejoice, therefore, O ye Heavens, and ye who tabernacle in them, and give Praise unto Him who sitteth upon the Throne in the midst of the thrones, the Eternal One, ever Blessed.'

Now, when the Dragon saw how he had been overthrown by Michael and the Angels, and cast out of the Heavens of the Earth, he was filled with wrath ; and he persecuted the woman who brought forth the Man-child.

And to the woman were given two wings, great as those of the Eagle, to enable her to fly unto her own place and be nourished until the time for the new manifestation.

350

NOTES.

revealed ; for the Rod of Power, which is said to have been in the Ark, which also divided the waters, blossomed, and brought living waters out of the rock, is the Power of the Divine Love.

[1] The Dragon symbolizes oppression and that which oppresses. It is the hieroglyph of the Western Mind, the materialistic mind that oppresses the Soul and destroys Christhood.

The Dragon or Materialistic Spirit always persecutes the woman— the Intuitional power within the system of the Soul. When applied in a Planetary sense it may readily be recognised ; and it will be most obvious when related to the ecclesiastical systems of the past and present, and the political systems which have oppressed all the nations. And in these latter days there may be witnessed the cumulative effects upon the peoples of these systems.

He has, by means of his power, brought down into his systems to follow His ways, even those who were as the Stars in the Firmament, Souls in whom the Light of Life once shone.

His seven heads are the seven planes of life upon which he has exercised his power ; and the ten horns are the five senses in their twofold manifestation, each having two modes, as these acknowledge the reign of the Dragon, for in doing so they become horns of power.

[2] The child born of the Woman is the Christ who, when manifested again, is to rule by the rod of Divine Power. But, until the day for the manifestation arrives, it must needs be that Christ be preserved within the Heavens of the Divine ; for the Dragon would seek to destroy Him.

[3] There are many things of a hidden order implied here. It means the changed state of the middle kingdom, for the woman to be preserved within it ; for it was that Kingdom that was as a Wilderness.

But it likewise signifies the work that had to be accomplished there because of the persecution of the Dragon, and the overthrow of that power within the Planetary Heavens.

[4] Michael and His Angels made war upon the Dragon and his Angels ; that is, the Lord as the Omnipotent One through the ministry of His Heavenly Hosts, drove out the Dragon-powers from the Heavens of the Planet, and threw them upon the outer planes to be ultimately destroyed. This process has been proceeding all through this era during which the Oblation has been accomplished, the effects of which are now manifest in the purification of the several spheres within the Planetary Heavens, and the breaking up of all the Dragon elements upon the lower spheres and outer planes. For the conflict is still in process, and the Heavens are now being fully cleared of all the evil principalities and powers that reigned therein.

[5] Herein is forcibly expressed the sublime acts of sacrifice made by the members of the Order of the Ancient Christhood when they

351

THE APOCALYPSE

But the old serpent, the Dragon, caused waters to pour forth after the woman to overwhelm her even as a river carrieth away those who cannot resist its current.

The Seven Angels with Censers of Fire

But the earth helped the woman, for it opened itself to receive the waters of the Dragon, and swallowed them : so the Dragon was more wroth with the woman, and made war with all who sought to keep the commandments of God, and hold sacred the testimony concerning Jesus Christ. And he waged his war against them upon the borders of the sea which encompassed the Earth.[1]

And I beheld yet another sign in the Heavens, which was marvellous in its meaning and great in its issues. Seven Angels had given to them seven censers containing the fire from the Altar of God within the innermost place. And these were to cast the contents of the censers upon the earth.[2]

And with this there appeared a sea of crystal wherein the fire was reflected ; and upon it there stood those who had overcome the influence of the Beast, who had not worshipped his image, nor borne upon them the mark of his number.[3] And they carried with them harps of praise to God, and sang the song of Moses and of the Lamb :

' Great and marvellous are Thy works, Lord of the Heavenly Hosts, Thou Almighty One ! Righteous and True art Thou, O King of all Ages ! Who would not have Thee in holy awe, O Lord Most High, and worship Thy hallowed name ! All the nations shall yet come and bow in worship before Thee, when the righteousness of Thine acts are made manifest.'

Then the Tabernacle of Testimony within the Temple was opened, and from out of it there appeared the Seven Angels who bore the seven censers of fire ; these were arrayed in white linen adorned with most precious stones, whose radiance was pure and bright, and girt about the breasts with golden girdles. And one of the four living creatures who were before the Throne of God, gave unto the seven Angels seven

352

NOTES.

yielded up the state of their Christhood which they loved so much, in order to minister unto the children of this Planet.

[1] The Woman who bears the Christ who also becomes the reigning One is the Virgin Soul; and to such a Soul is given the power to ascend unto her own Kingdom, for the Wings are Divine Powers in her.

The Waters poured forth from the mouth of the Dragon are Astral teachings. Waters are symbolical of truths. Poured forth from the Dragon who is the oppressor and deceiver of the Soul, the Waters signify impure or corrupted teachings; astral representations of Divine Things; the teachings of false science; the interpretations given by the materialistic systems which pose as the interpreters of the Divine Love and Wisdom; the false views of the meaning of Jesushood and Christhood, and the perversion of the vision of life given by the Master during the days of the blessed Manifestation. These are the waters the Dragon has spued out of his mouth ever since the Manifestation, and which, in great volume, have been even as a river carrying away all who were subject to the Dragon-power.

The awful cataclysms manifest upon the earth just now of a social and racial order testify how fully the prophecy in this vision has been fulfilled; for the outer planes are those where the Dragon now has his power. The Earth has received his outpourings, as he has been brought low by means of the Divine conflict in the Heavens. And though he yet has power to persecute, it is much more limited, and can only reach the outer planes or borders of the great Astral Sea.

The persecution and oppression of those who bear testimony for the holy estates of Jesus Christ, are manifest in our midst.

[2] Who were those Angels whose sacred office it was to take the seven censers containing the Fire of God from off the Altar that was within the Most Holy Place? They were the Elohim, the seven Creative Powers of the Most High, the seven great Redeeming Potencies operating within the Soul. They are more than Angels, or even Archangels; for by means of them Angels and Archangels perform their ministry. The Judgments of God are poured out upon the Earth by Himself; for upon every plane of experience and consciousness He manifests Himself through the Seven Divine Spirits.

The seven censers of Fire from the Altar symbolize the Fire of the Divine Energy accommodated to each plane of consciousness represented by each of the Elohe : for the Fire of God is none other than the Mystery of the Divine Love in operation upon each plane, purifying, energizing and illumining.

[3] The Sea of Crystal is a hieroglyph representing the Divine Sea of Knowledge within the Soul and the Planet. It was transparent, because Divine Knowledge is so beautifully spiritual that it is pure, free from all Astral and even Occult influences, and transcendentally greater than knowledges from those realms. And it reflected

353

THE APOCALYPSE

bowls full of the judgment of Him who liveth evermore. But the Temple became filled with the smoke from the seven bowls, that the Power and the Glory of God could no more be seen; nor could any one enter into the Temple again until the seven Angels had poured out the fires of judgment upon the earth.[1]

Then there spake a mighty Voice from out the midst of the Temple, and it commanded the seven Angels to go forth with their bowls of fire and pour them over the earth. And they went forth on their ministry.[2]

And the first Angel poured out the contents of his bowl: and the fire searched the lives of all men and women who dwelt upon the earth, and filled with pain those who had the mark of the Beast and who worshipped his power.[3]

The second Angel poured out his bowl upon the waters of the sea, which had become as blood; and in which all Souls had died; and the waters were deeply troubled at the outpouring of judgment upon them. But they were cleansed and the sea purified of its blood, so that Souls could live again within its waters.[4]

And the third Angel emptied his bowl upon the tributaries of the sea whose waters had been turned into blood, and the voice of the Angel said: 'Righteous art Thou, O most Holy One, and all Thy ways are done in righteousness. Upon these waters hath the blood of Thy prophets been poured out to purify them, for even Thy Saints have been drunken with the power of them. May these rivers of the sea once more become pure as in the days that were of old time.' And the Voice within the Temple spake from the altar, saying: 'Yea, O Lord God, the Almighty One; for Thy judgments are unto truth and righteousness.'[5]

The bowl of the fourth Angel was then emptied upon the fire which had searched all Souls and made many blaspheme the name of the Most High One; for it prevented them from repenting of their ways and giving themselves to the life that glorified God. And the power of the fire to search was destroyed, and its heats extinguished.[6]

The Seven Divine Judgments

354

NOTES.

the radiance of the Fire ; for Divine Knowledge truly reflects the Love, Radiance and Life of the Highest. But the Sea of Crystal likewise symbolizes the perfect conditions within the Soul in the high Christhood state in which all the elements before the throne of the Most High One reflect the glory of the seven sacred Fires.

[1] The opening of the Tabernacle of Testimony within the Temple indicates one of the most profound Mysteries of the Soul and the Planet. It is the opening of the Most Holy Place wherein are to be found all the records of the history of the Soul and the Planet. There may Elohim be found and known. The Seven Spirits of the Lord operate from within that Tabernacle. Their ministry upon all the planes proceedeth from that sacred centre. For in Christhood the seven are realized within the Soul, so that comes into the consciousness of the Divine Pleroma or Fulness. And in the Planetary Order they become the Angels of the Seven Spheres.

Their raiment was the Glory of God, the Light of His Radiance. And the precious stones are meant to express the seven sacred tinctures which they embody ; for each Elohe is one of the Divine Tinctures.

The Seven Bowls containing Judgment symbolize the Cup of Life upon the seven planes, and hence the ministry of each of the Elohe. The smoke simply implies the veiling of the Mystery of the Divine Way. Until the Divine Ministry through the Elohim upon the seven planes, no one could reach the high state of Divine Christhood so as to enter fully into the Temple.

[2] Whosoever has once heard that Voice will herein understand. It is not mythical as many suppose ; nor objective to the Soul, as many imagine. It is a most profound reality within the Soul ; and the Awe of it is overwhelming.

[3] God is a consuming Fire, but only in a purifying sense. The Tree of Life within us is enveloped in His Flame. The Fire energizes and illumines the Tree of Life within us ; and it also searches and tries the ways of man.

Who amongst men and women are truly blessed as they follow the ways of the Beast of materiality, and worship the things of outward sense ? The world is full of the groaning of their misery.

[4] The Astral and elemental waters : for the great sea of blood in which all Souls died in a spiritual sense, is the Astral. It is the Red Sea. Its waters are Astral knowledges and influences, full of impure desire and feeling and perverted vision. To purify that Sea within the Planet the Oblation was made ; and through its purification Souls are able to live again within its waters. Within the Soul system there is the correspondence to that Sea.

[5] All the Astral influences and powers of a material and elemental nature which have acted as tributaries or feeders of the Astral realm. These are as rivers to the inland Sea.

[6] This is a hieroglyph of the extinction of the Astral Fires, those

THE APOCALYPSE

The Seven
Divine
Judgments

Then did the fifth Angel pour out the fire which his bowl contained, and it fell upon the throne of the Beast, and upon his kingdom of darkness. For the reign of the Beast had filled many with sore disease, and made them cry out because of their pains, and to attribute these to the Most High One, so that in the darkness they blasphemed the name of the Holy One. And the throne of the Beast was consumed away, and his kingdom overthrown.[1]

And the sixth Angel poured out the fulness of his bowl upon the great river, the Euphrates, the waters of which had been dried up. And from its source the waters came again, and with their coming the way was got ready for the approach of the Kings of the East who come from the Sun.[2]

And at that time there went forth three evil spirits, one from the Dragon, one from the Beast, and one from the False Prophet ; and these worked signs and wonders amongst the people to deceive them, for they made war against the coming of the Day of God. And these evil spirits gathered the people who believed in them unto the place of Armageddon.[3]

When these things had been accomplished, the seventh Angel poured out his bowl upon the atmosphere ; and the Voice of Him who sat upon the throne within the Temple spake. And with the sound of His Voice the Temple was filled with the Light of His Glory, and the seven thunders spake, saying ; 'It is done.' And the earth was shaken in its foundations more greatly than it has been for ages upon ages.[4]

Then the Voice of Him who sat upon the Throne within the Temple spake, saying ; 'Behold ! I come to quicken and make new all things. Blessed be all who watch, and who keep their raiment unspotted. For these cover up the nakedness and shame of those who have been unclothed through the wickedness of all who have worshipped the beast.'

And amid the quaking of the Earth, the great City of Desolation fell, and with it all the kings and dominions in whom its rule prevailed.

356

NOTES.

fires kindled through misdirection and use of the passional nature and the desire. They are the fires that smite by day, and make the mind which should be as a Moon, to smite in its night.

[1] In the system of the Soul the Beast represents the lower mind in a fallen and degraded state, and in the Planet it symbolizes the fallen middle kingdom. The Beast, as elsewhere we have shown, is the hieroglyph for materiality and sensuality, and its throne is in the lower mind of the human system and the middle kingdom of the Planet. It is not a true part of the creative operation of Elohim, but the resultant of a wrong direction of mind and desire. And, as issues of the evil conditions, have arisen the gross materializing and sensualizing systems represented in the abattoirs, shambles, distilleries, breweries, wine-palaces, and the awful deeds of wickedness generated through the prevalence of these.

The diseases by which mankind has been afflicted have been begotten and maintained amid these terrible systems of evil. For the existence of disease is due to wrong spiritual conditions, indeed, to the inversion of spiritual polarity. Yet it is attributed to God!

All the true reform movements are contributing to the overthrow of the power of the kingdom of the Beast.

[2] The Euphrates is the great river of the Divine Spirit within the Soul whose waters are Life; and within the Planet it is the Divine Life-stream which nourisheth in a soulic sense all life. The waters had been dried up, because all spiritual power had been withdrawn on account of the reign of the Beast in high places.

The reflow of the Waters is the outpouring of the Spirit upon both the Soul and the Planet—the new Avatar; and, with that outpouring, the return of the Christs—the Kings of the East and the Sun.

[3] This trinity of evil corresponds to the inversion of the trinity of good, the degraded desire, the inverted love principle, and the perverted intuitive powers. The result is revealed in the false love of dominion and rule, the ambition that realizes itself through oppression and unrighteousness; the false concept of the uses of the beautiful love-principle and passional nature which have led to such disaster upon the whole of the planes of life; and the perverted vision of the meaning of life, both as to its origins and its ultimates, its nature and its transcendent possibilities, the path it should have followed and was meant to walk in, the only true way of attainment.

Armageddon is with us now. It has been fought upon the heights of the Astral realms; it is now being fought upon its lower reaches and outer planes. The evil trinity is being overthrown by the Divine Trinity: hate, darkness and death will be extinguished through the triumphant Love, Light and Life of God.

[4] Here the hieroglyph is difficult to express; for whilst the Planetary atmosphere is easily understandable, what is meant is

THE APOCALYPSE

The Beast that rose out of the Sea

Then I beheld a Beast rising out of the sea that encompassed the Earth, having seven heads and ten horns ; upon the horns were ten diadems, and upon the heads were written blasphemous things.[1]

The Beast was like a leopard in nature, he had the feet of a bear and the mouth of a lion : unto him did the Dragon give power, regnancy and authority.[2]

And one of his heads was as though it had been wounded unto death, but was healed again from its wounding ; and then all the dwellers within the Earth were filled with wonder, and worshipped the Dragon because he gave authority unto the Beast : for they said : ' Who is like the Beast for greatness and power, and who is able to make war with him ? ' [3]

And there was given unto the Beast a spirit that spoke things great and blasphemous, and he had the authority of the Dragon to continue his works for the forty times of the Oblation.

And he blasphemed the Name of the · Most High One, and the Tabernacle which He had fashioned for the dwellers upon the Earth ; and he made war upon the Saints that he might overcome them, and over every tribe and people, tongue and nation did he gain authority.[4]

And from all these did he claim worship ; and I beheld how those whose names were not found written in the Book of Life opened by the Lamb who had been slain, gave worship unto him.

Let him who hath the ear to hear, understand the mystery of the Beast.

Whosoever followeth the Beast, into captivity he goeth ; for the Beast maketh captive all who so willeth to follow him. And the sword with which he slayeth he causeth to pierce those whom he maketh captive. Herein is tried the patience and faith of the Saints.

Then I beheld another Beast coming up out of the Earth ; he had two horns like a Lamb, but he spake as the Dragon.

NOTES.

not that which is known as the atmosphere, but the Auric body. It is the atmosphere that surrounds the Soul itself upon the seventh plane ; and in the case of the Planet it signifies its spiritual realms. With the changing of that atmosphere within the Soul, new Heavens appear, and as a result new earth life. And so of the Planet. It is the issue of the conflict, the ultimate of the Redemption.

[1] The Sea that encompassed the Earth is the Astral, the sea of blood and mirages. It was the corresponding power to that of the Dragon, the one representing the sensualizing and materializing forces, the other the oppressive ruling mind. Both had seven heads, for they operated upon the seven spheres of the middle kingdom ; and both had ten horns or attributes, symbolizing the awful degradation of the attributes of the Soul and the Planet.

[2] He was cruel and treacherous as a leopard, stealthy and crafty as a bear, powerful and destructive as a lion ; just what all sensual things are. They are alluring and deceitful, treacherous and cruel, powerful to destroy and without mercy, the whole genius of the Soul and the Planet.

Even as the lower intellectual mind (the Dragon) has reigned, so has this sensualizing power, for he derives his authority and regnancy from the Dragon.

[3] The wounded head was the power that was broken by means of the Christhood ; for in the state represented by the Manifestation the power of the Beast was over-thrown for a time. There was one who conquered, and wounded the chief head of the Beast. And others overcame also, and in doing so wounded the Beast in his head. And had the Christhood been permitted to prevail, that wounding would not have been healed. But the betrayal of the Christ Vision enabled the Beast to have his wound healed. It prevented the arising of the Christhood and the overthrow of the sensualizing powers. It gave a false direction to the intuitional and passional natures, and brought down the things that were highest to become of the lowest. That of which the Manifestation was the prophecy was suspended in its realization until these days. Not until the Oblation had been fully accomplished could the prophecy find embodiment and fulfilment. And this could be done only through the overthrow of the Beast upon his own kingdom, and the wounding of all his heads by means of the changes effected in his seats of power (the seven spheres of the Astral), and the extinction by the process of transmutation, of the greater of his emissaries.

In both the individual Soul system and that of the Planet is this hieroglyph true ; and in the case of Him who bore the awful burden of the Oblation, it had a meaning such as no Soul could possibly imagine, and of a nature that we cannot chronicle.

[4] Here may be discerned the path of the Oblation in the Soul's

359

THE APOCALYPSE

And he had the like authority to the first Beast, and exercised it in his sight, and he influenced the dwellers on the Earth to give worship unto the first Beast.

The Lamb that spake as a Dragon

And the second Beast wrought great signs and made fire to fall upon men out of the Heavens of the Planet. By these signs he sought the worship of the dwellers upon the Earth, and did cause them to fashion an image of the first Beast.

And when the image of him was fashioned he gave life unto it, and power to speak, and he also made it to bring upon those who would not worship the Beast of which it was the image, much tribulation, pain, and sorrow.

He even gave unto it so great power that it imposed upon the weak and the strong, the rich and the impoverished, the freedom to make bondservants, and to cause them to commune and trade only with all those who had the mark of the Beast upon their foreheads, and who rendered unto him worship.[1]

Herein is Wisdom : who hath the understanding that can interpret these things ?[2]

For the Beast had a number which he marked upon the forehead of all whom he led into captivity, and who rendered worship unto him.

Now, the number of the Beast was six hundred, sixty and six.[3]

The Tribes of Israel

Then I saw the Lamb who had been slain standing upon the Mount Zion, and with him the one hundred, forty and four thousand of the children of Israel, twelve thousand of each tribe, and these had the Name of the Father-Mother written upon their foreheads.

They were garmented in the white linen which it becometh the Priests of the Most High to wear ; for they had washed their raiment in the Blood of the Lamb of God until it was without blemish.

Now these are they who have not defiled themselves in the Great Babylon by prostituting the woman in themselves, but have remained virgin, holding sacred the Life Eternal which the Lamb had bestowed upon

NOTES.

welfare with the emissaries of the Beast. The sensualizing powers spake blasphemous things through those who became subject unto them. And though the wounding of the Beast has been in process all through the days of the Oblation, yet he has prevailed to speak his will through the powers fashioned by him.

But within the Planetary Heavens his power is broken, and soon it will also be overthrown in the Soul.

[1] This other Beast signifies false religious systems. It had the appearance of a Lamb and had the two horns of the Ram, but had the voice and speech of the Dragon. It had the like authority given to it as was given to the first Beast, and wrought similar wonders to fill men and women with fear, and cause them to give worship unto the Beast.

There is a tragic history hieroglyphed here. The system that arose in the name of the Christhood took for its symbol the Lamb. In the Holy Name of the Most High One it spake ; but its voice was not that of the Lamb of God (the Divine Love), but that of the Dragon. It had two horns like a Ram, for it claimed to speak for God, and judge for Him. For the Ram is the hieroglyph of the Divine Kingdom, and the two horns represent the powers of the Divine Love and Wisdom—the power to redeem and the power to illumine.

Such has been the ecclesiastical system which grew up upon the Earth, arising out of earthliness, though claiming to have been begotten of God and appointed His vicegerent.

It has taught the doctrine of fire and filled all whom it has enslaved with dread. And by its ways it has emphasized the work and worship of the first Beast. For the image of the first Beast is nothing more than the sensuousness of an astral kind associated with the whole ecclesiastical system which has captivated and enthralled men and women. Its emblems, though most sacred in the esoteric sense, have been degraded in the service of the Beast. Like the Dragon, it has oppressed, whenever possible, all those who refused to bow down and worship its image.

[2] No one could interpret them unless it were given unto such an one from the Divine realms, for only thence can the true meaning come of these mysterious hieroglyphs.

They are Soulic, Planetary and Historical ; but the historical is only the objective expression of things which are first subjective, and related to the spiritual realms.

[3] In the Greek, the letters of the term used to express the lower mind have as their numerical value this number—666. But it could not possibly relate to the lower mind as such ; otherwise the Beast would be a necessary part of the human system, and to condemn that which is essential in life would be the height of absurdity.

There must be another meaning, and it is found in the *state* of the

THE APOCALYPSE

them ; for they have not believed in the lie of the false prophet, so that it has had no place in the testimony to the Word which they have borne.[1]

The Praise of God within Israel

These follow the Lamb of God whithersoever He goeth ; and they sing the song of the Praise of God which only they, of all who dwell upon the Earth, know .[2] and their voices are as the sound of many waters, and also as sweet Harps making melody.

And they follow the Lamb whithersoever He goeth, and worship the Lord, saying :—

' We praise and magnify Thy Holy Name, O Lord of the heavenly Hosts ! Thou wast, and art, and shalt be evermore the Holy One, the Redeemer of Thy Saints, the Saviour of all Thy Children.'

And at the sound of their Praise the Four-and-Twenty Elders bow down to worship the Lamb and the Lord, saying :

' Alleluia ! For the Lord Himself reigneth.'

And the Four Living Creatures likewise bow themselves before Him and worship, saying :

' Thine, O Lord, is an Everlasting Kingdom whose dominion is from the River of Wisdom unto the River of Thy Holy Love, and which encompasseth the whole Heavens wherein Thy Glory shineth and Thy Praise is heard.'

The Coming of the Messenger

Then an Angel flew from the mid Heavens to the Earth, carrying with him the Eternal Gospel ; and with a great voice he proclaimed the message. And it was made known unto all who could hear it in every nation, and tribe, and people, and in their own tongue.

And a great voice was heard crying : ' Fear God, and render the Glory due unto Him ; worship Him who fashioned the Heavens and the Earth, the Sea and the Great Deep. The hour is come when His judgment is to be made manifest.' [3]

Then there descended another Angel from the Heavens, and he cried unto the dwellers upon the Earth : ' Fallen to the depths of the abyss is Babylon the Great, for she hath made drunk with the wine of her fornications

NOTES.

lower mind ; and this corresponds to the Astral or corresponding Planetary mind.

[1] The Lamb is the hieroglyph for the Divine Love in its sacrificial capacity ; the Lamb slain is the sacrifice of that Love. To stand upon Mount Zion in a resurrected state symbolizes the restoration of the Christhood after the consummation of the Oblation. It is the recovery by the Soul of the consciousness of the Divine Love and Wisdom ; for Zion is the consciousness of the Divine Presence within, the Mount of the high spiritual estate, the Holy City of the Lord Presence.

The 144,000 of the Children of Israel represent the Ancient Christhood Order whose members were the Illuminati, the Seers, the Prophets, and the true Priests upon the Earth. They were all in Mediatiorial service in different ways upon the various planes. They were the true Children of Issa, the Holy Spirit ; for the Holy One was within them in great measure. They were the beautiful children of Ra, or Rei, or Rae ; for the Radiance of the Divine Countenance was within them. They were the beloved children of the Lord, children in whom were Elohim ; for the Lord (El) was the Glory of their life and the fulness of their days.

The very numbers are significant ; for 12 is the number of Christhood, being the Twelve Labours accomplished, the Twelve Gates entered and passed through, the Twelve Apostles attained, every attribute being an Apostle or one sent or consecrated for high service ; and so they are the Twelve Foundations of the Holy City, of which more hereafter.

These Children of Issa-Ra-El bore upon their brow the Name of the Father-Mother, by which we are to understand that His Radiance shone through them. In priestly raiment were they garmented, for the raiment of the Christhood is mediatorial. They were the Virgins of Zion, Souls in whom the true woman was never defiled amid the corrupting conditions of the Great City or system of Babylon ; for their intuition was never bought and sold in the religious market, but was held sacred, following the inner Light whithersoever it led. Though their outer garments were besmirched with the impurity of the conditions, their Soul remained Virgin. The false view of life proclaimed by the False Prophet—the materialistic systems, scientific and ecclesiastical, in their interpretations of life—found no deep response in them, and had no place in the testimony which they bore for God. They never had been materialists. Always were they the true Mystics, Souls who sought God not as mere knowledge, but in order to interpret His Love in all their teachings, and His Will in all their ways. And such are these Souls to-day in this hour of their awakening and arising into Christ-consciousness.

[2] Only they of all the dwellers upon the Earth know God ; for

THE APOCALYPSE

all whom the Beast hath made captive, and who have rendered worship unto him.'

The Messenger and the Harvesting

After this a third Angel spake with a great voice. saying : ' Whosoever hath the mark $_{of}$ the Beast, and doth bow down to worship him, shall indeed be made to drink $_{of}$ the wine $_{of}$ his wrath, even until the cup $_{of}$ life overflows with the bitterness $_{of}$ it, in the day whensoever that one shall seek unto God to drink $_{of}$ the wine $_{of}$ His Love.' [1]

Then a great Voice amid the Heavens spake, saying : ' Herein learn to be patient, O ye who are His Saints ; keep ye sacred His commandments to do them, and let your faith be undimmed, that ye may make manifest Jesus Christ.

Blessed are they who have died with their Lord · they rested not from their labours, and now their work is to follow them.' [2]

After this I saw a white Cloud, and upon the Cloud there sat One like unto the Son $_{of}$ Man : upon His head rested a golden crown, and in His right hand He held a sharp sickle. [3]

And the Angel $_{of}$ His Presence who was within the Temple spake unto Him who sat upon the Cloud, saying : ' Put forth Thy sickle and reap, for the hour $_{of}$ the reaping is come ; for that which is now upon the Earth for harvesting is dried up.'

And He who sat upon the Cloud put forth the sickle which was in His right hand, and reaped of the vintage within the vineyard $_{of}$ God great and many clusters $_{of}$ grapes from the Vine. And these were put into the winepress $_{of}$ God ; and when they had been trodden out, there issued from these wine like blood, so red and clear was it.

And the blood ran out even unto the bridles $_{of}$ the horses, from the inner shrine $_{of}$ the Temple unto the west gate that leadeth towards the city that is without.

But the vintage $_{of}$ the Earth had been taken by him who ruled over it, even the Beast whom the nations and peoples and tribes served and worshipped. For the vine-

364

NOTES.

they alone have arrived at the consciousness of Him within themselves.

[3] The Eternal Gospel is always the same in every age and in every clime. The Divine Love and Wisdom is to be again revealed and interpreted in the midst of all peoples and through the Great Religions. The beginning of this most blessed spiritual movement is at hand. In the heart of the nations and races and in the language and symbol of their own religious expression, shall it be accomplished.

[1] Never was anything relating to the human experience more truly expressed. Those who have followed the ways of the Beast shall come to know how profoundly true it is. The Soul in its return knoweth its own bitterness ; and all Souls who have been in captivity to the Beast know the wrath which is meted out to them when they essay to leave his ways and seek unto God. Souls who leave the worship of the Beast for the worship of the Eternal and Most Blessed One, who sever their connection with the venues of service employed in the worship of the Beast, such as abattoirs and shambles, distilleries and breweries, physiological laboratories and such centres of inhumanity, sensualizing social conditions and materializing institutions, in order that they may live the true life of the Soul, the life crowned with purity, humanity and love, are pursued by the wrath of the Beast and persecuted by all who are his emissaries.

[2] Here there is special reference to the Christhood Order, the true Saints, who died for the love they bore those to whom they ministered. They died with their Lord, for they were crucified with Him in the great city known as Sodom and Gomorrah. But with the restoration of these Souls, their work is to follow that of the Oblation. They are to continue the days of the Manifestation which were interrupted and suspended during the three Naronic Days during which the Oblation was made.

[3] This is the hieroglyph of the reigning and reaping Presence within the Soul and the Planet. He is the Cloud upon the Sanctuary, the overshadowing Cloud and Pillar of Fire. For the Son of Man is Adonai, the Head over all things within the Soul and the Planet.

[4] The reaping of the vintage of God is the ingathering to the Soul of all the good it has learned on its path, the true grapes of the vine ; for such a work is part of the true evolution and upbuilding of the Soul. But the reference here is to the ingathering at the end of the great cycle which has just been completed in the Planetary history ; and the vineyard with its vintage is none other than that of the Christhood. They know themselves to be members of the Vine of God. The gathering in of the fruits of their Soul travail issues in the Wine of God being poured out for the service of life. The Life-Stream of the Eternal Love flowed from their Souls even

365

THE APOCALYPSE

yard had been laid waste by him, and its vines destroyed; and in his wrath he had made many pass through his wine vat, and had them trodden under foot until they shed what wine they had.[1]

Then one of the Angels who carried the bowl with the sacred Fire, spake with me; and I beheld the great wilderness, and the Beast with the seven heads and ten horns.

The Beast was as the colour of scarlet, and he had names full of blasphemous things: and sitting upon the Beast there was one like unto a woman.

She was arrayed in robes of purple and scarlet, and gilded with fine gold, precious stones and pearls: in her hand she had a golden cup filled with many things which were abominations, even the unclean things of her fornicatory ways.[2]

Upon her forehead was written: 'Behold the Mystery. This is Babylon the Great, the Mother of harlotry and of all the abominations of the Earth.'

Then I beheld how the woman had become drunken with the blood of the saints who had borne their testimony for Jesus Christ and I wondered much that such things could be.

But the Angel who was with me said: 'Wherefore dost thou so wonder? This mystery must also be revealed.

The Beast that was, that is, and that is soon to be cast down into the bottomless abyss, is the mystery of iniquity by whose power the world hath been made full of sorrow.

His seven heads are seven mountains, for he hath acquired these by means of his power; and the ten horns are ten kings who have their power from him.

And the woman upon whom is written the mystery of Babylon, sitteth with these ten powers upon the seven mountains; and these have one mind, one power and one authority, even that of the Beast.

These all make war against the Lamb of God; but the Lamb shall overcome them, for He is King of

The
ystery
f
abylon

NOTES.

unto the bridles of the Horses ; for as the Horse is the hieroglyph for the higher mind, the bridles are the controlling powers of that mind. Thus the Wine or Life-Stream of the vintage of God in the Soul flowed from the Innermost Shrine where His Presence is, to the West Gate or outermost court, where all the service that has to be rendered in the Without is performed, so that the whole being, from the centre of the Within to the circumference of the Without, is consecrate.

[1] Here the meaning will be apparent to most readers. The spiritual in the Earth had long ceased to retain its magnetic power to respond to the Divine World ; for the elements had been so greatly changed that they lost their inherent magnetism to such an extent that they could not manifest according to the Divine Will. And as it was with the elements so was it with the Soul, for the Microcosm suffered in and with the Macrocosm. The terrible materialization of the spiritual qualities prevented the true development of Life ; and the accentuation of that condition by the various systems which arose and prevailed, systems represented by materialistic science and religion, brought about the states represented by the Dragon and the Beast.

The drying up of the spiritual upon the Earth was thus brought about. The materializing of all the Soul qualities and the consequent sensualizing of life, dried up the Life-forces which had their origin in the Divine Life within the Earth and Soul, until the Vines (Souls) were broken down, and the Vineyard (the spiritual system) was laid waste.

[2] The hieroglyph here is something more than a repetition of that concerning the Beast ; it is an amplification of the hieroglyph of the second Beast who rose out of the Earth having the appearance of a Lamb.

In the first place it is a picture of the fallen Intuition—the Woman in the system of the Soul—and the fearful issues upon the Earth of that fall. For through the fall of the Intuition, the woman has come to sit upon the Beast. She has reigned over the things which are of the sensuous world and made of them things sensual. The fallen Intuition has not been able to discern heavenly things. The intrinsic spiritual value of the qualities, quantities, and powers of the Soul, she has been unable to discern ; and when these have been presented to her she has repudiated them. The things of Jesus Christ she has rejected, knowing neither the vision of the Jesus state nor the glory of the light of Christhood.

But there is also this further meaning, and it was this that filled the Master with surprise as He beheld what was to take place whilst the Oblation was being offered. The fallen Intuition once more found its outward expression in the hierarchies which arose out of the betrayal of the vision of Jesus Christ given through the Master.

367

THE APOCALYPSE

The Fall of the Woman arrayed in Scarlet

all the kings, and Lord *of* all : they also shall overcome who are *of* Him, for they are the faithful ones, the called and chosen.[1]

And the waters *of* the sea out *of* which the Beast arose, surround the woman who sitteth upon the Beast, and these are of nations and peoples and tribes ; and by these waters shall the impoverishment and nakedness *of* the woman and the nations *of* peoples be made manifest.

For she is the great city by whom all the kingdoms *of* the earth have been and are yet ruled ; for she reigneth over them all. She is the great city Babylon.'

After these things I beheld yet another Angel descending out from the Heavens, who had great authority, and the Earth was made luminous with his glory.

With a mighty voice did he cry, ' Fallen one : O thou fallen one ! Thou art indeed a Babylon. Thine ancient glory is departed, and the glory which has come to thee is *of* the Beast ; for thou hast become the habitation *of* devils. Thou hast given shelter to the unclean spirits, and hast made *of* thy resting places coverts for the birds *of* prey. Through thee have the nations *of* the Earth fallen, for they have deeply drunk *of* thy fornicatory wines. By thy ways have the nations gone unto death, even whilst they thought to be enriching themselves.'[2]

I then heard the Voice from within the Temple in the Heavens, calling : ' Come ye out *of* her, all ye My people, and have no more any fellowship with her sins, nor carry the burden *of* her plagues ; for her sins have reached unto the lower Heavens, and her iniquities have been wrought before God and in His name.

According as she hath rendered unto you, so render ye unto her again, putting away her evils from you ; and as she hath wrought her works upon you to your undoing, so do ye redouble your works against her, that her iniquities may be overthrown : let her drink the cup which she hath mingled, even unto its dregs.[3]

Inasmuch as she hath glorified herself in wanton-

368

NOTES.

The Woman upon the Beast is the Intuition as very specially manifested through these systems, all of them professing to be great and essential to the world, forming one combined force for the triumph of the Beast, though each having separate power.

To those who know the meaning of Jesus Christ, it will be obvious that the great religious system in the West has been a gross betrayal of the sacred vision of life implied in those Soul states ; and this notwithstanding the fact that the Church has arrayed herself in all the garments and precious stones or attributes which belong unto a redeemed and restored Intuition.

[1] How true it is that the ecclesiastical systems have made themselves one with the Beast and the Dragon, history will confirm. The Church of the fallen Intuition found a great embodiment in the Church which rose in the name of the Master. Though she has claimed to sit in the Chair of Peter—the illumined understanding— her seat has been upon the Beast of all things sensuous, out of which have become many sensual things. In the sacred Name of the Most High One she has reigned, laying claim to universal power, yet through her fallen vision, her false concept of truth and righteousness, her misuse of power, her inversion through materialization of the Sacred Mysteries, she has made war against the Lamb of God (the Divine Love), and persecuted those who are of the Lamb of God in their ways and ministry.

[2] Here the appeal of the Angel is obvious. First the Intuition, then that which represents it in the ecclesiastical world. Once the Intuition was unfallen ; once there was a true Church of God. In her unfallen days the Intuition was beautiful in her devotion to the things of God ; and in those days the Church of God was the Church founded upon Petra—the Divine Illumination of Souls. There was no Beast then ; the Red Sea had no existence. The Astral Sea was pure ; its waters were full of life. But in the fallen state the glory departed. The Intuition became a bond servant ; the Church reared by it had no true Shechinah. She trafficked in all earthly things and changed the heavenly to the sensuous, and even that which was sensual. She became the house of low elemental powers ; even devilish spirits made of her their habitation. By means of her councils and councillors she wrought havoc upon the Soul, crucified afresh the Son of God and put Him to open shame. In the days of the Inquisitions, both Catholic and Protestant, she showed how greatly she was inflamed by those elemental and devilish spirits who had made of her their habitation.

[3] This appeal is very specially to the members of the Christhood Order. They were spoken of as the peculiar People of God, His Elect Ones. For she gathered them into her system, attracted by

THE APOCALYPSE

ness, so hath she inflicted pain and mourning upon all who have dwelt within her gates. Yet of herself hath she said : ' I sit as a queen, and am not alone, and mourning I shall not know.' [1]

But in that day when He cometh, death shall come to the plagues with which she hath afflicted the nations, and famine and mourning shall end ; for the Lord God Omnipotent shall judge her and purify her with His fires. [2]

And the Kings of the Earth who followed her fornicatory ways, shall weep and mourn when they behold her being consumed in the purifying fires, and fear shall make them stand afar off ; and they shall wail for her, and cry : ' Woe, woe hath overtaken the great city, Babylon the strong, for her hour is come : upon her judgment hath fallen.'

No more shall the merchants of the Earth who have communed with her, be able to buy and sell her wares ; and they shall mourn because of her, and that no one needeth their wares any more—their merchandise of gold, precious stones and pearls ; of fine linen and silk, purple and scarlet ; of ivory vessels made like those fashioned from the most precious woods ; of brass and iron and marble ; of spices, frankincense and ointment ; of wine, oil and corn ; of sheep, oxen, and horses with chariots ; of slaves for service, and the Souls of the people. [3]

The things which her merchants have thus lusted after shall perish ; and they also shall weep over her and cry : ' Woe, woe for the great city wherein we were made rich ; for she who was arrayed as in fine linen, with purple and scarlet robes adorned with gold embroideries, having pearls and other precious stones, is now made desolate.'

And everyone who owned a ship, and all who traded upon her sea and sought thus to enrich themselves, and those who were of the uttermost parts, also shall weep on her behalf and mourn that no longer are they able to engage in the traffic of her sea, and cry out : ' Woe, woe unto the great city unto which none has ever

The
Overthrow
of the
Ecclesiastical
Systems

370

NOTES.

the symbols of the Mysteries and the apparent great opportunities for service. What preserving power the Church has ever had has been due to their presence in her midst. The blood of the Saints has been the seed of the Church ; for it was through them that the Life-stream of the Lamb of God flowed for the healing of Souls. They have been the Saviours amid the scorpion-stricken people, the bearers-up of the Cross of God amid the wilderness made by the Church.

But now has come the day in which they must come out from her midst. The day of her overthrow has come.

[1] How true it has been in the whole spirit and action of the system known as the Church which professes to be the embodiment of the illumined Intuition, and therefore of the Word of God ! Each division of the Church of the West and East has in turn proclaimed by its spirit this very thing ; yet as truly as the barren Fig tree had to be replaced, namely the Jewish Church, so must it needs be with the Church of the West.

[2] " When He cometh " refers to the coming of the Lord Presence through the restoration of the Christ consciousness within all those Souls who once were in the high state of the Christhood. With the coming of the Christ Light, death shall fall upon the darkness which she has spread by means of her traditions and doctrines. The plagues of her false sacramentarianism, and the spiritual famine created by them, together with the Soul mourning she has occasioned through the false interpretations of life she has published abroad in her lack of true knowledge, will all be banished ; for through the Light of the Christhood, which is the Light of His Holy One within the Soul, God will judge her. He will make manifest what she has been, and purify her in the penal Fires of His searching. And the Fires will try her, burning up with unquenchable heat the wood, hay and stubble she has offered to Souls as the Bread of Life.

[3] The enumerations here are both literal and mystical. They are literal in respect of the Great City or materialistic system whose chief aim in life is such traffic in the lives of the Creatures and Souls of the people, and every material thing, changing their spiritually intrinsic values into mere merchandise for purposes of personal gain ; for these are the ways by which men enrich themselves. This awful system is to be overthrown.

And they are mystical, in that they all have esoteric meanings, inward significations, relating to the qualities, states and powers of the Soul. And in the Church of the West, all these most beautiful qualities have been changed, bought and sold. She, as an ecclesiastical system, has done with the most precious things of the Soul what the materialistic systems of the Nations have done with the

THE APOCALYPSE

been likened, for she is henceforth made desolate.'

The False Teachings Pass away

But the Heavens and the Saints, the Apostles and the Prophets, shall rejoice that God hath accomplished within her His righteous judgments.'[1]

Then one of the Angels took a stone like a great millstone, and cast it into her sea, and said . ' Through the might of this stone shall Babylon, the great city, fall ; for the slain of the Saints and Prophets are found within her, and the blood of all whom she hath slain upon the Earth.

No more shall the voice of her harpers and minstrels, flautists and trumpeters be heard within her, nor shall craftsman of any sort whatever be found in her, nor shall the sound of her millstones grinding her corn be heard any more.

Her lamp shall no longer shine within her, nor shall there be the rejoicings over those whom she accounts bridegrooms and brides ; for her merchants and princes shall have forsaken her, and the power of her sorcery to deceive and mislead shall be broken.' [2]

And a great voice sounded throughout the Heavens, even the voice of a great multitude, saying . ' Hallelu jah ! Salvation is of God. He hath wrought it out for all His children by His mighty Power, that all may behold His Glory. For His judgments are true and righteous. He hath overthrown the great City whose fornications had intoxicated the nations and

Henceforth the Lord Reigneth

corrupted all the earth. Hallelujah !' [3]

And the Four Living Creatures bowed themselves in lowly adoration and worshipped Him who sat upon the throne ; and they said . ' Amen ! Hallelujah ! Give praise unto our God, all ye who are His servants and who hold Him in Awe.'

Then there came the voice of the great multitude, like the sound of many waters, and as the voice of mighty thunders, saying

' Hallelujah ! The Lord God Omnipotent reigneth.

372

NOTES.

material forms.   She has failed to appraise the true value of a Soul, just as the commercial systems have done in regard to the pure gems. And this sad and terrible traffic in Souls is to be overthrown.

[1] This is in striking contrast to the mourning over the city by the multitudes who were traders in her wares.   But it is not the callous rejoicing over the downfall of Souls which has been a remarkable characteristic of those who did commerce with the great city.   The Heavens have no joy in any defeat or tragic sorrow that comes over Souls ; its joy is to help and heal.   And the Saints, the Prophets and the Apostles are the vehicles of the Heavens for the blessing of Souls.

But the Heavens and all who are citizens of the heavenly states, have true cause for rejoicing when the terrible systems, social, national and ecclesiastical, which have occasioned so great disasters to the whole earth are at last overthrown by the redeeming power of God. For, by means of these systems, Souls have been fearfully oppressed, deceived, betrayed and shut out of the Kingdom of the Heavens ; and the powers these systems represented have persecuted those who were the Saints of God, and His Prophets and Apostles.   The Scarlet Woman hath ever made war against them.

[2] This reveals the way of the overthrow of the great city with all its accessories.   For what is the stone cast upon the Earth by the Angel ?   It is the true Petra of the Illumined Understanding.   But the illumined understanding implies the restoration of the Christhood. This is the stone which the false builders despised and rejected.   It is the stone which is at once the foundation and the perfectionment of Life in the Soul.   It is the rock upon which the Church claimed to build itself up, but which it has utterly failed to understand.

"Behold ! Behold ! I lay in the City of Zion the stone which the builders refused ; whosoever buildeth upon the foundation of that stone shall never be confounded."

That is the stone that was cast into the sea by the Angel.   And it is now being accomplished.   For the Waters of the Sea by which the great City was encircled, were peoples and tribes and nations. And into the midst of them all is the blessed Christ vision coming, with its truly Illumined Understanding, to overthrow all the ways of the peoples, the nations and the professed religious institutions whose pride and arrogance, spiritual darkness and evil genius, unrighteousness and ambition, have led them to oppress and persecute those who would not become of them, nor receive the sign of the Beast, nor bow down to worship it even at the command of the woman arrayed in Scarlet robes.

[3] The Praise of the Heavens is indeed something to hear, so over-whelmingly glorious is it ; and it is of such a nature that when once

THE APOCALYPSE

Let us rejoice with exceeding great joy, and give glory unto Him. The marriage of the Lamb of God has come, for He hath made ready to receive His bride. And she is now adorned in white linen pure and glistening, even the raiment of her Christ. Blessed are all those who have entered into the marriage supper of the Lamb.' [1]

Then the Innermost Heavens opened ; and from out of their midst there appeared one riding upon a white horse. He was known as the Faithful and True One who doth judge in righteousness, and who doth make war against all that is untrue and unrighteous.

Like a flame of fire are His eyes : upon His brow are many diadems : Upon Him is written a name which no one can interpret but Himself.

His raiment is red-dyed as if in blood, or as one who has trodden the wine-vat. His name is to be called The Word of God.

Him do the armies of the Heavens follow, seated upon white horses, arrayed in the finest linen, pure and glistening ; and they go forth conquering and to conquer.

From out His mouth a sword proceedeth, sharp to divide asunder, as He ruleth the nations. For upon His Vesture there is written : ' King of all the Kings, and Lord of all.' [2]

Then I beheld yet another wonderful thing.

In the Heavens there arose one after another seven Arcs of Light more beautiful to behold than tongue or pen could describe, and these grew into the fulness and effulgence of the Sun.

The Sun was like very pure gold, and around it there were seven most wonderful circles, like the Rainbow when it encircles the Heavens, whose colours were beautiful, so full of softened splendour were they [3]

And there appeared within the Sun one whose form was that of an Angel in flight flying towards the Earth. [4]

374

NOTES.

heard, the Soul could never forget it. O how our whole being has vibrated to that Praise ! and how we long for the perfect realization of it once more !

[1] The Marriage of the Lamb of God is one of the most sacred functions in which the Soul takes part. For the Bride is the Soul. The hieroglyph has often been taken to represent the Marriage or Union of the Master with the Church ; for the Church has accounted herself His bride. And surely there never was a stranger contradiction in the history of life ; for the Church which vainly imagines herself to be the bride of the Master, whom she confounds with the Lord, has not only repudiated the Christ Vision and Life, but has actually persecuted Him during the lives lived by Him for the purpose of the work of the Oblation. He suffered much during the reign of the various Inquisitions, and has known great and bitter sorrow at the hands of those who professed to be the vicegerents of God.

The Church is the Bride of the Lamb of God ; but it is the Church within the Soul, the Church of the First-born and so of the Christhood. For it is the perfect sacred union of the Soul to the Divine Love.

[2] Another glorious vision of Adonai. It is the all-conquering Son of God who is hieroglyphed riding a White Horse—a Soul with a mind absolutely pure and beautiful. It is Adonai, the conquering Son of God, after the Oblation has been accomplished. The vision of the Soul's travail is implied in the saying that His raiment was red-dyed as if in blood, or as one who has trodden the wine-vat. For though the Master was the vehicle, the work was accomplished by Adonai. The Son of God goes forth to war ; but not as men and women conceive of Him or His warfare. The purified lives of His first-born children (the Christhood Orders) are the instruments of His power unto love and righteousness. In and through them He reigneth ; for He is King of all the Kings (the Kings of the East who come from the Sun), and Lord of them all.

[3] These seven Rays of Light are those of Elohim. They were seen in the form of Arcs of Light, for that symbolizes the Divine Spirit, and these seven sacred Arcs of Light are the Flames of the sevenfold Spirit. They were the Rays of the seven Tinctures. Together they formed the glorious Sun ; for the Sun in the solar world is not what it appears to be to man. Though science professes to know of what it is composed, and all about its nature, conditions and motions, yet it really knows nothing that is of real value ; for the Sun is not what it affirms. It is in reality the Divine World of this system ; not a physical body, but a spiritual Being of great estate. Elsewhere we will speak more fully of this Mystery.

[4] The Angel of the Divine Presence—Gabriel, the Angel of the Fulness of the Glory, the reflection of the seven Rays.

His stature was so great that He seemed to fill the circle of the Sun as He stood within it.

With veiled face and outstretched wings He came towards the Earth and cried in a voice whose sound was as that of the Seven Thunders, when they break upon the Heavens ; and he proclaimed unto all the dwellers upon the Earth that the Day of the Lord had come in which the Everlasting Gospel of the Divine Love and Divine Wisdom should be made manifest unto all peoples, that they who were in a state to hear it might come to know the Lord, as became His Saints.[1]

Then I beheld the Beast and the kings of the Earth who had derived their power from him, with all their armies, gathered together for battle ; and they made war against Him who sat upon the White Horse, even against the Faithful and True One, and all who followed in His train.[2]

But the Beast was taken captive, and with him the False Prophet who wrought wonders in his sight, with which he deceived those who had received the mark of the Beast upon their foreheads, and who worshipped his image ; and these were cast down again into the pit of the abyss that is without bottom, and there was found for them no more any foundation upon which to stand.[3]

And all their emissaries and all who had followed them and who had given worship unto the Beast, were overthrown by the double-edged sword of Him who sat upon the White Horse, even the Faithful and True One.[4]

After this I beheld another Angel descending from the Heavens, and he carried the key of the abyss ; and he laid hold on the Dragon, the old Serpent known as the Devil and Satan, and he bound him in such a manner that he was no more able to deceive.

And when he was bound, the Angel said that he must not be loosed from the powers by which he was bound until one thousand years had been fulfilled,

NOTES.

[1] In the Recovery, this vision, like many of those that have preceded it, was of an overwhelming nature. The Angel in very deed filled the Sun, so great was the fashion of Him. His face was not veiled in the vision, but as He approached the Earth it became veiled ; for it was necessary. As is the macrocosm so is it in the microcosm ; in the system of the microcosm, the Angel of the Lord encampeth round about those who have within them His holy Awe. And in a macrocosmic sense He is now encamping around the Planet. The New Avatâr is this Presence. Since the completion of the Oblation it has become possible.

The Everlasting Gospel is the story of the Divine Love towards this world and all her children, and the Divine Wisdom as revealed in the original purpose of that Love towards all Life, Planetary and Soul, and also that Wisdom as made manifest in the Celestial Hierarchies. For the end of creation is Christhood ; and in the higher degrees of that blessed and exalted state, all these things are known.

[2] The forces in the world that make for evil are not always what may be described as blind forces, unconscious and irresponsible. Though there are such, and these do work terrible mischief in the midst of the nations through their deleterious elemental influence, yet the worst powers of evil are conscious. They are minds wholly dominated by the elemental, and these make war against everything that is of God and the Soul. It is in that sense they make war with the Faithful and True One.

[3] The hieroglyph is difficult to express clearly. An abyss without bottom is inconceivable. That which is implied in the casting into the abyss of the Beast and the False Prophet with the Dragon, is the overthrow of the powers they represented. For the abyss is an evil state of the Astral world ; and through the power of the Highest that world has been and still is being changed, so that the powers which have prevailed throughout long ages are cast-out, and the elements and influences being changed, there is no more any foundation upon which evil can build its vast superstructures.

[4] The overthrow of all the powers which have warred against the Most High, is not to be accomplished by any material means. Men and women as represented in the nations and races, fly to earthy means to overcome the things in opposition to them. They fight with material weapons, or engage in intellectual conflicts, and they make use of principalities and powers to impose their will. But the Divine method is not that. The Son of God makes war against the evil dominations, but the conflict is spiritual. The enemy is overthrown by the sword of the Spirit, the sword that divides asunder, separating the dross from the gold, the evil from the good, the unrighteous from the righteous.

THE APOCALYPSE

after which he should be unbound for a season ; and that Angel shut up the abyss until the thousand years were fulfilled, and put his seal upon it.[1]

The First Resurrection

And there appeared with the Angel many thrones, and they who sat upon them ; and unto them was it given to make judgment manifest.[2]

And I saw those who had suffered martyrdom for the testimony of Jesus Christ, even the Word of God which He spake unto them through His servant whom He did send : these had not worshipped the Beast, nor borne his image, nor carried his mark upon their foreheads and in their hands, and these lived again upon the Earth and reigned with Christ.

This is the first resurrection : blessed indeed are they who have part in it, for over them that other death hath no power ; they shall be priests of God for His Christ, and they shall serve before Him in the thousand years.[3]

But the rest of all who had died, lived not so as to reign with Christ until the thousand years had been fulfilled.[4]

And I beheld the Great White Throne, and Him who reigned from it, before whose Presence the Heavens and the Earth melted away as if there were no room for them ; and before Him came all Souls bearing their books of life.

And these were opened ; and according to whatsoever was written therein, were they judged ;[5] *and the great sea gave up its dead, for Death and Hades found no more any place, because they were judged and cast down.*

NOTES.

[1] Here the mystical meaning deepens. The dramatic picture of the Angel laying hold of the Dragon, who is also known as the Devil and Satan, and shutting him up in the abyss for one thousand years, contains a profound mystery, having relation not only to the overthrow of evil, but also to the great changes ultimately to be effected in the planes of the Planet. Through the changing of the Middle Kingdom, now known as the Astral, the blotting out of the magnetic images upon it by means of the Oblation, the outpouring from the Divine World into that kingdom of marvellous spiritual magnetism, all forces and elemental powers and directions that make for evil are to be overthrown. Their power for wrong and hurt is to be taken away, and there is to issue a reign of comparative blessedness, increasing in intensity as the ages pass and the ways of the children of the Planet are purified. This is understood as the Millennium.

But after the thousand years are fulfilled, Satan is to be unbound for a season. Here we have a glimpse of what must needs be done after the Redemption of the Children of the Planet is fully accomplished. The outer planes of the Planet which became so fearfully changed as to bring hurt to the children after the great descent, have all to be brought back into their original state. There will be much done during the ages of the Redemption; but there are some things that must await its perfect accomplishment.

[2] The many thrones represent new Regnancies. It is said of Israel that they would sit upon the twelve thrones, judging the world. The new reigning powers are to be the twelve orders of the Christhood service, representing the twelve states or attributes of the Soul. Through the revelation of the pure, the true, the right, the path of love, judgment is made manifest.

[3] The first Resurrection is now. It is proceeding in the awakening and arising of all those who once were in the Christhood. They will again form a Kingdom of Royal Priesthood in mediatorial service for God, and with His Christ (the Lord of Glory in them) shall they reign upon the Earth, making manifest His Presence. Over them shall spiritual death no more have any power.

[4] What is here meant is that until the millennium had also been accomplished, none of the children of the Planet would be able to rise up into the consciousness of the reigning Christ within them. Those who had been far enough advanced in their spiritual evolution when the great descent took place, as to be on the threshold of spiritual Christhood, could share in the first Resurrection; but only these would be able to rise so high until the period indicated had passed.

[5] Each Soul has the Book of Life within itself. All the history of the Soul is written upon its walls, so to speak. It is a Mystery-Book which none can read until they reach that state of consciousness in which such power may be safely given to them.

THE APOCALYPSE.

SECTION IV.

*The Coming of New Heavens and the fashioning
of the Earth anew ; the full realization of the
New Avatâr, and the Overshadowing Presence
with the Soul ; the Vision of the Holy
City of Christhood as it is once more
to become, the outcome of the Over
shadowing Presence, and the most
blessed ministry that is to flow
through the Soul in that state unto
the whole Earth ; the bringing
unto all Souls the perfect
Healing by means of that
most blessed Ministry,
together with the
Restitution of
All Things.*

THE APOCALYPSE

After these things, I beheld the Heavens of the Earth become new, for their former state had passed away; and, through the new Heavens, I also beheld the fashioning of the Earth anew: for the great sea out of which the Beast had arisen was now no more.[1]

The New Heavens and the New Earth

And from out the Heavens there descended the Holy City of God, the New Jerusalem; and she was beautifully adorned, even as the bride is adorned for the bridegroom.[2]

Then I once again heard the Voice of Him who sat upon the Throne in the midst of the thrones, saying: 'Behold, now is the Tabernacle of God within man, and He shall dwell in him; and the nations shall be His people, and He shall reign in their midst and be their Lord. He shall wipe away sorrow from their eyes, for they shall no more know death, nor mourning for their dead, nor the pain and anguish of loss; for all these things have passed away. Behold! I shall make all things new.'

And I wondered much whether these things could again be, because of all that I saw. But the Voice of Him who sat upon the Throne said unto me: 'I am Alpha and Omega, the Arche and the Amen: and these things are faithful for they are true. I shall give unto him who is athirst, that he may drink of the waters flowing from the Fountain of Life. He who overcometh shall inherit all things; I will be again His Lord, and he shall be My Son.'[3]

And He spake unto me again, saying: 'Come hither; I will show thee once again the Bride who is made ready for her marriage with the Lamb of God.'

The Holy City

And the Spirit of Elohim carried me unto an exceeding high Mountain, and from it I again beheld the Holy City of Zion, radiant with the glory of God, descending through the Heavens.[4]

Within her burned the Seven Sacred Fires of Elohim, clothing her in a garment of Light.

NOTES.

[1] The Heavens of the Earth have had to be changed more than once during her history. The effect of the great descent known as the Fall was felt throughout her Heavens, for the elements became changed in their spiritual magnetism. Indeed, the lower Heavens were destroyed. New conditions had to be provided by the Solar or Divine World which practically constituted New Heavens. On three separate occasions even the magnetic plane was brought down, and after each disaster a new magnetic plane had to be provided. The original magnetic plane was brought down in what is known as the Deluge ; the second, when the Bow of the Lord set in the Heavens fell through the fearful conditions represented as those of Sodom and Gomorrah ; the third at a later period. Ever since that time the Divine Kingdom has been operating to create new Heavens around the Earth, and the Oblation, with its tragic history, was the last great act in this process.

What the Divine Love and Wisdom has done for this world is beyond telling, so great is it. Never were the Greatness and Majesty of Divine Love made so manifest as in the work of saving this human system.

The changing of the Astral Sea—the conditions of the middle kingdom so as to bring them to their original order and service—will enable the Divine World to create anew the Earth. Old and evil things will now pass away, so that the Earth will come to correspond to the New Heavens.

[2] This is a hieroglyph of the Redeemed Earth. The coming down out of the Heavens is the descent of the new realization for the Soul. For Jerusalem is this world as a spiritual system. It was a Mystery term in the days of ancient Israel, used to designate the spiritual household of the Planet. It was said that her ancient glory was great, but that she lost it through enemies who trampled her under foot. It has also been stated that her latter glory would be equal to her former splendour, indicating what would be the final result of the Redemption.

[3] So tremendous were the dramatic changes upon the Earth which eventuated in disasters, that as the Master looked upon them He could scarcely hope for the restoration to its former glory of this system. And it was only as He remembered who was with Him and all that He had done and was doing, that He was able to realize amid the dioramic pictures of unspeakable tragedy, how all-conquering that Love was.

[4] This is a vision of the Christhood restored, first to the Soul, and then to the whole Christhood Order. It was a vision of Zion in the midst of Jerusalem restored, the glorious outcome of the work of the Oblation.

THE APOCALYPSE

Her luminary was as a Jasper-stone whose facets are clear as crystal, and was therefore most precious.

The Holy City of the hristhood

Around her a wall was raised, exceeding high, and she had Twelve Gates, and at each Gate an Angel whose name was that of the House of Israel; three Gates looked towards the East and three towards the West, three towards the North and three towards the South.

And the wall of the City was built upon twelve foundations named after the Lamb of God, and they were the Apostles of the Lord.[1]

And the City lieth four square, whose length and breadth and height are equal, the measurement being that of a full-grown man—that is, of an Angel.

And the walls of the City were of Jasper; but the City itself was built of pure gold, transparent as glass.

And the foundations of the wall of the City were gar nished with every kind of precious stone—Jasper, Sapphire, Chalcedony, Emerald, Sardonyx, Sardius, Chrysolyte, Beryl, Topaz, Chrysoprasus, Jacinth and Amethyst.

And the twelve Gates were as twelve Pearls, each Gate being one perfect Pearl. And the City had no more any earthly Temples, because the Eternal One was the Overshadowing Presence and Temple, and the Lamb was its worship.

And the City required no more another Sun to lighten it, nor Moon to shine at night; for the Glory of God did lighten it through the worship of the Lamb.

And the Nations of them who are of the Redeemed Ones shall walk in the light of it, and the Kings of the East shall bring the Glory of the Lord unto it.

Its Gates shall not be shut at all by day, and there is no night in it.

NOTES.

[1] The high estate of a Divine Christhood is embodied in this most complicated hieroglyph. To those who have not entered into any deep consciousness of the blessed state, the full interpretation of it is impossible ; for to use mere terms will not convey anything of a definite and experimental nature to such. But to such as in the days of old knew by realization that most glorious experience, there will be found deep meanings in the symbology to which their innermost being will respond. To them it will be as Deep calling unto Deep.

The Seven Sacred Fires of Elohim are the seven Spirits of God. As Energy they are the sevenfold Fire ; as Light they are the sevenfold Ray ; as sound they are the seven Thunders, the sevenfold Voice ; as colour they are the seven most sacred Tinctures, the Divine Spectrum, of which the spectrum on the outer planes is but a dim imperfect expression. The Soul's luminary is the Lord Presence. Earlier in the series of visions, the Master looked upon that Presence, and thus it appeared to Him as the radiance of a combined Jaspar and a Sardius stone. This is a most remarkable combination, as it represents the first and last colours in the Urim and Thumim of Ancient Israel. But it is most highly significant in what it expresses of the glory and energy of that One.

The walls of the City represent the Divine Protection, the bulwarks fashioned out of the truth given from the Lord.

The twelve Gates are the entrances by which the Soul acquires. In the unfallen days they were known as the Gates of Initiation. And they are such still, though they have been confounded with the Twelve Labours of the Soul, as these are now understood. At each Gate was an Angel, and he bore the name of one of the Tribes of Israel. In the Christhood Order or Holy City of Zion, this Angel represented the Angel or Head of the Tribe ; but in the Soul system it represents the Initiation. But it also signifies an Attribute.

The four dimensions are within the City, for the Twelve Gates have a trine looking in each direction. The East is the Innermost of the Soul ; the West is the outer vehicle of service ; the North is the Higher Reason or pure Mind plane ; and the South the beautiful passional nature. Each has three Gates of Initiation and Service. In the Christhood all the Gates are entered ; life in its fourfold dimensions is acquired. And because they are Gates of Initiation and Service fully attained, they are said to be twelve precious pearls, each Gate a pearl ; for the pearl is the emblem of overcoming.

The foundations of the City were also twelve, and these are said to have been the twelve Apostles of the Lord. As an Apostle is one sent on service, there is significance in the statement ; for the Lamb of God is the Divine Love upon which all true Life is built.

All the precious stones with which the foundations were adorned are emblematic of the love of goodness and truth upon the four dimen-

THE APOCALYPSE

The River of Life and the Tree of Life

And the Angel of His Presence showed unto me a river of pure clear Water of Life, which reflected the Light of the Heavens like a perfect crystal, as it proceeded from the Throne of God and of the Lamb.[1]

In the midst of the stream of it, and upon each side of it, there grew the Tree of Life whose fruits were twelve, each in its season; and whose leaves were for the healing of the people.[2]

And wheresoever the river floweth there shall be no more anything accursed; but the Throne of God and of the Lamb shall be there, and all His servants shall enter into His service.[3]

And they shall behold His Face, and the sign of His Name shall be upon their foreheads.[4]

There shall be no night there in which the light of the candle is needed; for wheresoever the river floweth there shall be the Light of Life which proceedeth from the Lord as their Sun; and they shall reign evermore with Him.[5]

And His Angel saith: 'These Sayings are from the Faithful and True One who hath sent His Angel to speak of them unto His servants.'[6]

"BEHOLD! HE COMETH."

NOTES.

sions—the Human Estate, the Angelic Estate, the realm of the Immortals, and the Divine Kingdom, the full estate of the Four-fold Man.

[1] The River of the Water of Life is none other than the great magnetic Life-Stream proceeding from the Divine World.

In the Solar World or Divine realm of this system, it is the Magnetic Stream amid which the Earth and all the Planetary Worlds of this system once moved, that glorious stream that flows along the ecliptic or plane of the Divine Kingdom, and which is now only touched twice in the yearly round by our Earth at the period of the Vernal and Autumnal equinoxes.

In the system of the Soul it is the coming into the consciousness of the Divine Magnetic inflowing, a stream that passes from the Throne of God within the Sanctuary to fill the whole Being with the vibrations of the Divine.

In the realm of Thought or the purely spiritual planes, it is the River of Truth uncorrupted, reflecting the Life of the Heavens, and bearing healing unto all Souls.

[2] The Tree of Life is the Divine Principle in the Soul and the System, the emblem of God within us and all the Worlds, nourished from the Divine Life-stream and growing out from its midst into most beautiful manifestation, whose fruits are for the enrichment of the Soul, and whose influences (leaves of spiritual knowledge) are for the healing of the Nations.

[3] A picture of the effect of the new Life come into the Soul. The old Earth is passing away—the old conditions, and with the new vision that is coming healing will also come. The dark ages with their emissaries are expiring amid the throes of awful conflict, but the day of the new glory is breaking upon the battlefield. Soon there shall be no more accursed things.

[4] Those who live amid the streams of God fed from this Holy River, are His Servants. Of such are His Christs. These look upon His Radiance, for with unveiled vision do they behold His glory, and upon them is His sacred Name written, for they are Children of Love who bear upon them the fashion of His countenance.

[5] And with Him do they reign evermore ; for within them is His Throne ; the regnancy of the Kingdom within them is His. And His Presence is their Sun ; within them shall be no more Night. And this Glory the Earth shall know, for He shall reign upon the Earth through them, and all shall come to know Him.

[6] These Sayings are sent forth for the Elect ones, His servants. They are from the Faithful and True One, even Adonai. To-day they are restored that His Christs may understand who it is who speaketh again unto them ; who they themselves were and are ; what they are once more about to become ; and the profound and vital part they are to take in the New Age and the restored true Drama of the Soul and the Planet.

BB I

INDICES.

		Page.
1.	GLOSSARY INDEX	390
2.	SUBJECT INDEX OF THE LOGIA	395
3.	GENERAL INDEX	397

GLOSSARY INDEX.

An Index giving the References where may be found the Mystical, Spiritual, Esoteric, or Symbolic signification and meaning of the various Terms appearing therein.

Pages.

ABADDON	343
ABRAHAM	15, 108, 153
ABYSS, THE	343, 377
ADONAI	19, 61, 139, 311, 313, 317, 323
ADONAI, THE VISION OF	321
AGE, THE ADAMIC	172, 173
AGE, THE CHRIST	172, 173
AGAPÊ	169, 311, 319
ALPHA AND OMEGA	309
AMBROSIA OF THE GODS, THE	161
AMEN, THE	111, 307, 323
ANCIENTS	51, 161
ANGEL OF THE DIVINE PRESENCE, THE	375
ANGELS OF THE SPHERES	355
ANGEL OF THE SUN, THE	335, 376
ANNA	100, 101
APOSTLES, THE TWELVE	51, 383
ASIA	307
ASIA, THE CHURCHES IN	307
ARCHE, THE	87, 111, 307, 323
ARK, THE	127, 337, 347
ATMOSPHERE, THE SOUL'S	357
AVATÂR, THE NEW (see Second Coming)	377
BAAL	308, 309, 320
BABYLON	363, 366, 371, 373
BEAST, THE	305, 355, 357, 359, 361, 365, 367, 377
BEAST, THE SECOND	358, 361, 367
BEAST, THE MARK OR NUMBER OF THE	360-1
BEGOTTEN ONE, THE ONLY	87
BETHABARA	11
BETHANY	67, 211, 289
BETHLEHEM, THE	91
BETHLEHEM, CHILDREN OF	105
BETHLEHEM, THE CITY OF	69
BETHLEHEM, SHEPHERDS OF	91
BETHLEHEM, STAR OF	99
BETHPHAGE	67
BETHSAIDA OF GALILEE	123
BETRAYAL, THE	199
BOOK OF THE MYSTERY OF GOD, THE	347
BOOK OF LIFE	379
BOOK WITH SEVEN SEALS, THE	329
BOW IN THE HEAVENS, THE	159
BREAD OF LIFE, THE	199
BREAD, THE SHEW-	33, 199
BREATH, THE HOLY	75
BREATHS, THE FOUR	335
BREATHS, THE SEVEN	307, 311
BRIDEGROOM, THE	53
CAIAPHAS	247
CANAANITE	123
CANA OF GALILEE	191
CANDLESTICKS, THE SEVEN GOLDEN	309
CHRIST LIFE, THE	149, 151
CITY, THE HOLY	201
CITY, GATES OF THE HOLY	201

390

GLOSSARY INDEX.

		Page.
Cloud upon the Sanctuary, The	.. ..	365
Comfort of God, The ..	.. ..	203
Creatures, The Four Living	.. ..	327
Cross, The	.. ..	73
Cross, The Luminous ..	.. ..	287
Crown of All Things, The	.. ..	349
Crown of Life, The ..	.. ..	313
Darkness, The Outer ..	.. ..	89, 91
Day, The Fourth ..	.. ..	255
Days in the Tomb, The Three ..	.. ..	255
Death, Spiritual ..	.. ..	215
Decease of the Master, The	.. ..	181, 197
Dimensions, The Four ..	.. ..	385, 387
Dog, The	.. ..	123
Dove, The ..	.. ..	9
Doves, The Two ..	.. ..	101
Dragon, The	.. 305, 351, 352-3, 357, 359, 367, 371, 379
East, The	.. .. 99, 277, 285
East, A City in the	.. ..	99
Egypt	.. .. 105, 155, 157
Egypt, Descent into	.. ..	155
Egyptians	.. ..	103
Elect Souls, The	.. ..	141, 369
Elders, The Twenty-four	.. ..	327
Elim	.. .. 297, 341
Elijah	.. .. 129, 197, 199
Elohim	165, 309, 311, 353, 355
Elohim, The Seven Sacred Fires of ..	.. .. ..	385
Ephraim	.. .. 97, 121, 203
Euphrates, The River ..	.. .. 345, 357
Faith	.. .. 123, 129
Feet, The	.. .. 317, 349
Fig, The	.. .. 67, 69
Fig Tree, The ..	.. .. 25, 143
Fish	.. .. 33, 65, 279
Fishers	.. .. 65, 277
Forty Days of the " Temptation," The	.. ..	231
Gabriel	.. ..	335
Galilee, The Sea of ..	23, 113, 127, 277, 279, 293
Galilee, The Eastern Shore of..	.. ..	279
Gall	.. .. 217, 297
Garden of Gethsemane, The ..	.. ..	215
Gold, Frankincense and Myrrh	.. ..	99
Gold, Pure	.. ..	317
Golgotha	.. ..	247
Gospel, The Everlasting..	.. ..	377
Grace	.. ..	19
" Greater Works," The ..	.. ..	207
Hades	.. .. 308, 309
Hagar	.. .. 154, 155
Hail of Fire, The ..	.. ..	341
Hands, Unwashen ..	.. ..	27
Handwritings on the Middle Wall ..	.. .. ..	163, 233
Heaven, The Treasures of	.. ..	30
Herod	.. .. .. 105, 233, 247
Hills	.. .. 113, 139
Horse, The	.. .. 331, 345
Horses, The Bridles of the ..	.. ..	367
Horses, The White, Red, Black, Pale	.. .. 331, 333, 375
Hour, The Ninth ..	.. ..	247
Hour, The Tenth ..	.. ..	23
Hours, The Three Dark ..	.. ..	247

BB2

GLOSSARY INDEX.

Page.

HOUSE OF DAVID, THE 95, 329
HOUSE OF MARY, OR MARIA 191, 193
HOUSE OF MINDS, THE 323
HYACINTH, THE COLOUR 345

ILLUMINATI, THE 25
IMMORTALS, THE 173, 203
INNS 92, 93
INSPIRATION 305
INTUITION, THE 65, 263, 367
IOSEPH 93
IOSEPH-MARIA 99
ISAAC 15, 153, 155
ISCARIOT 283
ISHMAEL 154, 155
ISLE OF PATMOS, THE 305
ISRAEL 15, 97, 109, 151, 235, 305, 313, 347
ISRAEL, THE ANCIENT KINGS OF 25
ISRAEL, THE SEAL OF THE HOUSEHOLD OF 334-5
ISSA 363
ISSA-RA-EL 305, 335, 363

JACOB 15, 263
JACOB, THE HOUSE AND WELL OF.. 263
JESUS, JESUSHOOD, THE JESUS-LIFE 135, 149, 151, 335
JERUSALEM, THE CITY OF 15, 91, 154, 157, 215, 233, 267, 283, 383
JEZEBEL 316, 317
JOANNES THE SEER 307
JOHN THE BAPTIST 17
JORDAN, THE RIVER.. .. ..15, 289
JUDAH.. .. .. 15, 17, 187, 347
JUDAH, THE LION OF 329
JUDAH, THE TRIBES OR CHILDREN OF 318, 335
JUDAH, THE WILDERNESS OF 15, 35, 229

KINGDOM OF THE FATHER-MOTHER, THE 88, 369
KINGDOM OF THE HEAVENS.. .. ..64, 349
KINGS OF THE EAST AND OF THE SUN 357

LAMB OF GOD 19, 243, 319, 329, 369, 385
LAMB, THE PASCAL 41
LAMB, THE BLOOD OF THE 201, 243, 341
LAMB, THE MARRIAGE OF THE 375
LAZARUS 289
LOGOS, THE 19, 305, 309
LUCIFER 342, 343
MAN, THE SON OF 71, 115, 137, 139, 227, 229, 239, 309, 327, 365
MAN, THE COMING OF THE SON OF.. 53
MANNA 161, 199, 315
MARAH 297, 341
MARIA 91, 93, 191, 327
MARRIAGE OF THE LAMB, THE 375
MARTHA AND MARY 289
MARY MAGDALENE 291
MATTER 177
MESSENGERS 95
MIDDLE WALL OR PARTITION, THE 121, 135, 163, 233
MILLENNIUM, THE 379
MOON, THE 141, 333, 349, 355
MORTALS 173, 177, 203
MOSES 151, 161, 197
MOUNTAINS 113, 139
MOUNT OF GALILEE, THE, HIGH 293
MOUNT GERIZIM 267
MOUNT HERMON 195
MOUNT HOREB 161
MOUNT OF THE LORD 197

		Page.
Mount Moriah		195
Mount of Olives		..67, 215
Mount Sinai		103
Mount Zion		363
Mysteries, The Divine		59
Nazareth, Nazarene		25, 92, 93, 105, 293
Nirvana, The Day of		337
North, The		385
Numbers :—		
One, Three and Five		279
Nine		279, 335
Ten		51
Twelve		335, 363
Thirteen		51
" 153 "		279
" 144,000 "		.. 207 335, 363
" 666 "		361
Oblation, The		163
Paraclete, The Holy		239
Partition, The		121, 135, 163, 233
Pascal Lamb, The		41
Passover, The		..71, 283
Patmos, The Isle of		305
Patriarchs, The		161
Pearls		385
Peculiar People of God, The		369
Petra, Peter		197, 369, 373
Peter, The Chair of		369
Philosopher's Stone, The		315
Pilate		247
Pool of Siloam, The		77
Prophet, The False		305, 357, 363, 377
Priesthood, The Royal		329
Ra, Children of		363
Rachel		105
Radiance, The Divine		89
Ram, The		361
Rama		105
Red Sea, The		103, 159, 355, 359, 383
Resurrection, The First		379
Resurrection of the Lord, The		293
Revelation		307
River of the Water of Life, The		387
Rock of the Ages, The		160, 161
Rod of Power, The		351
Rod of God, The Measuring		347
Salvation		75
Samaria		135, 263
Samaritan, A		265
Sarah		153
Satan		177, 379
Saturn		315
Sea of Crystal, The		353, 355
Sea of Galilee, see " G."		
Sea, The Great		327
Sea, The Red, or Sea of Blood		103, 159, 341, 355, 357, 359, 383
Seal of the Household of Israel		334-5
Seraphim		337
Seven Loaves and Fishes, The		115
Sheckinah, The		305, 347
Shepherd, The Good		..37, 117
Silence, The Great		129, 337

393

	Page.
Simon	103, 271
Simon Iona	281
Simon Peter	23, 277, 281
Simeon	100, 101
Sin-Offering, The (see " Oblation ")	163
Sodom and Gomorrah	159
Son, The Eternal..	87
Son of God, The	61
Son of Man, The, (see " M.")	
Sophia	311
South, The	385
Spectrum of the Holy Spirit, The	165, 311, 385
Stars, The	141, 333, 341, 342, 349
Star, The Bright and Morning..	316, 317
Stars, The Twelve..	341-3, 348-9
Star " Wormwood," The	341
Stone which the Builder's Rejected, The	373
Stone, The White	315
Sun, The	141, 333, 349, 375
Sun, The Children of the	257
Sychar, The City of	267
Tabernacle of Testimony, The..	355
Tares	61
Temple of Herod, The	247
Temple of the Lord, The..	66, 195, 347, 349
Temple of Solomon, The	247, 347
Temple, The Courts of the	17, 349
Temple, The Porch of the	117
Thieves, The Two	195, 247
Thunders, The Seven	337
Tree, A	117
Tree of Life, The	387
Tribes of Israel, The	305, 335, 360
Tribes of Judah, The	335
Tribes, The Thrones of the Twelve	207
Truth..	19
Upper Room, The	47
Vinegar	217
Vine, The	201
Virgin	53, 360
Virgin Mary, The	99
Virgin Soul, The	353
Virgins of Zion	363
Watch or Day, The Fourth	255
Waters	353, 357
Waters of the Jordan, The	15
West, The	385
White Garments or Robes, ...	319, 333
White Stone, The	315
Wine	5
Wings..	327
Wisdom, The Heavenly	201
Witnesses, The Two	349
Woman	79, 133, 155, 263, 349, 351
Woman Clothed with the Sun, The	349
Woman in the House of Simon	271
Woman, The Scarlet	367, 369
Woman of Samaria, The	265, 267
Zion	103, 139, 159, 385
Zion, The Children of	159, 233
Zion, The Holy City of	382-3-4-5

SUBJECT INDEX
OF THE LOGIA.

	Page.
ALLEGORIES OF THE SOUL :	
Feeding the Multitude..	112
The Ship on the Sea	126
Stilling the Storm	126
The Marriage in Cana..	190
In the House of Mary ..	210
ALLEGORIES OF THE OBLATION :—	
The Woman who was healed..	132
The Anointing by Mary	210
The Temptations in the Wilderness ..	230
The Humiliation and Condemnation of Christ	246
The Crucifixion..	246
Going through Samaria	262
The Harvest	268
The Return of the Son of Man	268
The Christ in the House of Simon	270
The Seven Fishermen of Galilee	276
The Mysterious Soliloquy	280
The Feet Washing	282
The Sickness, Death and Resurrection of Lazarus	288
Mary Magdalene seeking the Lord, or the Recovery of Soul Vision	290
PARABLES CONCERNING THE DIVINE LOVE :	
The Good Shepherd	34
The Two Sons ..	36
PARABLES CONCERNING THE CHRISTHOOD OF THE SOUL :—	
The Marriage Feast	42
The Woman and the Lost Coin	46
The Unjust Steward	46
The Talents	50
The Virgins	52
Dives and Lazarus	54
The Sower	58
The Wheat and the Tares	60
PARABLES OF THE CHRISTHOOD ESTATE :—	
The Pearl of Great Price	62
The Hidden Treasure ..	62
The Net ..	64
PARABLE CONCERNING THE PLANET :—	
The Great Lament	232
THE STORY OF :—	
The Barren Fig Tree	68
The Pharisee and Tax Gatherer	80
Of going through Samaria	134
Of the Healing of the Lepers ..	134
Of the Good Samaritan	136
Of Abraham	150
TEACHINGS RELATED TO THE FOLLOWING INCIDENTS IN THE LIFE OF THE MASTER :—	
Blessing the Child Souls	28
The Enquiry of the Rich Young Man	28
The Healing of the Obsessed ..	70
The Interview with Nicodemus	73
The Sickness of the Ruler's Daughter	74
Healing of the Blind Man	76
Of the Woman taken in Adultery	78
Healing of the Leper ..	120
Healing of the Blind Man	122
Of the Syro-Phœnician Woman	122
Of the Demons and the Swine	124

395

GENERAL TEACHINGS CONCERNING :—

Titles	24
That which defiles	26
The Creatures	26
Offence	28
True Heavenly Treasures	30
The Soul, the Temple of God	66
Casting out Evil (Obsessions)	70
The Holy Breath	74
Marriage	80
The Law of Divorce	98
Prayer	84
Doctrine of the Logos	86
The Birth of the Holy States of Jesus, Christ, and the Lord	92
Witnessing of the Father-Mother	106
The Law of Ceremonial	116
The Works of God	118
Coming Events	130
The Days of the Regeneration	138
The Woes of the Prophets	142
The Elect or Called	148
The Divine Graciousness	158
The Mystery of God	162
The Gifts of the Spirit	164
Spiritual Discernment	166
Love Transcendent	168
The Veil of Moses	170
The Grace of the Lord	170
The Earthly and the Heavenly	172
The Rising from the Dead	172
The Imprisoned World	176
The Divine Conqueror	178
The Ransom (The Sin Offering)	180
The Burden of the Sin Offering	182
The Restoration of Israel	184
The Perfect Union and Unity	194
The Betrayal	198
The Manna of Life	198
The Lord, the Bread of Life	200
The Lord as the Vine	200
The Immortals (Beatitudes)	202
The Return of the Presence	204
The Night and the Dawn	206
In the Garden of Sorrow	218
The Burden of the Ransom	227
The Way of the Cross	228
The Passover	232, 234
The Recovery of the Logia	239
Preparations for the Return of the Son of Man	240
At the Eucharistic Supper	242
On the Eve of the Passover	244
The Power by which Sin is Remitted or Retained	248
In the Prayer for the Disciples	254
In His Great Request to the Father-Mother	256
In the Prayer of the Aftermath	294

ANCIENT SPIRITUAL HISTORIES :—

The Angelic Cohort at Bethphage	66
The Shepherds of the Bethlehem	90
Of the Magi	98
Of the Purification in the Temple	100
Herod and the Children of Bethlehem	104
Abraham and Sarah	150
Apocalyptic Visions (not only of the Past, but of the Present and Future)	301

396

NOTE.—Subjects not included in this Index may be found in Glossary Index.

	Page.
ABRAHAM	15, 108, 111, 154
ACTS OF THE APOSTLES, THE	5
ADONAI 17, 19, 37, 61, 87, 107, 139, 157, 171, 191, 239, 269, 305,	
307, 311, 313, 317, 319, 321, 323, 327, 329, 345, 365, 387	
AGAPÊ, THE	.. 169, 311, 319
AGE, THE NEW (AQUARIAN)	.. 143, 173, 241
AKASHIC RECORDS, THE	.. 329
ALCHEMISTS, DIVINE	.. 285
AMBROSIA OF THE GODS, THE	.. 161
AMEN, THE	.. 111, 307, 323
ANCIENT WISDOM, THE	.. 143
ANIMALS, see " Creatures."	
ANGELS	39, 40, 177, 353
ANGELIC KINGDOM, THE	.. 201
ANGEL OF THE LORD, THE..	.. 335
ANGEL OF THE PRESENCE, THE	.. 375
ANOINTING BY MARY	.. 210
APOCALYPSE, THE	6, 7, 301
APOSTLES	373, 383
ARCHE, THE	87, 111, 307, 323
ARK OF THE LAW, THE	199
ARMAGEDDON, THE	345, 351, 357, 377
ASTRAL WORLD AND KINDGOM, THE .. 37, 61, 95, 103, 105,	
119, 123, 127, 159, 163, 167, 171, 181, 185, 187, 219,	
221, 233, 237, 245, 247, 257, 263, 275, 283, 293, 295,	
305, 311, 315, 329, 341, 343, 347, 353, 355, 357, 359, 379, 383	
ASTRAL FIRES	.. 355-7
ASTROLOGY	.. 99, 143
ATLANTIS	333, 334
AVATÂR, THE DIVINE (see "Second Coming").	
BAPTISM OF THE HOLY ONE, THE	17
BAPTISM OF JOHN, THE	17
BEASTS, WILD	333
" BEATITUDES," THE	203
BENEDICTUS, THE	95
BETRAYAL, THE 199, 207, 217, 245, 269, 283, 359, 367	
BIRTH STORIES, THE..	91
BLOOD OF THE LAMB, THE	.. 201, 243, 241
BLOOD, THE VEIL OF	171
BREATH, THE HOLY	75
BROTHERHOOD, THE	167, 169
CELIBACY	.. 81
CELESTIALS, THE (see " Christhood Order").	
CEREMONIAL, THE LAW OF..	116, 117, 151
CHILDREN OF THE PLANET (see " Human Race.")	
" CHRIST AGE," THE	.. 173, 179, 205
CHRIST-CONSCIOUSNESS, THE 191, 269, 281, 283, 369, 379	
CHRISTHOOD ESTATE, THE .. 17, 43, 51, 53, 55, 61, 67, 73, 75, 85,	
87, 89, 93, 95, 105, 107, 108, 119, 121, 137, 149, 165,	
167, 171, 177, 183, 191, 197, 215, 217, 227, 247, 265,	
275, 279, 285, 299, 307, 313, 315, 319, 327, 341, 347,	
353, 355, 359, 367, 375, 377, 379	
CHRISTHOOD, THE DIVINE	322-3-4-5
CHRIST, THE ETERNAL } (see also " Adonai,") 17, 19, 133, 139, 305, 308, 335	
CHRIST, THE LORD	
CHRISTHOOD ORDER, THE ANCIENT 7, 15, 19, 25, 39, 59, 61, 69, 89,	
91, 95, 97, 99, 101, 103, 123, 129, 139, 141, 143, 147,	
151, 156, 159, 173, 175, 185, 195, 203, 205, 227, 233,	
235, 251, 257, 283, 305, 307, 311, 313, 315, 317, 319,	
321, 323, 329, 333, 337, 351, 363, 365, 383, 387	

397

GENERAL INDEX.

Page.

CHRISTHOOD ORDER, THE MISSION OF THE 251
CHRISTHOOD VISION (see "V").
CHURCHES IN ASIA, THE :—
   Ephesus 310, Smyrna 312, Pergamos 314, Thyatira 316, Sardis 318,
                           Philadelphia 320, Laodicea 322
CHURCH, THE ANCIENT HEBREW 69, 313
CHURCH, THE WESTERN (Christianity) .. 5, 8, 27, 31, 45, 93, 107,
        111, 115, 129, 131, 135, 137, 139, 143, 145, 167, 169,
        183, 199, 203, 207, 223, 227, 229, 239, 247, 255, 257,
        271, 287, 317, 361, 363, 367, 369, 371
CLAIRVOYANCE 25
COLOUR AND SOUND 309
COMING EVENTS .. 128, 129, 169, 179, 185, 239, 262, 269, 329,
                        365, 373, 383, 387
COVENANT OR TESTIMONY, THE NEW 243
CREATION 87, 179, 317, 327, 337, 377
CREATURES, THE 26, 27, 29, 93, 187, 371
CROSS, THE 23, 29, 33, 73, 97, 123, 125, 143, 167, 203, 211, 213,
                 246, 248, 285, 295, 311, 317
CROSS, THE LUMINOUS 287
CROSS, THE PATH OF THE 23, 33, 205, 228
CROSS, THE ROSY 285
CRUCIFIXION, THE (of the Master) 113, 131, 217, 219, 227, 246-7,
                      249, 251, 299
CRUCIFIXION, THE (of the Son of Man and of the Christhood), 128, 217,
               227, 246-7, 249, 267, 299
DEATH 315
DELUGE, THE 187, 383
DEVIL, THE 170
DISEASE 357
DISCIPLES, THE .. 22, 23, 67, 71, 89, 129, 131, 139, 143, 145,
       149, 157, 161, 163, 179, 193, 197, 199, 215, 227, 239,
               250, 267, 277, 283
DIVINE CONQUEROR, THE 178, 181
DIVINE GRACIOUSNESS 158-61, 170
DIVINE JUDGMENT, THE (see "J").
DIVINE LOVE AND WISDOM, THE 117, 125, 161, 169, 171, 177, 179,
      181, 185, 187, 199, 211, 225, 317, 341, 345, 377, 383
DIVINE MAN, THE 349
DIVINE REALM, THE 337, 387
DIVINE SPECTRUM, THE 165, 311, 321, 385
DIVINE VISION, THE (see "V").
DOG, THE 27, 123

ECCLESIASTICISM .8, 65, 93, 199, 203, 249, 259, 271, 305, 361, 369
EGYPT 14
EGYPT, THE FLIGHT INTO 104-5
ELECT SOULS (see also "Christhood Order") 7, 148, 150, 167
ELEMENTALS, ELEMENTARY SPIRITS 123, 127, 129, 163, 165, 313, 369, 379
"ELI, ELI, LAMA SABACHTHANI".. .. .. 216, 298
ELIJAH 129
ELOHIM .. 165, 309, 311, 326, 335, 345, 349, 353, 355, 363, 382
EPISTOLARY LETTERS (see "Pauline Letters").
ETERNAL LIFE 263, 269
EVANGELISTS, THE FOUR 3
EVIL AND THE POWERS OF EVIL 63, 177, 341, 343-5, 377
EVOLUTION, PHYSICAL 159, 177
EVOLUTION OF THE SOUL, THE 159, 165, 177, 281, 283, 337, 345, 379
EUCHARISTIC SUPPER, THE 211, 223, 242

FAITH 123, 129
FALL, THE 5, 15, 37, 91, 155, 173, 175, 177, 205, 235, 311, 331,
                      343, 379, 383
FALLEN SPIRITS 177
FATHER-MOTHER, THE DIVINE .. 17, 27, 75, 88, 127, 153, 202,
       206, 225, 248, 257, 311, 321, 345, 363

398

GENERAL INDEX.

Page.

FIRES, PURGATORIAL	55
FLESH EATING	27, 171, 187, 203, 239, 271, 317, 319, 365
GABRIEL	335, 375, 376
GETHSEMANE VISION, THE	183, 212, 215, 219, 245, 299
GIFT OF GOD, THE	263
GIFTS OF THE SPIRIT	164-6
"GLORIA IN EXCELSIS," THE	103
GOD, THE FIRE OF	353
GOD, THE MYSTERY OF	162-4
GOLDEN AGE, THE	187
GOSPEL RECORDS AND WRITERS	3, 169, 243
GNOSIS, THE	293
HADES	308, 333
HEALERS	71, 273, 319
HEAVENS OF THE EARTH, THE	383
HEBREWS, THE ANCIENT (see Christhood Order).	
HORSE, THE	27, 331
HUMAN KINGDOM OR RACE, THE	19, 89, 91, 125, 163, 175, 221, 233, 285, 295, 315, 319, 321, 333, 379
ICE AGE, THE	187
IDOLATRY, THE VEIL OF	171
IMMORTALS, THE (see also "Christhood Order"), 73, 111, 173, 177, 203, 206	
INITIATION	307, 385
INITIATION, THE GATES OF	201, 385
INQUISITIONS, THE	239, 369
INSPIRATION	109, 305
INTUITION, THE	8, 47, 65, 79, 101, 141, 171, 263, 275, 349, 359, 363, 367
IOANNES THE SEER	307, 347
IOSEPH	91
IOSEPH-MARIA	101, 105, 293
IRUSALEM, THE HOLY CITY OF	91
ISRAEL (see Gloss. and "Christhood Order").	
ISRAEL IN EGYPT	103
ISRAEL, THE RESTORATION OF	184-7, 207, 251
JESUSHOOD AND THE JESUS-LIFE	9, 17, 21, 29, 75, 93, 103, 119, 135, 143, 149, 155, 167, 175, 181, 183, 267, 279, 297, 353, 367
JERUSALEM	195
JEWS, JEWISH NATION AND RELIGION	6, 15, 17, 19, 27, 69, 75, 77, 79, 95, 101, 107, 117, 125, 137, 143, 145, 149, 151, 185, 207, 227, 305, 371
JOHN THE BAPTIST	199
JOHN THE SEER	6
JUDGMENT, THE DIVINE	8, 51, 63, 139, 143, 205, 353, 355, 371, 378
KARMA	33, 63, 77, 273, 275
KINGDOM, THE DIVINE	227, 305, 341
KINGDOM OF THE FATHER-MOTHER, THE	88, 269
KINGDOM OF GOD, THE	23, 31, 85, 108, 269, 349
KINGDOM, THE HUMAN	29
KINGDOM OF THE HEAVENS, THE	28, 31, 44, 51, 61, 64, 85, 193, 273, 349
KINGDOM, THE MIDDLE (see "Astral World").	
LAMENT, THE GREAT	232
LAW OF THE DIVINE LOVE, THE } (see also "Karma")	33
LAW OF RIGHTEOUSNESS, THE	
LIBERTY, TRUE	179
LIFE, THE ONE	88, 279
LIFE, THE RIVER OF THE WATER OF	387
LIFE, THE TREE OF	387
LOGIA OF ST. JOHN, THE	4, 5, 6
LOGIA OF ST. MATTHEW, THE	4, 17
LOGOI OF GOD	341

399

Lord, The	141, 143, 191, 197, 201, 305
Lord, The Body of the	166, 167
Lord, The Coming of the (see " Second Coming ")	17
Lord Consciousness, The	167, 267
Love Transcendent	168

Magi, The	99, 153
Magnetic Plane of the Earth, The	383
" Magnificat, The "	96
Mammon	313
Man of Sorrows	219
Manifestation, The (by the Master)	19, 67, 81, 93, 105, 121, 133, 137, 141, 167, 169, 187
Marriage and Divorce	78, 80
Marriage of the Soul, The	191
Mary, The Virgin	99
Mass, The	223
Master, The	6, 17, 19, 25, 37, 103, 107, 117, 119, 121, 125, 129, 135, 139, 141, 145, 163, 171, 181, 183, 185, 197, 207, 217, 219, 247, 271, 281, 307, 347, 375, 383
Master, The Great Request of the	256
Master, The Mission of the	121, 193, 227, 248, 251, 253
Master, The Offices of the	167
Master, The Return of the	101, 139, 141, 255, 267, 268, 271, 279, 291
Materialism and Materialistic Systems	7, 8, 305, 315, 351, 353, 363, 367, 371, 377
Materialism, The Veil of	171
Matter	177
Mercy	203
Message, The Divine	119
Messengers, The	14, 89, 95, 112, 201, 205, 250, 263, 268, 269, 291, 307, 337, 343, 345, 347, 349
Michael	351
Middle Kingdom, The (see " Astral Kingdom ").	
Middle Wall or Partition, The	121, 135, 163, 323
Mind	65, 97, 103, 121, 141, 165, 281, 333, 357, 359
Minds, Evil	377
Minds, The House of	323
Mind, The Higher (or Reason)	127, 215, 293, 315
Mind, The Lower or Intellectual	359, 361
Mind of the Planet, The	233, 331
Miracles (see also Subject Index)	113, 207
Monastic Systems	55
Mortals	173, 177
Moses, The Veil of	170
Motherhood of God, The	153
Mountains (see Glossary Index).	
Mysteries, The Ancient and Sacred	59, 65, 67, 99, 143, 155, 169, 185, 195, 201, 237, 277, 279, 307, 345, 347, 355, 369, 383
Mystery, The Hidden	162, 277
Mysteries, The Lesser	115
Mystics and Mysticism	59, 121, 149, 247, 279, 315, 363
Mystery of God, The	162-4, 201
Naros, The. Naronic Cycles	7, 113, 115, 131, 205, 211, 213, 233, 247, 255, 269, 277, 281, 289, 347, 365
Nature	179
Nirvana, The Day of	337
Numbers (see Glossary Index).	
Nunc Dimittis	101-2
Oblation, The (The Sin-Offering)	5, 7, 19, 71, 85, 95, 101, 104, 121, 131, 133, 135, 137, 139, 157, 163, 167, 171, 179, 181, 183, 185, 197, 203, 207, 211, 217, 219, 221, 229, 237, 239, 245, 247, 249, 253, 255, 257, 263, 269, 273, 279, 283, 287, 289, 295, 299, 319, 321, 329, 337, 341, 347, 351, 355, 359, 365, 383

400

OBSESSION 71, 123, 124, 125
OCCULTISM AND OCCULT POWERS .. 25, 29, 65, 181, 229, 279, 285,
293, 329, 333, 353
ORDERS OF SOULS, THE 175
OX, THE 27

PAPAL SEE, THE 231
PARACLETE, THE HOLY 238-9, 245
PARABLES (see Subject Index).
PASSION, THE DIVINE 277
PASSOVER, THE .. 71, 133, 197, 226, 237, 240, 243, 244, 251, 283, 299
PATH, THE THREEFOLD 23, 33, 93
PAUL 4, 5, 147, 169, 243, 281
PAULINE LETTERS, THE EPISTOLARY OR 3, 4, 5, 149, 153, 169, 173, 281
PETROS, PETER 129, 131
PHILOSOPHIES, DELUSIVE 163
PLANET (EARTH) AND THE PLANET SOUL, THE .. 9, 15, 35, 59, 103,
109, 111, 119, 125, 139, 147, 154, 157, 159, 161, 177,
179, 187, 205, 215, 235, 239, 241, 273, 277, 283, 305,
329, 331, 333, 337, 351, 353, 383, 387
PLANET, THE CHILDREN OF THE (see " Human Race ").
PLANETARY HEAVENS, THE 333
PLEROMA, THE DIVINE 153, 355
PRAYER 33, 81, 84, 183
PRAYER OF THE AFTERMATH, THE.. 294
PRAYER, THE LORD'S 84
PRAYER OF THE MASTER, THE INTERCESSORY 253, 256
PROPHETS AND SEERS 61, 109, 111, 117, 143, 164, 165, 205,
233, 275, 305, 373
PROPHETS, THE SCHOOLS OF THE 143
PROPHETS, THE WOES OF THE 143
PURGATORIAL FIRES.. 55
PURITY 187

RAINBOW, THE 326
RANSOM, THE WORK OF THE 180
RECOVERY, THE AGE OF, AND THE DAY OF THE 239, 295, 297, 299, 377
RECOVERY OF THE LOGIA, THE ANTICIPATED 238
REDEEMER, THE 103 162, 167, 235
REDEMPTION, THE .. 5, 7, 8, 33, 41, 59, 89, 93, 101, 117, 121, 145,
149, 154, 163, 171, 172, 177, 178, 179, 183, 187, 203,
227, 233, 235, 237, 251, 253, 287, 319, 337, 359, 379, 383
REFORM MOVEMENTS, THE 357
REGENERATION, THE 7, 41, 59, 139, 159, 235, 251, 337
REGENERATION (and the Recovery), THE DAYS OF THE 138, 141,
142, 181, 237, 238, 239, 255, 257, 287, 295, 297
REINCARNATION .. 29, 73, 77, 97, 133, 137, 253, 255, 273, 275, 283
RELIGIONS, THE GREAT 89, 95, 185, 187, 363
RELIGIOUS SYSTEMS, FALSE 361
RESTORATION OF ISRAEL, THE 184-7, 207
RESTORATION OF THE PLANET, THE 349
RESURRECTION, THE.. .. .. 7, 172-6, 293, 379
RETURN OF THE MESSENGER, THE (i.e., of the Master) 101, 139, 141,
255, 267, 268, 271, 279, 291
RETURN OF THE SON OF MAN, THE (see " Second Coming ").

SACRAMENTS OF THE CHURCH, THE 115, 233
SALVATION 35, 95, 103, 133
SATAN 170, 376
SAURIANS, THE 125, 159, 233
SCIENCE 329, 353
SECOND COMING, THE (of the Son of Man), 115, 139, 141, 143, 205, 240-1,
247, 255, 268, 269, 320, 321, 322, 359, 377
SECOND COMING, THE (of the Master), (see " Return ").
SEERS (see also " Prophets ") 108, 164, 165, 205

401

Page.

SENSES, THE FIVE 265, 279, 351
SINS, THE FORGIVENESS OF 95, 249, 273
SINS, THE REMITTANCE OF 248
SIN, THE WILDERNESS OF 14
SIN OFFERING, THE (see " Oblation ").
SIN OFFERING, THE EXPERIENCES OF THE 180-3
SIN OFFERING, THE BURDEN OF THE 182-5
SIN OFFERING, THE WORK OF THE 163, 219-21
SODOM AND GOMORRAH 383
SONS OF GOD, THE (see " Christhood Order ").
SON OF MAN, THE 53, 128, 137, 139, 191, 227, 228, 356-7
SOPHIA, THE DIVINE 26, 47, 107, 117, 311
SPIRITS, EVIL (see also " Elementals ") 124, 356-7
SPIRITUALISM, MODERN 165
SOUL, THE   33, 35, 37, 47, 53, 59, 63, 65, 67, 71, 75, 77, 81, 85,
               88, 97, 99, 101, 103, 105, 115, 135, 137, 139, 149, 151,
               153, 155, 159, 163, 165, 171, 173, 175, 177, 187, 191,
               195, 201, 217, 239, 269, 279, 281, 283, 289, 307, 319,
                    323, 327, 337, 341, 345, 347, 355, 373, 379
SOUL, THE GENESIS OF THE 327, 345
SOUL, THE EVOLUTION OF THE 159
SOUL, THE VEHICLES OF THE 17
SOUL THE MOTHER OF THE LORD, THE 191
SOUND AND COLOUR.. 309
STONE, THE PHILOSOPHER'S 315
SUPPER OF THE LORD, THE 211, 223, 242

TEMPLE OF HEROD, THE 247
TEMPLE OF THE LORD, THE (the Soul) 17, 66, 67, 195, 347, 349
TEMPLE OF SOLOMON (the Christhood Estate) ..119, 227, 247, 253, 347, 349
TEMPLE, THE PORCH OF THE 117
TEMPLE, THE TABERNACLE OF TESTIMONY IN THE 355
THREEFOLD PATH, THE 23, 133
TRANSFIGURATION, THE 196
TREE OF LIFE, THE 355
TRIBULATION, THE GREAT 139, 335, 337
TRINITY, THE HOLY.. 88
TRINITY, THE DIVINE 356-7

UNDERSTANDING, THE SPIRITUAL 8
UNITY, THE PERFECT 194
URIM AND THUMMIM, THE 385

VEILS, THE THREE 171
VIRGIN (see Glossary Index).
VIRGIN MARY, THE 99
VIRGINS OF ZION 363
VISION OF ADONAI, THE (of the Eternal Christ)   19, 89, 197, 307, 308,
                                            321, 326, 327, 349, 375
VISION OF THE CHRISTHOOD ESTATE, THE   67, 71, 129, 137, 143,
                                            169, 207, 229, 341
VISION OF GETHSEMANE (see " G ").
VIVISECTION 7, 29, 203, 317, 319, 365

WESTERN WORLD, THE   27, 45, 131, 139, 145, 183, 201,
                       231, 249, 253, 269, 271, 273, 275, 351
WILL, THE 165
WISDOM, THE HEAVENLY 201
WOES OF THE PROPHETS, THE 165
WOMAN (see Glossary Index also) .. 79, 133, 155, 263, 349, 351, 360
WORLD, THE IMPRISONED 176-8
WORK, THE GREAT 225

YOGISM 165, 285

ZION, THE HOLY CITY OF 195, 382-3-4-5

402

THE ORDER OF THE CROSS.

AIMS AND IDEALS.

To attain by mutual helpfulness, the realization of the Christ-life, by the path of self-denial, self-sacrifice, and absolute self-abandonment to the Divine will and service :—

It is of these things that the Cross as a symbol speaks. It stands for the Sign of the Order of the Cross, because its three steps are those which have to be taken in order to arrive at that Estate which it symbolizes. It speaks of the quest after the humble spirit and the pure heart. It speaks also of that further state of realization, when the Soul gives itself in absolute abandonment for the Divine Service. The three steps are—

> Purity of Living.
> Purity of the Mind.
> Purity of the Soul.

Thus to endeavour by example and teaching to win all men to the love of Truth, Purity and Right-doing

To proclaim the Brotherhood of Man, the essential one-ness of all religious aspirations, and the unity of all living creatures in the Divine. To teach the moral necessity for humaneness towards all men and all creatures :

To protest against, and to work for the abolition of all national and social customs which violate the teachings of the Christ, especially such as involve bloodshed, the oppression of the weak and defenceless, the perpetuation of the brutal mind, and the infliction of cruelty upon animals, *viz.* : war, vivisection, the slaughter of animals for food, fashion and sport, and kindred evils :

To advocate the universal adoption of a bloodless diet, and the return to simple and natural foods :

To proclaim a message of peace and happiness, health and purity, spirituality and Divine Love.

The Journal is supplied gratuitously to many Public Institutions in this and other lands, such as Free Libraries, Institutes, University Colleges, etc.

All Official Correspondence in connection with the work of the Order of the Cross should be addressed **TO THE SECRETARY,** to whom Cheques and Postal Orders should be made payable.

" The Herald of the Cross "* is published monthly. It can be obtained direct from Headquarters for 2/6 per annum, post-free, or from the Publishers, Messrs. PERCY LUND, HUMPHRIES & Co., LTD., 3, Amen Corner, London, E.C.

The issue of this Journal is temporarily suspended during the Publication of larger works of the Order.

EXECUTIVE COUNCIL.

ROBERT H. PERKS, M.D., F.R.C.S. (Eng.), *Secretary*, Ferndale, Woodland Park, Paignton.

J. TODD FERRIER, *Editor*, Roselle, Woodland Park, Paignton.

All Offices of the Order are Honorary.

Publications of the Order of the Cross.

PAIGNTON, ENGLAND.

The Official Journal of the Order, "The Herald of the Cross," published on the first of month. Price 2d., postage 1d., or 2/6 per annum.

A Journal whose teachings appertain to the Gospel of the New Interpretation, setting forth the Evolution of the Soul as a spiritual process, and the nature and meaning of Christhood as the Crown of the Soul's Evolution. Also giving the true readings of the Ancient Hebrew Scriptures and the Teachings of the Christ, in which Purity in Diet. Thought and Feeling, and Love made manifest in Compassion unto all Souls and Pity unto all Creatures, were set forth as essential to the Pure and Good Life.

Volumes I. to VII. (1905 to 1911).
Bound in imitation parchment. Price 3/6. Postage—British 1/6, Foreign 2/10.

Only sold in sets, except Vol. I.

What is a Christian? By the Rev. J. TODD FERRIER. Paper Covers, post-free, 4d. each ; 2/6 a dozen ; 15/0 a hundred. Bound in Art Linen, 9d. each, post-free.

Concerning Human Carnivorism. By Rev. J. TODD FERRIER. In Art Linen, post-free 1/6 in United Kingdom, 1/8 abroad.
An historic plea on behalf of Purity of Living, and Humaneness towards the Creatures.

Its six chapters deal with The Records of History, The Testimony of Science, Some Economic Problems. Dynamic Value of Pure Food, A Plea for Humaneness and The Voice of Religion.

The New Avatâr, or the Second Coming. Post-free, 7d.

Why I Condemn Vivisection. By ROBERT H. PERKS, M.D., F.R.C.S. (Eng.), 24 pages. Revised Edition, 55th thousand. One Penny, or 3/- per hundred, post-free.

The sketch is a rich and welcome contribution of Anti-Vivisection literature, and should be ready at hand for referance of labourers in the cause, and for circulation among those floundering in the dismal mazes of illusion and the evasive indifference of neglect. The Author fortifies his position with ample authority from the writings of physicians, clerics, and thinkers and writers of eminence, and there is nothing in his treatment of his subject to harrow the susceptibilities of the timid or emotional servant of the Master, in behalf of whose creatures, and the justice due to them, the author is a conspicuous and conscientious labourer.

Dietetic Difficulties. ROBERT H. PERKS, M.D., F.R.C.S. Price 1d. 2/6 per hundred, post-free.
The pamphlet is a guide for those adopting pure diet, in the selection of suitable foods to replace flesh meats.

Leaflets.

By the Rev. TODD FERRIER.

Vivisection: an Inquiry into its Real Nature. Post-free, 2/6 per 100.
The Habit of Flesh-Eating. Post-free, 2/6 per 100.
How to Realize the Divine. Post-free, 2/6 per 100.
Christmas, a Vision of Hope. Post-free, 1/6 per 100.
The Path of Discipleship. Post-free, 1/6 per 100.
The Divine Man. Post-free, 1/6 per 100.

By Dr. R. H. PERKS.

Vivisection, or True and False Science. Post-free, 2/6 per 100.
Humaneness. Post-free, 1/6 per 100.

WORKS BY THE SAME AUTHOR.

THE MASTER,

KNOWN UNTO THE WORLD AS JESUS THE CHRIST:

His Life and Teachings:

BEING RECOVERIES BY THE WRITER THROUGH ILLUMINATIONS, VISIONS, AND EXPERIENCES, WHEREIN ARE SET FORTH THE INNER MEANINGS, OF THE MASTER'S TEACHINGS AND THE NATURE OF HIS JESUSHOOD AND CHRISTHOOD.

The Volume treats of the following important questions:

1. DID THE MASTER LIVE AS A MAN?

2. THE MASTER AS HE WAS.

3. HIS MISSION, AND HOW HE BECAME JESUS, THE CHRIST AND THE LORD.

4. THE INNER MEANINGS OF HIS TEACHINGS SET FORTH IN

   (a) The Birth-Stories.

   (b) The Allegories of the Soul, wherein the Nature, History and Redemption of the Soul are revealed.

   (c) Allegorical stories of the Passion, in which the true meaning of the latter is portrayed.

   (d) The Logia of the Passion, embracing those of the Gethsemane, the Upper Room and the Cross.

The Teachings set forth the meaning of the profound Mystery of the Sin Offering, why it had to be accomplished, and how it was accomplished; and they reveal the inner significance of Christhood and the Jesus state, showing that they are conditions within the soul, states of spiritual consciousness, and how these states may be attained by all souls. And the Teachings explain the meaning of the New Age upon which we have entered, and the reason for the remarkable spiritual phenomena so obvious in the heart of all the Great Religions.

Ryl. 8vo., pp. 540.

Sacrifice a Necessity. 3/6.

Concerning Human Carnivorism. 1/0.

What is a Christian? 3d. and 9d.

The New Avatâr, or the Second Coming. 6d.

The New Interpretation, relating to the History of the Earth and all Souls, given in "The Herald of the Cross," Vols. I. to VII. 3/6 a Volume. In Sets only, except Vol. I. Postage 1/6.

Price, 7/6 nett, Postage, British 7d., Foreign 1/2. To be obtained from

"THE ORDER OF THE CROSS," PAIGNTON, ENGLAND.

UNIVERSITY OF CALIFORNIA LIBRARY
BERKELEY

Return to desk from which borrowed.
This book is DUE on the last date stamped below.

JAN 22 1948

6 Nov '63 MM

REC'D LD

NOV 4 '63 - 8 PM

INTER-LIBRARY
LOAN

JUL 30 1970

INTERLIBRARY LOAN
DEC 28 1983
UNIV. OF CALIF., BERK.

Received in Interlibrary Loan
JAN 27 1984

LD 21–100m-9,'47(A5702s16)476

Printed in Great Britain
by Amazon